Churchill in
North America, 1929

# Churchill in North America, 1929

*A Three Month Tour of Canada and the United States*

Bradley P. Tolppanen

McFarland & Company, Inc., Publishers
*Jefferson, North Carolina*

LIBRARY OF CONGRESS CATALOGUING-IN-PUBLICATION DATA

Tolppanen, Bradley P., 1966–
Churchill in North America, 1929 : a three month tour of Canada and the United States / Bradley P. Tolppanen.
   p.   cm.
Includes bibliographical references and index.

ISBN 978-0-7864-7922-1 (softcover : acid free paper) ∞
ISBN 978-1-4766-1504-2 (ebook)

1. Churchill, Winston, 1874–1965—Travel—Canada.  2. Churchill, Winston, 1874–1965—Travel—United States.  3. Prime ministers—Great Britain—Biography.  I. Title.
DA566.9.C5T59 2014        917.304'916—dc23        2014009385

BRITISH LIBRARY CATALOGUING DATA ARE AVAILABLE

© 2014 Bradley P. Tolppanen. All rights reserved

*No part of this book may be reproduced or transmitted in any form or by any means, electronic or mechanical, including photocopying or recording, or by any information storage and retrieval system, without permission in writing from the publisher.*

On the cover: Churchill in Edmonton (Glenbow Museum NA-1234-5); background image: the CPR private car Mount Royal (second car from left) at the Quebec Conference; Churchill travelled aboard the car in 1929 and again in 1943 (Canadian Pacific Archives NS. 4646)

Printed in the United States of America

*McFarland & Company, Inc., Publishers*
*Box 611, Jefferson, North Carolina 28640*
*www.mcfarlandpub.com*

For Mum and Dad

## Table of Contents

*Acknowledgments* — ix
*Preface* — 1
*Introduction* — 3

1. The Departure, August 3 — 5
2. Planning the Trip, June–August — 7
3. The *Empress of Australia*, August 3–9 — 18
4. Quebec, August 9–12 — 28
5. Montreal and Ottawa, August 12–15 — 39
6. Toronto and Niagara Falls, August 16–17 — 58
7. Northern Ontario, Winnipeg and Kenora, August 17–20 — 70
8. Regina and Saskatoon, August 21–22 — 82
9. Edmonton, Calgary, and Prince of Wales Ranch, August 23–26 — 92
10. The Rocky Mountains, August 26–September 1 — 107
11. Vancouver and Victoria, September 1–6 — 118
12. Seattle to Napa Valley, September 6–9 — 132
13. San Francisco to San Simeon, September 9–16 — 141
14. Los Angeles and Santa Barbara, September 17–21 — 158
15. Los Angeles and Catalina, September 21–26 — 170
16. Yosemite to Chicago, September 27–October 5 — 181
17. New York City, October 6–18 — 193

| | |
|---|---|
| 18. Virginia, Washington, and Pennsylvania, October 19–23 | 211 |
| 19. New York, October 23–29 | 222 |
| 20. The Return to England, October 29–November 5 | 229 |

*Chapter Notes*     235
*Bibliography*     251
*Index*     257

# Acknowledgments

I would like to thank the staff of the following institutions for their assistance with this project: Churchill Archives Centre; Archives of Ontario; Canadian Pacific Archives; Glenbow Museum; Library and Archives Canada; Library of Congress; National Churchill Museum; Provincial Archives of Alberta; Parliamentary Archives; Seeley G. Mudd Manuscript Library, Princeton; Bancroft Library, University of California; University of Arkansas Libraries; and the Vancouver City Archives.

Special thanks are extended to the staff of the interlibrary loan service at Booth Library, Eastern Illinois University, for their efficient efforts in locating the many different sources required for this book.

A large debt is owed to my wife, Lori, for her unfailing support and encouragement over the long course of researching and writing this book.

# Preface

Winston S. Churchill always desired to see people and places firsthand. Such was the case with the subject of this book—his three-month holiday trip to North America from August to November 1929. While there is an extensive body of literature on Churchill, including studies of his travels, as well as his relationship with Canada and the United States, the 1929 trip remains a little known event in his long career. This present book is the first detailed full-length study of his expedition to North America. Churchill made the trip as a private individual while Parliament was in recess, with the goal of learning about the countries he was visiting. This trip merits study because it was his most leisurely visit to the continent, made without the fatigue of a lecture tour or pressure of the high-level political discussions and negotiations experienced when visiting as British prime minister. It was on this trip that the British statesman had the time and opportunity to see and gain an understanding of the two countries first hand, meet their leaders in a variety of fields, and form opinions about Canada and the United States that would guide his decision-making in the Second World War. This work also studies the themes of Churchill's efforts to promote Anglo-American cooperation in his public speeches and private conversations on the trip, his speculation in the stock market, and his relationship with his brother, son, and nephew, who accompanied him on the tour.

A variety of sources have been used to tell the story of Churchill's long tour of North America, including newspaper accounts of the trip. The statesman's visit to a city was front-page news, especially in Canada, from large-city newspapers to small-town weeklies. Articles from the *Bakersfield Californian* and *Fredericksburg Free Lance-Star* to the *Los Angeles Times* and *Winnipeg Evening Tribune* provide interesting and new information on Churchill and his visit. Other sources consulted include the private papers of Churchill and other individuals, the articles about the trip written by Churchill, the memoirs of both Randolph Churchill and John Churchill, and other published sources.

# Introduction

Winston Churchill was an avid traveler. France was his most frequent destination, as he crossed the English Channel dozens of times in his life, but he also traveled across the rest of Europe as well as to Africa, the Middle East, Asia, and North America. From completing a walking tour of Switzerland at the age of 18 in the company of his brother Jack and a tutor, to flying to Moscow to meet with Soviet leader Josef Stalin during the Second World War or quietly relaxing as a guest at Lord Beaverbrook's villa in the south of France during his twilight years, Churchill always showed a great enthusiasm for going abroad.

Churchill traveled for profit, politics, or pleasure, and on some trips he managed to combine all three pursuits at the same time. Such was the case with his visits to Canada and the United States. The first trip came in 1895 when as a young cavalry officer, he visited New York City (which impressed him greatly) before proceeding to Cuba for the exciting adventure of observing the rebellion against Spanish rule as a correspondent for the *Daily Graphic*.

After this first visit Churchill crossed the Atlantic Ocean 17 more times. Twice he came to the continent for lecture tours, in 1900–01 and in 1931–32. The first tour was not as lucrative as he initially hoped, and the second had a disastrous start when he was struck and nearly killed in a traffic accident in New York City. However, after recuperating in Nassau in the Bahamas he recovered to complete the six-week tour that took him as far west as Minneapolis and as far south as New Orleans. Churchill traveled to the continent six times during the Second World War for conferences with President Franklin D. Roosevelt. The first was aboard American and British naval vessels off the coast of Newfoundland, followed by three conferences at Washington, the first of which also included a visit to Ottawa for meetings with Prime Minister William Lyon Mackenzie King and an address to the Canadian House of Commons, and two conferences at the Citadel at Quebec City. After the war Churchill returned to North America in 1946 and 1949, making the famous "Iron Curtain" speech at Fulton, Missouri, on the first occasion. In his second term as prime minister in the early 1950s, Churchill visited North America on three occasions to confer with American and Canadian leaders in Ottawa and Washington. He also crossed the Atlantic in 1953 for the Bermuda Conference with President Dwight Eisenhower and French Prime Minister Joseph Laniel. During his retirement Churchill visited twice more, the last being a brief visit in 1961 at the age of 86 following a cruise of the Caribbean aboard Aristotle Onassis' luxurious yacht the *Christina*.

Churchill's three-month trip to North America in 1929, the subject of this book, was his longest visit to the continent. Already an internationally famous figure as a British politician and writer, he visited Canada and the United States with the purpose of seeing the countries and meeting its leaders in politics and business. Taking a month to travel west across Canada from Quebec City to Victoria, he then spent a further three weeks enjoying California. Crossing the continent eastward, Churchill paused briefly in Chicago before continuing to New York where he stayed for the remainder of the visit, save for a hectic scramble to Washington to call on President Herbert Hoover at the White House and tour Civil War battlefields in Virginia. It was on this long tour that Churchill felt he really was able to get to know the two countries, the "Magnificent Dominion" and "Great Republic" as he called them.

… 1 …

# The Departure, August 3

"It is purely a pleasure trip I am going on and I am looking forward to it with the keenest joy," Winston Churchill told the journalists that had gathered at Waterloo Station in London on the morning of August 3, 1929, to report on his departure to North America. He was relaxed, smiling, and appeared to be "care-free." Wearing a brown lounge suit, a soft collar and bow tie, a brown trilby hat, and brown shoes with white spats, Winston was carrying a brown Malacca cane with a silver knob. He continued, "I shall be away for three months, and during that time I shall travel through Canada, and return via the United States."[1]

Waving goodbye to his friends who had also assembled at the station to see him off, Winston, along with his party, boarded the train bound for the southern England port of Southampton. The train departed Waterloo at 9:26 that morning.[2] Traveling with Winston on this trans-continental tour of North America were his only son Randolph, his brother Jack, and his nephew Johnny. Two of Winston's daughters, Diana and Sarah, went with them on the train, but were only going as far as Southampton.

The train reached Southampton before noon, and the Churchill party went aboard the Canadian Pacific ocean liner *Empress of Australia*. Aboard the ship Winston happily posed for a newspaper photographer with a group of cadets who were traveling on the liner to Canada to participate in the Canadian Bisley, a shooting competition. To the correspondent of the *Southern Daily Echo* he remarked that this trip to North America would be his first visit to that continent in thirty years.[3] Churchill had twice previously crossed the Atlantic, first in 1895 to visit New York City and to observe the war then underway in Cuba, and then again in 1900–01 to complete a lecture tour of the eastern United States and Canada. On his previous visits he had been no further west than Winnipeg, Manitoba. On this trip, however, he intended see the entire continent. Traveling mostly by train, the Churchills planned to cross Canada all the way to Victoria, then travel down the Pacific Coast to Los Angeles before re-crossing the continent to New York by way of Chicago.

The *Empress of Australia*, a yellow-funneled ship flying the red-and-white-checkered house flag of the Canadian Pacific steamships, departed from Berth number 30 of the port of Southampton's Itchen Quays at 1:30 that afternoon.[4] Even though he was embarking on a pleasure tour, Winston wrote his wife Clementine that he felt "melancholy twinges" as he watched the figures of Diana and Sarah slowly disappear as the ship sailed. The liner plodded across a calm English Channel to call at the French port of Cherbourg, where Winston posted his first note of the trip to his wife, before turning west to sail for its ultimate destination of Quebec.

Winston was off on his trip. It would be a holiday of Churchillian proportions. Over the next three months, until he reached England again on November 5th, Winston would crisscross a continent. In the course of the journey he would visit North America's great cities; meet the American president and Canadian prime minister, as well as a host of other politicians; become friends with Charlie Chaplin, the most famous man in the world; visit the fantasy castle of William Randolph Hearst, the most influential man in America; meet leaders of finance and industry; marvel at the scenes of natural beauty; be entertained by famous movie stars in Hollywood; walk the great battlefields in Quebec and Virginia; deliver speeches to enthusiastic audiences, including one to a crowd of 20,000; endure American prohibition laws; and gamble a small fortune on the stock market.

... 2 ...

# Planning the Trip, June–August

In 1929, more than a decade before he became Great Britain's wartime prime minister, the 54-year-old Winston Churchill was already a world famous figure as a soldier, war correspondent, biographer, historian, member of Parliament, cabinet minister, war leader and world statesman, not to mention as an orator, polo player, painter, and brick-layer. Winston possessed dynamic energy, a brilliant mind, great vision, and an enormous capacity for work. This made for a life on an epic scale. One of the most controversial men in Britain, Winston in 1929 was thought a great man by his supporters and a reckless gambler and untrustworthy self-promoter by his detractors. By the time he departed Southampton on his trip to North America he had already been, as the *Ottawa Journal* would write, a "household word throughout the Empire for a generation."[1]

A descendant of John Churchill, the Duke of Marlborough, Winston was born at Blenheim Palace on November 30, 1874. He was the son of the meteoric politician Lord Randolph Churchill and his American wife, the former Jennie Jerome. Winston served as an officer in the British army, seeing war service on the Northwest Frontier of India and in the Sudan, before becoming a war correspondent to report on the Anglo-Boer War. In South Africa he was captured by the Boers and won worldwide headlines by his daring escape from the prison camp where he was being held. Quite indefatigable, Winston also wrote books on the British military campaigns he had participated in, including *The Story of the Malakand Field Force* and *The River War*, as well as one novel titled *Savrola*. Of the novel, he later said he always urged his friends to avoid reading it. Winston would continue to produce a torrent of writing, including books as well as newspaper and magazine articles, throughout his life.

Elected to Parliament in 1900, Winston bolted from the Conservatives to the Liberals in 1904 over the issue of protection and free trade. He always would be an ardent free trader. As a Liberal, Winston successively served as president of the Board of Trade, home secretary, and first lord of the Admiralty. In 1908 he married Clementine Hozier. They would be married for more than 56 years until Winston's death and have five children. Sacked as first lord after the failure of the attempt to storm the Dardanelles in the First World War, an operation which he had instigated, Winston eventually resigned from the government and went to France to command a battalion of the Royal Scots Fusiliers in the trenches on the Western

Front for several months in early 1916. In David Lloyd George's wartime ministry Winston returned to high cabinet office as minister of munitions. After the armistice he was appointed secretary of state for war and for air and later colonial secretary. In 1922 Lloyd George's coalition collapsed, and in the subsequent election Winston went down to defeat at the polls. Just before the election campaign began he had been stricken by illness and had his appendix removed. The collapse of the Liberals, his own defeat, and the medical operation prompted him to quip, "In a twinkling of an eye I found myself without an office, without a seat, without a party, and without an appendix."[2] Out of Parliament, Winston plunged into writing the *World Crisis*, his mammoth history of the First World War. The first volume appeared in 1923, and the fifth and last volume was published in 1931.

After two more election defeats, Winston was returned to Parliament at the 1924 general election as a member for the Epping division after running as a Constitutionalist. In a surprise move, Winston was appointed chancellor of the exchequer, an office once held by his father, by the newly elected Conservative Prime Minister Stanley Baldwin, thus completing his return to the Conservative Party after an interval of two decades. As chancellor, Winston delivered five budgets, negotiated war debts settlements with some of Britain's wartime allies, and edited the news sheet *British Gazette* during the 1926 general strike. In office he followed financial and economic policies for the country that were generally accepted and orthodox at the time, such as the now much discredited return of Britain to the gold standard.[3]

Baldwin's Conservatives ran for reelection in 1929 under the confident slogan of "Safety First." The voters, however, were not interested in safety. Expecting to be comfortably returned to office, the government suffered a shocking setback at the general election held on May 30, 1929. Winston was reelected, but the Conservatives were reduced to 260 seats against Labour's 288. The Liberals had won 59 seats. Rather than make an alliance with Liberals or be seen trying to cling to power by forcing Parliament to meet and turn the Conservatives out of office, Baldwin chose to resign immediately, thus making way for Britain's second Labour government under the new premier Ramsay MacDonald.[4]

Before the government had even resigned and he had been officially deprived of his cabinet office, Winston had already decided to take a trip to Canada and the United States. On the afternoon of June 3, Baldwin's cabinet met for the final time. After the meeting Winston walked in the garden at 10 Downing Street with his cabinet colleague Leo Amery. Despite the surprise defeat, Winston was in "tearing spirits" and excited about a holiday in Canada and the United States.[5] The news that he was to make a trip to North America quickly became known, as by the next day he received a letter from the Cunard Steamship company offering their services for his trip across the Atlantic.

In typical energetic fashion Winston had quickly decided on how he would spend his time now that he was out of government. Over a period of years he planned to write a monumental biography of his most famous ancestor, the Duke of Marlborough, a great military commander. Plunging straight into the project, he hired an assistant to help in the work and sold the serial rights to Lord Camrose for publication in the *Daily Telegraph* for 5,000 pounds.[6] A more immediate venture was, however, embarking on the trip to North America. In June and July Winston hastily made the arrangements.

Winston's eagerness to travel to Canada and the United States after an interval of nearly three decades was motivated by a desire for rest and pleasure, and to see the "wonderful countries, of which I have heard so much."[7] He wanted to see again the places he had visited three decades before so that he could observe and note the changes that had occurred. As well, Winston wished to see the West, where he had not been on his previous trips. In Canada and the United States he also hoped to meet the leading men of each country. As he wrote to Bernard Baruch, his friend and a wealthy American financier, he wanted to see the United States and meet the "leaders of its fortunes." He also assured his friend that he had no political purposes in making the trip, writing that he had "no axe to grind."[8] The pleasure aspect of the tour was emphasized by Winston when he wrote to another friend, Lord Beaverbrook, "What fun it is to get away from England, and feel one has no responsibility for her exceedingly tiresome and embarrassing affairs."[9]

While it is true Winston primarily undertook the 1929 trip for pleasure, such a multifaceted and forceful figure could never be restricted to merely one purpose. As his daughter Mary Soames notes, Winston was "good at combining pleasure with profit," and on this occasion the trip soon became "part holiday and part a programme of speeches."[10] The tour eventually combined many of Winston's interests, from enjoyment of travel to that of journalism, lecturing, promoting his latest book *The Aftermath*, and even painting. Although not planned as a painting holiday (as some of his later excursions were after the Second World War), Winston would bring his painting supplies along just in case opportunities to paint presented themselves.

Winston had previously found it profitable to write about his travels. While in Cuba as a war observer he had written articles for publication in the *Daily Graphic* newspaper, and he had published a book, *My African Journey*, about his 1907 trip across East Africa from Mombasa, Kenya, to Alexandria, Egypt. It is thus not surprising that Winston, having lost his ministerial salary with the election result, sought to subsidize the cost of his trip by writing and selling articles of his observations of Canada and the United States. Before Winston left England he had negotiated a deal for the British rights to ten articles on Canada and the United States with Lord Camrose of the *Daily Telegraph* for the sum of 2,500 pounds.[11] However, initial approaches to the Hearst newspapers, the *New York Times* syndicates, and the *Star* newspaper service in Canada failed to generate any interest in the proposed articles. Eventually, after Winston was already in Canada, the American and Canadian rights were sold to the Bell Syndicate, who agreed to pay $750 per article for ten articles of 1,500 to 2,000 words apiece.[12] The syndicate wanted perhaps one or two articles on Canada and another devoted to Winston's impressions of Prohibition. Winston agreed but noted in a letter sent from California on September 20 that the final selection of topics could not be made until the tour was finished. From California he suggested such possible themes as Prohibition, Hollywood, the Grand Canyon, Chicago, Ford's Works, California, Canadian development, American-Canadian relations, American newspapers, the great stock market craze, the American South, Washington, New York, and Anglo-American cooperation. Dutch and French rights to the articles were also sold, as were rights for South Africa, Malaya, and Australia.[13]

Being proficient at reusing material for later publications, with one example being his newspaper articles that were later published in book form under the title of *Great Contemporaries*, Winston had hopes of publishing the articles about the tour as a book. The proposed book would have been titled *American Impressions*, but neither Thornton Butterworth nor Scribner's, Winston's publishers, were interested in the project, and the idea was eventually dropped.

In planning the trip, Winston called on his family and many friends for advice on what to do and see in North America, introductions to the important figures of the two countries, and for assistance in making the travel arrangements. The generosity of wealthy friends was sought to assist with the travel and lodgings, a generosity Winston was always quick to repay by welcoming visitors either to his home in London or to Chartwell, his beloved estate in Kent. The Canadian portion of the trip was rather quickly arranged, with the Canadian Pacific Railway (CPR) agreeing to lend him a private car in which to travel across the country from Quebec to Vancouver. This private car could be hooked to any CPR train as they traveled across Canada, allowing the traveling party to stop wherever they liked.[14]

The Canadian Pacific was a huge company, with a chain of grand hotels and a fleet of ocean liners to complement its core business of railways. Having been lent the private car for no charge, the party would pay their own fares when traveling to Canada aboard a Canadian Pacific ocean liner and when staying at the company's hotels during the trip. Further hospitality would be happily provided to Winston by Canada's vice-regal representatives and Canadian politicians, many of whom Winston already knew quite well.

The United States leg of the trip took longer to put together. Prominent among those lending their assistance was Bernard Baruch, who was traveling in Europe in the summer of 1929 when the trip was planned. Having become friends during the First World War when they were, respectively, the British minister of munitions and the head of America's War Industries Board, Winston and Baruch had forged a close friendship since the war. Winston later recalled that they first became friends as they exchanged official cables during the war and remained so with the onset of peace.[15] Through June and July the pair exchanged a series of cables and letters as the details of the trip's itinerary were worked out.

The general scheme was for Winston to travel to Los Angeles after he completed his Canadian tour and spend two or three weeks in California. He would then go on to New York, with a stop to marvel at the Grand Canyon. How long Winston remained in America after reaching New York would depend on the political situation in England. He hoped to stay away several weeks, but that would require political events at home remaining uneventful.[16] With the Labour government holding only a minority of seats in Parliament, rapid political developments were always a possibility once Parliament convened.

Winston did not want a fixed itinerary or to take on many speaking engagements in the United States, as he wanted to be free to relax and get to know the country. He emphasized this to Baruch, writing, "One must have time to feel a country and nibble some of the grass."[17]

As the travel plans developed, Winston proposed visiting Salt Lake City, Denver, Chicago, Detroit, Pittsburgh, Cleveland, Richmond, and Washington as he crossed the country from California to New York City. He hoped to visit Detroit, since he had previously promised Henry Ford a visit to inspect his factories; while Baruch further offered to make arrangements for Winston to see the great lumber mills and sea ports in Washington and Oregon at an earlier stage in the American leg of the trip. Baruch advised Winston to spend a day among the Redwoods of California and to travel by motor car rather than train from San Francisco to Los Angeles (and, indeed, all over the state of California). He said that an automobile could be arranged for Winston by one of his friends in the Golden State.[18]

Baruch wrote to Winston in July that he wanted him to meet privately with all the political leaders in Washington and volunteered to make the necessary arrangements. He would arrange meetings with both Democratic and Republican politicians, as he would like

## 2. Planning the Trip, June–August

Winston to meet people from "both sides of the political fence" while in the American capital. Baruch also pledged to arrange for Winston to be conducted over the battlefields of Virginia by an expert who knew the battles thoroughly.

Although Baruch was planning on remaining in Europe until September 23, at which time he would be returning to the United States, Winston was eager to have his American friend join him for at least the last portion of the tour. Baruch readily agreed. Winston wanted him to join the traveling party as early as possible and hoped to meet up with him either in California or as he journeyed east, the farther west the better. He wrote to Baruch that he would immensely enjoy traveling under his "aegis" in the United States.[19] In the end Baruch agreed to meet Winston in Chicago.

Baruch was keen to ensure Winston had a smooth trip. He wrote to him that "I would have you taken in hand by some fine fellow at each point."[20] To this end Baruch cabled his friends and business associates across the United States, telling them of Winston's planned visit and suggesting that if they were interested they might send the British statesman an invitation. As a result of Baruch's efforts a host of offers of hospitality were cabled to Winston, including invites from the former American secretary of the treasury William Gibbs McAdoo in Santa Barbara and William H. Crocker of San Francisco. Both of these offers were accepted. To Crocker, Winston excitedly replied that he was enormously eager to see the sea lions which he had heard so much about and ended humorously, "but please, no earthquakes!"[21] Other associates of Baruch also volunteered to host Winston, including Henry M. Robinson in Los Angeles and Donald R. McLennan in Chicago. The latter wrote Winston that his "good friend" Baruch had informed him of the upcoming visit before proceeding to offer an invitation to dinner, which was also accepted.

Winston wished to meet the American newspaper titan William Randolph Hearst during the California leg of his visit. He asked both Baruch and Lord Beaverbrook, a Canadian-born British newspaper baron, to inquire if a visit for a few days with Hearst could be arranged.[22] Beaverbrook dutifully helped Winston by cabling Hearst in mid July suggesting that if he wished to meet Winston an invitation should be offered. Hearst was indeed interested and cabled Winston from his magnificent estate at San Simeon on July 18 saying it would be his great pleasure to have the traveling party as his guests. Hearst went on to add, "I can guarantee the climate and the thrill of the earthquake and will try to provide other entertainment in matters more immediately under my control." Winston was pleased with the invitation, telling Beaverbrook that it would be "most amusing."[23] He also assumed, quite correctly as it turned out, that Hearst would look after him for the rest of his stay in California once he had reached San Simeon, while Baruch assured him Hearst would introduce him to Hollywood and the movie industry.

The news that Winston would be traveling to the United States produced a shower of other offers of hospitality and invitations to dinners, including one from Percy Rockefeller for Winston to use his flat for his stay in New York City, and another from the financier Otto Kahn proposing to arrange a dinner at his home at which Winston could meet leaders of American finance and industry. The Kahn invitation was accepted, while the Rockefeller offer was eventually declined in favor of staying at a hotel, for which Baruch apparently paid the bill.[24]

Others sought to aid with planning the trip, including Freddie Guest, Winston's cousin and himself a member of Parliament. Guest contacted Richard Tobin, a banker from San Francisco who was at that time serving as the U.S. minister to the Netherlands, for recommendations. Tobin immediately replied that he had written to several people on Winston's behalf, including Crocker and another San Francisco businessman, William Van Antwerp. Tobin also contacted the director of the Lick Observatory, located near San Francisco, asking for Winston to be invited for a night. The proposed visit to the observatory caught Winston's imagination, as he thought it would be very absorbing.[25]

In the United States Winston also wished to renew his acquaintanceship with Charles Schwab, the president of the Bethlehem Steel company. The two had known each other since the first frantic days of the First World War when they had arranged a deal for Schwab to deliver twenty submarines to the Royal Navy. They had remained in touch since. In a letter to Baruch on July 28 Winston wrote that he would like to meet Schwab during the trip and made a not-so-veiled suggestion that some action to this end on Baruch's part would be appreciated, as he wrote that "I expect he is a friend of yours."[26]

While in Washington, Winston desired a meeting with the president of the United States, Herbert Hoover. To this end, he asked the Foreign Office to inform the British ambassador in Washington that he would be in the American capital during the trip and would like to pay his respects to President Hoover.

A pressing concern that had still not been resolved before Winston sailed on the *Empress of Australia* was the question of a private rail car for the English travelers once they reached the United States. In mid-July, still without a private car to bring them east from California, Winston asked the CPR if its car could go past Vancouver and be hauled over American lines if it could be arranged without any additional expense to the company. No matter the reply, Winston wrote to Freddie Guest that they would certainly pay for their own tickets.[27] To Winston's disappointment the Canadian Pacific was unable to allow the private car to be used beyond Vancouver, and an alternative had to be found. On Winston's behalf, Guest cabled his American brother-in-law Jay Phipps about possibly arranging a private car, asking if some American magnate could bring Winston east from the Pacific coast. Phipps consulted the New York Central and Pennsylvania lines through some friends who indicated they would do everything they could to help, despite the federal law against the provision of free train travel. Tobin at The Hague also joined the effort but warned that the "private car is more difficult but I will give it some thought." Baruch was greatly concerned with the problem, telling Winston that traveling by private car "robs the journey" of much of the wear and tear.[28]

As soon as it became known that he was going to Canada and the United States, Winston was besieged with requests for him to speak. Both before and during the trip Winston's secretary was kept busy declining speaking invitations. The Mid-Day Luncheon Club of Springfield, Illinois, the Dutch Treat Club, the Los Angeles Advertising Club, and the Ontario Magistrates Association were just some of the organizations that desperately wanted to hear him speak. Many of the organizations persisted with multiple invitations after the initial approach was declined, while others approached Winston for a speaking engagement through the British Ambassador in Washington or with the support of an American politician.

Winston, however, did not want to speak a great amount while in Canada and the United States. He was determined to limit his speaking engagements to the minimum. Unlike his visit in 1900–01, or when he returned to the United States in 1931–32, this visit was not intended as a lecture tour. When he departed England he had only four speaking engagements scheduled, all in Canada (at Montreal, Toronto, Winnipeg, and Vancouver). This small series of speeches had been arranged in the interest of the National Council of Education and the Overseas Educational League. This league was dedicated to erecting a hostel in London for use by Canadian teachers and students along the lines of one in Paris that had been opened three years earlier by the Prince of Wales. Winston requested that the proceeds of his four speeches be donated for furnishing the hostel.[29]

On the day he sailed from Southampton, Winston had no speaking events at all planned or officially scheduled in the United States. At the most he wanted to speak two or three times. He had told Baruch that he did not want to undertake any public events except for those of a purely honorary nature. If the circumstances were favorable, he might be willing to possibly make one or two speeches while in the United States.[30]

Baruch, on the other hand, was very keen on Winston speaking to the Institute of Politics at Williamstown, Massachusetts. This event would have taken place in August. Both Baruch and the officials of the institute tried to persuade the reluctant British statesman to take up the invitation that had been proffered. Although Winston was scheduled to be traveling across Canada during that month, Baruch suggested he break his Canadian trip to make a dash down to Massachusetts to speak. Winston must have found it difficult to decline an invitation that was so favored by his friend Baruch who was doing so much for him, but he was equally reluctant to commit to speaking fixtures. In the end, Winston's itinerary for the Canadian tour had already been set, and it was impossible to alter it. Using this excuse, Winston was able to opt out of the invitation without, apparently, offending Baruch.[31]

Taking care of various matters as he prepared to embark, Winston had a notice appear in the "Court Circular" section of *The Times* on August 3 requesting that all of his correspondence, except that of a purely personal nature, be sent to him care of Patrick Buchan-Hepburn at the Travellers' Club until the end of October. Buchan-Hepburn, who had been an unsuccessful Conservative candidate in the May election, had just recently been taken on as Winston's new private secretary. He was only interviewed by Winston at Chartwell on June 21. As Winston's secretary, Buchan-Hepburn would send him occasional letters during the trip, catching him up on the political situation in England.[32]

The composition of the party that would accompany Winston to North America was one of the most difficult issues to be resolved. The first person recruited to join the expedition was Winston's brother, John Strange Spencer Churchill. Known as Jack, he was a "quiet man, courteous, and good-looking."[33] Six years younger than his older brother, Jack was born in Dublin in February 1880. Some of Winston's biographers have claimed, probably incorrectly, that he was Winston's half-brother. Whether they were full or half brothers, Winston and Jack loved each other and were close throughout their lives. Jack has been described by Winston's wartime secretary John Colville as being "loyal, affectionate, and scrupulously honourable," and possessing "natural humility." He was always proud to be Winston's brother. More unkindly, Jack has been dismissed as "vague, quiet, inoffensive, the classic 'little man' somewhat bemusedly adrift among eruptive consanguineal peaks."[34]

Jack had attended Harrow, where he shared a room with his brother, and later served with the army in the South African War. On arriving in the country, he joined the South African Light Horse regiment and was wounded in his first skirmish with the Boers. To recover, Jack was transported to the hospital ship, which had been organized and brought to South Africa by his mother. After recovering from his wounds, Jack rejoined his regiment.

Returning to England after the war, he pursued a career as a stock broker, as well as manager of his mother's convoluted financial affairs. Upon the outbreak of the Great War, Jack rejoined the British army, seeing service at Gallipoli on General Sir Ian Hamilton's staff, a campaign that had been instigated by Winston and which almost destroyed his political career, as well as on the Western Front. Jack ended the war with the rank of Major and had received the Distinguished Service Order.[35]

In 1929 Jack was a stock broker in London as a partner in the firm of Vickers da Costa. This firm was also Winston's brokerage firm. Jack had been married since 1908 to Lady Gwendeline Theresa Mary Churchill, known in the family as Goonie. They had three children, Johnny, Peregrine, and Clarissa. His daughter recalled a firmly established routine on the part of her father that did not leave much time for the children. Jack, she said, would leave early in the morning for the City and not return until late, whereupon he would go into the library and open the *Evening Standard*. Only then would she be allowed about fifteen minutes with him.[36] Every August, however, Jack and Goonie would go to Horsey Hall in Norfolk for their holidays where, Clarissa recalled, she would see more of her father. Among Jack's hobbies was fishing and photography. He was also a pianist who regularly attended concerts in London.

An early plan for the grand expedition to North America had been for Winston and Jack to make the trip accompanied by their wives, Clementine and Goonie. However, Goonie was not interested in making such an arduous trip. For her part, Clementine could not undertake the trip due to ill health. She had been sick with mastoid in 1928 and had suffered recurring bouts of illness since then.[37] In early July 1929 Clementine had gone into a London nursing home to undergo a tonsillitis operation. By August she had not recovered enough to even contemplate leaving on the trip. Winston, however, still hoped she would be able to join him for at least part of the tour.

Even after he had embarked on the *Empress of Australia* he was still hopeful in this regard. He wrote to her on August 3 from the ship, admitting it would have been "madness" for her to undertake the journey when she had not regained her strength. Winston, after recommending she devote the next six or seven weeks to calm and rest, urged her not to exclude the possibility of joining the tour in the United States. Again in a letter from the ship five days later, Winston wrote that he would greatly like to make plans for October, although she must get fit and well for those to be arranged.[38] Only after the tour of Canada was a week old did Winston finally accept that having Clementine join him was unrealistic and unwise. He wrote her from Ottawa, conceding that the trip would be tiring and taxing even for him, and that it would have been impossible for her with her recent illness.[39] Instead of joining Winston in North America, Clementine eventually went with her daughter Diana to Italy for a more restful trip that October. Winston and Clementine would celebrate their 21st wedding anniversary on September 12, separated by the Atlantic Ocean and the entire continent of North America.

Although Winston and Clementine spent a great deal of their married life apart, and Winston in the summer of 1929 did not delay his departure on a long trip until his wife was fully recovered, there is no reason to doubt the strength of their marriage.[40] Winston accurately summed up the couple's relationship when he wrote that they married in 1908 and "lived happily ever after." Winston missed Clementine a great deal while on the North American tour and confided that he thought of her all the time. He kept her up to date on the party's progress with a series of long letters, and begged Clementine to cable him with the latest news on her fortunes and how she was getting on.

With Clementine too weak from illness and Goonie just not interested, Robert Boothby was briefly penciled in for the party. The then–29-year-old Boothby was a Conservative member of Parliament who had been Winston's Parliamentary private secretary for the three years until the defeat at the election. Boothby was soon scratched.

With Boothby out, the party of tourists became an all–Churchill affair. Winston's 18-year-old son Randolph was added to the party in place of his mother fairly early on in the planning, while Jack's eldest son Johnny appears to have been a last-minute addition. Only in late July does Winston first mention in any of his correspondence that Johnny will be the final member of the traveling party.

Beyond merely wishing to enjoy the company of his son and nephew on the tour, Winston hoped that bringing them along to North America would broaden their horizons. He wrote as such to Hearst, saying that he wanted the boys to see these "mighty lands at a period in their lives when the proportion of things are established in the mind."[41]

Randolph Frederick Edward Spencer Churchill was born on May 28, 1911. He was Winston and Clementine's second child and their only son. By 1929 Randolph had attended Eton and completed two terms at Christ Church, Oxford. He was described by Colville as a "bewitching companion," while others observed that "no one ever found Randolph more abominable than during the first half hour of acquaintance."[42]

As a young man Randolph was very handsome and a great success with the ladies. He was "dazzlingly handsome, dazzlingly opinionated, a fierce partisan of his father and ardently studying to follow in his footsteps."[43] Throughout his life Randolph could be charming as well as arrogant and quick with abuse. As Winston never punished or even made him apologize for being rude, Randolph made being rude a habit, thinking it was "clever."[44] Randolph's charm, budding arrogance, and rudeness would all be displayed on the tour of North America.

The relationship between Winston and his only son was a difficult one, marked in later years by terrible rows and much bitterness. Having suffered greatly from the neglect of his own father, Winston was determined to avoid those mistakes with Randolph. The results, however, were unhappy. Rather than neglect his son, Winston spoiled him terribly and encouraged frightfully high aspirations in him. In 1928 Randolph appeared to assume that he would be the youngest prime minister in history, as "it seemed only too easy for a Churchill with his talent."[45]

From his early teens Randolph was allowed to dine and argue on equal terms with Winston's friends, including such giants as Lord Birkenhead, David Lloyd George, and Beaverbrook. Winston ignored all warnings from his wife, as well as his friends Brendan Bracken and Professor Frederick Lindemann, that he was spoiling the boy.[46]

In 1929 the great unpleasantness between father and son mostly lay in the future. The seeds of the future problems, however, were in evidence on the tour, with Winston occasionally indulging Randolph and encouraging him as a mere 18-year-old to address packed audiences and speak on equal terms with the worthies they met on the trip.

Winston and Randolph had been travel companions many times before the trip to North America. From the time Randolph was twelve his family had traveled abroad nearly every summer, usually driving through France. On one occasion they had gone to Biarritz and then motored through the foothills of the Pyrenees to Carcassonne and then on to the French Riviera. In 1927 Winston, Randolph, and Jack had made a trip to Italy, Greece, and France, during which they had separate audiences with Mussolini and Pope Pius in Rome. The next year Winston and Randolph had traveled to France together for a holiday.[47]

The tour of North America would be a rare time in his life that Randolph kept a diary. Winston noted during the trip that his son was regularly writing in it. Randolph, however, keenly protected its contents and would not let his father read it.[48] Despite the enthusiasm in keeping the journal, the diary excerpts included in Randolph's book *Twenty-One Years* are not very detailed and somewhat unreliable, especially in regard to dates. The most interesting portions of the diary were, unfortunately, probably left out of the book.

The last member of the party, who would occasionally be omitted from newspaper reports about the party's progress, was John George Spencer Churchill. Born May 31, 1909, he was always known in the family as Johnny. Johnny was friendly and charming, but among Jack and Goonie's three children he was the "odd one out, fun-loving, mischievous, and irresponsible."[49] An excellent swimmer, diver, and acrobat, Johnny's first interest was art. At Harrow he was an eager art student and specialized in watercolors. His passion for art was not at all understood by his father, who Johnny claimed thought art was merely "playing the ass in the gutter."[50] Johnny has been described as "moon-faced, musical, artistic, cherubic, and with just a trace of the satyr in his eyes."[51]

In 1929 Johnny was a 20-year-old student at Oxford who, by his own admission, did not know what he was studying or to what purpose. Jack had attempted to resolve his son's vague plans for the future by suggesting he could have a good career with British Petroleum or a similar company. Such a career would, in Jack's experience, require an initial posting to Mesopotamia or another such remote outpost for ten years to learn the business. Johnny recoiled at the idea, which led to his maddened father asking what he would like to do. Johnny recalled, "In my heart I wanted to answer: music, painting, and sculpture, but felt it was fatuous to even consider this." As there was no money in it, a career in art would not be tolerated. Johnny could thus only answer his father's question with an infuriating, "I don't know."[52] Jack's solution was that if his son refused to do anything sensible, he could at least be expected to join his office at the stock exchange. The stock exchange, Jack claimed, was an "easy life" in which for the signing of a few documents a man could be kept in port and cigars.[53]

In the meantime, before he went into the stock exchange, Jack thought it still worthwhile to send his son to Oxford in the hope he might develop "in a definite direction." After one disastrous exam result and the ensuing help of a crammer, Johnny managed to pass into Oxford and go to Pembroke College.

At the time of the tour, Johnny was in love with a girl named Sophie, who was herself in India. While in North America he would write to her constantly in his spare moments. Johnny's declared affection for Sophie did not prevent the young man from showing a great interest in many of the young ladies that he met on the tour.

Randolph and his cousin Johnny were quite close in 1929. During the Great War, when the two cousins were still young children, the two families had lived together in a house at 41 Cromwell Road in London.[54] Additionally, the families had frequently been together at Winston's "weekend haven" of Lullenden near East Grinstead. Johnny was already at Oxford by the time his cousin arrived there. Randolph later remembered that upon reaching Oxford he called on Johnny at his rooms at Pembroke College only to find him lying on a high platform painting one of the murals that adorned his rooms. He had not been down from the platform for three days and was having his food and drink passed up to him. Not surprisingly, Randolph thought that Johnny "cut a considerable figure" at Oxford with his many unusual ways. In turn, Johnny considered Randolph a "sort of Nordic or Anglo-Saxon equivalent of Rudolph Valentino."[55]

Being undergraduates together at Oxford gave the cousins a renewed closeness. Johnny felt a special rapport with Randolph, as he, quite self-servingly, thought that their respective fathers always made them both feel like children.[56]

Although the two cousins planned to leave the tour early to return home for the start of the new Oxford term, Randolph later wrote that it was "with immense excitement that Johnny and I set out on this adventure."

On the two nights in August before Churchill left on his tour, Victor Cazalet, MP, joined Winston for dinner. Winston was in fine form. On the first night he held forth on the history of Parliament since 1881, the Dreyfus case, *The Ring and the Book*, and his American tour, along with playing Bezique until two o'clock in the morning. On the second night he talked about the Duke of Marlborough until a slightly earlier hour of 1:30 in the morning.[57] The trip and planned biography of the Duke of Marlborough were his two main preoccupations that summer.

## ... 3 ...

## The Empress of Australia, August 3–9

The ship that would be Winston's home for the next six days was the *Empress of Australia*, a 21,850-ton liner. Launched in 1913, the vessel had originally been the *Tirpitz* of the Hamburg America Line. Turned over as war reparations, the ship had been bought from Britain in July 1921 by the Canadian Pacific for its Pacific Ocean run. After being briefly renamed the *Empress of China*, the ship finally became the *Empress of Australia*. It was 615 feet in length, 75 feet in breadth, and could steam at over 20 knots. The ship was capable of carrying nearly 1,500 passengers, including 400 in first class. On September 1, 1923, the *Empress of Australia* had been docked at Yokohama, Japan, when an earthquake struck. The ship remained in port and assisted with the rescue efforts. After 22 round-trip Pacific voyages the *Empress of Australia* went in for a refit, and when it emerged in 1927 it reentered service on the North Atlantic route.[1]

The *Empress of Australia* was a luxurious ship. It had seven decks for passengers, two elevators, a gymnasium, a Pompeiian swimming pool, a writing room, and a smoking room, as well as a lounge on the promenade deck, a drawing room, a swimming pool on the deck, and a Verandah café. The first-class dining saloon sat 330 people at tables for two to six diners. The suites on the ship consisted of a bedroom, sitting room, sun room, baggage room, and a private bath and toilet.[2]

Winston judged the ship "very comfortable," and the cabins the party had been assigned were marvelous. While the ordinary first-class ticket on the *Empress of Australia* cost 50 pounds, the Churchills paid an extra 100 pounds to get the best accommodations. As the Canadian Pacific was providing him with a private rail car in Canada, Winston wrote Clementine that he could hardly quibble about their cabins on the ship.[3]

The captain of the *Empress of Australia* for the voyage was Robert "Jack" Latta, who was well known on the "North Atlantic and throughout the world."[4] The then–56-year-old had been born in Scotland and joined the Canadian Pacific in 1904 as fourth officer on the *Montezuma*. He achieved steady promotion and commanded the Canadian Pacific ship's *Monmouth*, *Sicilian*, *Grampain*, *Scandinavian*, and *Mount Royal*. In 1927 he had taken command of the refitted *Empress of Australia* on the service between Southampton, Cherbourg, and Quebec. That same year Latta carried the Prince of Wales and Prime Minister Stanley

The CPR liner *Empress of Australia* carried the Churchills from Southampton to Quebec City (Canadian Pacific Archives NS.1075).

Baldwin to Canada for the 60th anniversary of the dominion's confederation. After completing a record crossing of the North Atlantic on another voyage, Latta was made an honorary chief of the Iroquois and given the name Tetoniatarakakowa, which translated as "swiftest rider of the mighty water."[5] Latta would remain with the *Australia* until appointed to command the *Empress of Britain*, the flagship of the Canadian Pacific Fleet, upon her entry into service in 1931. Captain Latta, Johnny later recorded in his memoirs, was an entertaining host at his table and had a great collection of stories to tell.

Aboard the *Empress of Australia* for the crossing to Quebec were several leading figures in different fields that would have held some appeal to Winston's interests. These included the former Chinese minister to London, Dr. Wellington Koo; a leading British throat specialist, Sir George Badgerow; the wife of the Canadian high commissioner to London, Jean Larkin, and her daughter Aileen; and a host of Canadian businessmen. Also aboard were George Lawson Johnston, the first Lord Luke, and his wife Edith. Luke was a noted food manufacturer as chairman of the company Bovril.[6]

Although Winston was probably introduced to many of the other passengers during the crossing, he spent a great deal of the voyage speaking with his former cabinet colleague and political rival Leo Amery, who was also traveling. At five-foot-four-inches, Amery was a short, brilliant, bespectacled, pugnacious man who had once been fined two pounds for boxing the ears of a political opponent who had refused to apologize for calling him a liar.[7]

Traveling separately on the same train from Waterloo, Amery had also boarded the *Empress of Australia* at Southampton. Like Winston, he was going to Canada for a holiday, with the possibility of giving a few lectures. Amery was planning, however, after landing at Quebec to go directly to the Rocky Mountains where he intended to be the first to climb the 10,940-foot-high Mount Amery, which had been named in his honor two years earlier. Aside from being an accomplished scholar and politician, Amery was an outdoorsman and mountaineer who had scaled the Matterhorn several times. Mount Amery in Canada would be one of three mountains that were named after him, the other two being in South Africa and on Kerguelen Island.[8]

Although Winston and Amery had known each other since first meeting under inauspicious circumstances as schoolboys at Harrow in 1889, they had never been close. They always had a difficult relationship. Disagreeing on a range of issues, including free trade, the gold standard, naval strength, the empire, America, and India, Winston and Amery could never quite be friends. As Robert Rhodes James noted, "there was always a definite restraint, a lack of warmth, a noticeable caution and reserve" between the two.[9]

The nature of their turbulent relationship was set for life in their dubious first meeting at Harrow in which Winston pushed Amery into a pool. Like the other schoolboys, Winston had thought it was great fun to push unsuspecting boys into the water. Amery recalled being greatly surprised at being knocked into the pool by a foot to the middle of his back and even more surprised to discover a younger schoolboy had been the perpetrator. A furious Amery climbed out of the pool and, after catching a fleeing Winston, hurled him into the deepest part of the water. Upon emerging from the pool himself, Winston found that despite being small in stature, Amery was in the sixth form, head of his House, a champion at gym, had received his football colors, and was holder of many other such impressive titles. Winston was "convulsed not only with terror, but with guilt of sacrilege."[10] He was determined to apologize and explain that he had been unable to tell Amery's importance due to his victim's short stature.

Winston duly approached Amery the next day and said, "I am very sorry. I mistook you for a Fourth Form boy. You are so small."

Not surprisingly, Amery was not placated by this explanation, but Winston retrieved the situation when he added, in what he thought a brilliant recovery, "my father, who is a great man, is also small."

At that point Amery laughed and, after chiding Winston for his "cheek" and warning him that he best be more careful in the future, indicated the matter was closed. In his memoirs Amery would remember that although a great wrong had been committed in his being dunked by a younger boy, he had the "permanent consolation" of Winston's "delightful apology."[11]

Elected to the Parliament in 1911 as a Conservative, Amery had entered the cabinet as first lord of the Admiralty under Andrew Bonar Law eleven years later. He was appointed colonial secretary by Baldwin in 1924 and served in cabinet alongside Winston who was chancellor of the exchequer. The two constantly disagreed. In cabinet meetings their battles were so continuous that Baldwin claimed half the time was taken up by Winston's speeches and the other half with Amery's rejoinders. Amery was not an effective communicator, prone to speaking too often and too long. It was quipped that Amery might have been prime minister had "he been half a head taller and his speeches half an hour shorter."[12]

Amery considered Baldwin's appointment of Winston, a stubborn free trader, as chancellor of the exchequer to be a disaster for both the nation and the Conservative Party. He thought Winston was an "unrepentant Victorian" at heart on the important issues of free trade and protection, while ignoring the problem of unemployment. In 1927 Amery had urged Baldwin to move Winston from the exchequer and give him authority to coordinate the three fighting services, and two years later had again unsuccessfully advised the removal of the domineering Winston, this time proposing to shuffle him out of the way to the Foreign Office.[13] In the aftermath of the 1929 election defeat, Amery quite readily agreed with his Labour successor at the Colonial Office, James Henry Thomas, that it was "certainly Winston that killed you."[14]

Aboard the *Empress of Australia* Amery would devote much time to gymnastics, swimming, and reading, as well as having long talks with Winston on the many subjects in which they were interested, including honest and frank chats on their differences. The two recently deposed cabinet members had their first talk of the voyage after lunch on the day the *Empress of Australia* sailed from Southampton. The weather seemed threatening but the waters were quite smooth to Cherbourg. As they walked around the deck, Winston told Amery about the prices he had received for writing articles, such as 500 pounds a month from *Cosmopolitan*. Amery seemed taken aback that his colleague had gone on writing and selling articles all the time he was in office as chancellor of the exchequer.[15] In 1923–24, before entering the cabinet, Winston's earnings from his literary efforts had been 16,448 pounds. Once chancellor of the exchequer, he had indeed continued to write but not, of course, with the same rate of productivity.[16]

Winston invited Amery to join their table that night, but his fellow member of Parliament had already accepted an invitation from Captain Latta. Amery did go on to join the Churchill party afterwards and spend the evening with them in Winston's sitting room. A routine was thus established for the duration of the voyage. The next day, August 4, the Churchills and Amery talked until nearly midnight on various topics, including whether one is really afraid of death when it does come and whether one would stand up straight in the face of a firing party.[17] Although Winston and Jack's relationship with their respective sons was far from perfect and would have their own problems in the future, Amery might have envied the Churchill fathers and sons spending three months happily traveling across North America. By 1929 Amery's eldest son John was already exhibiting the instability that would plague his parents until he was ultimately executed by hanging for treason in 1945 for having made pro–German broadcasts from Germany during the Second World War.

In one of their conversations aboard the ship, Randolph recalled his father and Amery discussing school life at Harrow. Winston said, "I have always had the greatest sympathy for convicts, and when home secretary always strove to reduce their sentences as I myself have undergone eleven years of penal servitude in the private and public schools of Britain!"[18]

Both aboard the *Empress of Australia* and throughout the tour of North America, Winston would remain in contact with England by cables and mail. His correspondence on political and business matters, as well as letters from family and friends, would follow him as he progressed through the trip. On the ship Winston considered the wireless a great advantage as he had been able to hear regularly from Horace Vickers, Winston's personal stockbroker, about trading on the stock market. The news in that regard was entirely satisfactory.[19] Winston sent several cables, he called them Marconigrams, to Clementine and was delighted to receive her cabled replies. As the ship neared Quebec he urged her not to hesitate to cable him, as it saved a fortnight in time over the mail, and such a message of 20 or 30 words was not that expensive. He compared the price to what one spends on the stalls at the theater, and yet a cable gives so much more joy.[20]

As Martin Gilbert has noted, for the entire three-month trip Winston was removed from British politics and thus unable to influence Conservative party policy-making, most especially on two issues about which he cared very deeply: free trade and the Empire.[21] A form of trade protection was again being proposed when Winston left for Canada. On this occasion, Beaverbrook, Austen Chamberlain, and Amery were leading calls for Empire free trade, which Winston always firmly rejected.

Another issue that reached the boiling point shortly before Winston departed was Egypt's constitutional status. Before leaving England, Winston had reacted angrily against the Labour government's proposals for new negotiations over that country's position. This new approach on Egypt had begun with the unceremonious dismissal of Lord Lloyd as High Commissioner. Lloyd, who was a friend of Winston, had been acting in Cairo more as a proconsular than as a high commissioner. Winston emerged as Lloyd's principal defender and spoke against his sacking in the House of Commons. This was an unpopular position and was poorly received, garnering hostile reactions even from the Conservative benches. Foreshadowing their future break over India, Stanley Baldwin sat silently as Winston spoke. It was evident that on Egypt Winston was "almost alone in the House."[22]

Although unable to save his friend in 1929, Winston rehabilitated Lloyd in 1940 when, as prime minister, he appointed him colonial secretary. Winston would brood about free trade and Egypt with his traveling party aboard the ship and debate the issues with Amery, all as a precursor to his returning to these subjects in his speeches to Canadian audiences.

On August 5 Winston and Amery had a long talk by themselves, as Jack had retired to bed early, and Randolph and Johnny had slipped away to dance. The two politicians, rather than debate generalities, talked about their immediate differences. First among them was free trade. In his diary Amery complained that no argument on the topic made any difference to Winston and accused him of being exactly where he was 25 years before. Winston was just repeating the "old phrases, of 1903." In Amery's opinion, Winston thought in phrases and the only way to get home with him was to produce "equally striking counter phrases" rather than detailed arguments.[23] Winston told Amery that in 1903 he had tried to convince himself Joe Chamberlain was right on trade but had been unable to do so. They also discussed Joe Chamberlain's Board of Trade speeches against free trade and Baldwin's maneuvering on the issue in 1923. Winston thought Baldwin was only trying to position himself politically in the event Lloyd George started such a fiscal campaign, while Amery protested that the move was genuine, as Baldwin was worried about unemployment and sought a remedy. Later writing in the margins of his diary, Amery conceded that Winston was correct about Baldwin's motives, and it was only his own "innocence" that left him unable to decipher Baldwin's true intentions.[24] The two also disagreed about the political value of their respective positions on trade. Amery claimed the only way to win an election was to fight on a protective and preferential policy, while Winston thought it "incredible" that anyone would dare face the cry of "food tax."

Amery told Winston of how he had often wished to leave the Baldwin government and possibly should have, but now in opposition he was not going to be "muzzled." Winston replied that if Amery succeeded in his plans he would retire from politics and devote himself to making money. Regardless, Winston added that he had achieved all he had ever wanted in politics short of the "highest post," which he saw no prospect of ever reaching. Besides, he complained, politics was not what it had once been, with the level now much lower. There were no great men like Gladstone, Salisbury, and Morley, or even Harcourt and Hicks Beach. These Victorians, Amery said, were "relatively small men making a lot of to do about relatively small matters." Winston was willing to admit the issues were "less titanic," but the men themselves were "much greater."[25]

This discussion closed about eleven that evening. As Amery got up to go, Winston started to dress for bed, donning a long silk nightshirt with a wooly tummy band over it. Amery started smiling, and Winston asked why he was grinning.

"Free trade, Mid-Victorian statesmanship and the old-fashioned nightshirt, how appropriate a combination," Amery chuckled as he left.

In his diary that night Amery wrote that the key to Winston was that he was "Mid-Victorian, steeped in the politics of his father's period, and unable ever to get the modern point of view." This fact was only disguised by Winston's "verbal exuberance and abounding vitality."[26] For his part, Winston thought he had made progress with Amery aboard the liner, both personally and politically. After he landed at Quebec he wrote Clementine that Amery had been pleasant company on the voyage and (more unlikely) that, perhaps due to his arguments, Amery had strongly criticized the Empire free trade campaign in an interview with the Canadian newspapers.[27]

While willing to concede that the *Empress of Australia* had spacious accommodations, Randolph did not enjoy the ocean crossing. He thought it was boring. On Monday August 5, two days out of Southampton, he wrote in his diary that he could never remember a weekend passing so slowly and quoted Dr. Johnson that "being on a ship is like being in prison with the extra chance of being drowned." Randolph would only suggest modifying the quote to substitute sick for the word drowned. The next day he, a budding snob, wrote that he sighed for the company of his friends and claimed, probably referring to the other passengers, that the "vast majority of one's fellow-men and women are dull, graceless, unattractive, gauche, and boorish." He was willing to grant that if one knew these people they would probably be very charming and even generously conceded that they "no doubt serve some useful function." Randolph fervently hoped that something interesting would soon happen, but such hopes faced an "uphill fight till we reach firm land once more."[28]

Unlike his son, Winston had no such difficulty in keeping busy. Rather than devoting himself only to rest aboard the liner, he intended to do a great deal of work. A goal was set of reading extensively on Marlborough and completing two articles which he had agreed to write. In a letter to his friend and former private secretary, Eddie Marsh, Winston reported on August 7 that the ship was splashing along and that he was hard at work as usual.[29] The result of his labors aboard the *Empress of Australia* included writing an article on Lord Morley. Pronouncing himself very pleased with the biographical profile, it was probably dispatched to London and New York from Rimouski on the morning of August 9. This article was published in the November 1929 issue of *Nash's Pall Mall*. Winston did not finish the other article he intended to write aboard the ship — "Will the British Empire Survive" for *Answers* magazine. He decided to complete it later on the trip and wrote Clementine that he "dared say [the British Empire] will last as long as that."[30] This article was duly finished before he reached Banff late in the month and published in the October 26, 1929, issue of the magazine. For both of these articles Winston received 750 pounds. Although Winston would revise and polish his articles many times before he was satisfied, he always ensured the articles arrived on time.

The goal of completing a large amount of work on Marlborough was likewise accomplished. Winston enjoyed the prospect of undertaking such a massive project as the one he had planned for his illustrious ancestor. It was wonderful to have the contracts settled, he told Clementine, and have two or three years of pleasant work before him. To ensure the project was completed in the manner he wished, Winston had decided to spend money on what he termed expert assistance. From the ship he wrote Rear Admiral Kenneth G.B. Dewar, recently placed on the retired list, asking if he was interested in assisting with the book by studying and discussing the naval aspects of the War of the Spanish Succession. He also planned to hire a military officer to study, under his direction, the land campaigns. After reading several histories of the War of the Spanish Succession, Winston wrote his wife that he was confident he could "tell a tale which will rivet attention." The published literature he had read was lacking "colour, structure, drama & simplicity."[31]

The one pressing task that Winston did not undertake on the crossing of the North Atlantic was preparing the speeches he was to give in Canada. He confessed to Clementine that he had done nothing about the speeches but did have some ideas formed. It would be better, he thought, to wait until he landed to see what the atmosphere was, and then he would have all of Sunday as well as Monday morning to work on his first speech, which he was to give to a luncheon audience in Montreal.

Beyond his hard work, Winston also relaxed aboard the *Empress of Australia* by playing a great deal of Bezique with Jack. He boasted that he inflicted many cruel defeats on his brother, "marking over 1,000 points in my favour." Randolph and Johnny spent an hour and a half each day in the ship's swimming pool where the young people, both male and female, played water polo. It was an interesting game, since when the ship "reels to and fro tremendous waves are hurled from one side of the pool to the other." Winston did not risk the pool and stuck to the "hot water."[32]

During the Atlantic crossing Winston believed he had met with partial success in enforcing discipline upon his son. He tried to get Randolph out of bed in the morning and off to bed at a reasonable hour each night, as well as ensuring that a certain amount of reading was being done.

Winston's talk with Amery on the evening of August 6 was mainly about the failed Dardanelles campaign of the Great War. After recounting the series of missed chances that just prevented the British from getting through the straits, Winston said in jest that it was his conclusion that God had wished the war to be prolonged in order to sicken mankind of war and thus interfered with his project designed to bring it to a speedier conclusion. Winston's other evidence for the deity in this conversation with his fellow Parliamentarian was the very existence of Lenin and Trotsky, for whom a hell was needed. As the talk shifted to Field Marshal Douglas Haig, the controversial overall British commander on the Western Front for the last three years of the war, Winston said that Haig's conduct since the war had made him sometimes wonder whether he was quite so hopeless a general as he had thought at the time.[33]

On August 7 Randolph recorded in his diary that utterly nothing had happened that day beyond the usual water polo he had played in the pool. At dinner that night Winston called the attention of those at his table several times to record his opinion that there would soon be grave trouble in Egypt. This country was at the time only nominally independent and firmly under British rule. Egyptian nationalists were, however, demanding both full independence and the withdrawal of the British military from the country.[34] That day Winston was appalled by the information received via a news telegram that the British foreign secretary, Arthur Henderson, had announced a new Anglo-Egyptian treaty that incorporated many of the demands of the Egyptian nationalists. The draft agreement ended British occupation of Cairo and Alexandria, and pulled all British troops back to the canal. Winston was doubly angered, as he felt Henderson had lied in a House of Commons debate when he had said no negotiations were underway, but then almost immediately a new treaty had been published, "cut and dried." The entire plan of withdrawing to the canal and leaving the rest of Egypt "to go to hell" was doomed, in Winston's view. He predicted that disorder would soon ensue and the British would be forced to resume their "abdicated responsibility." This would all occur after possibly serious bloodshed. Although Winston was very upset about Egypt at dinner, Randolph noted that some 1865 brandy cheered him up.[35]

During that evening's talk with Amery, Winston recalled his escape from Pretoria after he had been taken prisoner during the South African War. To escape he had only to scramble over a lattice work and drop over the side. As Winston told it, he had given the other two prisoners who were trying to escape with him every chance to come with him and had urged them as they spoke through the lattice work to follow him. They would not take the chance, while Winston was unable to come back inside as they wished. After receiving their blessing, he set out alone, but told Amery "he never felt so lonely as the next day when he dropped off the train and was alone in the veld." Winston could only think about how less than two months before he had been lunching with Ernest Cassel, a financier and friend, at the Savoy and prayed to God for help. He thought his prayers were being answered when he reached a friendly house whose occupant aided his escape.[36]

Amery was very familiar with Winston's escape from the Boers, as he had been with Winston on the morning that he had been captured by the enemy. Both men were in South Africa as journalists, Amery as a *Times* correspondent and Winston working on behalf of the *Morning Post*. They had dined one evening with an army colonel and arranged to go out with a British armored train the following morning. That morning it was pouring rain when they were called in their tent by Winston's Indian servant. From inside his sleeping bag Amery said it was no possible use rushing about and getting wet in the rain, as the train, although scheduled to depart at six o'clock, would never leave before eight o'clock. Winston volunteered to go ahead and find out about the train at the rail siding, which was just 300 yards away. In fact, Winston only just caught the departing train. Two hours later Amery was woken by the sound of gunfire and, in the company of the *Manchester Guardian*'s correspondent J.B. Atkins, rushed towards the scene. He met the returning train carrying the survivors of the fight with the Boers, who were full of praise for Winston's bravery during the action.

Years later Amery reminded Winston of that morning in South Africa and told him that the early worm was apt to get caught. To which Winston replied, "If I had not been early, I should not have been caught. But if I had not been caught, I could not have escaped, and my imprisonment and escape provided me with materials for lectures and a book which brought me in enough money to get into Parliament in 1900—ten years before you." Amery admitted Winston's rejoinder was excellent but with the qualifier that in actuality he did not even think of standing for Parliament until the issue of imperial preference was raised by Joe Chamberlain in 1903.[37]

The talk was shorter than usual that evening, as both members of Parliament attended a concert, at which Winston presided. At the concert Randolph thought his father made quite a good speech. The concert itself, however, was dismissed as "bad" by the younger Churchill. The poor performance was balanced out somewhat by Randolph meeting an attractive Canadian girl. By the end of that day he was quite tired as he wrote his diary entry in the cabin that he shared with Johnny, who was also anxious for sleep.[38]

From midnight to daybreak on August 8 the *Empress of Australia* sailed carefully, wary of drifting icebergs. In Winston's words, a "most vigilant watch was kept" for several dangerous growlers, low-lying icebergs that were not only difficult to spot but also capable of fatally injuring a fast moving ship. The ship ahead of the *Empress of Australia* had reported several such growlers, but the night was clear and speed could be maintained. Had there been fog, the ship would have been forced to stop and wait for daylight.[39]

At half-past-six o'clock that morning Captain Latta roused Randolph and Johnny out of their beds to see a large iceberg that the ship passed at no great distance. It was 160 feet high. No one woke Winston for the excitement, and he missed seeing the iceberg, which he thought was a shame. That day the *Empress of Australia* reached North American waters. After the bleakness of the North Atlantic, Winston was pleased to see the "green shores of Labrador." That day the ship passed the site where the *Raleigh* was wrecked two years earlier and the desolate island of Greenly off the Labrador coast, where on April 13, 1928, the exhausted aviators flying a German Junkers aircraft had landed after completing the first crossing of the Atlantic Ocean from east to west by airplane. As the *Empress of Australia* passed the Straits of Belle Isle between Newfoundland and Labrador, Winston was writing a long letter to Clementine in which he reported that the ocean passage had been very good, with only one day of rough seas. Despite the good passage, he told Clementine that he had been rather sad at times as he thought of her lonely and miserable in England recovering from her illness.[40]

The Gulf of the St. Lawrence, which Winston called a "great inland sea," lay before the ship.[41] The weather was getting warmer and the sea was quiet. By eleven o'clock on the morning of August 9, the *Empress of Australia* was sailing in the St. Lawrence River, which Winston called a "noble estuary," into the heart of Eastern Canada. Five hours later the inbound ship was southeast of Crane Island, about 50 miles east of Quebec.[42]

As the ship approached its destination, newspaper reporters came aboard to interview Winston and Leo Amery. Before he had even set foot ashore, Winston received his first requests for interviews. These requests would continue unabated for the duration of the tour. In Canada Winston would usually accept the requests, although not always giving anything more than routine answers; while in the United States, on the more private leg of the trip, he was very likely to decline the demands for interviews.

After the Churchill party posed for a photograph on the deck of the ship, Winston gave his first newspaper interviews of the trip in the ship's smoking room for reporters from Quebec and Montreal newspapers. He answered their questions while gazing out the windows at the panorama passing by. The inevitable "very big cigar" was evident throughout. In the corner of the room Amery "beamed benevolently" as he watched and listened.

"I came to Canada 30 years ago and saw it under a blanket of snow. That impression naturally persisted. I have come out this time to correct it, to see Canada in its summer dress, in all its beauty, to learn about Canada," Winston remarked.[43]

Although Winston proclaimed as he watched the passing scenes that he would like to go up to the bridge and see the lovely scenes, he did remain long enough to answer questions on a wide array of topics. He would not hazard a guess on how long the Labour government would survive but said their tenure in power would depend on whether they forgot "a lot of its silly nonsense" they had been proposing. Winston also commented on such issues of the day as deploring the ongoing Lancashire cotton strike (then in its third week), opposing restoring relations with Russia, doubting that Labour would nationalize the coal industry, stressing the importance of the Singapore naval base, remarking on the naval negotiations between the United States and Britain, and giving his support to the position of his successor as chancellor of the exchequer, Philip Snowden, in opposition to the Young Plan on war reparations. He declined to express an opinion on the developments regarding Egypt, as he had not yet read the agreement, and would not comment on free trade, as that would be the topic of his first speech in Canada in Montreal. On Canada, Winston said he had always been impressed by the country's natural wealth and was pleased to have this opportunity to see its great possibilities first-hand.[44]

"But I must, I really must, get up on deck and see all this," Winston told the reporters as he waved his hand towards the window. "You won't mind, will you?"

With that, Winston was gone, with his cigar a-tilt, as E.J. Archibald of the *Montreal Daily Star* observed. Having listened to Winston's interview, it was Amery's turn to answer the questions, including the ones on free trade and Egypt. Winston and Amery's willingness to be interviewed led the *Quebec Chronicle-Telegraph* to write that the two "have something to say and are not afraid to say it." It was thus light work for newspapermen.[45]

In reporting the interview, Archibald commented that in Winston and Amery there were two happy men who came to Canada aboard the *Empress of Australia*. The electoral defeat and loss of cabinet offices apparently had not caused either of them great concern.[46]

Winston was eager to break off the interview, as Captain Latta had earlier invited the Churchills to the bridge when the ship entered Quebec so that they could see the arrival from the best viewpoint. After being 12 miles wide a mere 32 miles below the city, the St. Lawrence River at Quebec narrows to a width of only 1,000 yards. Quebec was situated on the north bank of the St. Lawrence, with the Lower Town on the banks of the river and the Upper Town on the heights above. Winston thought there was much to strongly recommend, both in the view and Quebec City itself. He later wrote, "[The] romance and charm of the City of Quebec is matched by the singular beauty of the surrounding country. It is Scotland at its best."[47]

Johnny thought the "spectacle of entering Quebec" was outstanding but claimed a family controversy marred the affair, as Randolph missed the view from the bridge. He could not be found anywhere, and his father was left to growl, "Where has he got to?" Although probably an exaggeration, Johnny claimed that Randolph was still missing when the ship docked, and the other members of the party went ahead and disembarked without him. Johnny maintained that Randolph eventually turned up at the hotel in a taxi with a "wonderful excuse about being locked in a bathroom." He was then thoroughly ticked off by his father.[48]

... 4 ...

# Quebec, August 9–12

If Winston was looking forward to seeing Canada again after the passing of thirty years, Canada was equally looking forward to seeing him again. In advance of his arrival in each city on the tour, his visit would be hailed as that of one of the Empire's greatest figures. Newspaper sketches would praise his career as "amazing" and "meteoric," calling him the "most restless, dynamic, and spectacular personality in British public life" and the "most interesting phenomenon of our time."[1] The *Victoria Daily Colonist* wrote that Winston was one of "that rare type of men bound to succeed in any walk of life," while the magazine *Saturday Night* headlined their profile on him as "Churchill, the Man of Courage."[2]

On his one previous visit to Canada during his lecture tour of 1900–01, Winston had spoken in Montreal, Ottawa, Toronto, and Winnipeg. In the thirty years since he had been in Canada, the country had grown from a population of 5,371,000 and seven provinces in 1901 to 9,796,000 and nine provinces and two territories in 1929, covering a total area of 3,684,723 square miles. Granted dominion status in 1867, Canada had celebrated the 60th anniversary of confederation in 1927. The enthusiastic reception given to Winston's rousing speeches on the British Empire was evidence that Canadians in 1929, or at least English-speaking Canadians, strongly identified with Britain and the Empire. The dominion sent a large contingent to fight in the First World War, with the Canadian Corps gaining a reputation as an elite formation on the Western Front. After the sacrifices of the Great War, then–Canadian Prime Minister Robert Borden won a role in the Paris Peace Conference, with the prime minister leading a Canadian delegation. A landmark in the gradual pursuit of greater political independence from Britain had taken place at the 1926 Imperial Conference in London. The conference had agreed that the self-governing dominions of the empire were of equal status and autonomous within the Empire and in no way subordinate to another or the British government.[3]

Winston began his tour of Canada at Quebec City. In doing so he gave the island colony of Newfoundland and Canada's three Maritime Provinces a miss, for which he was reproached by some he met on the trip.[4] This omission would be partially repaired years later when Winston went ashore in Newfoundland for an afternoon during the conference with President Franklin D. Roosevelt held off the island in 1941, and by landing at Halifax in 1943 to entrain on his way to the Quebec Conference.

At ten minutes after nine o'clock on the evening of August 9, the *Empress of Australia* docked in the harbor at Quebec. First class passengers and returning Canadians were allowed to disembark on the ship's arrival. The remaining passengers would spend another night aboard the *Empress of Australia* and land the next morning. That morning three liners disembarked 849 settlers at Quebec.[5]

As merely a British member of Parliament and ex-minister on a private holiday, Winston's arrival in Canada was an unofficial occasion. According to one newspaper account, a big crowd was on hand to greet the two famous Parliamentarians, Winston and Amery; while another newspaper disagreed, writing that the four members of the Churchill party descended the gang plank almost unrecognized. The latter account described a "faint cheer" after he came ashore, but it quickly died away and Winston was soon lost in the crowd. Neither the mayor of Quebec City nor the lieutenant-governor of Quebec were on hand to welcome Winston as he arrived. His arrival was not entirely officially ignored, however, as Arthur Beauchesne, the clerk of the House of Commons and the secretary of the Canadian branch of the Empire Parliamentary Association, was present to welcome him to Canada again after three decades. Beauchesne had received a cable from Sir Howard d'Egville, general secretary of the Empire Parliamentary Association at London, asking him to meet Winston and Amery at Quebec as they came ashore. Also dockside was R.A. Benoit, secretary to Quebec Premier Louis Alexandre Taschereau, who welcomed Winston on behalf of the province. Benoit explained to the English visitor that Taschereau was prevented by other engagements from being there in person to meet him. Winston replied that he was glad the premier had not been inconvenienced by his arrival, as he was "just out on a little holiday."[6] Beyond these political representatives, the traveling party was also met by officials of the Canadian Pacific Railway, which was taking such a large role in the Canadian leg of the trip.

"It is 29 years since I was in Quebec and I am delighted to once more have the pleasure of visiting Canada. When I was here before, Montreal had a population of only 60,000," Winston told the newspaper correspondents on his arrival. He went on to say that he hoped to visit the Isle de Quebec, Wolfe's Cove, and the Plains of Abraham.[7]

On coming ashore, Winston parted company with Amery. While Winston would leave the ship and spend the weekend in Quebec, Amery would spend another night aboard the *Empress of Australia* before leaving for Montreal by train in the morning. From Montreal he traveled west to the Rocky Mountains where he would successfully climb Mount Amery. For the next decades Winston and Amery would remain wary friends in British politics. Amery would at last exact a measure of revenge for being pushed into the pool as a schoolboy in a Parliamentary debate with Winston on the conduct of the government minister Samuel Hoare on June 13, 1934. Winston, by then in the political wilderness, spoke first and was immediately followed by Amery, who ended his speech by referring to Winston with the words, "at all costs he had to be faithful to his chosen motto: 'Fiat justitia, ruat caelum,'" which translates as "let justice be done though the heavens may fall." Winston, who had failed to overcome Latin in his school days, immediately demanded a translation. Amery, who "had hardly expected my fish to swallow the fly so greedily," was pleased to pounce. To great enjoyment on all sides of the House he wittily rendered the translation as "If I can trip up Sam, the Government is bust." That night in his diary Amery gloated that he had given Winston the best "ducking" since the incident at the Harrow pool. Although he did admit that Winston "remains unsinkable and will, no doubt, bob up again after a bit."[8]

During the 1930s Amery and Winston were bitterly divided over the issue of India's constitutional status, but would find themselves allies in opposing Neville Chamberlain's appeasement policy. Despite not being a great orator, Amery delivered two famous calls in the House of Commons during the early stages of the Second World War. In September 1939 he shouted during a debate, to cheers from all sides, for Arthur Greenwood, who was rising to speak on behalf of the Labour party, to "Speak for England." Months later Amery finished off the tottering premiership of Neville Chamberlain with a devastating House of Commons speech that ended with him quoting the terrible words from Oliver Cromwell's address to the Long Parliament: "You have sat here too long for any good you have been doing. Depart, I say, and let us have done with you. In the name of God, go!" In Churchill's wartime government Amery would be, however, somewhat disappointed at serving in the important but secondary post of secretary of state for India.

Soon after their arrival, the Churchills were whisked off to the Chateau Frontenac, where they would stay during their visit to the provincial capital. The hotel, designed in a French chateau style, was a majestic structure with towers, turrets, and cornices. Located on Cap Diamant, it formed an impressive part of the view of Quebec, as it overlooked the St. Lawrence River and towered over the old city of Quebec. Owned by the CPR, the hotel had been intended to rival any European hotel in luxury when it first opened in 1893. Additions and new wings had been added to the hotel in 1898–99, 1909–10, 1915, and 1920–24. A fire had destroyed a wing on January 16, 1926, but it had been rebuilt in only 127 days.[9]

Winston was very pleased with the Chateau Frontenac and thought it an excellent hotel.[10] While staying at the hotel the party occupied the suite numbered 1301 on the thirteenth floor.

That night R.E. Knowles, a reporter for the *Toronto Star*, had a brief unsatisfactory interview with the Churchill party. Other than learning from Randolph that his father's principle physical exercise was bricklaying, the reporter gained little that would be of any use. Winston, however, graciously told Knowles to come back at eleven o'clock the next morning and bring his questions with him.

Among the cables awaiting Winston at the Chateau Frontenac was probably one from Charles Schwab that had been sent that day saying he had just learned from Baruch of Winston's visit to Canada and the United States. He was sending his assistant, Joseph Larkin, on a special trip to Quebec to meet Winston and determine what Schwab could do to make his trip more "enjoyable and comfortable." In the cable Schwab said he was eager to reciprocate the kindness Winston had previously shown him.[11]

Randolph, if one believes Johnny's story, finally turned up at the hotel. He made it to his bed and wrote in his diary around midnight of his excitement at having reached Quebec. Within a week of starting out on the trip from Westerham, Wolfe's birthplace, the party had reached the scene of his death at Quebec. Below him Randolph observed that the St. Lawrence was "bright with the lights of a hundred vessels."[12]

In Quebec City and then in Montreal, Winston would have had the opportunity to use his command of French in speaking with the French-Canadians he met. As he had great confidence in his command of the language and did not hesitate to speak it, he undoubtedly took advantage of the chance. Although he had studied the language throughout his school years and even spent a few weeks living with a family in France in 1891–1892 to improve his facility, his French would have left the French-Canadians puzzled at best. Winston's French, for all his self-confidence in his abilities in the language, was questionable if not just poor. His friend Venetia Stanley judged it the "worst French you or anyone has ever heard," while the British ambassador to France, Eric Phipps, commented that Winston's "French is most strange and at times quite incomprehensible."[13]

On Winston's first morning in Canada he was visited at the hotel by Schwab's assistant, and the vexing issue of the private rail car to take the Churchills east across the United States was resolved. The 41-year-old Larkin, whose card he gave to Winston identified him simply as Assistant to President, offered cordial greetings from his boss. He soon proved that he was indeed empowered to make the Churchills' trip more comfortable, as he conveyed an offer from Schwab to put a private rail car at their disposal for the whole tour of the United States. As Winston reported to his wife, the Churchills hesitantly suggested they pay the haulage, but this was fortunately dismissed with a pained look from Larkin. With the question of payment out of the way, the offer was quickly and happily accepted.[14] Larkin suggested the private car meet the Churchills in Seattle, but Winston felt that was unnecessary, as they planned on traveling by train only as far as San Francisco. After that they would follow Baruch's advice and motor through California. Larkin and Winston thus arranged for the private car to meet the Churchills at the Grand Canyon on September 28. Eventually Winston would alter the plans, with Larkin's approval, and have the private car instead meet the party at Los Angeles. Winston was quite pleased to have this problem resolved, as the private car would be comfortable and make the trip much easier. He cabled his news about the private car to Baruch and declared it "all beautifully arranged." Had Schwab not stepped forward with his car, all would not have been lost, as a week later in Ottawa, Winston received a cabled offer from the Baltimore and Ohio Railroad offering to place a special car at his disposal. With everything arranged, this offer was politely declined, with many thanks.[15]

At eleven o'clock that morning Knowles from the *Toronto Star* arrived promptly on time for the interview which had been agreed to the previous evening.[16] The interview would take the best part of an hour, with Winston consuming a long black cigar for the entire duration. Knowles found Winston wearing colored shirt sleeves, with slippers "still in evidence." During the interview Knowles sat at the end of a long sofa, while Winston, a "dynamo of energy," shifted between the other end of the sofa, an armchair, a rocking chair, and a corner of a table. Most of the time, however, Winston was pacing up and down the room.

"Go ahead," Winston ordered to begin the interview.

Knowles started with following up on an assertion he had received from Randolph the previous evening that his father's principal exercise was bricklaying. Winston grinned and said he used to play polo, but was older and heavier now and welcomed all forms of sedate exercise. He was then asked if he enjoyed relaxation.

"Of course I do. Do you know that for nearly 20 years, ever since 1905, I have been entrusted with high office. And high office means hard work. I can't tell you what this trip to Canada means to me," Winston replied.

The reporter then suggested the room the Churchills were occupying in the Chateau Frontenac was a happy omen for Winston, as Ramsay MacDonald had stayed in the same suite almost a year earlier and within 12 months became prime minister.

"Tut, tut," Winston broke in. "What on earth put that into your head."

Knowles next told Winston that a fortnight earlier Lord Queenborough, while at the

Ritz in Montreal, said a man would be a fool to bet that Winston would never be prime minister.

"All very good for a bit of chaff," was Winston's response. He added that 10 Downing Street would be a lovely place to live; but as he stopped his "to and fro careen" around the room to gaze out the open window on the "noble" St. Lawrence river below, he said, "My word, but this taste of freedom is good. There are just two things I have my mind set on now—one is to have a jolly good rest, the other to learn all I can about your wonderful Canada and her place in the imperial plan."

Winston gave a "real-honest born laugh" when Knowles asked why he was not knighted and thus "Sir Winston." Remaining on the same topic of his name, Knowles noted that in his published diaries Herbert Asquith called him Winston.

"Oh, yes I was never anything but 'Winston' to Mr. Asquith," the British statesman remarked.

After being asked whether he regretted not having given his life to literature, the future winner of the Nobel Prize for Literature wheeled around and stood in front of Knowles and demanded, "Why should I regret that?" The *Toronto Star* journalist explained that, given the high quality of his works, a pen might provide a greater life's work than an eloquent voice and a political genius.

Taking the question very seriously, Winston said it was an old debate and that he was more at home with a pen than on the platform. "To speak in public takes a great deal out of me. I never excelled as a platform speaker."

In the remainder of the interview Winston proclaimed that his friend Lord Birkenhead was a far better orator than he was, recalled his love of journalism, referred to the novel he had written, and said he was still best of friends with David Lloyd George, despite now being in different political camps. The interview concluded with Knowles asking about the outlook of the Labour government, to which Winston replied that the Baldwin government had given good service to the country and that the new government would reap the fruits of their labor.

That afternoon the Churchills undertook a sight-seeing tour of Quebec. Accompanied by Arthur Beauchesne and a party of leading citizens of Quebec, they visited by motor car points of interest in the ancient capital.[17]

As every English schoolboy knew about James Wolfe and the British victory over the French under Montcalm at Quebec, it was no surprise that, with Winston's interest in military history, the first place he wanted to visit was the battlefield at the Plains of Abraham.[18] The battle fought there was the climax of a summer-long British siege of Quebec. Wolfe had been unable to force the French position at Quebec and, with time quickly running out due to the approach of winter, had decided on a daring maneuver. On the night of September 12–13, 1759, the British army was embarked on boats in order to pass the river in the darkness under the watch of the French sentries and make an amphibious landing on the enemy-held shore at the cove of Anse au Foulon. The British scaled the 175-foot cliffs without loss and formed up for battle on the open ground on the Plains of Abraham. In the final battle the British shattered Montcalm's army. Wolfe was wounded three times in the battle and died, as did Montcalm, who had been mortally wounded. Five days after the battle the French capitulated and the British entered Quebec.

In his memoirs, written 33 years after the tour, Johnny probably exaggerates the ignorance on the part of their hosts about the battle when he writes, "Wolfe? Montcalm? Nobody seemed to have heard of them. Amidst confusion we descended into a fleet of cars and set off."[19]

Winston wanted to start the tour of the battlefield at the bottom of the heights that Wolfe's men had scaled so he could understand the difficulties they had faced. Again Johnny contends that their hosts were baffled by this request to see the place that ever since the battle had been known as Wolfe's Cove. Maps had to be sent for. After consulting the maps, the party arrived at a spot below the rugged cliff.

"Ha, why yes!" Winston exclaimed as he gazed at the cliff and brandished his walking cane. Johnny thought his uncle seemed to recognize the place.

Randolph and Johnny had already guessed what would happen next, and they were soon proven correct. "You two are General Wolfe's army," Winston ordered as he pointed at them. "Climb the Heights and the rest of us will engage you at the top."

Climbing the cliff in shirtsleeves in daylight was exhausting for Johnny, and he realized how "dreadfully difficult" it must have been for Wolfe's soldiers scaling the cliff at night while carrying guns and other equipment. On finally reaching the top of the cliff, the boys scrambled over the rim only to be greeted by Quebec's leading citizens advancing towards them, representing the French formations under the direction of Winston who had taken the role of Montcalm. With the mini-reenactment completed, Winston ordered the sight-seeing party back to the cars. "He had seen what he wanted to see. He was satisfied."

After seeing the battlefield first-hand, Winston was impressed with Wolfe's audacious maneuver. "Genius is akin to madness," he declared in one of his articles for the *Daily Telegraph* as he wrote approvingly of the succession of grave risks Wolfe took on that night in September 1759. The British politician seemed amazed that with only luck and darkness in his favor, Wolfe had divided his force and rowed his army upstream past the French positions in order to land at the bottom of the cliff, which his men had to struggle up. All with the purpose of engaging a much larger French army on ground from which Wolfe would have no avenue of retreat, either by land or river.[20] During the Second World War, Winston, in his dual role of prime minister and minister of defense, would forever seek and demand such genius and daring from what he considered his reluctant and unadventurous generals, admirals, and air marshals.

The dramatic view from the Plains of Abraham also captured Winston's imagination. He was again reminded of Scotland. The view of the St. Lawrence held for him an "uncanny similarity" to that of the Firth of Forth when seen from the gardens of Hopetown House, Lord Linlithgow's stately home. It had the same bluffs, vegetation, atmosphere, and "even the same vast cantilever bridge."[21]

So fascinating was the bridge at Quebec that the party drove over for a visit. The bridge was 3,239 feet long in terms of steel length and had required 1,066,740 field rivets to build. In the company of their hosts, the Churchills gave it a close inspection and walked across it. In the process they would have learned about the struggle to build this engineering marvel across the St. Lawrence River. The attempt to build a bridge suffered two disasters. The first attempt ended in tragedy in 1907 when the partially-built bridge collapsed into the river, at a cost of 75 lives. The second attempt to build the bridge suffered a setback in 1916 when the center span, which was being maneuvered into position, suddenly failed and fell 200 feet into the water, this time with 11 dead. The engineers persevered and finally finished the bridge in late 1917. Originally the completed bridge consisted of two rail tracks, with two pedestrian sidewalks on each side of the structure. With the demand for vehicle traffic, construction had begun in May 1929 to convert one of the rail tracks to a concrete roadway. This work was underway at the time of the Churchills' inspection. It would be finished a few weeks later, as the bridge was open to automobiles on September 23.[22]

On the day of their visit to the structure, the Englishmen were able to claim that they had walked across a bridge that had the world's longest span of any design, as well as the longest cantilever span in the world. Unfortunately, only one of those two distinctions lasted very long, since the Ambassador Bridge linking Detroit and Windsor was completed in November of the year and became the longest bridge span in the world. The cantilever span distinction, however, remained with the Quebec bridge. Winston also observed the bridge's terrible height above the water to allow for the largest ships to pass underneath. Indeed, the highest point on the entire structure was 343 feet above the water.

Among the other sites the party visited in Quebec that afternoon was the Citadel, located at Cap Diamant. The imposing military fortification, with its 24-foot-high ramparts, was built by the British army between 1820 and 1831 to protect the city. The impressive structure led Charles Dickens to call Quebec the "Gibraltar of North America." Since 1872 the original officers' quarters at the Citadel had been used as the summer residence of the governor-general of Canada.[23]

The party then left Quebec City and motored about eight miles through the countryside, which Winston thought magnificent, to the Montmorency Falls. The hour's run from Quebec to the falls took the party into the enchanting valleys of the Jacques Cartier. Winston soaked in the atmosphere, "the meadows expand amid wooded heights; clear streams descend on every side, from lake to lake and pool to pool, all abounding in fish, to swell the broad, fast-flowing river. Water-power, timber, farming, sport, glorious scenery, buoyant air!" He thought it would be a wonderful place to live, save for the menace of winter.[24]

Although a much smaller body of water, the Montmorency Falls are, at 274 feet, about 100 feet higher than the famous falls at Niagara. The Quebec hosts of the Churchills had intended the visit to the great falls at Montmorency to be a fishing trip. Jack loved fishing and was pleased with the opportunity, while the others had little enthusiasm for the pastime. Unless, that is (in Johnny's words), one is after something big, such as a whale or shark.[25] In which case there was then a great interest on the part of his uncle. While Jack happily fished, Winston and Johnny brought out their sketchbooks and canvases, and took the opportunity to sketch the beautiful scene. Winston also had a chance at Montmorency to observe another old battlefield dating from the British siege of Quebec. In 1759 the Montmorency River had formed the left flank of the French lines, and it was here that Montcalm scored a great defensive victory early in the siege when he repulsed the British attack across the river, made in conjunction with a separate landing against the French entrenchments facing the St. Lawrence River.

The day of sight-seeing accompanied by their hosts ended with a small dinner party, with Winston as the guest of honor, at the exclusive Garrison Club located on Saint Louis Street in Old Quebec.[26] Originally founded by militia officers in 1879, the private club's membership was limited to the political and economic leaders of the city.

The next morning Winston spent several hours in his hotel suite working on his Montreal speech that would be delivered in two days. In preparing the speech, Winston was concerned with saying too much or covering too many topics in one speech. At Winston's special request, Frank Carrel called on him at his suite. Carrel was a prominent businessman, the editor and proprietor of the Quebec *Chronicle-Telegraph*, and a member of the Legislative Council of Quebec. The two spent an hour in conversation. As Carrel was one of Canada's leading proponents of inter-empire trade, the discussions no doubt covered the issue of free trade.[27]

During the various discussions he had with the officials he met at Quebec, Winston sought comments on the subjects of the speech he would make in Montreal. These discussions also led Winston to believe that most of the people he was speaking with thought Beaverbrook's campaign for empire free trade was mischief and would, in fact, actually set back the cause for which he was campaigning. He had also already been warned to be very careful of what he would say in his Canadian speeches, as he might comment on matters that might become issues in a Canadian general election, which could come on short notice. A prime example was the issue of the American tariff that was hurting Canadian agriculture. The ruling Liberal government of Prime Minister William Lyon Mackenzie King wanted to find new markets, while the leader of the Conservative opposition, R.B. Bennett, wanted a retaliatory tariff. An ardent free trader, Winston's views on the subject, had he expressed them, would no doubt have been against the protectionists. Although the Canadian election did not, in fact, come until the following year, Winston had rightly decided that "above all things I must keep clear of local politics."[28]

For lunch, the party dressed in their most formal attire to dine as guests of the lieutenant-governor of Quebec and his wife, Henry George Carroll and Amazelie Carroll, at Spencewood, their official residence. Carroll, formerly a distinguished judge, had held the position of lieutenant-governor of the province only since April 2, 1929. Winston thought Carroll was charming. Carroll had read Winston's war books and was quite admiring of them.[29]

Spencewood, which had been finished in 1863, had originally been the residence of the governor-general of Canada before being given to Quebec in 1870 as the residence of the province's lieutenant-governor. The two-storey building was two miles from the walls of Quebec and situated on the banks of the St. Lawrence River. A Doric portico ran the length of the river side of the residence.[30]

As the lieutenant-governor was the King's representative to the provincial government, the luncheon was more of a formal state occasion. The affair, held in honor of Winston and the other members of the party, was attended by many of the leaders of Quebec politics and society. These included William Molson Dobell, a lumber merchant; Joseph Edouard Caron, formerly minister of agriculture for Quebec; Cyrille F. Delage, the province's superintendent of public instruction; two Quebec judges, C.E. Dorion and Adjutor Rivard; Charles Lanctot, the Quebec deputy attorney-general; and the Churchills' host in the city, Arthur Beauchesne. Winston was impressed, as everyone at the luncheon made themselves very agreeable. Perhaps Winston should not have been impressed by everyone, since Lanctot was arrested a decade later for embezzling $107,000 from the government.[31]

At three o'clock that afternoon, as the luncheon was concluding, a violent and impressive thunderstorm struck the Quebec area. The storm lasted ninety minutes and brought with it heavy rain, chain lightning that illuminated the whole city and surrounding district, and fearsome thunder. An inch of rain fell and numerous trees were brought down, while the city's trams were forced to halt operation, and the electric power and lights were off throughout the duration of the storm. Randolph, however, was disappointed the storm did not come closer.[32] A second heavy storm hit the area at eleven o'clock that night.

Later that afternoon, after the poor weather had passed, the Churchills went for a drive in an open motor car. Prior to the storm the atmosphere had been terribly humid, but in its wake the air was nice and cool. During this expedition, which Winston described as going "off twenty miles into the blue," the party viewed the countryside close up. They saw hills and forests that looked barely explored by man, as well as every kind of tree and lakes full of fish. Randolph was so inspired by what he saw that he announced that he wanted to buy land and build a house on it, renouncing society and ambition in the process. In a letter to Clementine, Winston joked that a final decision on this had been delayed until all of the other places could be considered. A little bungalow with four or five motor cars parked beside it attracted the interest of the party, and they stopped to visit. They found that the bungalow was a "country club" for fishing whose twenty members were of "modest circumstances." Winston commented that it was "quite Arcadian." Even here Winston was recognized, and the members of the club gave him the warmest of welcomes, complete with champagne.[33]

The Churchills made it back to the hotel that evening for another, more official engagement than the impromptu soiree at the modest bungalow. That night Winston returned the lieutenant-governor's hospitality by entertaining him as his own guest at a dinner at the Chateau Frontenac.

Back in their suite before they went to bed, the Churchills could see from the windows on the 13th floor the lights of the Rothermere paper mills burning brightly in the darkened sky. Having seen the magnificent scenery of the forests, Winston was moved to remark, "Fancy cutting down those beautiful trees we saw this afternoon to make pulp for those bloody newspapers, and calling it civilization." Randolph, who recorded the comment in his diary, agreed that the wonderful sights of the countryside they had seen induced a "great reaction against the modern highly developed existence."[34]

On Monday, August 12, after a quiet morning in their rooms at the Chateau Frontenac, the Churchills left the hotel at 11:30 for the train station where they would embark for Montreal.

"I have enjoyed my vacation in Quebec immensely," Winston remarked to the reporters gathered at Union Station. In summarizing his visit to the provincial capital, he went on to elaborate by again noting Quebec's striking similarity to Scotland, and that the Quebec bridge was almost a copy of the Forth bridge. Asked to comment, he also said that he was impressed by the amount of "Old Country" news found in Canadian newspapers. As he posed for the photographers with the other members of the party, Winston jocularly said the travelers could be called the "Churchill Troupe."[35] A few days later, in its coverage of the Churchills' visit to Toronto, the *Globe and Mail* would seize on the comment about the "Old Country" news and said it hoped Winston, on his return to England, would express surprise at the small amount of Canadian news carried in British newspapers.[36]

In being interviewed himself by a newspaperman at Quebec that day, Jack recalled his war experiences both in the Anglo-Boer War and the Great War. In South Africa he had served under Julian Byng, who went on to command the Canadian Corps in World War One and serve as governor-general of Canada. During the Great War Jack said he had served for a considerable part of the war with the Australians, including the remarkable achievement at Villers Bretonneux in March 1918 when they held the position against determined German assaults.

The CPR private car *Mount Royal* (second car from left) as seen at the Quebec Conference. Winston Churchill traveled aboard the car in 1929 and again in 1943 (Canadian Pacific Archives NS.4646).

Jack praised the Canadian and Australian soldiers in the war as terrific, saying the "Germans felt that the British were people they could understand, but they couldn't quite fathom the fellows from the Dominions."[37] He also told the newspaperman that he looked forward to renewing his friendship with Sir Arthur Currie, Canada's great general of the war, while in Montreal. As principal of McGill University, Currie lived in Montreal, but whether the hoped for meeting with Jack and the other Churchills took place was not recorded.

At Union Station the Churchill party went aboard the CPR's private car that would carry them across the continent to Vancouver and be their base for the next three weeks. They were immediately delighted. Randolph thought the car was "palatial," and it possessed every "convenience and comfort." With the provision of the car, the party was being treated in a "princely fashion."[38]

The private car, named the *Mount Royal*, was built in 1927 by the CPR's Argus shops at a cost of $78,862.65. At 77 feet in length, the 12-wheeled car had four bedrooms, a sitting room, a large dining room, bathrooms and lavatories, kitchen, secretary's room, steward room, and observation area at the back. For the first 15 years of its service, until 1942, the *Mount Royal* served as the official car of the CPR's vice-president. The vice-president at the time of Winston's visit, and the one who lent the car to the Churchills, was Grant Hall. The private car was staffed with a cook and waiter, with the *Mount Royal*'s steward for the trip west being a CPR employee named George Grant.[39]

The comfort of the *Mount Royal*, which he thought was superb, certainly would have appealed to Winston's love of luxury. His sophisticated tastes were acknowledged by his closest friend, Earl of Birkenhead, who said, "Mr. Churchill is easily satisfied with the best." Winston's love of luxury, which he was required to pay for with his own hard work throughout his life, was evident on the North American tour in the first-class ocean liner rooms, the top hotels stayed at, the exclusive private cars traveled aboard, and the ever-present food and drink that included champagne, brandy, and cigars.[40]

At 1:30 in the afternoon the train departed Union Station at Quebec. Winston would return to the city as British prime minister during World War Two for the two Quebec conferences in 1943 and 1944. Rather than staying at Suite 1301 of the Chateau Frontenac, Winston would stay on those occasions in the equally majestic surroundings of the Citadel. While the Citadel served as the location for the main meetings of the conferences, the Chateau Frontenac would be used to house members of the attending delegations that could not be accommodated alongside Winston at the Citadel.

## ... 5 ...

# Montreal and Ottawa, August 12–15

As the train steamed west, following the course of the St. Lawrence to Montreal, the Churchills settled into the *Mount Royal*. They unpacked their clothes and arranged themselves in the private car. Winston and Jack each had a large bedroom with big double beds and their own private bathroom, while Randolph and Johnny had rooms which Winston described as being like a regular compartment in a sleeping car. With the convenience of their own private car, they planned to take only one suitcase each when they left the car at their various stops during the trip. In each room there were three or four fans, and there was a wireless set that could play in the car's sitting room and dining room at the mere press of a button. Once aboard, Randolph effused that "one could not travel in more luxurious fashion."[1]

Winston thought that the fans in the private car were definitely going to be needed. The day was as warm as a very hot day in England, but with the fans the air was cool. Even with the *Mount Royal* at his disposal, he foresaw that the trip was going to be a strain and expected they would "have enough of our land yachts before we are finished."[2]

On this trip to North America there is no mention in any of the memoirs, correspondence, or newspaper accounts of the amount of luggage that Winston brought with him. It was most likely a great deal. He was never a light traveler. Phyllis Moir, who worked for Winston on his 1932 lecture tour, commented that when traveling he "carries enough baggage for a regiment."[3] On that tour she observed that Winston's rooms in New York were filled with trunks and packing cases, with filing boxes, stationery, and correspondence heaped on every table and chair. Although this 1929 trip was not an official visit or working tour, Winston still planned to deal with his always voluminous correspondence, prepare articles, and compose speeches. As such, it was most likely that he would need the necessary supplies and brought them along. When traveling after the Second World War, a functionary noted that the former prime minister always wanted his office to be fully functioning upon his arrival at a location, and that he traveled with "typewriters, paper clips, pencils, ink, paste, scissors, pins, envelopes, sealing wax, seals, and string."[4] As his many letters sent to his wife from North America in 1929 were almost always typed, it can be determined that Winston always ensured he had ready access to a typewriter and a typist.

The need for a typist was met by the CPR for the Canadian leg of the tour. Beyond loaning the Churchills his official private car with staff, Vice-President Grant Hall also loaned Winston his secretary, Mr. J.H. Baker, for the trip. Either at the Chateau Frontenac or when he first came aboard the *Mount Royal*, Winston met the secretary that was temporarily loaned to him. As the train traveled to Montreal, Winston decided to use the dining room as his office and began dictating more of his letter to Clementine, using his newly acquired secretary. The use of a secretary was an essential requirement for Winston. As he admitted in the letter to Clementine, the provision of a secretary was a wonderful development, as without him he did not know how he would have been able to deal with all his correspondence and speeches.[5]

Baker probably, like many of his secretaries, found working with Winston to be a challenge. The aforementioned Moir thought her employer in 1932, who required her to work the hardest and fastest she ever had in her life, to be demanding and impatient and given to fits of irritation. She wrote scathingly that to him a "secretary is a completely impersonal adjunct, a machine that must have no personal needs—for food, rest, or recreation, somebody who must be on call when he wants them, a being anonymous, perfectly efficient and completely dedicated to the service of Winston Churchill."[6] Elizabeth Layton was one of Winston's wartime secretaries, from 1941 to 1945. Although admiring him greatly, Layton also thought working for Winston was definitely not easy, and that he was hard on his staff, describing that he went off like a rocket when a secretary made a mistake. Another wartime secretary, Mary Thompson, believed being Winston's secretary required patience, intense concentration, a good memory, above average speed in shorthand and typing, and the constitution to work long hours.[7] Unlike Moir, Thompson, or Layton, Baker did not produce a memoir of working for Winston, so it can only be speculated on how much he enjoyed being employed by a demanding boss.

Winston always dictated straight to the typewriter. Layton records that he would pace up and down the room, working on a cigar as he dictated. It was not easy to hear him. From Layton's experiences she thought that until one got used to his voice it was almost impossible to catch everything he would say. Her finished typing would come back to her from Winston to be retyped, with alterations in red and occasionally remarks about her education and hearing.[8]

Baker had a great deal of work ahead of him as he started taking dictation from Winston. All of Winston's speeches usually had to be retyped several times over until he was satisfied. The drafts would come back from him to the secretaries as he polished the speech. Each version would have many corrections and alterations, with words crossed out and new sentences written in above the typed lines. Baker also had to learn his temporary master's preferred method of arranging the typed page. Correspondence could be typed with single spacing, minutes had to be typed with double spacing, while speeches were typed in what Winston called the psalm format, with each succeeding line indented.

The letter to Clementine that Winston dictated to Baker as they headed to Montreal described the visit to Quebec and remarked on the immense size of Canada, with its rich agricultural soil that went on for thousands of miles. The unlimited possibilities of the land prompted Winston to philosophize that it was "silly for people to live crowded up in particular parts of the Empire when there is so much larger and better a life open here for millions. Half the efforts of the war would have solved all these problems. However, the world is known to be unteachable."[9]

Winston also gave his wife an update on his efforts to keep their son in line. Randolph was thought to be behaving very well, and Winston was ensuring that he studied for several hours each day. Although he tried to get him down to breakfast, Winston found that even if Randolph went to bed before midnight he still slept until ten o'clock in the morning. Winston, however, decided there was no harm in this.[10]

Aside from working on the letter to his wife on the trip to Montreal, Winston also gave an interview to W.W. Murray, a staff writer for the *Canadian Press*, and also probably continued working on his speech. An unnamed member of Winston's entourage assured the reporter, rather optimistically as it turned out, that no two of the speeches delivered in Canada would be alike.

The train completed the 180-mile journey and arrived in Montreal at 6:30 on Monday evening. In 1929 Montreal had not yet been surpassed by Toronto and was still Canada's largest city, with a population of 618,506. There was not an official reception for the Churchill party at the train station, but a small crowd was still on hand to welcome them to the city. The crowd included several friends from the old country. Disembarking from the *Mount Royal*, Winston waved "adieu" to the crew of the train engine that had drawn the train from Quebec to Montreal and started for a waiting motor car.[11]

Harry Stafford of Montreal crashed enthusiastically through the crowd to grasp Winston's hand and "warmly welcome" him. Described in a newspaper report as a "small man," Stafford claimed to be a former captain of the Manchester United football team who had worked on Winston's behalf in Manchester in 1906. The unlikely former football captain made eager enquires about Winston's health and that of his children, to which Winston was said to reply with appreciation.

After exchanging salutes with the policeman on duty at the gate, Winston and his party made their way to the waiting motor car, stopping only to allow a press photographer to take their picture. While in Montreal, the party would stay at the Ritz-Carlton hotel and went there from the train station.

Despite the interest his trip generated in the press and the attention he occasionally received from members of the general public, Winston was not accompanied by any bodyguards on his "vacation jaunt."[12] His long-time detective, Inspector Walter Thompson, did not accompany him on the trip. Despite having until only two months earlier held one of the most senior offices in the government of the world's great power, Winston was thought not to be in any need of special protection. Indeed, there were no security threats or incidents during the trip. He was a private traveler unburdened by any concerns for his safety. Two years later, however, when he returned to North America for a lecture tour, he had by then aroused the active hatred of Indian nationalists by his opposition to India's constitutional progress and was considered a possible target of assassins. On that trip he was joined by Inspector Thompson.

Montreal's Ritz-Carlton Hotel was located at 1228 Sherbrooke Street West and was called the "Grande Dame of Sherbrooke Street."[13] Opened on New Year's Eve 1912, the hotel had been built in the "Beaux-Arts style" at a construction cost of three million dollars. A hotel in the European tradition, the building was 10 floors and had 261 rooms. The manager of the hotel at the time of the visit, having been appointed in 1924, was Emile Charles des Baillets, a tall bearded Swiss nicknamed "Rasputin."

After a short time at the hotel, the Churchills departed for the exclusive Mount Royal

Club further along Sherbrooke Street where a dinner in Winston's honor was held that evening. The dinner was sponsored by Edward W. Beatty, the president of the CPR. Beatty had participated in the planning of the Prince of Wales' visit to Canada in 1919 and had probably helped in the CPR's preparations to carry Winston across the country.[14] The dinner was a private affair, with the press excluded. Fifty of the most prominent businessmen in Montreal attended the event, at which Beatty presided and Winston gave a 35-minute speech. This speech was considered by Winston to be a "preliminary canter" for the following day's address, which was open to the public, as well as for all of his other speeches in Canada. It was a success. Randolph thought the speech was excellent and welcomed by the audience. On this occasion Winston broke with his usual practice and spoke without notes. Randolph, who thought the effect on the audience was greater when the speech was given spontaneously, believed his father was coming around to his point of view and relying less upon notes.[15]

Having succeeded in the first outing at the Mount Royal Club, Winston left his hotel the next day, August 13, to deliver his first major speech of the tour. As the Churchills departed the Ritz-Carlton they were photographed by the waiting newspapermen. Winston was to speak to the Canadian Club of Montreal, which had been founded in 1905.

While the speeches given in 1929 in Canada and the United States were of little importance in comparison to his great wartime speeches, it is still true nevertheless that Winston put a great deal of time into their preparation. He always worked very hard on his speeches. The text of the speeches would be written out and then revised and polished. As he reread the speech and rehearsed, even further revisions would be made to the text.[16]

A major topic in the news in August 1929, which Winston had already commented on in his newspaper interviews and would remark on in many of his speeches, was the Young Plan for a new settlement of the reparations that had been imposed after the Great War. The proposed plan was named after Owen D. Young, the American chair of the committee that had negotiated the agreement. For the British, Winston included, the question of reparations had always been tied to the issue of the war debts incurred by the Allied nations during the war. By 1920 the United States was a creditor who was owed ten billion dollars, while the British was also a net creditor, having borrowed four billion dollars from the United States but having lent a further eight billion dollars to other nations. Even though it would theoretically cost Britain money, the British government had always favored an all-round cancellation of debts. The Americans were, however, unwilling to agree and viewed such proposals as an attempt by the debtors to "wriggle out" of their commitments. With the United States refusing a cancellation, Britain had established a policy of collecting from her debtors no more than what she owed the United States. Two years after Winston's trip, in 1931, Britain had paid $1,911,798,300, which represented three-quarters of all debt payments that had been made to the United States.[17]

The Young Plan was supported by the United States, France, and other countries, but strongly opposed by Great Britain. The new plan was not only a setback for British efforts to win an all-around cancellation, but would see their share of the reparations significantly reduced. At The Hague Conference in August 1929, Winston's successor as chancellor of the exchequer, Snowden, refused to accept the Young Plan as it was written. During the 1929 election campaign Snowden had accused Winston of reaching "over-generous" debt settlements with France and Italy, and, now in power himself, was determined to be intransigent in the negotiations.[18] Although he was enjoying his North American holiday, Winston must have envied the excitement his successor was having in the high drama of the ongoing negotiations at The Hague.

The luncheon was scheduled for one o'clock that afternoon, but well before that time the tables in the ballroom of the Windsor Hotel were already filled. The aisles between the tables quickly became packed, and the overflow crowd filled the corridors outside the ballroom. Additional tables were laid out in the corridor and adjacent rooms. By the time the official program began, a crowd of 1,400 people had assembled in the ballroom, while several hundred more were listening through loudspeakers set up in the adjacent rooms. A *Montreal Herald* report of the speech called the throng gathered at the hotel a "grinding and almost uncountable crowd," while another English-language newspaper, the *Montreal Gazette*, reported "Ballroom, Rose Room, galleries, corridors and platforms were filled in every available niche where a chair could be placed." Even then, hundreds more had to be turned away.[19]

The 38-strong head table featured the "political, ecclesiastical, industrial, professional, and financial life of the city and country." Winston himself sat between James Robb, Canada's minister of finance, and Major J. Colin Kemp, a businessman who presided at the luncheon as president of the Canadian Club. Jack, Randolph, and Johnny were seated elsewhere at the head table. Other notables at the table were the premier of Quebec, Louis-Alexandre Taschereau; Montreal mayor Camillien Houde; Anglican Bishop of Montreal John Farthing; and an array of leading politicians and business figures, including the province's reform-minded minister of agriculture Joseph-Leonide Perron; Senator Wilfrid Laurier McDougald; the publisher of the *Montreal Gazette*, Senator Richard Smeaton White; the former president of the Saar Valley Commission George Washington Stephens; and the president of the Canadian Chamber of Commerce W.M. Birks. Lord Luke, the Churchills' fellow passenger from the *Empress of Australia*, was at the head table, as was their host from the previous evening, Edward Beatty.[20]

During the luncheon Winston took a glass of white wine with his meal, smiling as it was poured. He was also observed to spend a few minutes in thought before lighting a huge cigar. Winston also took the opportunity to discuss the subject of trade with James Robb, his tablemate and someone who, as Canada's minister of finance, would have been greatly interested in the topic. Kemp began the proceedings by introducing Winston with a short tribute in which he referred to the Englishman's many "versatile gifts" and successes as first lord of the Admiralty and chancellor of the exchequer. When Winston rose to speak he received prolonged applause, with the audience rising to its feet. After the warm welcome he began speaking in a slow and deliberate manner as he warmed to his subject.

"I have come to Canada to learn from those men who are making and guiding the destinies of this country, what their problems are, what their anxieties are, what their hopes are and how they think we in the Mother Country can best help and cooperate in the fulfillment of their desires," Winston said to begin his speech after thanking Kemp for his introduction and the audience for its friendly welcome. As he spoke, he grasped the lapels of his coat in typical fashion.[21]

Winston turned first to the greatest of all the joint interests of the British Empire, which he said was the maintenance of world peace. He said that no other association among men had a greater interest in peace than the British Empire, and that he rejoiced that the state of the world is so peaceful and its mood so pacific. As he turned from the topic he added that it could be taken as a practical assurance that there was now to be a long period of peace.

Winston went on to discuss disarmament and the special case of France on the issue of disarming, hailed the Locarno Treaty as the greatest step towards attaining an international understanding since the Great War, and endorsed Snowden's position against the Young Reparations Plan at The Hague conference. In a theme that he would return to in all of his Canadian speeches, Winston patriotically rebutted suggestions of British weakness and the false impression those abroad may have of the island's true situation. He said Great Britain's position had never been better. It was the greatest creditor nation in the world, greatest exporting nation of manufacturers, still built half the world's ships every year, and still carried the bulk of the world's trade.

To loud applause, Winston defended his home country. Britain was a "remarkable island," he said. At this time in history it was "more populous, more prosperous, richer, more comfortable, more healthy, more educated, than it was ever before."[22]

The *Montreal Gazette* thought that Winston adapted his "linguistic gait," wishing to avoid problems with the "disc in front of him." The loudspeakers, nonetheless, on one or two occasions caused minor interruptions in the speech.[23]

Toward the end of the speech Winston paid tribute to this "magnificent Dominion of Canada," declaring the country had made great progress. Returning to Montreal for the first time after 29 years he had found the city was five times as large and probably 20 times as wealthy as when he was last there. In describing the bonds of the Empire he said that after several days crossing the great wastes of the Atlantic it was with a thrill that he landed in a new hemisphere and found himself at home; despite crossing a quarter of the globe, he immediately found himself among friends.

Referring to the desire for a friendly association between the British Empire and the United States, Winston ended his speech by urging the "two gigantic powers of human society" to cooperate, so that together they could resolve many of the world's problems. He concluded by saying that this resolution of the world's problems could only be achieved by the Empire, "founded on freedom and faith," remaining united and "sharing fair and stormy weather hand in hand."

The audience gave thunderous and long applause at the speech's conclusion. The overwhelming response of the attendees was echoed in the accounts of the speech in the Montreal newspapers. The *Montreal Gazette* called the speech, "clear, concise, deliberate, and, above all else optimistic," and found the most satisfying element of the address to be that the future could be faced with "undiminished confidence." The *Montreal Herald* reported that the "widely focused" speech was "comprehensive and masterly," while the *Montreal Daily Star* wrote that Winston had spoken "quietly, decisively, and well." The latter newspaper editorialized that the speech teemed with British patriotism, explained recent British foreign policy, and delivered praise for Montreal and the Dominion that every loyal-hearted Montrealer "takes secret delight in hearing." All of the newspapers had reservations, however, with the *Herald* saying the speech avoided controversial subjects and would upset "no apple carts"; while the *Daily Star* noted that, contrary to expectations, Winston had not spoken on free trade or Egypt. The *Gazette* remarked that those in the audience who wanted "flame and spirit" were disappointed, as Winston knew the time, place, and occasion for the "famous aggressive Churchill touch."[24]

The spirited defense of Britain's progress that Winston made in the speech would be repeated in all his speeches and newspaper interviews across Canada. In England after the tour, he said that he had been confronted with anxious inquires from Canadians about the situation in the Mother Country. Winston explained that he had attempted to reassure the many Canadians who were under the impression things were ill in Britain and "that we were all on the dole."[25]

That his speech was a success was not a surprise, as Winston was, of course, a great orator. He had a "complete mastery of the language" and as an orator was able "to put the right words in the right order, at the right time, and in the right place."[26]

Montreal was not a successful stop merely for the two well-received speaking efforts. It was also financially lucrative for Winston. In a letter to Clementine he reported that 600 copies of his book the *World Crisis* had been bought in the city and by special arrangement he would be paid in cash for these sales. Winston ventured a hope that if these sales kept up in other cities he would make a small windfall on the tour.[27]

After less than twenty-four hours in Montreal, the Churchills departed by their private rail car bound for Ottawa. They arrived at Union Station in the nation's capital after a short journey at 7:30 on the evening of August 13. At Ottawa the traveling party set foot in Ontario, Canada's wealthiest and most populous province, with 3,271,000 people. About 200 citizens of the city had gathered in the station's concourse to get a glimpse of Winston. Ottawa had learned about the British statesman's impending visit from coverage in the local newspapers in the days prior to his arrival. The *Evening Citizen* had carried an editorial recounting his career and calling him a "brilliant debater" and "indefatigable worker."[28]

A group of Ottawa newspapermen who boarded the train on its arrival were disappointed with the results. Although received politely, Winston indicated to them that he was not "disposed" at that time to answer questions. As he had already given a major speech in Montreal that day, Winston was probably tired and not in the mood to be pestered with interviews. In addition, he had little time to spare for the journalists, as a dinner had been scheduled for the Churchills by the governor-general of Canada. To reporters that nevertheless tried to ask their questions (for example, on the possible evacuation of French troops from the Rhine before Christmas), Winston replied that he was not aware of the reports in that day's press.[29]

However, when an *Ottawa Journal* reporter asked if he had ever been in Ottawa before, Winston smiled, "Sh, sh. That would be before most of you were born." A question about Canada was answered with a happy, "It's a wonderful country you have here, and your people have been more than kind to me."

The Churchills were officially met at the station by Captain R.J. Streetfield, aide-de-camp to the governor-general. During their stay in Ottawa the party would be the guests of Viscount Willingdon, the current governor-general, at his official vice-regal residence in the capital Rideau Hall. This would not be Winston's first time staying at the hall, as he had previously spent Christmas 1900 there as the guest of the then governor-general and his wife, Lord and Lady Minto.[30] For his arrival in Ottawa, Winston was wearing a brown suit, light green shirt and soft collar, a blue and white spotted tie, and a felt hat.

As Streetfield escorted the party through the station to the waiting automobile, Winston removed his hat, walking through the concourse with his "characteristic stoop." With a bared head he acknowledged the cordial welcome he received from the gathered crowd. He appeared genuinely gratified by the reception, and bowed and smiled to those on hand in the station. In turn, as the newspapers formally recorded, the men in the crowd raised their hats and the women politely smiled their own welcome.[31]

At the waiting automobile outside the station, Winston shook hands with a Joseph Gamble of Ottawa, who told him that they had previously met thirty years earlier at a political meeting in Rhyl, Wales. Winston remembered the occasion, as David Lloyd George had been in the seaside town that same evening to address a separate meeting. Asked by a reporter if Winston was a Conservative at that time, which indeed he had been, Gamble responded with a laugh, "Oh, Winston has changed a lot of times but still he's all right."[32] Streetfield and the English travelers in his charge then drove by automobile directly to Rideau Hall and the waiting dinner.

Freeman Freeman-Thomas, Viscount Willingdon, had been governor-general for three years since assuming office in August 1926. The largely ceremonial position was in 1929 still the preserve of British appointees; the first Canadian to hold the office would not be named until well after the Second World War. The then 62-year-old Willingdon had attended Eton and Trinity College, Cambridge, before being elected a member of Parliament in 1900, the same election that saw Winston win a seat in the House of Commons. He was appointed governor of Bombay in 1913 and next became the governor of Madras in 1919, where he remained until he came to Canada. The charming Willingdon was married to the dynamic

Governor-General Viscount Willingdon and Viscountess Willingdon of Canada hosted the Churchill party at Rideau Hall in Ottawa (Library of Congress).

Adelaide, and as a couple they made for a "handsome, close-knit pair." An avid golfer, the governor-general was also King George V's favorite tennis partner.[33]

The Willingdons had had a busy three years in Canada. Apart from holding office during Canada's Diamond Jubilee celebrations in 1927, they had toured across Canada, including visits to the Maritimes and two trips to the west coast. Additionally, Willingdon had made the first official visit of a governor-general to Washington. After his service in Ottawa, Willingdon would return to India as viceroy, having been elevated to an Earldom.

Rideau Hall had originally been built in 1838 as a private estate overlooking both the Ottawa and Rideau rivers. Since becoming the governor-general's official residence in 1864 when the capital of Canada was moved to Ottawa, both the grounds and the original hall had undergone many changes. The hall itself had been enlarged with new additions and its interior greatly renovated. Improvements to Rideau Hall were an ongoing concern during the Willingdons' tenure. Adelaide found the hall in great need of repair and had managed to extricate more money for such renovations from Prime Minister King than any other governor-general. While Adelaide improved the interior of Rideau Hall with imperial tapestries, chests, lamps, and rugs from Baghdad, a new tennis court was added to the grounds in 1927, no doubt reflecting the governor-general's sporting interests.[34]

At Rideau Hall the Willingdons had already hosted the Prince of Wales, European royalty, and the prime ministers of Great Britain, Australia, New Zealand, and Ireland. A few weeks after the Churchills' visit they hosted their second visit of a sitting British prime minister when Ramsay MacDonald arrived in Ottawa following his official visit to the United States.

That the Churchills were going to spend two nights at Rideau Hall had not pleased everyone in official Ottawa. Prime Minister William Mackenzie King, who also acted as his government's secretary of state for external affairs, had complained about it to Willingdon the previous day. In one of their regular meetings the prime minister had grumbled about Government Houses all over Canada being used as "boarding houses for English visitors." As the traveling party was to stay at Rideau Hall, as well as a string of Government Houses in the provincial capitals all the way to Victoria, Winston was quite guilty of this trespass. Beyond English visitors filling the guest rooms of Canada's Government Houses, the prime minister was also irritated by the social events such visitors required. In his diary entry for August 12 he further carped that it was a "shame" to have to give up the entire week for visitors from the old country and having to fuss about their entertainment. He nevertheless arranged to have Winston for lunch during the visit to Ottawa. Although King dreaded the social commitments, he expected it would "all go well."[35]

The dinner in honor of Winston and his party at Rideau Hall started around eight o'clock that evening, with Viscount and Lady Willingdon and Prime Minister King welcoming the Churchills. It was a small affair, with the other guests being Vice-Admiral Sir Cyril T. Fuller and his Flag Lieutenant Commander Evelegh. Fuller was the Royal Navy's current commander-in-chief, North America and West Indies, and had arrived to stay at Government House that morning. Also arriving that morning, and probably in attendance at the dinner, were the Willingdons' son and heir to the family title, Inigo Brassey Freeman-Thomas and his wife Maxine Frances Mary Forbes-Robertson, known as Blossom. At the dinner King sat between the governor-general and Randolph. The prime minister was charmed by Winston's son. He described him in his diary as a "fine looking young fellow & most intelligent &

clever."[36] During the party, King also thought he had had a pleasant few words with Winston and Rideau Hall's other visitor, Admiral Fuller.

The next morning Randolph began his day with a thrilling speedboat ride on the Ottawa River. One of the governor-general's aide-de-camps, probably Captain Streetfield, who had met the party at the train station, took him out for a fun jaunt on the river in his speedboat. They cruised along in the boat at about 35 miles per hour.[37]

While Randolph was enjoying the river, Winston spent the morning at Government House.[38] Making up for the previous night's omission, he agreed to be interviewed by a group of eight to ten newspapermen. Although the reporter from the *Evening Citizen* thought him unwilling to give off-handed answers to studied questions, on the issue of reparations Winston did say, "What we want in Britain is to secure from Europe what the British taxpayers has to pay the United States." He warned that the British government would have to consider what would happen in the event of a complete breakdown of the reparations system. This, he said, would be a very serious business. On a less important issue, when asked about his current literary works, he said he was writing a biography of the Duke of Marlborough but that it would not be published for several years. Nor, he told the journalists, would he be able to work on it during the present tour. After making progress on the project aboard the *Empress of Australia*, the rigors of the trip required him to set the project aside.

It had already been arranged that for lunch that day the Churchills would be guests of Prime Minister King at Kingsmere, his country estate in the Gatineau Hills outside of Ottawa. Winston and the Canadian prime minister were already friends, having first met in December 1900 during Winston's stop in Ottawa on his lecture tour. They had renewed their acquaintanceship on King's occasional official and private visits to England. The visiting Englishman had told the newspapers that King was a "friend of many years" and that he had been looking forward to meeting him in Ottawa.[39] The two politicians had much in common. Both were born in 1874, enjoyed dogs, were balding, owned treasured country estates, were successful in politics, and had famous ancestors. In King's case his famous relative was his grandfather, William Lyon Mackenzie, a radical and reformer who had led the failed rebellion in Upper Canada in 1837.

King, however, was a vastly different type of politician than his visitor. Prime minister since 1921, save for a brief three-month interruption in 1926, he was cautious and avoided taking risks. He would delay decisions rather than act, and as a natural conciliator and mediator always searched for common ground within his cabinet, party, and country. Eventually serving as prime minister for more than two decades, his greatest ability was to gain and hold political power. As prime minister, King pursued greater Canadian autonomy and independence in foreign affairs, resisting all attempts at greater centralization within the British Empire.[40]

Despite his public image as a dull and plain figure, the bachelor King was actually a complicated man with great interest in spiritualism, numerology, séances, fortune tellers, and dream interpretation. Impressed by coincidences, he always noted if he happened to look at a clock when the hands were together, opposite, or at right angles. For all his interests in such matters, they never influenced his political decisions.[41]

King had a mixed opinion about Winston. At times he admired him, but on other occasions he did not trust him. Once in speaking to Stanley Baldwin, King had been told that the three most dangerous men in the British Empire were David Lloyd George, Lord Birkenhead, and Winston. No doubt to King's immense bemusement, Baldwin later placed two of these dangerous men, Birkenhead and Winston, in prominent positions in his government of 1924–1929. During the British general strike of 1926, when Winston's actions were, as usual, quite controversial, King wrote that as "for Churchill I feel a scorn too great for words. He has been the evil genius in this."[42]

The greatest difficulty between the two politicians had occurred during the Chanak Crisis in September 1922 when Winston was colonial secretary in Lloyd George's government. At the height of the crisis with Turkey, the British cabinet had requested pledges from the Dominions to send fighting contingents in the event of war. These requests for troop commitments were also made public in emotional statements released to the press. Exasperated about the request being made public, King sent a distinctly cold response to London and sought to delay a decision by saying such a commitment required Parliament to be summoned into session for the measure to be debated and approved. Unlike Australia and New Zealand, who readily offered troops, King rebuffed several attempts to secure a promise of support. He wrote in his diary at the time, "It is a serious business having matters in hand of a man like Churchill—the fate of an Empire!"[43] King thought, correctly as it turned out, that the Turks would back down and believed that by holding back Canadian support he had aided the peaceful outcome.

William Lyon Mackenzie King, Canadian prime minister and friend of Winston Churchill (Library of Congress).

The Churchills went by motor car the 15 miles from Ottawa to Kingsmere for lunch with Canada's prime minister. The estate, which at the time was about 400 acres, was the "true, abiding passion of King's life." Modeled after a British country estate, he wanted to build Kingsmere into the finest estate in Canada. King spent his summers at Kingsmere and often had his staff make the journey out from Ottawa so that he could work at his estate. Like Winston and Chartwell, Kingsmere was for King a "refuge from the pressure of public life."[44]

Since purchasing his first lot in 1903, King had built up the estate by accumulating more land holdings and making continual improvements. He enjoyed planning the developments but agonized over every detail as the cottages and other buildings were constructed, an entrance and drive designed, trees and shrubs planted, flower beds and rock gardens laid out, lawns seeded, roadways put in, and walking trails cut in the woods. Over the years King had stone and wood fences built, flagpoles added, garden furniture laid out around the grounds, and a pergola, boat house, and wharf constructed. By 1929, work on King's main residence on the estate, which he called Moorside, had been finished. This formerly small cottage had been transformed into a "large, rambling summer home on the scale of a modest English country home."[45] Kingsmere was a "scene of British pastoral delights: rolling lawns, meadows filled with grazing sheep, woodland trails, flower gardens, and the deep mystery of the forest."[46]

At the time of Winston's visit, work was still underway at Kingsmere. In 1929 King had purchased another 100 acres to add to the estate, and also begun buying statuary for the grounds. Work was also then underway on the rose garden, which would not be completed until 1931.

King enjoyed showing visitors around Kingsmere, including in 1927 when he had Prime Minister Stanley Baldwin and his wife visit the estate. As a present he had given Baldwin a cane with a gold band engraved "Kingsmere 4.8.1927."

While he did not receive an engraved cane on his visit to Kingsmere, Winston must have found much to fascinate him about the estate. He too was a dedicated owner of a country estate, having purchased Chartwell for five thousand pounds in 1922 and spent another 18,000 pounds renovating and expanding Chartwell Manor. Like his Canadian colleague, Winston found his estate in Kent to be a safe haven and playground, and greatly enjoyed planning and directing the outdoor works. He cleared the grounds, built cottages, constructed walls with his own hands, redirected streams, and created lakes. At Chartwell Winston worked late into the night in his study on his books, articles, and speeches, entertained visitors, and relaxed with his brick-laying, painting, and other pastimes.[47]

After a half-hour journey, the Churchills arrived at Kingsmere. Randolph was impressed with the estate, calling Moorside and the grounds, a "sweet little house in lovely surroundings."[48] To join them for lunch, King had invited Ernest Lapointe, General Andrew McNaughton, and his friend, Dr. Arthur Doughty. As minister of justice and the government's unchallenged leader in Quebec, Lapointe was King's most trusted advisor and lieutenant. Like Winston, he was an excellent Parliamentary orator.[49] The British visitor and Lapointe had met previously, at the 1926 Imperial Conference held in London. Doughty, who had an interest in the Battle of the Plains of Abraham, had held the position of Dominion Archivist and Keeper of the Records since 1904.

McNaughton, a brilliant artillery officer in the Great War, had become Canada's chief of the general staff at the age of 41 on January 1, 1929. He had met Winston previously. In 1916, while Winston had been commanding the 6th Royal Scots Fusiliers in France, McNaughton was commanding a nearby artillery battery and had been invited over as a guest to his mess. The Canadian army officer had not been overly impressed by the fine dishes and wine served in the mess, and further had been annoyed by the presence of one "Foghorn" MacDonald, a profane Canadian attached to Winston's headquarters. Apparently kept around because he made Winston laugh, MacDonald offended McNaughton by his language, and McNaughton was dismayed at seeing a Canadian officer playing the role of a court jester. Although McNaughton would command the Canadian army in Great Britain during the early years of the Second World War and meet Winston many times, he recalled to his biographer that he always nursed an antipathy toward Winston over the MacDonald affair.[50]

Shortly after the Churchill party arrived it started to rain quite heavily, and everyone was forced to have lunch indoors in the "little conservatory." One of King's household staff, a servant named Frank, attempted to undertake the service for the lunch by himself. The prime minister thought this was a mistake, as the guests were kept waiting for every course. King was concerned with the day being a success and later worried in his diary, "Had the day been a fine one the visit would have been a real joy. As it was I was sensitive feeling that things were not just as I would have liked them, and receiving little aid from my guests in the matter of conversation."[51] One topic that was discussed over lunch was the Chanak crisis. The Canadian position in the crisis was explained to Winston, and, according to McNaughton, the British statesman conceded he had been wrong to interfere in Canadian affairs in such a manner.

Both at the lunch and later while strolling in the woods of Kingsmere, Winston and King discussed the speech the visiting statesman was to give the following day at the Chateau Laurier in Ottawa. Winston found his host in agreement with his views on the need to avoid rigid agreements on naval armaments as well as on Empire trade. No objections were offered from King on Winston's suggestion that Empire businessmen should be allowed to meet and develop a report on ways to expand trade that could be offered to their respective governments for action. Winston, however, could see very little being gained from holding an Imperial conference on trade. King and the Canadian government had been anxiously hoping to hold such a conference that fall, although by August 1929 this was thought less likely to happen.

Following the lunch, with its delayed servings, Winston was shown the grounds of Kingsmere by its squire. Though the walking was bad after the earlier rain, Winston and King went all over the estate, save for the farm portion. They were joined on the walk by King's dogs and were photographed as they strolled with the animals. On the estate King had diverted a stream with a series of small dams to create a "picturesque meandering stream," with "small pools and cascades" being created in the process. Five wooden bridges had been built across the stream. Winston was "keenly interested" in the dams and was able to provide his own experienced advice on these works.[52] The prime minister proudly recorded that his visitor liked the small cottages and lakes, and quite correctly felt his guest was "greatly taken with the property."[53] Winston was indeed taken with Kingsmere and later wrote Clementine that it was "just the sort of place you would like to buy for me, a tiny bungalow three hundred acres of hills and forests with a large lake and Scotch Burn, all just the right size for me."[54] In October 1934 Winston would host King at Chartwell, showing him all over the house and grounds.

The Churchills stayed until five o'clock that afternoon, when they left for Rideau Hall. Despite the problems with the lunch service, they had been pleased with the estate, and the visit seemed to have gone well. King still complained in his diary, however, about the succession of British visitors, writing the "summer has been eaten into right & left by people from the old country."[55]

Randolph had enjoyed his second meeting with the prime minister and pronounced him "most interesting and enlightening about Canada," as well as a "very thoughtful and purposeful man." For political purposes, he later wrote in his diary, King and the Liberal government were made out to be disloyal to the Empire and friendly with the Americans. But Randolph thought that was not so.[56]

That evening the Churchills attended a large dinner of thirty people at Government House. After the dinner there was dancing. Randolph found it to be an enjoyable evening. He noted that Blossom Forbes-Robertson was present and found her to be "very attractive in fact almost beautiful."[57] There seems to have been common agreement among the Churchills about the appearance of Forbes-Robertson, as Winston, in writing home, refers to her as being rather striking. William H. Clark, who had been Winston's private secretary back in 1908 and was now in Ottawa as the British high commissioner to Canada, was at the party. Winston reported to Clementine that Willie was now married and that he and his old secretary had a very pleasant conversation.[58]

The second major speech of Winston's tour of Canada was given the next day on the afternoon of August 15 at a Canadian Club luncheon held in the spacious main dining room of the Chateau Laurier in Ottawa. The 500 available tickets to the luncheon, the first of the club's new season, were all sold in advance, and the dining room was packed. The influential audience included members of Parliament, senators, and justices.[59]

In the speech that Winston had prepared he would discuss the need for Anglo-American cooperation and the related issue of reaching a naval understanding with the United States. He would return to this issue in his public speeches and newspaper interviews, both in Canada and the United States. After the creation of the "Special Relationship" during the Second World War, it is difficult to recall that Anglo-American relations were in a rather poor state during the 1920s. An assortment of issues, including war debts and reparations, naval rivalry, Ireland, the British alliance with Japan, the American policy of isolationism, and the United States' rejection of the League of Nations had contributed to a deterioration in the relationship from the alliance of the First World War. The tensions between the two countries could, however, be exaggerated, as friendship with the Americans was a fundamental element of British policy, and actual hostilities was always completely "unthinkable."[60]

Anglo-American disagreements had been temporarily reduced by the agreement reached at the 1921 Washington Conference. At the conference the British terminated their alliance with Japan and agreed to naval parity with the United States, thus giving up forever British supremacy on the seas. The agreement was a recognition by the British that they could no longer economically maintain the leading naval position. The Washington treaty that established parity between the British and American navies only applied to aircraft carriers and capital ships. The Americans were eager to extend the agreement to other classes of naval ships. An attempt to reach an agreement on cruisers had been made at the Geneva Conference in 1927. The United States and Britain viewed the cruiser issue from differing strategic perspectives. As a continental nation, the United States wanted larger long-range cruisers, while the British, needing to protect their commercial lifelines in times of war, wanted smaller ships with lighter armaments. At the conference the two sides could not agree on the number of cruisers, tonnage figures, and the comparative strength of the American cruiser against the British cruiser. The ill feeling created by the failure of the conference was further strained by the 1928 Anglo-French naval compromise. The text of the agreement between the British and French was leaked to the anti–British Hearst Press in the United States, which published the documents on September 21, 1928. The publication created further "antagonism and suspicion" between the British and Americans. While publishing the secret document was a great coup for the Hearst Press, the French government was not impressed. They did not forget the incident and exacted a measure of revenge a few years later when they expelled William Randolph Hearst from their country after he had arrived for a visit.[61]

After reaching a nadir in 1928, relations between the two countries were already improving by the time Winston reached North America. The newly elected president, Herbert Hoover, and the likewise newly elected prime minister, Ramsay MacDonald, were already preparing for a rapprochement. Anglo-American conversations were quickly overcoming the recent coolness and mistrust, and by later 1929 a "political basis" for Anglo-American cooperation had been established.

Winston and his party, accompanied by the governor-general, were at the hotel waiting to go into the dining room by one o'clock that afternoon. King arrived exactly on time at the hour of one, only to find everyone else already in place waiting for him.

The luncheon was presided over by T. D'Arcy McGee, the president of the Canadian Club. The head table was twenty-strong. It included the governor-general and members of his suite, the prime minister, Ernest Lapointe and other federal cabinet ministers, all four visiting Churchills, the former prime minister Robert Borden, Vice-Admiral Fuller, William H. Clark, and General McNaughton. The head table and audience lacked some Canadian political notables, as Parliament was at the time enjoying its summer recess. Many members of Parliament and most members of the cabinet were out of the city for the break. The most important person missing from the head table (and Winston's other engagements in Ottawa) was Robert B. Bennett, the leader of the Conservative party, who was then making a tour of Canada's western provinces. Bennett, who was also a close friend of Lord Beaverbrook, would displace King by winning the next Canadian election and assuming the prime ministership in a year.

In what was noteworthy for a Canadian Club meeting, ladies were present for Winston's address. Shortly before he was to speak, Viscountess Willingdon and her daughter-in-law, the aforementioned beautiful Blossom, escorted by Captain Streetfield, entered the dining room to warm applause from the audience.[62]

D'Arcy McGee, who had recently been elected club president, was in the chair for the first time. He began the proceedings but quickly made way for Winston, as he said it would be "superfluous" for him to provide a long introduction. There were several minutes of applause when Winston rose to speak.

The themes of Winston's 35-minute speech were naval disarmament and Empire trade. During the speech, which was punctuated by frequent applause, he expressed the desire for peaceful relations between Great Britain and the United States. Every British government, he said, both before and since the war, had sought to remove all roadblocks to Anglo-American friendship.

On the issue of a new naval disarmament agreement between the two countries, he asked whether such an agreement would really resolve any problems and actually bring about a reduction of expenditures on armaments. A rigid disarmament agreement controlling the ships to be held by each country would be a complicated affair. It would create much confusion and lead to quarrels, as naval ships varied as much as a human being, with variations in speed, armor, guns, and age. Any such pursuit of an agreement for naval parity had to take into account the differing circumstances of the two powers. The United States was a continental power with the means of prosperity within its own borders separated by thousands of miles from potential danger, while Britain was an island an hour away from Europe and dependent on sea trade for its life. Rather than have the "spectacle of two large costly navies, rigid replicas of one another, jealously scrutinized by experts across the ocean, measured in their last detail and advertised by the press," Winston suggested both nations go their own way, acting in friendship and goodwill.

Turning to the vital question of trade, Winston proclaimed himself a free trader. He said Great Britain could not tax imports, while Canada and Australia could not be expected to abandon the tariff barriers which had allowed their industries to grow. Although saying he did not wish to meddle in Canadian politics, Winston did modestly propose the calling of a conference of Empire businessmen that he had discussed the previous day with King. This conference, he said, would drag the issue of trade out of the arena of party politics and lift it to a more reasonable platform.

Winston finished his speech by making a forceful call for the unity of the British Empire. Divided the empire would fall into shattering ruin, he said, but in unity the empire would unquestionably have a "foremost place in the onward march of men."[63]

There was prolonged cheering and applause throughout the room when he finished speaking. The club president then rose and declared the address they had just heard to be "most interesting, inspiring and instructive," before calling on King to speak. The prime minister extended Winston a hearty welcome to Ottawa and the Dominion, and said it was a source of pride that, upon being released from office, he had chosen to visit Canada. He assured Winston that he had not upset the sensibilities of Canadian politics, saying, "If all of Mr. Churchill's addresses in Canada are as carefully guarded and as beautifully worded as that to which we have listened today then there will be only thanks to him for his visit." At the call of King there was another spirited outburst of a treble round of cheering for Winston.[64]

Before the meeting closed with a "full-throated" singing of the national anthem, there was a presentation. Colonel R.M. Blair, V.D., who sat at the head table, had the previous month won the King's Prize and the Grand Aggregate Cup at the rifle shooting competition at Bisley against the Empire's 1400 greatest shots.[65] In recognition of this accomplishment, King presented Blair with a piece of silver plate with an inscription. Blair, the commanding officer of the Seaforth Highlanders of Canada, made a modest reply after the presentation.

Winston's speech was praised in the local newspapers, with the *Evening Journal* calling it a "brilliant address," and the *Evening Citizen*, although doubting Winston would ever look at economic matters from anything but an orthodox doctrinaire point of view, supported his proposal for an economic conference. The most important man listening to the speech, Prime Minister King, thought it a very good one, a "very fine & very true peroration." King noted that the speech had been "very carefully prepared, notes quite complete and as I could see 'exact' in his own handwriting."[66]

After the luncheon, Prime Minister King took the English visitors to Parliament Hill, a short walk from the hotel, and gave them an extended tour of the Houses of Parliament. The gothic-style Parliament buildings had been rebuilt since Winston was last in Ottawa. The original buildings overlooking the Ottawa River had been constructed after Queen Victoria had chosen Ottawa as the capital of Canada in 1857. A three-hour fire in 1916 had destroyed all of the original buildings, save for the library.[67] Work had quickly started on a new building, and the new Parliament buildings had opened in 1920.

On the tour of the building, the traveling party was shown the Memorial Chamber that was in memory of the Canadians who had died in the First World War. It had been dedicated by Prime Minister King on the tenth anniversary of the Armistice on November 11, 1928. The floor of the chamber was made of stones from all the areas where Canadians had served, with brass plates set in with the names of the major battlefields, including Ypres, Somme, Vimy Ridge, Hill 70, Passchendaele, and Amiens. Other stones in the chamber, such as the altar steps, had been gifts from the people of France and Belgium. On the Altar of Sacrifice was the Book of Remembrance, sitting on a 24-karat gold frame, bearing the names of every one of the 66,657 Canadian war dead.[68] Winston was "visibly deeply impressed with the memorial chamber." He took the time to read all of the inscriptions and tablets in the chamber, such as the carved marble wall panels describing the achievements of the Canadian military in the war.[69]

A visit was made to the Senate chamber, called the Red Chamber. The paintings in the Senate would have been of great interest to Winston, as they were from a collection given to Canada by his great friend Lord Birkenhead. The Churchills also climbed up the Peace Tower that also honored the sacrifice of the Canadian war dead and had been dedicated by the Prince of Wales in 1919. On each corner of the tower were ten-foot gargoyles which have been described as "weird, gnome-like creatures, clutching mandolins." Additionally, the tower had a four-faced clock that measured 16 feet in diameter, 53 bells, and a lookout that gave views of Ottawa and the surrounding area. The Churchills climbed to the lookout and took in the view, as well as inspecting and hearing the carillon bells. Percival Price, the Dominion carillonneur, was on hand and played two or three selections on the carillon for their benefit.[70]

Back on the ground, the party visited the council chamber where Winston took pleasure in being seated in the chair King occupied as prime minister at the council table. Likewise, in the House of Commons chamber, Winston again took the chair that King sat in as prime minister. The commons was called the "Green Chamber," and if Winston had observed the Speaker's chair in the chamber he would have found it very familiar. It was an exact copy of the one in the House of Commons at Westminster. The chair, which was 13 feet, six inches high and included old oak taken from the roof of Westminster Hall, had been given to Canada in 1921. Winston thought the Houses of Parliament were much better cared for than his own, and that the carillon was one of the finest in the world.[71]

At the foot of the steps of the Houses of Parliament, the habit of Winston running into men he had not seen in thirty years continued. Thus far men had come up in twos and threes at every place to shake his hand. As they were leaving the Parliament building, a thick-set little man approached the party.[72]

"Mr. Churchill, I would like to give you this box of cigars in admiration of your achievements," the man said.

"Thank you so much," Winston replied as he accepted the gift. In a letter to Clementine he described the man as a former Sergeant of the Engineers who had helped him in 1898 make plans at the battle of Omdurman. Johnny's suspect dialogue recounted in his memoirs, however, continued the conversation as, "We have met before, I think. It was in India in 1897, when I was with the Fourth Hussars."

"Yes, I was regimental trumpeter," the man said, evidently surprised that he had been remembered after three decades.

"I remember you well," Winston explained. The man appeared to be in humble circumstances, and Winston was "greatly touched." He thanked him again for the gift by adding, "How very kind!"

Johnny, who probably himself did not recall the incident absolutely accurately, thought this was a prime example of his uncle's ability to remember faces.

In their discussions that day, Winston had told King that he dictates his books and then revises, often six times. Additionally, he declared that the *World Crisis* had thus far paid 40,000 pounds. Out of these books, Winston explained, was "made the wherewithal for public life."[73]

After again reaching Rideau Hall later that day, Winston wrote to Clementine.[74] He was somewhat drained after making the speech, as well as from the anxiety that went into preparing it. Although he wrote that he was enjoying his stay in great comfort with the governor-general, Winston said the journey was very tiring. He had taken great pains with his two major speeches in Montreal and Ottawa due to the "unfamiliar atmosphere and also because of the delicacy of the topic." Winston promised to send copies of the speeches to Clementine. The audiences at the speeches, however, were large and enthusiastic. Contrary to his initial plan to avoid speaking too much, Winston told his wife that he had agreed to take on three more speeches in Canada. These addresses were to be in Regina, Edmonton, and Calgary. They would not, fortunately, require much additional preparation.

After being in Canada for about a week, Winston described in the letter that the "immense size and progress of this country" impressed him more each day. The population of nearly 10,000,000 could be expected to at least double in the next twenty-five years. Although the United States was "stretching their tentacles out in all directions," the "Canadian National spirit and personality is becoming so powerful and self-contained that I do not think we need fear the future."

In the usual report on Randolph, Winston said he was conducting himself in a "most dutiful manner and is an admirable companion." He was praised for an intelligent interest in everything and being a "remarkable critic" of the speeches Winston had made and the people they were meeting. The other members of the troupe, Jack and Johnny, were also thoroughly enjoying themselves.

At seven o'clock that evening the Churchills were entertained at a dinner party for about 15 people held by Robert Borden in Winston's honor. Winston had long known his host; when first lord of the Admiralty, Churchill had worked with then Prime Minister Borden over the Canadian government's plan to pay for the construction of three dreadnoughts for the navy. The issue, mired in controversy, never came to pass.[75] Several of the guests at the dinner that night were men he had already met, including Prime Minister King, T. D'Arcy McGee, Major-General McNaughton, and most likely Eric Mieville, the secretary to the governor-general. Among the other guests Borden had assembled were Charles Stewart, the former premier of Alberta and current minister of the interior in King's government, Supreme Court Justice Edmund Leslie Newcombe, Major Newson of the United States legation in Ottawa, Senator Napoleon Antoine Belcourt, and Alfred E. Fripp, a former Conservative member of Parliament.[76] Winston and Borden found much to discuss, including their reflections on past events. Even though Johnny thought Borden was a striking individual, both he and Randolph had little interest in this talk of bygone matters and affairs. With this in mind, Johnny records that Borden gave the two young men a large collection of speeches he had made and pamphlets he had issued in his political career to look through and keep them occupied. Randolph again enjoyed meeting Prime Minister King, calling him "one of the most delightful men I have ever met. He was very kind to me, and took great trouble to be agreeable."[77]

After the party was over, King drove with the travelers back to Rideau Hall and then to Union Station for their departure for Toronto. The prime minister and the aide-de-camp of the governor-general went with the Churchills to their private car, which would be attached to the Toronto train. As they arrived at ten o'clock, nearly an hour before the train was to depart, King was able to spend a few minutes in the car with the Englishmen before he took his leave.[78] Later that night, after returning from the train station, King read aloud to two of his friends the last chapter of the *World Crisis*. He thought it was very fine writing.

The Canadian prime minister wrote in his diary that he had found Winston to be "exceedingly pleasant and companionable," and "enjoyed him with the boys & the way he spoke to them, was very strong in impressing on them the need of hard work, mastering due books, etc." Although he had liked the visit, at a lunch on August 17 with Viscount Willingdon and his wife, King returned to his complaints about Winston using Government Houses across the country during his visit. The prime minister said such use of Government Houses by visitors from Great Britain would eventually raise the question of abolishing the "whole lot." He confided to his diary that he had "little sympathy with the whole social side of Govt. House life whether in Ottawa or elsewhere. Its patronizing attitude shrivels me up completely."[79]

The train pulling the private car left Ottawa and made the short trip to Toronto on the night of August 15. Winston would return to Ottawa three more times in his life, most famously in December 1941 when he delivered his "some chicken, some neck" speech to the House of Commons. The friendship and working relationship with King would also continue, especially when both men were in power in their respective countries during the Second World War. As the two Quebec conferences were taking place in his country, King, while excluded from the main decision-making, attended and held meetings with Winston and President Franklin Roosevelt.

… 6 …

# Toronto and Niagara Falls, August 16–17

At seven o'clock on the morning of August 16, the Churchills' private car arrived at Union Station in Toronto at the start of their two-day visit to the city. The stay in Toronto would include a major speech and a side trip to Niagara Falls. The private car had been pulled from Ottawa attached to Train No. 33. The party was still asleep when the train arrived, and the assembled newspapermen had to wait two hours until Winston finally emerged from the *Mount Royal*. In that interval Lieutenant-Colonel Alexander Fraser, the aide-de-camp to the lieutenant-governor of Ontario, went aboard the private car and waited as the party dressed and prepared themselves to leave the car. Fraser had a Government House motor car waiting and, after welcoming them to the city, was to escort them to Government House. A Toronto tailor also arrived and went aboard the private car. He brought with him a couple of suits of clothes that Winston had ordered by cable, specifying his measurements and needs.[1]

During the tour of North America, Winston had to forgo his usual schedule. His routine when at home in England was to wake at eight o'clock in the morning, have breakfast in bed, and work from his bed for the rest of the morning. Lunch would usually never take less than an hour and a half (or, if guests were present three hours). In the later afternoon he would take a siesta for an hour or two before dressing for supper. With the last meal out of the way by 10:30, he would then concentrate on work for several hours, usually toiling till well past midnight. On the tour, with the need to adhere to his hosts' timetables and train schedules, he had to, for the most part, dispense with his usual practices.

Awaiting Winston when he disembarked from the private car was a small army of newspaper representatives on the station platform, including photographers and movie men to film him. Although it is unknown whether he was wearing the new clothes brought to him by the Toronto tailor, the newspapers reported he was wearing a brown suit with light green shirt and matching tie. For the benefit of the photographers and camera operators, Winston took off his hat and posed as the cameras clicked and movie film rolled. Led by the lieutenant-governor's aide, the party, save for Randolph, who was still in the private car, left for the waiting motor car.

Although Winston declined the request for interviews from the newspapermen and said he would not have the opportunity to give such appointments, he did talk with the reporters when peppered with questions while walking through the train station. Asked about his impressions thus far of Canada, he said he had not had the time to form any, as he had been too busy making speeches. When asked about politics, he avoided the question by saying that anything he had to say on such matters would be said in his speeches.

Three days before Winston reached Toronto, the city's police force had used mounted police and motorcycles to scatter a large crowd of local Reds that were trying to mount a demonstration at Queen's Park.[2] The police rout of the communists was still fresh in everyone's minds, and Winston was asked about the incident. Proving that he had been reading the Canadian newspapers, he replied, "Oh, yes ... I see you had some sort of rumpus and the police were rather rough. What did they do? Did they actually hold a meeting?"

The newspapermen told Winston that the Reds had been prevented from holding their meeting by the police.[3]

"And did they use their truncheons? And chased them out of the park?"

After being told that the police had indeed chased the Reds out of the park, Winston was asked what he made of all this.

"Well, you must not expect me to get mixed up in your difficulties. I have enough of my own," Winston replied with a smile.

A reporter persisted and asked if Reds could hold a meeting such as this in London. Winston said, "Of course, they could. They have a perfect legal right to hold a meeting to discuss their views, hold a demonstration or even run a candidate. They should give notice to the police authorities that the meeting is to be held."

"This is usual?"

"Yes," Winston confirmed, before adding, "but they are a poisonous breed."

What if they talked sedition, the *Toronto Star* representative ventured. Winston replied that was then a different matter.

As Winston entered the great hall of the new station, he suddenly stopped and gazed about in amazement. "What a magnificent station—a splendid hall," he remarked. As he looked at the ceiling, he asked, "How high is that?"

The reporters then asked Winston what he would say in his speech in Toronto, to which he replied he would touch on the Egyptian situation. He then changed the conversation by remarking that he had been blessed with fine Canadian summer weather on his trip.

At that point the cameramen asked for another picture, this time in the shade. As Winston had already been "snapped" about a dozen times since emerging from the private car, he said, "Well, you've had a good many chances." Nonetheless, Winston relented and allowed his picture to be taken again, with a "sunny smile."

While Winston was handling the newspapermen with patience and politeness, Randolph ensured that the traveling party's arrival in the capital of the province of Ontario was not without a display of bad temper. Before the party was even out of the train station the younger Churchill had a spat with a Toronto reporter that made the front page of the newspaper.[4]

A journalist from the *Toronto Telegram*, apparently noticing that Randolph was not with the party when they left the *Mount Royal*, went aboard the private car to seek him out. Randolph was found in the middle of "hectically" collecting odds and ends for his bag. To the reporter's request to speak with him, Randolph said he was busy and tossed a suitcase to one side.

"Right-o, I'll wait for you outside," the reporter said.

When Randolph eventually emerged from the private car attired in a grey suit and Panama hat, the reporter attempted to start a conversation by asking, "What was your impression of waking up at the station here—you know, the noise, bustle, and activity?"

"I didn't hear anything," Randolph replied, which the reporter found non-encouraging. In his diary Randolph said the slight fracas began over the reporter asking him about the first sound he had heard on arriving in Toronto.

The representative of the *Telegram* tried a different subject and asked if Randolph had heard many of his father's speeches.

"I am not answering any questions. The Toronto papers ask a lot of foolish questions and write silly replies. One Toronto paper sent a man 500 miles to interview my father; he asked two or three absurd questions, and his report wasn't any better," the eighteen-year-old announced.

And with that "peroration" out of his system, Randolph, in the words used in the *Telegram* article, hurried off after his "distinguished father." Although not the article the *Telegram* reporter had expected, the exchange with Randolph provided a story for that evening's edition. It was headlined "Too Busy Packing to Talk and Prefers Silence Anyway—Didn't Even Hear Toronto" and opened with the observation that Randolph "is not the sort of traveler who is a delight to interview." Randolph recorded in his diary that Winston was quite angry with him over the fracas and the paragraph in the article that made out that he had been extremely rude to the reporter.

Accompanied by Fraser, the party left Union Station and drove by motor car to Chorley Park, the Government House of Ontario. Located on a 14-acre estate, this house, in the romantic chateau style of Canada's railway hotels, was "easily Canada's most splendid Government House."[5] During the stay at the residence the party was probably given use of some of the guest bedrooms (there were 22 of them in all) in which to refresh and relax.

The party breakfasted at the official residence with the lieutenant-governor of Ontario and his family. The current lieutenant-governor was William Donald Ross, a 60-year-old who had made a career in banking before becoming lieutenant-governor in 1926. Winston, who, along with Clementine, had previously met and spoken with Ross at Ascot, found him to be very pleasant during their stay in Toronto.[6] The lieutenant-governor's wife, Isabel, and daughter were present for the visit and joined the Churchill party for the later trip to the Royal York. They were photographed with all the English visitors, save for Winston.

The lieutenant-governor had arranged for a luncheon to be held for the visitors at Government House the next day. This disrupted the itinerary the party had planned, and new arrangements had to be made. Originally it had been planned that they would spend Friday night at the vice-regal suite of Toronto's Royal York Hotel and on Saturday visit the university, before driving by motor car to Hamilton and Niagara Falls. They would return to Toronto Saturday night, again by motor car, and board the train for the 36-hour journey west to Winnipeg. In order to accommodate the lieutenant-governor's luncheon they would now leave for Niagara Falls by train on Friday evening, visit the falls Saturday morning, and return to Toronto in time for the luncheon.

That afternoon Winston addressed a joint meeting of the Canadian Club of Toronto, the Empire Club, and the Toronto Board of Trade. The meeting was facilitated by the National Council of Education. It was held at the Royal York Hotel, located at 100 Front

## 6. Toronto and Niagara Falls, August 16–17     61

Winston Churchill (left) with the lieutenant-governor of Ontario, William Donald Ross, in Toronto (C322-1-0-6. Archives of Ontario).

Street West in Toronto. The Royal York, a CPR hotel, had only been in operation for two months when Winston gave his speech, having opened on June 11 after a two-year construction period, costing 16 million dollars.[7] With 28 floors and 1100 rooms, it was at the time one of the largest hotels in the British Empire and one of the tallest structures in the world. With roof gardens, cafes, dining rooms, and dance floors, the hotel had 1300 employees.

    1929 was a banner year for the Canadian Club, as the speakers that followed Winston at later meetings that season included Leo Amery on September 20; Prime Minister Mac-Donald on October 16; and the past and future prime minister of South Africa, General Jan Smuts, on January 3, 1930. All three of these men were personally known to Winston, with Smuts being a very close friend whose advice and guidance he often sought during World War Two.

    The Royal York's banquet and concert halls were decorated with flags and flowers for the occasion of Winston's speech. For the luncheon portion of the program, 950 attendees were in the banquet hall and another 700 in the concert hall. Throughout the luncheon the concert music of Rex Battle and his orchestra was broadcast from the main dining room of the hotel. After the lunch was over, the 700 people in the concert hall moved into the banquet hall to hear the speeches. The *Globe and Mail* claimed it was one of the largest audiences addressed by a visiting statesman, while the *Telegram* wrote that the "exceptionally large audience" included prominent men from all walks of Toronto's "industrial and commercial life." Winston agreed with the newspapers' assessments, writing that the audience was the "keenest looking fellows I ever saw."[8] Loudspeakers were also set up in the hotel to broadcast the speech to those who could not gain entry to the crowded banquet hall. By that means the members of the Rotary Club who were in the hotel for their weekly luncheon also listened to the speech. Those not actually at the Royal York had the opportunity of listening to a broadcast by radio over the CFRB station in Toronto from 1:10 to 3:10 that afternoon. Winston's own estimate was that 3,000 attended the luncheon, with many more listening to the speech by radio.

The Toronto speech included Winston's support for the naval base at Singapore. For most of the 1920s British plans for an impregnable base at Singapore, supported by the rapid deployment of the British fleet to Singapore in the event of an actual war, had proceeded quite slowly and haphazardly. The project had been cancelled under the first Labour government and resumed again under Baldwin's Conservatives. Winston feared it would be cancelled a second time by the recently elected Labour government. While he had always supported the construction of the base, as chancellor of the exchequer he had been very reluctant to commit the necessary money. After being delayed but not cancelled by Prime Minister MacDonald, the base would eventually be completed.[9] As a naval base, Singapore would prove to be far from impregnable, and its surrender to the Japanese would be the greatest and most humiliating British disaster of the Second World War, a horrible defeat for which Winston has often been blamed and chastised.

The luncheon was presided over by A.W. Scripture, the president of the Canadian Club for the 1929–30 season, and had the by-now usual illustrious turn-out for the head table at one of Winston's speeches in Canada. In Toronto the 23-strong table included Lieutenant-Governor Ross; Ontario Premier George H. Ferguson; former premier of the province, Ernest C. Drury; the president of Canadian General Electric, D. Clarence Durland; a former Canadian minister of finance, Sir Thomas White; industrialist Thomas A. Bradshaw; art collector Harold Tovell; and Brigadier-General Arthur H. Bell. Sir George Badgerow, a fellow passenger on the *Empress of Australia*, was seated at the table, as were the three other members of the Churchill party.[10]

Winston would have been pleased to again meet Sir Joseph Flavelle, who was also seated on the platform. The two were old friends and had worked closely together during the war when Winston was minister of munitions and Flavelle was the chairman of the Imperial Munitions Board in Canada. The British minister valued his Canadian counterpart, and in 1917 when a scandal was engulfing Flavelle, who was quite unpopular with the public, Winston sent his counterpart a supportive cable urging they both carry on with their task. By the end of the war, Flavelle's Imperial Munitions Board had filled 240,000,000 pounds worth of orders placed by the British government and had produced 60,000,000 shells among its military production. Flavelle, while on a visit to London, had been invited to, and attended, a reunion dinner for the senior men at the Ministry of Munitions, hosted by Winston in 1923.

It can be hoped that Flavelle was more at ease speaking with Winston in Toronto than he had been on a previous occasion. In 1916, on a trip to London to discuss Canadian war production, Flavelle had attended a glamorous dinner party with Margot and H.L. Tennant, Winston, and Edwin Montague. The conversation was brilliant and repartee witty, but Flavelle felt very out of place, "a fish out of water." He was able to flee the party early and left at 11:30 pm.[11]

A.W. Scripture began the speaking portion of the program by calling on Hugh S. Eayrs, the president of the Empire Club, to introduce Winston. In the introduction, Eayrs described him as a "gentlemen of superb courage" and a "great ambassador of the British Empire." With the introduction over, Winston rose to speak and was met by a now-expected rousing ovation.

After speaking on peace in Montreal and naval disarmament in Ottawa, the focus of Winston's address to the Toronto audience was imperial ties.[12] To frequent bursts of applause he delivered a "plea for Empire unity." Winston began the speech by saying he was going to speak on subjects of general interest to "patriotic British citizens in every part of His Majesty's domains." On the issue of the Singapore naval base, Winston said the completion of the base was vital for the defense and protection of the Empire's lines of communication. The base at Singapore was not a menace to Japan's security, and he claimed the continued friendly British relations with Japan proved this to be correct. The abandonment of the base by the new British government would be a terrible setback for Australia and New Zealand, who had already contributed money for the base and considered it to be an essential spot from which the Empire could come to their aid should danger threaten. To "vociferous cheering," Winston said that just as Australia and New Zealand had come to Britain's defense, "if anything arose to endanger their safety down under the Southern Cross, we must be sure we could go to their aid with all the strength we could muster."

After proclaiming that he was no opponent to self-government, and reminding the audience that he had put two "daring experiments" in self-government through the British Parliament—the Transvaal and the Irish Free State—Winston said he had serious reservations about the proposals for Egypt's constitutional development. He did not think Egypt was capable of any more stability in 1929 than it had been 50 years before when Britain had first stepped in to the country. Murder and conspiracy were rampant in Cairo, and the public services already turned over to Egyptians had worsened under their control. Under the British administration, he judged, these public services had greatly improved. The proposed withdrawal of the British garrisons from Cairo and Alexandria to Suez was condemned as the shirking of Britain's duty to the Egyptians. It was a cowardly and feeble policy. Rather mischievously, he recommended in the speech that the dominions be consulted on any Egyptian developments before the British government proceeded.

A decade before the outbreak of the Second World War, Winston told his Toronto audience that peace was now securely established between the world's "civilized nations." The prospect for peace, he said, was better than it had been for 50 years among these nations. Disturbances might well still occur, he observed, "in the barbarous parts of the world where the Bolsheviks come in contact with other nations." In the same vein, Winston also warned against subversive movements masquerading as pacifists.

Also in the speech Winston returned to his familiar themes, including Empire trade, and repeated his call for an Empire conference of business leaders and reiterated his belief that any naval disarmament agreement between the United States and Great Britain had to recognize the differing needs of the two powers. He warned against too gloomy appraisals of Great Britain's strength, and, indeed, proclaimed her strength, prosperity, and interest in peace. In an appeal to local sympathies, Winston called Toronto an important center of the

Empire and a "stronghold" of the United Empire Loyalists. Since the Imperial Conference of 1926, which recognized the independence of the dominions, Winston said the Empire had been held together by the firm ties of tradition and common interest. Although these bonds were not understood by Europeans, it was these that had "drawn millions of men from the far corners of the earth to the battlefields of France, we must trust them to continue to draw us together."

After Winston had concluded, Scripture of the Canadian Club called on John A. Tory, the president of the Toronto Board of Trade, to move the vote of thanks for the speech. In his remarks Tory said no statesman in the empire had more appeal to Canadians than Winston, and "we not only admire him as a great servant of the Empire, but also as one who sees eye to eye with Canadians."

The *Globe and Mail* proclaimed Winston's speech to be eloquent, while the *Telegram*, whatever their views of Randolph, called it a "stirring address." In its editorial on the speech, the *Globe and Mail* agreed with Winston's stand on Egypt and said his warnings were "worth heeding." In disagreement with Winston was the Liberal Party–supporting *Toronto Daily Star* which wrote that Canada was not directly interested in the affairs of Egypt and had no desire to be consulted over its constitutional development. *Saturday Night*, a Canadian magazine, called the address "very interesting" and wrote that the proposal for a conference of businessmen "one of eminent practicality."[13]

About one and a half years later, at the young age of nineteen years old, Randolph returned to Toronto to make his own address to the Empire Club of Canada. This speech was part of the speaking tour he was conducting of the United States and Canada. In the talk on April 23, 1931, Randolph spoke on the subject of peace.

After the speech, Winston retired to Government House, where he spent most of the rest of the afternoon in the gardens on the grounds. He wrote to Clementine, updating her on the progress of the trip and saying that he had just returned from the Toronto speech. It was a marvelous event, and he thought it was his best speech thus far in Canada. Winston closed by telling Clementine he often thought of her and the "kittens," and hoped they were well. He added, "Do write & wire & forgive me using short hand. I cd not possibly tell you about things otherwise."[14] The rest of the afternoon Winston also worked on preparing the next speech he was to give, this one in Winnipeg.

That night the lieutenant-governor hosted a dinner for Winston. At the affair Winston managed to accomplish one of the goals he had set out for the trip—to meet the leading figures of the places he visited. The guests included many of the individuals who had attended his speech earlier in the day, as well as the founder of the British American Oil Company, Albert L. Ellsworth, former Canadian Minister of Finance Sir Henry Drayton, provincial cabinet minister William Finlayson, publisher Samuel B. Gundy, recently retired Major-General Sir Casimir van Straubenzee of the British Army, and an array of businessmen and politicians.[15]

With rumors swirling of an impending provincial election to be called for the fall by the premier in the days before the Churchills reached Toronto, Winston likely discussed electioneering with Ontario's premier at the dinner. Ferguson, who was a Conservative and had held office since 1923, had not been denying the election rumors too firmly. The province did go to the polls in October, and the Conservatives won reelection in a resounding triumph.

Also attending was Vincent Massey, who had served in Prime Minister King's cabinet and would in 1952 become the first Canadian to serve as the country's governor-general. At the time, Massey was serving in Washington as Canada's first minister to the United States. Winston and Massey would exchange occasional cables during the Churchills' trip about the arrangements for the visit to the American capital.

With his interest in the market for the articles he wrote, Winston would have had useful conversations with John B. Maclean, the leading Canadian magazine publisher, who was also in attendance. Maclean had established the magazine that bears his name in 1911.

In accordance with their recently changed travel plans, Winston and his party departed Toronto in their private car attached to a train shortly before midnight for Niagara Falls. After traveling the short distance to the falls, the Churchills spent most of the night of August 16–17 aboard the *Mount Royal* at the Canadian National Station at Niagara Falls.[16]

The sightseeing tour of Niagara Falls began at eight o'clock on the morning of August 17. Winston had last seen the falls 29 years earlier, during the winter. Instead of being the planned day-long visit, the outing would now be a short two-hour dash. John H. Jackson, general manager of the Park Commission, met the party at the station and escorted them around the falls. The party of 12, including all four Churchills and the local officials, embarked into three waiting motor cars and were conducted on their tour. A group of Canadian and American newspapermen and photographers were waiting for Winston, but he rebuffed their requests for interviews with "abruptness." Denied an interview, the newspaper men doggedly trailed the visitors around the falls for the entire visit. One of those reporters observed that Winston appeared to be interested in anything and everything.[17]

With very little time at their disposal, the party was driven all over the park and viewed the falls from both sides of the river. To make up for the limited time, they were driven at a high rate of speed and made only brief stops at each point. First they were taken to Falls View and Chippewa, where short stops were made. The Englishmen then went on to Table Rock House for another stop. On his previous visit to the falls, Winston had descended down a step-ladder to a ledge under the "roaring water." By 1929, however, the step-ladder and the ledge itself were gone. Instead, there was now an elevator and a scenic tunnel in place.

"I was scared last time. There was no protection," Winston commented as he saw the changes. Thrusting his hands into his pockets and with a feigned look of disgust, he said with exaggerated gravity, "Ah, that's better. How time alters things. If I had only, thought of this thirty years ago, if I'd only got the concession, I'd be a millionaire. One dollar a visitor—suppose there were only 100,000 visitors a year—that would mean more than 30,000 pounds, and it takes only about four people to operate the thing. Yes, I missed my chance—I might have been a millionaire."

As he listened to his father, Randolph smiled.

"I mean it," Winston thundered.[18]

Bypassing the elevator, the party entered and descended the long and winding scenic tunnel to one hundred feet below the Horseshoe Falls. The tunnel had "openings scooped out" to see the "foaming waters sheering downwards." After returning to their cars the tourists moved on with the tour and next boarded a tram to cross over the "boiling waters" of the Whirlpool, which was three miles below the falls. They were in a tram, called the Spanish Aero-Car, which, as Winston described it, ran along 600-yard-long wires. It looked "alarming but was really quite safe."[19] The tram was 1,800 feet long and stretched between Thompson's Point and Colt's Point. It was named for the Spanish engineers and investors who had completed the project in 1916. While both ends of the cable were in Canada, the cable car briefly passed through American territory as it completed its run. From the tram car the traveling Englishmen could see the Whirlpool down below, a "maelstrom, a vortex of water, swirling in gradually narrowing circles."[20] They also enjoyed the scenery of the Lower Rapids.

Embarking again in the motor cars, the Churchills then drove across the Falls View Bridge to the American side. Winston thus set foot in the United States for the first time since February 2, 1901, when he had sailed from New York City. This return to American soil was only temporary. On the United States side of the Falls the travelers drove around Goat Island with a brief stop at the Cave of the Winds. After further viewing of the falls was made from Goat Island, and Prospect Point, they then crossed back into Canada. According to the *Niagara Falls Gazette*, the party also made a hurried visit to the power plant of the Ontario Hydro Electric Power Commission at Queenston. According to this report, the party was shown through the plant by Jackson, who was aided by Hydro Electric employees. However, the *Niagara Falls Evening Review* reported that while Winston expressed great interest in the development at the falls, he did not have the time to see the plants. With only limited time, Winston wished to spend it viewing the scenic beauty of the falls rather than inspecting its industrial aspects.[21]

Very soon it was already ten o'clock in the morning and, with only a few minutes before their train left, the party rushed back to the train station to board their private car. After ignoring the newspapermen during the visit, Winston spoke to them as he was about to board the train. After warning them that his trip was one of pleasure entirely and that he would not make any political comments, he provided the reporters with the comments they needed. He was quoted in the resulting articles saying that the trip was a success, expressing delight with the visit, remarking on the great development that had occurred since his last visit and on the amount of water going over the falls.

"It appears to me that the falls are becoming more beautiful all the time. Both myself and the other members of my party believe that this is the most beautiful sight we have seen or will see on our trip," Winston said.[22] He went on, "There seems to be more water going over the cataracts now than twenty-nine years ago, when I visited here."

When a reporter tried a serious question about the feelings of British people toward the proposed naval conference, Winston waved his cane with a "defensive air" and laughed, "Nothing doing. I don't know anything about politics. I am having a good time and don't want to get mixed up in any arguments that might spoil it. That's work and work doesn't agree with persons on their vacation."[23]

With the duty to the newspapers dispensed with, the party boarded the private car and left by a Canadian National Railway train for Toronto at 10:10 a.m. from Niagara Falls. The beauty of Niagara Falls must have appealed to Winston, as he again returned for a third visit on August 12, 1943.

The Toronto-bound train made a stop at the Canadian National Railway station on Stuart street in Hamilton for a few minutes, just long enough for passengers to embark and disembark. As soon as the train pulled into the station, Randolph was the first passenger to alight. He ran into the station to make a purchase. While he was gone on his shopping mission, a reporter and photographer from the *Hamilton Herald*, who were waiting on the platform, climbed aboard the *Mount Royal* and went through the door of the private car. Winston was found on a davenport reading a magazine. The reporter asked Winston if he would be able to pose for the *Herald* photographer. Winston agreed with a smile. Dropping the periodical, he stepped out onto the platform. After being photographed alone, Winston then asked Randolph, who was back from his quick shopping expedition, to step into the frame for a further photograph. The photograph of a happy father and son ran on the front page of the newspaper.[24]

At Niagara Falls and on the train back to Toronto, Winston observed the fertile and cultivated lands of Ontario. These lands were excellent for growing fruits and vegetables, and supported many farms and villages. In sharp contrast to the territory the Churchills would observe as they passed through northern Ontario the following day, these more southerly regions had been "definitely subjugated by man."[25]

The Churchill party reached Toronto and returned to Government House at 12:30 in the afternoon of August 17. They were in time for the luncheon hosted by the lieutenant-governor. The guests invited to meet Winston included several members of the provincial Parliament, William D. Black, George H. Gooderham, Lincoln Goldie; as well as such business leaders as bank president Sir John Aird; president of the Toronto Carpet Manufacturing Company, F. Barry Hayes; and Charles Burton, who was president of Canada's second largest department store. The greatly accomplished Sir William Mulock, then 85 years old, was at the social event. During his career he had been a successful lawyer, member of Parliament, cabinet minister, and judge. Mulock had the distinction of having launched the political career of William Mackenzie King when he had appointed him the first deputy minister of labour two decades earlier.[26]

Also present were Senator William H. McGuire and Ontario's minister of public works and highways, George S. Henry. In 1930, upon the resignation of Ferguson, Henry would become the new provincial premier and hold office during the difficult years of the Great Depression. Winston had possibly met one of the guests at the party previously, as both he and Sigmund Samuel had attended the Dominion Day celebrations at Canada House in London in 1926. Samuel was a millionaire businessman in sheet metals who was a philanthropist and collector. Having traveled aboard the *Empress of Australia* with his mother and sister, Winston and Jack now had the opportunity to meet Gerald Larkin, the son of the Canadian High Commissioner to London. One of the most intriguing people for Winston to speak to at the luncheon was Charles Trick Currelly, an archaeologist who had worked on sites in Egypt, Crete, and Turkey, and was the director of the Royal Ontario Museum.

Winston was a good talker, both in quality as well as quantity. He enjoyed talking, whether at his own table at Chartwell or across the Atlantic Ocean on his tour in 1929. As a talker, his sentences would flow more quickly than in his speeches, with "casual epigrams" and "quick verdicts on men."[27] In such situations he almost always dominated the conversation and was forceful in arguments. A friend of Randolph's who visited Chartwell the same year of the visit to North America captured a vignette of Winston as talker when he wrote:

> We remained this evening at the round table until after midnight. The tablecloth was removed. Mr. Churchill spent a blissful two hours demonstrating with the decanters and wine glasses how the Battle of Jutland was fought. He got worked-up like a schoolboy, making barking noises in imitation of gun fire, and blowing smoke across the table in imitation of gun smoke.[28]

In an attempt to repair the damage done in his initial unsuccessful meeting with a member of the Toronto press, Randolph was interviewed on Saturday afternoon at Government House while his father and uncle were enjoying the luncheon. This was the first lengthy interview the 18-year-old Randolph had ever given to the newspapers, either at home in England or anywhere else. It was, however, the first of a great many such interviews he would give in his life. The interview was with Miss D.K. Livesay of the *Toronto Daily Star*. She asked him about the "silly question" remark at the train station and what he meant by silly.[29]

"What is a silly question? A question that makes me seem presumptuous. I do not see the point of asking me who my favorite author or politician is. It makes me seem presumptuous. What if my English friends saw it? They would laugh at me," Randolph explained.

The *Star* representative then asked if the majority of young Englishmen sympathized with Labour or the Conservatives.

Randolph, who had told Livesay that he was at Oxford in order to become a statesman, lit a cigar before saying, "Well, I don't really know. Oxford, you see, is very conservative." He added that he did not know if young Englishmen were interested in politics.

Asked about how he found Niagara Falls, Randolph said it was quite up to expectations and that Canada was very beautiful. To a further question on whether Canada was more like Great Britain or the United States, he said that he had not yet been to the United States but expected Canada would be more like Britain.

Possibly ranging into territory that Randolph might consider in the silly category of questions, Livesay asked him if he had ever considered having a Canadian wife.

"I don't know. I haven't met many Canadian girls so I cannot tell you what I think of them. We have been chiefly entertained by men."

"And do you regret that?"

"Oh no. It has been very interesting," Randolph replied without even a smile.

At that point in the interview, Tommy Church, M.P., came up to them, smiling and holding a copy of that day's *Saturday Star*, which had a picture of Randolph. Church volunteered that it was a "fine picture. Fine picture. And fine hat too. Isn't that a fine hat he's wearing?"

As Livesay agreed that it was a fine hat, Randolph looked embarrassed.

The interview continued, with the reporter asking Randolph if he approved of women in politics. Without pausing to consider that Canadian women had won the right to vote in 1920 and a woman had been elected a member of the Canadian Parliament in the 1921 election, Randolph replied emphatically, "No. I do not." He proceeded to explain that the presence of women "creates a certain lack of dignity. Women have as good minds as we, yes, but they do not fit in Parliament."

"So forty years hence, when you are a statesman sitting in Parliament you won't want to see any women around?"

"Now that's a silly question," Randolph rebuked. As the reporter begged his pardon, Randolph explained, "Don't you see how absurd it would sound in a newspaper if I was reported as saying that I did not want to sit in Parliament with women? Of course I do not mean that absolutely."

By this time the guests at the lieutenant-governor's luncheon had left Government House, and Randolph was standing almost alone on the portico gazing at the green lawns and bright gardens. Puffing on his cigar, he abruptly ended the interview with, "I think I have answered enough questions."

"I think you have," Livesay replied.

Randolph and Livesay then shook hands. With his visit to Toronto almost over, the youngest Churchill added a further plea: "And please don't be silly."

… 7 …

# Northern Ontario, Winnipeg and Kenora, August 17–20

Winston and his traveling party departed Union Station in Toronto at ten o'clock on Saturday night, August 17 aboard the *Mount Royal*, attached to Train No. 3, bound for Winnipeg. Montreal and Toronto had each met with Winston's approval. Since he last visited three decades before, the cities had each grown greatly in both population and wealth. The two cities were centers of "immense economic and social development," and were connected to the rest of the continent and world by a first-rate system of sea and rail communications.[1]

Over the next day and a half the Englishmen traveled 1200 miles across northern Ontario to Winnipeg, the capital of Manitoba. With the heavily populated regions receding behind them, they would, in Winston's words, leave behind the settled regions of Ontario and plunge into a "No Man's Land." It was a huge "rocky barrier" that "cut the continent in twain."[2] Winston recalled that for hour after hour they traversed by train "scenes of savage but desolate beauty." He watched as the *Mount Royal* passed through impenetrable forest marked by a nearly endless succession of rocky hills and countless lakes. The only sign of human activity was the harvested timber floating on the occasional "swift-flowing river." Apart from the logging, the remainder was a "wild tumult, stern and lonely."[3]

Very early on Sunday morning the train reached Sudbury, a center of Canada's nickel-copper production. It had been nearly 50 years since the discovery of mineral resources in the district. By 1933 a total value of $500,000,000 of nickel and copper would have been mined, with hundreds of millions more tons still underground yet to be extracted. In the "paling dawn," a captivated Winston looked through his window and saw scattered to the horizon the "flames of furnaces and the pouring pale smoke of chimneys." It was a "bleak, stern panorama."[4]

A train conductor noticed Winston looking through the window so intently and interjected that this is where a great many fortunes had been made in recent years. "Yes, Sir! This is International Nickel."

Leaving Sudbury the train pressed on for the shore of Lake Superior. It would follow the north side of the lake for several hundred miles until it reached Port Arthur and Fort

William at the lake's head. Winston was up at six o'clock on the Sunday morning with the train on the north shore of the lake, admiring more of the "grimly beautiful but unhospitable" terrain they were passing through. The train went through Nipigon, where Winston said he would have liked to have stayed on longer for a visit. He spent all of Sunday watching the scenery from the window of his private car and found it mesmerizing. Lake Superior also dazzled Winston. He wrote it was a "mighty inland sea" with "limpid waters, clear and blue" and rocky islands. In the early evening the lake was "marvelously tinted by the sunset." While on the lake side there was an occasional hamlet or boat, out the other side of the train was the neverending harsh wilderness.[5]

The train reached the station at Port Arthur, Ontario, on the evening of August 18. The usual cluster of reporters were awaiting Winston. Going beyond his usual politeness to Canadian reporters, on this occasion he welcomed them aboard his private car and chatted amiably with them as the train traveled between Port Arthur and Fort William. The two cities were located close beside each other and would later be amalgamated as the city of Thunder Bay. As the train passed between the two cities, the lights were turned off in the private car so that the harbor works could be viewed by the moonlight. It was exceptionally brilliant that night.

As was his custom, Winston refused all questions about politics, save for providing a few phrases and themes from the speeches he had already made in Canada. However, he was happy to comment on his trip, remarking that "this is the most enjoyable day's traveling I have ever had." Most of the trip between the two cities was spent not with the newspapermen interviewing Winston, but with the English statesman questioning *them* about the region. He asked "all number of questions" about the harbor, industries of Port Arthur and Fort William, the grain handling facilities, and the manner in which the people in the district lived. Winston told the reporters that he was able to get more information about the country from newspapermen than he would otherwise have been able to obtain. He regretted not passing through the two cities in daylight so that he could see the elevators and grain storage plants. He vowed, however, that "this will not be my last trip."[6]

Based on his trip through Port Arthur and Fort William, and at least in part on his interrogation of his temporary newspaper traveling companions, Winston described its fine harbor in his later *Daily Telegraph* article as part of a vast mechanized enterprise for shipping grain. Wheat brought from Manitoba was stored in the array of huge elevators at the harbor before being loaded aboard the grain ships that would carry the product to the great cities of the Great Lakes, as well as through the system of canals to the St. Lawrence River and the ocean beyond.[7] The Canadian wheat production which Winston referred to (and which he would study in more detail in the Canadian West) was worth $346,502,000 in 1929, on a production of 299,520,000 bushels.[8]

Wearing a dark, silk-faced overcoat, Winston left his private car when the train reached Fort William. At the platform he was met by a Mr. Chisholm, the district engineer of the CPR, who asked if everything possible was being done for him.

"I was never so comfortable in my life," Winston replied.

Winston then walked out of the train station and passed a number of people on the street without being recognized. At a nearby confectionary he made a purchase and then returned to the train.[9]

As the train completed its run to Winnipeg, the Churchills had been traveling aboard the *Mount Royal* for almost 36 hours. This was the first long leg aboard the train, after the relatively short earlier jaunts that had been made in Quebec and southern Ontario. Had the *Mount Royal*'s steward, George Grant, and the other staff of the private car not been exposed to Winston's demanding needs, they probably found out about them on the long trip from Toronto to Winnipeg. At home in England, Winston's valets lasted about a year with this impatient master before they had to depart his service. Valets were expected to appear as soon as he rang for them and have everything arranged exactly right or be told of their errors in "very plain language."[10] Among the many essential tasks the valet was expected to perform was to wake him, bring him breakfast, hand him his newspaper, run his bath, dry him after the bath, put out his clothes, insert his cuff buttons, help him dress, tie his tie, hand him his hair brushes, help him on with his shoes and tie them, hand him his cigars, and be ready to meet him at the door upon his return from his journeys. The demands continued until Winston retired to bed. Walter Graebner, one of Winston's publishers, wrote that he never saw him pour his own drink and could not imagine him without a valet. Although Winston was on holiday, and without the stresses of high political office or the demands of his career, Grant and the other staff aboard the private car no doubt found serving Winston to be a taxing experience.

By the morning of August 19 the train emerged from the harsh barren lands of northern Ontario and reached the plains. They soon arrived at Winnipeg. Winston proclaimed the city a "metropolis of the corn plains." For the next 800 miles, until reaching the Rocky Mountains, the party would travel, as the British statesman noted, across the corn belt with its "vast surfaces of waving crops." It was an "ocean of cornfields as far as the eye can reach." On either side of the rail car there would be nothing but the growing wheat crop, or corn crop in Winston's terminology, with only the infrequent small farm house.[11] This bed of a now "long-vanished sea" had rich, deep, black soil. He estimated the soil was capable of bearing crops for 30 to 40 years without manure. The "frozen north in its brief five months becomes a very volcano of food."[12]

As the train neared the Manitoba capital, Winston gave a long interview to C.D. Pyper of the *Winnipeg Evening Tribune*.[13] The reporter wrote that the British statesman was recognizable at once as he stood on the platform of his private car wearing a light-grey suit, a long cigar in his mouth, plump, round-shouldered, round-cheeked, and his head held slightly forward. Prior to boarding the train at one of the stops before Winnipeg, Pyper had observed Winston with his hands thrust in his overcoat and cigar in his mouth as he talked to policemen and strangers and bought a few cigars at a dry goods store.

As the porters had yelled "all aboard," Winston remained waiting, with his hand on the rail on the platform. He later explained to Pyper that he never gets on until the train starts.

Approached aboard the train in his private car with a request for an interview, Winston attempted to beg off. Pyper, however, persistently reminded him that he himself had once been an interviewer, and Winston relented.

"What was it you wanted to know?" Winston asked with a smile.

After declining comment on Egypt and providing only a brief answer on Snowden and reparations, Winston turned to Jack and started discussing the flower in his buttonhole. The flower was apparently a present from a resident of Fort William who admired Winston. He then asked Pyper what sort of meeting he would encounter in Winnipeg and was informed the theater was already sold-out.

"What sort of audience will it be—mostly men?" Winston asked.

Pyper replied that it would include many women and used the question as an opportunity to remind Winston of his problems with the suffragettes, and ask him about women and the vote.

"Well, they've got it. They've got it," Winston replied as he grinned. After considering the question more deeply for a moment, he continued, "Women are a very great help in politics. Liberal women, Conservative women, Labour women—they all help their parties immensely."

Prefacing his next question with the explanation that Winston and Napoleon had taught him the "value of audacity," Pyper said he was going to ask a personal question—at which point Winston leaned forward and listened attentively.

To the question of whether he may one day be prime minister, Winston answered with "No."

Pyper then asked about his reputation for possessing one of the most brilliant brains in the political world, but at the same time being somewhat erratic.

"It's not true," Winston replied with another grin. This grin, Pyper thought, was a "cheerful, boyish grin that would make you like him even if he were erratic."

"Actions are greater than words," the statesman answered to the question about which gave him the greatest satisfaction—being a famous writer or a hero of whom writers write about.

The interviewer then asked Winston what he considered the greatest thrill of his career, and followed up with whether he liked soldiering.

"The mobilization of the fleet for war," Winston replied without any hesitation to the first question; while to the second he said, "Well, I was brought up to be a soldier, was a soldier and naturally took a great interest in it."

"You are asking a great many questions," Winston interjected, but he allowed Pyper to continue with the interview. He even answered political questions that he usually tried to avoid. Questions were asked and answered on free trade, unemployment, and whether Labour would pursue a scheme of nationalization (to which Winston replied that Parliament would not let them).

"The British system of government is the soundest in the world. It is based on freedom and is capable of being changed as circumstances demand," Winston said in answer to a question about changes to the electoral system.

"You are asking a great many questions," Winston observed for a second time.

Pyper reminded Winston again that he too had once been an inquisitive journalist and then added that he had only one or two more innocuous ones to put to him. Winston relented and listened as Pyper asked who Winston considered to be the greatest Parliamentarian of his time.

"Lord Balfour is the greatest statesman, certainly in the last 15 years," Winston replied.

Having given Pyper more time than was his custom, Winston ended the interview. The newspaperman told him that he was glad to have met him, as he always admired him, even though he had once hated him.

"Tell me when you hated me," Winston said with a smile.

When told that it was when Pyper was an Ulsterman, Winston replied, "Oh, but the Ulster people have forgiven me."

Pyper managed to get in two more questions as he rose from his chair to leave the *Mount Royal*, the first on how Winston was getting on with his painting and the second on Lord Asquith's amusing references in his book to Winston's "priceless French."

"I haven't any time for it now," Winston batted away the first question; and to the second he said, "Oh, one must do the best one can."

That same morning of August 19 the Churchills arrived in Winnipeg, capital of the province of Manitoba and then the third largest city in the dominion, with a population of 179,087. This was Winston's second visit to the city. He had been in Winnipeg once before, in January 1901, for a stop on his lecture tour. That visit to the city had taken place during the height of winter. As Winston recalled, he had emerged from the train and boarded a horse-drawn sledge, with the temperature far below zero.[14] In Winnipeg in 1901 he had delivered his lecture, complete with slides on the South African War, to a full house at the old Winnipeg Theatre. Before the curtain went up that night Winston had looked through the peephole and asked the manager of the theater for an estimate of the evening's box office. On the afternoon before the lecture Winston had bought a coon coat at a Hudson's Bay Company store and was wearing it the next morning as he boarded the train for St. Paul. Winston was in Winnipeg when the news arrived that Queen Victoria had died, bringing an end to the long Victorian age.[15]

Back in Winnipeg after three decades, Winston marveled at the changes that had occurred. As he recalled in one of his *Daily Telegraph* articles, Winnipeg was now a large, up-to-date city, with imposing buildings and bustling streets that were packed with motorcars and lined with hotels, stores, and theaters.[16]

The train reached Winnipeg at nine o'clock that morning, and Winston was greeted at the station by a delegation of Winnipeg's leading citizens, as well as the usual gathering of newspapermen. To the reporter from the *Manitoba Free Press* who came aboard the private car, Winston repeated that he was here to see Canada and the men who are shaping the country, as well as how Canada and Britain could help each other.

Beyond that, Winston pointed to a chair facing him and said, "Sit there. I'll give you five minutes—now what would you like to know?"

Winston pulled on a black cigar (the reporter commented on how "deftly" he manipulated it between his teeth) and sat back a little deeper in the chair. With his eyes half-closed he was ready for the questions. He discussed the prospects of the Labour government, which he said was in office but not in power, his support for Snowden's efforts over the Young Plan, and Canada's place in the empire. Asked about what he would say in his speech, he asked instead, "What would you like to hear?" More informatively, Winston said he would allow the opinions he gathered locally in Winnipeg to guide him on his subjects.[17]

At the train station to meet the Churchill party were several illustrious citizens of the city, including James A. Richardson; Major A.B. Allard, aide to the lieutenant-governor of Manitoba; E.D. Cotterell, the general superintendent of the Canadian Pacific Railway; and Dr. Robert Fletcher, representing the National Council of Education. On the train platform a photograph was taken of Major Allard, Winston, James Richardson, Jack, Randolph, and Dr. Fletcher.[18] The photograph ran on the front page of the next edition of the *Winnipeg Evening Tribune*.

The 44-year-old Richardson was Winston's host on this leg of the trip. He impressed Winston, who described him to Clementine as a "very good specimen of a new world business

The Churchills pose for newspaper photographers with their local hosts at the Winnipeg train station after disembarking from the *Mount Royal*. From left: Major A.B. Allard, Winston, James A. Richardson, Jack, Dr. Robert Fletcher, and Randolph (Library and Archives Canada).

man."[19] Coming from one of Canada's leading business families, Richardson was a successful and visionary businessman. Joining the family firm of James Richardson and Sons after university, he became president of the company in 1918. Under his guidance the company became a leader in the grain business and also expanded into such fields as securities, communications, and aviation. The firm was a member of all of the stock exchanges across Canada and had offices throughout the country. To transmit orders and information between the offices the latest "advanced equipment" was used. These machines might have been demonstrated by Richardson for the English tourists, including the teletype machine (which had been introduced in 1928). In 1926 Richardson had formed Western Canadian Airways, which by 1929 was the second largest air transport company in the Empire. He also moved into radio when he established a 500-watt transmitter at Moose Jaw in 1925. Richardson was a director of such firms as the Canadian Bank of Commerce, Canadian Pacific Railway, Canadian Vickers Limited, and International Nickel Company. His position as a CPR director probably led to his involvement in the Churchill visit to Winnipeg. While in the city, Winston also met Richardson's wife Muriel, who would become president of her husband's company after his death in 1939. She headed the company for 27 years.[20]

The Englishmen and their hosts left the station and embarked on a tour of Winnipeg. In short order they visited the grain exchange, located in the Grain Exchange Building at the corner of Rorie and Lombard in Winnipeg, where wheat was traded. This structure, in a reflection of the power of the exchange, was claimed to be the largest office building in the Dominion. The Winnipeg Grain and Produce Exchange had opened in 1887 and was one of the continent's leading commodity markets. A seat on the exchange cost up to $25,000 in 1929. Trading grain at the exchange was a spectacle, with the traders once said to have been "barking like dogs and roaring like bulls in a most undignified and excited manner."[21]

Richardson, a former president of the exchange, gave the British visitors a tour. An expert on the trade, Richardson once said, "Success in the grain export business requires the constitution of an ox, an enormous capacity for hard work, and the peculiar qualifications which belong to a trader."[22] As Winston observed the floor of the exchange that day, "frantic dealers screamed and gesticulated as the telegrams from all the world recorded the ceaseless fluctuations of wheat prices."[23] From his hosts Winston learned that it would be a profitable investment to buy wheat for the October delivery, as with the current price of $1.50, a profit of 50 percent could be expected in just a few months. However, as Winston wrote his wife, the travelers did not have the money available at that moment for such an extra investment.

At noon the party was Richardson's guests at an informal luncheon attended by many of the city's prominent citizens. In the afternoon they toured the provincial Parliament buildings.

Randolph took note during the trip across the country of the general prosperity that he observed. He later wrote that there were "no beggars in Canada. No one is destitute. All can earn a satisfactory living."[24]

In Winnipeg Winston continued his habit of meeting old comrades in Canada. During the visit to the city he met James Dyer and W.L. Robertson, both formerly of the 4th Squadron, the Queen's Own Hussars. Dyer and Robertson had been in the regiment along with Winston in India.[25]

That evening Winston was the guest of honor at a dinner at Government House hosted by the lieutenant-governor of Manitoba, James D. McGregor. Built in the 1880s, the house was adjacent to the Manitoba Legislative Building and close to the Assiniboine River. At half-past eleven that night the Churchill party returned to the train station and boarded the *Mount Royal*, attached to a special eastbound Canadian Pacific Railway train, in order to retrace their steps back into Ontario for a brief visit to Kenora and the Lake of the Woods. On this overnight trip to Kenora, the Churchills were accompanied by their Winnipeg hosts. Richardson, Robert Rogers, James B. Coyne, and others traveled with the party in the *Mount Royal*, while D.C. Coleman, who was vice-president of Western Lines for the Canadian Pacific Railway, came along in another private car. Rogers was a Conservative member of Parliament for a Winnipeg constituency who had served as minister of public works under Prime Minister Borden. Additionally, he owned a 200,000-acre ranch with 10,000 head of cattle and 2,000 horses near Medicine Hat, Alberta. A successful Winnipeg lawyer, Coyne participated in the Citizens' Committee of 1000 that opposed the 1919 Winnipeg General Strike.[26]

Mayor Earl Hutchinson of Kenora had cabled Winston on August 16 that he had learned of his planned visit to the district, and extended a welcome and offered any assistance to make his visit more enjoyable, saying he would make any arrangements for a reception or holiday. In reply, Winston thanked the mayor for his "charming" message, but said he could not alter his itinerary without inconveniencing his hosts.[27]

After traveling overnight, the special train arrived at Kenora at ten o'clock in the morning. It departed again at half-past two that afternoon, after a four-and-a-half-hour visit, in order for Winston to return to Winnipeg in time for his speech that evening. Shortly after arriving at the station, the party left for the Lake of the Woods. They spent a great deal of their time on the lake, which is one hundred miles long and 40 miles wide, with thousands of islands. Winston guessed that twenty or thirty thousand islands were dotting the beautiful water of the lake. Several hundred of these islands had summer homes. Winston wrote that the lake was the "country club and playground" of the Winnipeg magnates. These "victors of the mart of Winnipeg" owned nice summer homes on the lake where they rested and enjoyed themselves on the weekend. He also noted that motor boats careened across the lake at great speeds, causing "fierce furrows [that] toss the canoes of the Indians (real) about like corke."[28]

Winston experienced the speed of the motor boats first hand as the party roared around the lake in one that was considered the fastest of all the boats. Randolph and Johnny swam in the lake and also tried to surf. The Churchills visited the camp belonging to James Richardson and later had lunch at the summer home of Rogers and his wife, Aurelia, a residence Winston thought was a "palatial Peter Pan Bungalow." As they enjoyed a leisurely lunch, the wireless was tuned to a ceaseless report of the latest trading and developments on the Winnipeg Grain Exchange which they had visited the previous day.[29]

One of the topics Winston and Richardson talked about during their time together, either in Winnipeg or at the Lake of the Woods, was investing. The Canadian suggested that his organization was available should Winston wish to do any business or make any investments while in North America. This offer was soon to be taken up by Winston.

The Lake of the Woods rivaled or supplanted in the minds of the Churchills the countryside of Quebec, where Randolph had previously imagined himself settling down. Winston and Randolph now gave notice that they intended to buy one of the islands. That was unless, of course, they found somewhere they liked better as the journey continued. Winston thought any of the thousands of islands at the Lake of the Woods could be made into a "most beautiful summer residence." Winston or one of the party with him told the newspapers of this intention to purchase an island, and it was duly reported in Canadian newspapers.[30]

Winston thoroughly enjoyed his relaxing visit to the Lake of the Woods, later writing Richardson that above all else during his stay in Winnipeg he had remembered his wonderful time at Kenora.[31] To Clementine he wrote that the day at Kenora and the Lake of the Woods was one she would have really enjoyed, and that the "brilliant aspect of this lake has left a strong impression on my mind."[32] He added that one day he would show her the beautiful lake. Winston's enthusiasm for the Lake of the Woods was shared by another British politician, Ramsay MacDonald, who had also been much pleased with Kenora on his trip through the region.

Had his Canadian trip only been intended for relaxation and pleasure, Winston said he would have changed his travel plans and spent three or four days at the Lake of the Woods. The days spent at Kenora would have been gained by giving Winnipeg, Regina, Edmonton, and Calgary only a quick inspection from the train. The trip was, however, also intended as a means to learn and lecture. Learning about Canada required that he not bypass these "brand new cities."[33]

Winston's prior commitment to deliver an address to the citizens of Winnipeg that evening forced him to abandon the pleasures of the Lake of the Woods and travel back over one hundred miles to Winnipeg that afternoon. The speech in Winnipeg was scheduled to start at 8:30 that evening and would take place at the Walker Theatre on Smith Street in Winnipeg. The speech was again delivered under the auspices of the National Council of Education and the Overseas Educational League. It was a "monster gathering." Like his last speech in Winnipeg, the address was delivered to a full house. The audience was large, warm, and brilliantly-colored, with Union Jacks draped on the balcony rails. Others beyond those at the Walker Theatre were able to hear the speech as it was broadcast, while still others could read it, since, like many of his Canadian speeches, an almost complete transcript of the speech was published the next day in the local newspapers.[34]

For the occasion Winston wore a black coat, winged collar, and grey striped trousers, with a link of thin gold shining on the black background of his waistcoat. A reporter thought he was a "picturesque, unusual, and brilliant gentleman," with a "round, plump, little–Jack-Horner sort of face you might find on a friendly gnome in the depths of an enchanted forest." Altogether, Winston, like other British politicians, had a "peculiar appearance" of oddity, simpleness, innocence, and naïveté. All of which was a "curious mask," as Winston came from British fighting stock.

Leading the platform party at the event was Archbishop Samuel Matheson, president of the Overseas Educational League, who wore a purple apron that glowed "royally in the footlight's soft glare." On the platform Winston sat beside Matheson. Also on the platform was James Richardson, "heavy and stern in full dress," Lieutenant-Governor J.D. McGregor, Mayor Dan McLean, Dr. Robert Fletcher, and Major A.B. Allard. Randolph, described as "handsome as a sculptor's model" by one newspaper account and as a "slim, handsome boy" in another, sat on the right wing of the platform delegation. With such a very large audience in attendance, hundreds of spectators were seated on the stage itself behind the "celebrities" of the platform party.[35]

Premier John Bracken of Manitoba was also on the platform. Winston had probably met him during the previous day's tour of the Parliament buildings and dinner at Government House. A university professor and principal of the Manitoba Agriculture College, Bracken became premier in 1922, even though until that moment he had had no previous interest in politics. The United Farmers of Manitoba, having won the most seats in the provincial election and in the position to form a government, lacked a leader. They approached Bracken, who was shocked by the offer, but after an initial refusal accepted the proposition and became premier. He held the office for the next two decades. Winston was impressed with the 46-year-old Bracken and later told Richardson that he had taken a liking to the brilliant politician.[36]

His Grace Archbishop Matheson was presiding and introduced Winston in a set of remarks thought to be "genial and witty." He recalled the speaker's previous visit to Winnipeg and then called him "one of the greatest of Modern Britishers—a great statesman, a great writer and a very great personage." He was an ex-chancellor, an ex-soldier, and an ex-prisoner of war, an excellent statesman and one of the most versatile England had ever produced.[37]

As Winston rose to speak, he received an enthusiastic reception when everyone in the audience rose and cheered loudly. As he stood by the table on the stage to speak, a reporter observed, "There he was exactly like Low's cartoon of him."[38]

Having already delivered three major addresses in Canada—in Montreal, Ottawa, and Toronto—the speech in Winnipeg did not see any new themes introduced. Instead, he covered the old ground of the previous addresses with phrases borrowed and repeated. The speech, however, was still delivered with vigor. With his passionate delivery, patriotism, and positions that found popular appeal with the audience, the speech was interrupted repeatedly with loud applause and at the end was cheered "to the echo."

As he started, Winston looked "puckishly" into the crowded, darkened theater and then, clutching both of his coat lapels near the collar, began speaking in a "thin refined voice touched faintly with a dainty little lisp." The voice would take edge during points in the speech, and the "gnome is suddenly a figure of menace, the humorous tabby, we perceive with a thrill, is a stalking feline."[39] C.B. Pyper, who had interviewed Winston the day before, was in the audience for the speech. He noted that Winston's voice was "pleasant and clear," and that while he spoke he stood with an "easy and natural attitude," using few gestures.[40]

Winston spoke without "exertion" and opened with the familiar reference to his coming to Canada in search of knowledge and then referring to the three decades that had passed since he had previously been in the city. He remarked that these almost 30 years had certainly been a long time and were marked by stunning change. Scientific developments had transformed the world, and war had led to the collapse of all the German, Russian, Turkish, Chinese, and Austro-Hungarian empires. All the world's great empires had shattered, save for the British one. Winston said the "whole organization has changed—new ideas, new spirits, new values, have been instituted among men, all in these 30 years. But we have come through them safely. Let us be thankful for that. Here we are. The British Empire came through the fire, came out of the struggle intact, stronger than ever." The audience interrupted with applause.

Winston then remarked that he had read in the newspaper that in his previous speech in the Manitoba capital he had told his audience that the city was a "winner." Reflecting on that, he said, "Well, I think on the whole, I was right. It was prophetic!" The city of 40,000 Winston had visited in 1900 now boasted a population of a quarter of a million and was Manitoba's "great productive capital and centre."

Pyper observed Randolph while his father spoke. He thought him a "good looking boy" who was "perhaps the most interesting thing in the meeting." While Winston delivered his speech, Randolph's attention was divided between "loyally" leading the applause and making "nervous little smiles" to friends in the audience.[41]

In the speech Winston again refuted the notion that Britain was "down and out," agreed with President Hoover's statement that the outlook was more favorable for peace than at any time in the history of the world, warned against subversive propaganda aimed at destroying the empire, "ridiculed" the idea of a breakdown in relations between Britain and the United States which would be the most disastrous mistake in human history, and repeated his concerns over naval armaments negotiations with the United States. On reparations and the Young Plan, the "thin voice was suddenly exciting. He had mounted a horse, and flashed out a saber and whirled off Mr. Young's head by the simple inflexion of his tones. Here was the famous Winston, the hero of a hundred high dramatic scenes and misadventures." He also stood against the Egyptian proposals as leading the country to disaster, called for continuing the Singapore naval base, and supported the constitutional decisions taken at the 1926 Imperial Conference of each dominion having equal status.

The Empire, Winston assured his audience, belonged to Canada and Australia as much as it did to Britain. He proclaimed, "It is your Crown, your empire as much as it is ours, and we are sure that you will guard and cherish it as we have always tried to do."

As Winston neared the end of his talk, his son became very busy making notes with a pencil and paper for several minutes.

Winston ended the speech with a rousing patriotic closing. The ties that bound the dominions to the empire centered on the crown, he said, which could be traced back to the "Tudors, the Plantagenets, the Magna Carta, Habeas Corpus, Petition of Rights, and English Common Law—which links us inseparably over all the massive stepping stones which the people of the British race shaped and forged to the joy, and peace, and glory of mankind."

Matheson thanked Winston for his speech after the last ovation had subsided, calling it a "delightful address." He then called on Randolph to reply to the vote of thanks. Eager both for the spotlight and to emulate his father, "Churchill the Younger" rose and stood before the audience with his hastily scribbled notes in his hand. "Swaying slightly as he stood," a reporter observed that Randolph "delivered his speech in a clear, cultured, and flexible voice."[42]

The audience applauded and laughed at the appropriate moments during Randolph's speech. While his son spoke, Winston's face was a "study." His "laughter turned to a smile and then the smile faded away. He looked up thoughtfully out of the corners of his eyes at his son." Pyper thought Winston looked a "little fearful for the boy" and appeared to want to reach out and pull on his son's coat and whisper, "That's enough for this time, Randolph; wind it up now and sit down."

"I, too, have come here in search of knowledge," Randolph said as he began his short speech gracefully. He told the audience that in Ottawa he had seen a picture in the archives of Winnipeg in 1870. The city then consisted of eight houses. The modern Winnipeg that he was visiting left him, he said, "in even greater astonishment than that experienced by my father. Like him I have been greatly impressed by the astonishing growth, vitality, beauty, and hospitality of Canada. I think it is a pity that more young men from England do not visit Canada and that more young men from Canada do not visit England, and thus do their part in strengthening the link between us, of which my father had spoken."[43]

Randolph sat down to applause. He looked a "little flustered, a little doubtful whether this was what he had striven for."

Pyper thought it was a "nicely phrased little speech" and that Randolph had "done well for a beginner." After hearing the son, this newspaper writer concluded that not only was the British premiership still within the bounds of possibility for Winston, it was also a possibility for the younger Churchill. Winnipeggers at the Walker Theatre that night, he suggested, may have heard "two members of one family, father and son, both with the premiership in their knapsacks."[44]

The *Free Press* effused that Randolph had won the hearts of the audience. The same newspaper additionally expressed thorough approval of Winston's appearance in Winnipeg. It summarized that during his long career in which he had dealt with warlords and rulers in deciding the fates of nations, Winston had gone down "to bite the bitter dust of defeat" but had come back again. Now in opposition ranks, Winston was "in good fighting order and with all his weapons shining." That same newspaper's editorial wrote that Winston spoke eloquently, wisely, and with "directness, force, and even passion." His arguments on some subjects were "masterly and convincing." In expressing his deeply held set of opinions, he could be criticized for discussing partisan and controversial questions and for giving the Canadian government advice over Egypt. The Canadian audience, however, "appreciated, enjoyed, and applauded the performance," as he spoke on important issues with "freedom and directness." The editorial noted, with great prescience for his future relations with Baldwin and the Conservative party, that on such matters as Egypt Winston was speaking for himself rather than his party. Winston's emphatic declarations in favor of the new conception of Empire relations embodied in the Imperial Conference should, the newspaper editorialized, "have a highly enlightening effect upon those Canadians who think that the Balfour report is a treasonable document wrested from a reluctant British government by truculent, scheming, Dominion premiers."[45]

The *Evening Tribune* editorial said that Winston was "temperamentally incapable of a non-controversial speech." He expressed his point of view on the subjects covered in the speech with frankness. His discussion of the Empire had "refreshing candor and force." It was "like a breath of fresh air" to hear a statesman who did not apologize, or appear to apologize, when he used the word Empire in reference to the association of British nations, colonies, and dependencies. It concluded that Winston's visit to Canada could "awaken in the Canadian people the sentiments of pride in their Imperial inheritance and desire to assume fully the responsibility and obligations of Empire Citizenship."[46]

Although Winston's speeches had been very well-received at each stop, both by the audiences and in the local newspapers, the *Ottawa Journal* was moved to complain about his addresses in its August 20 edition. It said that in the content of his speeches he was "transferring a British political platform to the hospitality of the Canadian Club." According to the newspaper, speakers at the Canadian Club were not supposed to "talk politics," and Winston should have refrained from speaking about issues such as Egypt and naval disarmament. Canada was "not a good place" for debate on such matters.[47] The pleased Canadian Club officials and thrilled audiences at the speeches, for their part, were apparently unaware that their hospitality was being so abused by Winston.

This criticism of Winston's Canadian speeches was echoed by the *Star*, an evening Liberal newspaper in England. Writing that they knew him better than his audiences in North America, the newspaper labeled as "mischievous" his attempts to turn Canadian opinion against the Egyptian settlement, and recalled what they termed his frantic flag waving at the dominions during the Chanak Crisis. All of this the *Star* said was "merely the ebullience of the irresponsible boy who is still behind Mr. Churchill's 55 years."[48]

Winston was so fascinated with the grain industry he had observed in Manitoba that he devoted one of his eight *Daily Telegraph* articles to it in a piece entitled "World's Greatest Grain Emporium." He had seen first-hand the "golden fields of illimitable cultivation," visited the grain exchange, befriended in Richardson one of the leading grain magnates, and before that passed by the grain ports at Port Arthur and Fort William on Lake Superior. Winston noted in his article that Manitoba's grain exports were worth fifty million dollars annually, a sum that enriched the producers and expanded production. This was the crop that brought "cheap food to far-off unthinking millions."[49]

Winston and the other members of the traveling party left for Regina from the Winnipeg train station at 10:30 on the night of August 20, shortly after the speech at the Walker Theatre had been completed. In reporting the departure, the *Winnipeg Evening Tribune* overestimated the scale of the Churchillian holiday that was being undertaken. After accurately reporting that the party would travel on to Vancouver and then down to San Francisco, it then incorrectly said an extensive tour of South America would follow before the Churchills returned to England. Perhaps the reporter misunderstood, or someone in the party was having some fun telling the reporter the trip would carry on all the way to another continent.

... 8 ...

# Regina and Saskatoon, August 21–22

Aboard the *Mount Royal* the party traveled from Winnipeg through the night to Regina, the capital city of Saskatchewan. The province in 1929 had a population of 866,700 and covered an area of 251,700 square miles. In their private car attached to the CPR train they would cross the three prairie provinces of Western Canada in stretches of 300 or 400 miles at a time. After hours and hundreds of miles of traveling through the seemingly unending cornfields, Winston wrote they would arrive at one of the new cities—Regina, Edmonton, and Calgary. These cities were entirely up-to-date in every way. In 1929 these three cities were still comparatively new and small, with populations of 34,432, 58,821, and 63,305, respectively. As they traveled farther west, Winston wrote that the golden wheat fields were framed "only on distant horizons by the blue or purple-grey silhouettes of mountains."[1]

As was by now inevitable, a Regina journalist from the *Leader-Post* boarded the train on the morning of August 21 and delivered himself to the door of the *Mount Royal* to beg an interview.[2] He found Winston examining a mass of telegrams and dictating replies to his secretary. Most of the correspondence were expressions of regret at being unable to accept the great number of invitations that were now showering him. Despite his predisposition to avoid such interviews while in Canada, he once again gave the newspaperman a few minutes of his time just as the train neared Regina.

The reporter was immediately impressed by Winston's "alertness and physical and mental vigor." He was immediately put at ease, even as a stranger, by Winston's "courteous and affable" manner.

"A startling contrast to the scenes we passed through two days ago. This is very different from the country north of the Great Lakes, which is impressively beautiful but fierce," Winston told the reporter in describing his opinion of the territory they were passing. As he spoke he glanced out the window of the private car at the landscape. Winston added that he could not offer his impressions on Saskatchewan as he had not been to the province yet. As in other interviews, Winston tried, for his part, to gain information from the reporter and asked if this was the heart of the corn belt.

From the interview the newspaperman reported that Winston was on holiday but was finding it anything but relaxing. Even on the train he was kept very busy replying to correspondence from all over Canada and the United States inviting him to all sorts of functions. That the trip thus far had been tiring rather than relaxing was a theme echoed by Winston himself that day. In a letter he wrote that the trip had been very interesting but quite demanding, as they were now traveling every night and speaking every day.[3]

As was normal, Winston was guarded in answering questions on international issues, declining to comment at all on the reparations conference at The Hague. He was, however, quite interested in the latest developments at the conference. The reporter showed him the latest press dispatch from The Hague in that morning's edition of the *Leader-Post*. After he lit an enormous cigar, Winston carefully read the article.

"Well, obviously there is nothing to be said, because it is all hanging in the balance," Winston remarked after he read the dispatch.[4]

On other issues, Winston offered some comments to the reporter. These included the British system of government, Lord Balfour as the greatest British statesman, the future of the Liberal party, unemployment, and women in politics. He also declared the British Empire to be the "greatest show in the world."

When the reporter attempted to ask about international affairs, Winston turned down the opportunity to discuss such issues. "Really, there is nothing I can add to what I've said already at meetings in the East. You know my views on the Singapore base, on naval reduction, and on development of trade within the Empire." There would not have been any time to discuss such issues even if Winston had been willing, because at that moment the train was pulling into the Union Station in Regina.

While aboard the private car, the newspaperman noted that several books were lying on a table in the car. These included *Overtones of War* by Edmund Blunden, *Three Centuries of Canadian Story* by J.E. Wetherell, a volume of Macaulay's history, and *Birds of Western Canada* by Percy A. Taverner. This last book, the "most comprehensive work" on the subject, had been presented to the party while they were in Winnipeg. Another volume present was a short book on Winnipeg's anti-mosquito campaign.

The train was scheduled to reach Regina at 10:30 in the morning.[5] They would spend less than one day in Regina, during which time the party would tour the city, dine with the lieutenant-governor, and attend to another speech.

The city of Regina had been formerly known as Piles of Bones. It had been the capital of the Northwest Territories, and when Saskatchewan became a province on September 1, 1905, it became the new province's capital. The history of Regina had been closely associated with the Royal Canadian Mounted Police. Although the force's headquarters had been moved from the city to Ottawa in 1920, Regina continued to be home to a large RCMP establishment that trained all its new police recruits. Rather surprisingly, Winston did not visit the RCMP depot in Regina. Given his interests and romantic outlook, he probably would have thoroughly enjoyed everything he would have seen. Perhaps it was a question of time.

A large crowd of citizens were on hand at the train station in Regina to welcome Winston and his party to their city. Among the officials greeting the Churchills were Lieutenant-Colonel A.G. Styles, DSO, on behalf of the lieutenant-governor, and D.J. Thom, KC, representing the Canadian Club. The party was enthusiastically welcomed by the citizens of Regina as they left the *Mount Royal*.[6]

The Churchill party was then driven to Government House, official residence of the lieutenant-governor of Saskatchewan, where they were to be guests until they departed the city that evening by train for Saskatoon. The house had been designed by Thomas Fuller, the dominion architect, and built in 1890–91 for a cost of more than $50,000. A ballroom had been added to the south end of the building in 1928 for a cost of $36,000. Winston's one-day stay in Regina had not been the shortest by a prominent British visitor. The Duke and Duchess of York, the future King George V and Queen Mary, had been entertained at a "lavish banquet" at Government House during a three-hour visit to Regina on September 27, 1901.[7] All four Churchills signed the Guest Book at Government House during their stay.

The lieutenant-governor of Saskatchewan at the time of Winston's visit was Henry Newlands. A lawyer and judge on the Territorial Supreme Court and Saskatchewan Court of Appeal, he had held the post of lieutenant-governor since 1921. He had only a few months left in his tenure, as he would resign on October 30, 1929, due to illness. In the performance of his official duties, including hosting formal dinners and receptions, Newlands was assisted by his daughter Edina (as his wife Mary had to reside in the United States due to her poor health). It is likely Edina was present for the Churchills' visit. If she indeed was present, both she and Winston would have had flying to talk about as a common interest. Winston had had an early interest in flying and pursued pilot training both before and after the Great War until forced to abandon the effort after a crash and the disapproval of Clementine. Edina Newlands did not have such a restraining hand and would shortly, on November 19, 1929, receive her pilot's license. She would be the 12th woman in Canada to receive her license, the first being awarded only a year and a half earlier, on March 22, 1928. Edina was instructed in a Cirrus Moth and flew out of the Regina Flying Club at the Regina Air Board's six-plane municipal aerodrome.[8]

The first visit to Government House that morning was probably necessarily brief, since the speech to the Canadian Club of Regina was to be at a luncheon in the ballroom of the Hotel Saskatchewan. The hotel was on Victoria Avenue, facing Victoria Park. Built in a modern classical style, the 12-storey hotel had opened over two years earlier on May 23, 1927.[9] The Canadian Club had planned for 450 guests at the luncheon, and the *Morning Leader* reported that "every square foot" of the ballroom was filled for the speech.[10]

A selection of politicians, businessmen, judges, military officers, and clergy sat alongside Winston at the 26-place head table in the ballroom. They were led by Lieutenant-Governor Newlands, Saskatchewan Premier John G. Gardiner, and three provincial cabinet ministers: Thomas C. Davis, George Spence, and William J. Patterson (the last of whom would become premier himself in 1935). The judges included James Mackay, William Ferdinand-Alphonse Turgeon, William M. Martin, and Chief Justice of the Court of King's Bench for Saskatchewan James T. Brown; while the soldiers at the head table were Brigadier-General J.N. Ross and Lieutenant-Colonel Alfred G. Styles, who had received a DSO in France during the war. John F.L. Embury qualified as both a judge and soldier, as he had been a brigade commander in the Great War and was then a judge on the Saskatchewan Court of King's Bench. Anglican Bishop Malcolm T. McAdam Harding, the Reverend E.W. Stopford, and the Reverend Dean George N. Dobie were present, as were Regina bank manager J.J. Galloway, businessman and former mayor of Regina James Grassick, Alderman Wes Champ, and Royal Canadian Mounted Police Superintendent G.S. Worsley.[11]

A Regina lawyer and president of the Canadian Club, Douglas J. Thom, introduced Winston, who received a "tremendous ovation" as he rose to speak. He received repeated applause throughout the speech and, as reported by the *Morning Leader*, spoke impressively, eloquently, and persuasively.[12] The speech covered the by-now well-established topics for Winston's Canadian speeches. As he wrote to Clementine, he had spent a great deal of time preparing his first speeches in Canada but was "now working over old ground as in an election campaign."[13] Britain's position in the world and at home, Anglo-American relations and naval disarmament, and Egypt were all discussed. While the speech was resoundingly cheered and applauded, the audience for most of the speech listened "in a dead silence, electric, tense, and expectant." The news account reported that there was a "thrill" when Winston repeated his declaration of traveling so far but still being able to find himself among friends and fellow citizens, and that "this, too, is my home." At the conclusion of the speech Winston received a degree of applause that no previous Canadian Club speaker had probably received. The speech was approved by the audience as well as in the editorials of the local newspaper. The latter wrote that the speaker they had seen at the luncheon was a "confident, buoyant, progressive, forward-looking imperial and world statesman." They found little in the speech, which was printed in full in their newspaper, to quarrel with except for possibly Egypt and the pessimism he held for a naval agreement with the United States. Thom of the Canadian Club, in writing to Winston to thank him for the gift of an autographed copy of *The Aftermath*, called the speech the most successful event in the history of Regina's Canadian Club.[14]

Quite likely after the luncheon Winston and the rest of the party went to the top of the Hotel Saskatchewan to take advantage of the view it offered of the city and surrounding country. In the *Daily Telegraph* articles he reported that in each of the provincial capitals in western Canada, the Churchills would go up to the top of a large hotel to see the great scenery.

That afternoon, after the luncheon at the Hotel Saskatchewan, the Churchill party visited the Parliament buildings. The party was accompanied by Styles and other local dignitaries on the visit, while Premier Gardiner led the tour. As the party came to the visitor's book, which was on a desk placed outside the entrance to the legislature, Winston met another old colleague. Larry Lett, sergeant-at-arms of the Provincial House, was on duty, and both he and Winston instantly recognized each other.[15] They had met in South Africa during the war when Winston was a war correspondent and Lett was a Sergeant-Major with the British army. Lett, who was serving as a scout and knew the terrain, had at one point in the war led Winston and another army officer across the "hostile South African veldt." A Regina newspaper account of their earlier meeting misplaced the time of the event to that of Winston's escape from the Boer prison in Pretoria. Nonetheless, when Winston and Lett parted at Honing Spruit, Winston gave him a note asking Lett to call upon him in England. This invitation was, in fact, never acted on. Lett, however, kept the note in his possession over the years.

"I wish I had it with me today to show you," Lett said.

Winston chuckled as he recalled the incident, and both men had a "long chat" about their "old experiences."

A political impasse was underway in Saskatchewan politics at the time of the Churchills' visit to Regina. The election two months earlier, on June 6, 1929, had proved inconclusive. The governing Liberals under Gardiner had won 26 seats, with 46 percent of the popular vote, while the Conservatives had won 24 seats and 36 percent of the vote.[16] The remaining 11 seats were split between the Progressives and Independents. The Liberals had the largest number of seats, but a coalition of all their opponents could form a majority and oust the party that had held power in Saskatchewan since 1905. After consulting with his party, Gardiner refused to resign and advised the lieutenant-governor to call the legislature into session, proclaiming only that body had the right to dissolve his government. With the Conservatives, on the other hand, demanding he immediately dismiss the government based on the election result, Newlands was in a difficult position. The lieutenant-governor did not dismiss the sitting government and instead called for the legislature to meet for the first time since the election in early September. As Winston noted, some drama was expected at the opening of the legislature.[17]

During the day the Churchills spent in Regina, Gardiner spoke to Winston about the political situation he was facing. At the time he had been premier for over three years, having previously been a farmer, headmaster, backbench member of the legislative assembly, and provincial cabinet minister. Gardiner had a reputation for being ruthlessly partisan in politics. With his visitor's vast experience in politics, Gardiner consulted with Winston about what he should do. This would be an interesting query for the Englishman, who had just seen Stanley Baldwin resign immediately after an indecisive election result in order to avoid being seen trying to cling to power. On other occasions Winston had recommended the Conservatives reach an agreement to keep the Socialists out of power. In this case Winston's advice to Gardiner unfortunately is unknown.[18]

That evening Winston and the rest of his party were guests at a dinner party hosted at Government House by Lieutenant-Governor Newlands. After being entertained at the party, the Englishmen departed Regina, bound for Saskatoon, shortly before midnight aboard their private car, which was attached to the CPR Tri-City express.

Having gained first-hand knowledge of the political affairs of the province from the lieutenant-governor and current premier in Regina, Winston was probably eager to meet the Conservative leader, Dr. James T.M. Anderson, at his next stop. The party leader was the host of the Churchill party in the city of Saskatoon, which was reached by the *Mount Royal* at half-past six o'clock on the morning of August 22. Anderson was a 51 year-old who had been leader of the provincial conservative party since 1924. Joining Anderson as host was Frank R. MacMillan, a former mayor of the city.[19]

The visit to Saskatoon was a restful day without a speech and no public appearances. This stop had not been included on the final itinerary that had been prepared as the party had been about to leave England. It had originally been intended for the party to spend the night of August 21–22 in Regina and travel directly to Edmonton, giving Saskatoon a miss. No information is available to indicate why the itinerary was altered, but perhaps Winston thought it would be both appropriate and interesting to meet Anderson, given the local political impasse. The Saskatoon newspaper the *Star Phoenix* regretted that Winston's visit to the city did not include a speaking engagement, but recognized that one day without an address to deliver would be a "welcome relief" to even someone so energetic as Winston.[20]

That morning the party and their hosts drove by motor car to points of interest in Saskatoon and in the surrounding district. At the University of Saskatchewan they were met by Dr. Walter Charles Murray, the university president. Born in New Brunswick, Murray had been the Canadian Gilchrist Scholar at the University of Edinburgh and also briefly studied in Berlin. After holding professorships at the University of New Brunswick and Dalhousie University, Murray had been appointed the first president of the University of Saskatchewan in 1908, a post he held until retirement in 1937.[21]

On the tour of the university the Churchills were shown the gardens and the experimental aspects of the agricultural college, which Winston was reportedly much interested in. They also went through the main buildings on the campus. He noted that the schools, colleges, and universities across western Canada were so prominent as to be actually "out of proportion to other developments." This, he reasoned, was due to the attitude of "for what is the good of cultivating the soil if you do not cultivate the men who till it?"[22]

The Churchills next toured the forestry farm in Sutherland, near Saskatoon. Operated by the Forestry Branch of the Federal government's Department of the Interior, the farm grew trees suitable for the Canadian prairie. It had opened in 1913. The forestry farm, with its landscaped grounds, was popular for walking and picnicking. From the farm the party drove to Pike Lake and also took in the view of the Saskatchewan River. Winston was pleased with the scenery after not seeing much water for some time. He had likewise enjoyed the forestry farm.[23]

At some point during the visit to Manitoba and Saskatchewan, most likely on the visit to Saskatoon, Winston saw a combine at work. He sounded quite fascinated with this new machinery and gave attention to it both in a letter to Clementine and in one of his *Daily Telegraph* articles. A combine, he noted, was three times as big as a loaded hay-cart and was pulled by a petrol tractor. In one operation it cut and threshed the crop before sending it in a "stream of golden grain" into the back of a large grain truck. The grain was then transported to the towering grain elevators located along the railway lines for loading aboard the trains bound for the ports at the head of Lake Superior. These rail wagons, he observed, were of such a size that "would delight Lord Beaverbrook."[24]

Probably this same day, outside Saskatoon, Winston discussed the combine's effectiveness with a farmer he met and spoke with. The farmer told him that he and his son had harvested 70 acres the previous day. The new machinery was being put into use on such a scale over the previous year that the 20,000 men employed in the harvest were no longer required. Although interested in the new machinery, Winston wrote ruefully to Clementine in a rather Luddite tone that this was yet another lost opportunity to employ labor from home. Based on what he had seen and heard, he concluded that Canadian farming was like manufacturing, with a need for chauffeurs and mechanics rather than farm labor.[25]

With the brief tour complete, the party returned to the *Mount Royal*, which was on a sidetrack at the station, for lunch. Anderson and MacMillan came aboard the private car as guests for the meal. During the stop in Saskatoon, James Anderson and Winston discussed the political drama underway in the province.

Having met Anderson in Saskatoon, Winston had now spoken with all three of the leading players in the unfolding drama in the province's politics. He wrote Clementine to tell her he had learned about Saskatchewan politics, which were undergoing a "political and constitutional crisis of the first magnitude."[26] Gardiner had explained his problems to Winston in Regina, telling him that with only a minority of seats in the legislature, he expected to be defeated when the legislature met. In turn, Anderson revealed that he feared the Liberals would cling on to power long enough to find a way to win the support of some of the wavering Independents. After having an unbroken monopoly on the reins of government since the founding of the province, Winston thought the Liberals did not want anyone else to have a chance. After meeting and sizing up the current premier and opposition leader, Winston was more receptive to the Conservative leader. He left the province thinking Anderson was "in every way the bigger man than the present ruler." Winston's judgment may have been influenced by Gardiner being a teetotaler and a prohibitionist.

Anderson and MacMillan departed after lunch, leaving the Churchills to spend a quiet afternoon aboard their private car. Johnny, unlike the rest of the party, however, ventured out to go swimming in the municipal pool. It was a hot day in Saskatoon, with the temperature reading 89 degrees at two o'clock that afternoon. The high temperatures may have made the afternoon a little difficult. Winston had not found the heat thus far on the trip to be severe. However, he told Clementine that he only noticed the heat when the train was standing on a siding.[27]

That afternoon in Saskatoon Winston dutifully gave a half-hour of his time over to talking with the *Star Phoenix*. He declined to discuss reparations, as he did not want to do anything that would embarrass Snowden in his negotiations at The Hague. These negotiations had reached a crucial stage. Among the topics covered were the desirability of British immigration to western Canada and the strenuous nature of Winston's present trip. On the last point the reporter thought, however, Winston showed no signs of weariness.[28] On British trade with Canada, Winston said the British must wake up to the Canadian market.

Remarking on the changes he had seen in Canada since his last visit in 1901, Winston commented, "Then it was a common idea that Canada would split apart into two halves, could not hold together. Today your provinces are linked by railways and industry into one economic whole."

"Most certainly I see many evidences of a national spirit in Canada," he answered when asked if Canada had developed a personality. "Of course, Canada and the other Dominions are now nations of equal status with Great Britain, and stand in the same relation to the King. Your country has all the advantages of a national position, and of a partnership in the Empire as well—a most enviable situation."

Winston asked the reporter to tell him about the recent opening of the Hudson Bay rail route. He was no doubt interested in this route both for its economic potential as well as the fact that it culminated at Churchill, Manitoba, on the eastern coast of Hudson's Bay. This location had been so named in honor of the Duke of Marlborough in his capacity as a governor of the Hudson Bay Company. The newly built Canadian Pacific Railway line to Churchill was much in the news in August 1929, with articles in all of the Canadian newspapers that Winston was reading on his holiday. The first shipment of grain was to be sent by train to Churchill in late August for loading aboard the Hudson Bay Company steamer *Ungava*, which would sail for Liverpool. When told of the mileage from Saskatoon to Liverpool via Montreal compared with the distance via Churchill, Winston said it was very remarkable. Winston noted later that the port named in honor of his famous ancestor was now "awake and is again on the move."[29] Perhaps based on the information he learned from the *Star Phoenix* reporter, Winston told his *Daily Telegraph* readers in his article entitled "Across Canada to the Pacific" that in the months the bay was navigable it was possible for great ships sailing from Southampton or Liverpool to reach Churchill sooner than they reached New York. Churchill was an entirely new outlet for food and minerals to be sent to Europe from one of the world's great centers for both of those products. The Hudson Bay route for food, Winston thought, would be one of the most significant in the world.

Towards the end of the conversation with the *Star Phoenix* representative, Randolph came aboard the private car with a half-dozen assorted fly swatters that he purchased from some Saskatoon "emporium." Winston chose one of the stouter ones and had at the flies about him. He scored three hits out of a possible five.

When asked for his opinion on the Canadian Wheat Pool that may raise its price and increase the price on bread, Winston thought carefully before replying. He took a long pull on his cigar and said the British were mostly unaware of the Wheat Pool, but that he would not mind if the pool raised the price.

When the conversation turned to his book on the Duke of Marlborough, Winston replied with enthusiasm, "Yes, I have entered the dangerous field of historical writing, beset as it is with ferocious monsters which pounce on you if you make a mistake. This life will take me three or four years, and will be a full-length account. There is a whole library of books about Marlborough, but none which is at once modern and complete." The reporter left Winston aboard the private car "quietly enjoying his Canadian holiday" and "happily greeting every caller at his car."

Two more reporters, these from the *Edmonton Journal*, appeared at the *Mount Royal* shortly before the private car was to be hauled away and connected to the west-bound train. The pair had traveled down from Edmonton to interview Winston as he traveled on the train to their city. They approached Jack, who was on the platform, and asked him for an interview with his brother. Jack went and relayed their request to Winston and returned to tell them they could have their interview at seven o'clock that evening on the train.

At 4:35 that afternoon the Churchills departed Saskatoon by train for Edmonton. The political impasse in Saskatchewan was resolved two weeks after Winston left the province. Newlands called the legislature into session, and it met on September 4. As expected, the Liberals were defeated by the opposition coalition. Anderson became the new premier of Saskatchewan, a post he would hold for five years before being replaced by Gardiner at the next election.

All of the political maneuvering and fighting for power excited Winston's interests. He thought it was great fun. These provinces had "all the buoyancy of an expanding world and all the keenness of the political game played out with true Eighteenth century rigour."[30]

On August 22, probably that evening while traveling aboard the *Mount Royal*, Winston wrote a long-delayed letter to Clementine. He had been planning to write her five days earlier back at Lake Superior but had no time, as he had been traveling, speaking, and meeting so many people.[31] Winston was quite happy with the welcome he had been receiving thus far and wrote that people were pleased to see someone they had heard about. In the letter he described their adventures and then recalled, only towards the end of the letter, that he had nearly forgotten to tell her about their morning spent at Niagara Falls, which was now two thousand miles behind them. On his speeches he wrote that he was rather pleased, since he had addressed packed houses with everyone of consequence in attendance. Having started out on his trip intending to make four speeches in Canada, he had now consented to do ten. Six were done and four were left. They were a source of anxiety, but he thought they were making a contribution to the common cause of the empire.

At seven o'clock the two representatives of the *Edmonton Journal* presented themselves at the door to the *Mount Royal* but were put off for another two hours. "Oh, I'm so sorry gentlemen. I'm really not ready now. Could you come back after I have my dinner, say at about nine o'clock," Winston said.

Promptly at nine o'clock the persistent reporters tried again and were told by the steward of the private car that Winston was now through with dinner and would be ready for them shortly. After five more minutes the steward brought word that Winston was at last ready.

"Come right in, gentlemen," Winston said as he opened the door of the *Mount Royal* himself. "Please have a chair."[32] Winston was wearing a broadcloth shirt open at the neck and appeared comfortable, informal, and hospitable to the two reporters. After the hot day in Saskatoon, he seemed to be enjoying the cooling breezes that evening as the train traveled to Edmonton. Winston motioned the reporters to sit down while he took a cigar from a case and lighted it. It was big and black and looked "as though it would be a task in itself to smoke." He offered cigars to his guests. One took the proffered cigar and was still smoking it an hour-and-a-half after the interview. The other, however, declined the cigar and dared ask for a cigarette. The request sent Randolph rushing away to get one, and he returned with a box of cigarettes and then lit a match for the cigarette-smoking reporter.

The representatives of the *Journal* had a sheet of questions to ask for their interview, but Winston suggested it might be easier if he read the questions and gave his answers verbally. As they sat in the lounge of the *Mount Royal*, Winston was "at his ease" sitting on a chair with "big deep cushions." Puffing on his cigar as he proceeded through the questions, Winston's answers were short, but each "contained a wealth of knowledge and understanding." Along with the usual questions about unemployment in Britain and so forth, Winston said he favored British immigration to western Canada in order to "make a British country here." He did not support the abolition of appeals from the dominions to the privy council in London, calling it a "retrograde" step.

When asked about his impressions of western Canada, Winston said he was struck by the great expanse of deep, fertile soil, and went on to observe that the people were buying light cars for communication with trading centers, combines for harvesting, as well as telephones and radios for their use. He elaborated on this theme in one of his *Daily Telegraph* articles, writing that the major inventions of the first three decades of the century had made the economic development of vast regions of Canada possible, and life tolerable for the farmer and miner who lived there. The motor car, tractor, thrashing machine, telegraph, telephone, radio, and aeroplane had all been great advantages in building the region.

Randolph sat near his father during the interview, with a fly swatter dangling in his hands. He was quite interested in the interview and watched his father "with admiring eyes." Jack sat reading quietly in a corner while Winston was being interviewed. The reporters noted Randolph was wearing slippers, while Jack was also wearing slippers but over bare feet. Johnny, perhaps tired of Canadian journalists, was elsewhere on the train during the interview.

Reaching the last of the prepared questions, Winston stood up to indicate the interview was over. When asked about his buying a farm in Alberta, Winston replied that something was bought wherever he went in Canada, and by the time he reached England again there was no saying what he might own.

Questioned about what his Edmonton speech would contain, Winston laughed for a moment and replied as he smiled, "Well, I am very much afraid that I won't be able to have anything for an address. You've asked me about everything I know and I have nothing left to talk about."

The reporters then requested an autographed picture of Winston, to which he said with another chuckle, "No, I'm sorry that I haven't one with me. However, I think that I have had about 400 taken since I arrived in Canada." Winston walked the reporters to the door of the private car and opened the door for them as they exchanged good nights.

An avid reader of newspapers, Winston's normal routine at home in England was to begin the day by reading the newest editions. Newspapers were always piled high by his bed. In Canada Winston kept in touch with developments by reading the latest editions of the newspapers. At Saskatoon it was reported that he had a "full supply of all editions," and shortly after the train departed the station for Edmonton late that afternoon Winston called for copies of the *Edmonton Journal*. In typical fashion, on arriving in Edmonton the next morning he received copies of all the local daily newspapers.[33]

The night of August 22–23 would be the seventh successive night the Churchill party had spent in the *Mount Royal*. The following night, as they traveled from Edmonton to Calgary, would make it the eighth. The private car was meeting their needs, with Winston still thinking it was luxurious. His only mild grumble was that the baths were very short, too short for lying "on one's back with one's paws in the air." Even so, a good dip could still be obtained.[34]

… 9 …

# Edmonton, Calgary, and Prince of Wales Ranch, August 23–26

Two women, three children, a CPR constable, two or three railway employees, three camera men, two photographers, two reporters, and a cat were on hand to welcome Winston to Edmonton and the province of Alberta as he descended to the train platform on the morning of August 23. Of all the provinces the traveling party visited during the trip across Canada, they would spend the most time in Alberta. This province seems to have captured Winston's imagination in 1929, with its rising cities, oil industry, and beautiful scenery.

Winston emerged from the *Mount Royal* at half-past ten in the morning for his unofficial welcome to the city after a false start a few hours earlier. The train that conveyed the Churchills to Edmonton had arrived at the train station at 6:50 that morning. An official party was then on hand to greet the train, along with a contingent of private citizens and newspapermen. The official program for Winston's day in the city, which had been published in the August 22 edition of the *Edmonton Journal*, specified the train arriving at that time, with the party proceeding ten minutes later to Government House for breakfast. This program had apparently not been communicated to the Churchill Troupe, as they did not appear when the private car came alongside the platform at the Canadian Pacific station. With no sign of Winston, the committee on hand to welcome him eventually decided to depart and return later.

By half-past eight that morning Winston and the other members of the party were finally having breakfast aboard the *Mount Royal*, and an hour after that Mayor Ambrose U.G. Bury of Edmonton, Colonel A.C. Gillespie from Government House, and G.S. Dawson, the Edmonton manager of James Richardson & Sons, returned to the station. The Irish-born Bury was a lawyer who had previously served in the House of Commons as a Conservative member of Parliament. In 1929 he was nearing the end of his term as city mayor. The Edmontonians were now received by Winston and went aboard the private car. John Blue, the secretary of the Edmonton Chamber of Commerce, had been present for the first attempt to greet Winston but was not among those who were able to return to the station for the second try.[1]

Winston was smoking the "inevitable" cigar and wearing a grey suit with a felt hat as

## 9. Edmonton, Calgary, Prince of Wales Ranch, August 23–26

he stepped onto the train platform. He was accompanied by the other three members of his party, as well as Mayor Bury and the rest of the welcoming committee.[2] Winston told the newspapermen he was "adverse" to giving interviews. The article that ran in the *Edmonton Bulletin* without a byline overcame the visitor's unwillingness to be interviewed by recycling word for word the statements Winston gave to C.B. Pyper at Winnipeg, claiming they were made on his arrival in Edmonton. On the platform and on leaving the train station Winston allowed a photographer to take his picture and then accommodated a motion picture operator by walking with Jack, Randolph, and Johnny toward the cameraman. He gave the operator "every chance to take good picture." He also posed for another picture after he had climbed into Mayor Bury's motor car. Through all the photographs the long black cigar remained firmly in his mouth. Nor did he remove his felt hat.

Driving in Bury's motorcar, the party went to Government House, the official residence of the lieutenant-governor of Alberta, where they were welcomed by the current occupant of the office, Dr. William Egbert. Having been trained as a teacher and doctor in eastern Canada, Egbert had moved to Calgary to establish a medical practice in 1905. Twenty years later he had been appointed lieutenant-governor of the province.

The grounds of Government House were entered through iron gates off 102nd Avenue in Edmonton. Built on 28 acres of land on the bank of the North Saskatchewan River, the official residence was a three-storey building that had been constructed in 1911–1913. The

Winston Churchill outside of Government House in Edmonton, with (from left) Mayor Ambrose Bury of Edmonton, Jack, Johnny, Randolph, former lieutenant-governor of Alberta Robert Brett, lieutenant-governor of Alberta Dr. William Egbert, and unidentified (Provincial Archives of Alberta).

Englishmen were probably shown to the guest rooms on the second floor of the house and encouraged to enjoy the green park, gardens, and stables that comprised the grounds.[3] The party remained at the residence until time to depart for the luncheon.

In Edmonton, probably that morning, Lord and Lady Rodney came to see the Churchill party.[4] Lord Rodney was Winston's cousin once removed, as his grandmother was Cornelia Guest, who was also one of Winston's aunts. The 38-year-old George Bridges Harley Guest Rodney was the 8th Baron Rodney of Rodney Stoke, a peerage that had been created in 1782. The 1st Baron of Rodney had been the great British admiral Sir George Rodney, who had decisively defeated the French under the Count de Grasse at the Battle of the Saints on April 12, 1782. The 8th Baron had married Lady Marjorie Lowther in 1917 and emigrated from England to Canada after the war.[5] Lord and Lady Rodney lived on a farm outside of Edmonton, and arrangements were quickly made for the visitors to come for tea after Winston's speech was over.

Like elsewhere on the Canadian tour, the address in Edmonton was eagerly awaited by the local citizenry. On the day of the speech the *Journal* had written of Winston that few in the course of British political history have had such heavy and varied responsibilities as he had. Only Pitt the Younger had had these responsibilities at such an early age. To hear Winston speak, the newspaper assured its readers, was an "exceptional privilege," and the people of Edmonton and the Dominion were "delighted" at such an opportunity.[6]

On the day before the speech, the Mayor's office in the city had been busy with the previously reserved tickets to the civic luncheon being picked up in person and paid for. Upon learning of the large demand for tickets, the provincial government and the management of the Hotel Macdonald, where the speech was to take place, agreed on short notice to set up a loud speaker system to allow those without tickets to the luncheon to hear the speech. Vernor W. Smith, minister of railways and telephones in the provincial government, offered use of the government's loud speaker system free of charge, and the hotel likewise made available the terrace at the rear of the hotel to locate the loud speakers for no charge. Three hundred tickets for the terrace were printed by the city government and made available beginning at nine o'clock on Friday morning for those who wanted to hear the speech. These tickets were free and on a first come first served basis. Mayor Bury made clear no favoritism was being shown in distributing these tickets, and no reservations would be taken. The luncheon program was also to be broadcast to the city and surrounding area by the *Journal*'s radio station CJCA.[7]

Winston gave a "thrilling address" to the civic luncheon that began at 12:30 that afternoon, with the speeches commencing 45 minutes later. The luncheon was held in the main dining room of the Hotel Macdonald, which was located on McDougall Street overlooking the North Saskatchewan River. This Canadian National Railway hotel had opened in July 1915 and was built in the chateau style, with a "commanding view over the North Saskatchewan River."[8]

Approximately 1,000 people were at the hotel for the speech, with 550 in the main dining room and at least 300 more on the terrace. The main dining room was full a half-hour before the luncheon was to start, and by the time the program began there were no vacant chairs in the dining room or the corridors. After the lunch portion was over, many of the tables were removed to allow for more chairs to be set out so that more people could gain admittance to the main room. The *Edmonton Bulletin* devoted an entire article of their cov-

**Winston Churchill in Edmonton (Glenbow Museum NA-1234-5).**

erage of the speech to reporting that a large number of women were among those present to listen to the address, both in the dining room and on the terrace.⁹ The turnout by so many women was said to reflect their interest in "public questions."

The entire assembled audience rose in his honor when Winston entered the room with the other members of the head table. There were several familiar faces at the table for Winston, who was not only joined by Jack, Randolph, and Johnny, but also Lady Rodney and even J.H. Baker, his private secretary for the Canadian tour. Other people seated at the table that he had already met were Colonel Gillespie, Mayor Bury, Lieutenant-Governor Egbert, and most likely Egbert's wife Eva and daughter Ethel. Other notables invited to the dais were the first premier of the province, Alexander Cameron Rutherford, Senator William Griesbach, former federal Minister of the Interior Frank Oliver, Anglican Bishop of Edmonton Henry Allen Gray, former Lieutenant-Governor Dr. Robert G. Brett, Justice Thomas Tweedie, and Mrs. Bury, the wife of the Edmonton mayor. Also present was Richard G. Reid, who was the provincial treasurer and minister of municipal affairs, and at the moment acting premier in the absence from the capital of Premier John E. Brownlee. Although his wife was present and representing him at the head table, Brownlee himself was near Lac La Biche on a tour of the province. He planned on driving back to Edmonton in time to have dinner with Winston that evening.¹⁰

Mayor Bury presided over the civic luncheon and introduced Winston, proclaiming to applause that "one of the most brilliant men in Great Britain is Lord Birkenhead and the other is our honoured guest." The reception was "deafening" when Winston rose to speak.

"They have a way with them, these politicians," Winston said early in his remarks as he stood in front of the microphone. He was referring to the city mayor's efforts to get him to come and speak in Edmonton. The speech covered the customary topics of naval disarmament, the British need for peace, the prospects for peace, reparations, and Empire relations. The audience responded at the end of the address with "thunderous applause." The newspaper reaction was glowing, with the *Journal* proclaiming the speech a "triumph" and a great pleasure, and it being most stimulating to hear Winston speak. Their newspaper competitor, the *Bulletin*, editorialized that no audience could be disappointed in "so richly gifted a speaker."[11]

After the luncheon and speech were over, the Churchill party motored twenty miles northeast of Edmonton with Lord and Lady Rodney to their farm at Fort Saskatchewan for tea. Winston thought George was a "fine young fellow" and Marjorie was a "pretty little woman."[12] Lord Rodney had been educated at Eton and Oriel College, Oxford, and had served in the First World War. Beyond his peerage, Rodney also had the distinction of being one of the first members of the movement founded by Lord Robert Baden-Powell that became the worldwide scouting movement. Along with his three brothers, Lord Rodney was one of the twenty boys who were part of the experimental camp at Brownsea Island in 1907. Rodney had been a patrol leader. Unable to attend the 1928 reunion of the surviving Brownsea Scouts, George had sent a letter in which he called the experience a "landmark" of his life. Lord and Lady Rodney were both active in the Scouting movement, with Marjorie becoming the first provincial commissioner for Girl Guides in Alberta.[13]

The Rodneys had been in Alberta for almost ten years. George had worked as a laborer before they bought the farm, which then had only a small cabin on it. They lived in the shack for two years as they cleared and cultivated the ground. Having received money from George's grandmother, Cornelia Guest, they were able to build the wooden house they currently lived in with their four children, 11-year-old George, nine-year-old John, five-year-old Diana, and three-year-old Michael.

The farm stood on a bluff of the Saskatchewan River, which Winston characterized as a "broad, muddy pewter coloured flood which runs between scrub covered banks." The farm itself was "dusty and unlovely," with no attempt to beautify it or plant a few trees. It was a place of toil, and Winston appeared taken aback by the amount of labor George had to put into the farm. He wrote Clementine that "it seems incredible that anyone could do so much work." With one permanent man and one or two others taken on for the harvest, George had "ploughed, sowed, and reaped" 750 acres of the 1,000-acre farm. The other 250 acres were left fallow. The harvest was a "season of great hope," as all the labor and efforts of the year reached their culmination. That year the Rodneys hoped to have 20,000 bushels, with a profit of one dollar per bushel. Although George and Marjorie seemed tired to him, he also observed that they were immensely happy "living in this primitive way."[14]

Winston quoted an unnamed farmer's wife, who was most likely Marjorie, in his *Daily Telegraph* article.[15] The wife told her visitor that they could not afford to go south for the winter, as they still had to save for their children's education. A fire six years earlier had burned to death 22 of their horses, which even though they only use tractors, was still, nonetheless, a terrible setback. Before that they had suffered a cyclone, and before that had been the war. Perhaps some day in the future, the wife said, they will be able to go south for a winter holiday.

At the Rodney farm the Churchill party helped cut the grain. They used a piece of machinery which Winston only described as "one of these complicated machines," meaning a combine, which he had first seen in operation in Saskatchewan.

Winston met the four Rodney children and found them quite pleasant. The two oldest children were soon to make the journey to England to attend the recently established Stowe School. They would make the trip from Fort Saskatchewan to Buckinghamshire in England entirely alone, despite their young age.[16]

Probably with the Rodney farm in mind, Winston later wrote about the homesteads in western Canada in his article for the *Daily Telegraph* titled "Across Canada to the Pacific." These he described as simple and austere, with only a few occasionally being sheltered by trees. The farms were "workshops" for the production of food on a large scale, with the goal of creating wealth for the "lonely, thriving families." The dirt roads that crossed this countryside were made passable in the summer by the drought and in winter by the frost.[17]

On returning to Edmonton, the Churchills found that their dinner plans had been altered. The dinner originally planned for eight o'clock that evening at Government House had to be switched at the last moment to the Hotel Macdonald due to Lieutenant-Governor Egbert suffering what was called a "slight indisposition." A group of about 25 sat down to dinner with their honored guest. The guests were the "leaders of the professions, legal, medicine, the church, province, city and of the business men of the city."[18] Many of them Winston had already met at his speech, while George Rodney was there with a late invitation from the Alberta government.

With his plans including a visit to Banff and Lake Louise, Winston would have found a conversation with Dr. Richard Brett, who had been at the luncheon as well as at the dinner, quite useful. After working as a surgeon on the construction of the CPR in the area, Brett had become interested in the sulphur hot springs and settled in Banff in 1886. He eventually built a hospital and hotel to treat patients with the hot mineral waters that were receiving 2,200 guests a year before 1900.[19] Another guest Winston or Jack might have had an interesting conversation with was Senator Griesbach, who had served at Vimy Ridge and Passchendaele, and been promoted to brigadier-general in 1917 at the age of 39.

It is most likely, that Premier Brownlee was unable to return to Edmonton from his tour in time for the dinner and thus missed meeting the famous traveler. Brownlee's career would end a few years later in scandal amid charges that he had seduced an 18-year-old named Miss Vivian MacMillan.[20] Upon Brownlee's resignation as premier in 1934, Reid, who had met Winston in Edmonton, became premier.

After the dinner, the party engaged in informal conversation. Winston was not impressed. The speeches he judged boring, and he was not happy with the water he was provided with. The speeches did not improve as the evening progressed, but Winston was at least pleased that "some kind friend, however, put something better in my tumbler."[21]

In Edmonton that night, probably at the dinner, Winston learned about the forest fires raging in southern Alberta that might interfere with his plans for the next day. The fires were ravaging the Bow River Forest, which was 45 miles south of Calgary and 12 miles west of the oilfields at Turner Valley.[22] Winston was rather worried until he reached Calgary that the forest fires would upset his intention to visit the oilfields.

A new lighting scheme for the legislative buildings in Edmonton was turned on at dark on Friday evening in honor of Winston's visit to the city. The Alberta government's electrical department had installed a series of 34 flood lights on the corners of the four wings of the buildings, and eight floodlights with an amber shade hung in the dome of the tower. The lights ranged from 200 watts to 1,000 watts, with the dome lights controlled from the main rotunda and the other lights controlled from the basement. The new system, which was finished earlier that day, was intended for use on special occasions, such as Winston's visit and when the legislature was in session.

While there is no evidence that Winston had an actual tour of the legislative building in Edmonton, he probably at least was shown the new lighting scheme from outside the building. Of the legislative buildings he had seen in successive provinces, he wrote that they were each worthy of comparison with the Tate Gallery. Each was spacious and would be worthy of provinces that expected to have a population of five million inhabitants in the future. The Parliaments of western Canada were complete with "speakers, mace, serjeants-at-arms, House of Commons procedure, Constitutional crisis, party politics, caucuses, wire-pulling, Government and Opposition, ins and outs, Tories and Liberals, Farmers' party, religious questions, social questions, labour questions, Socialist sproutings, Communist fungi— in fact, the regular British outfit."[23]

The Churchills departed Edmonton aboard their private car attached to the Calgary-bound train shortly after midnight. A small group, described as Edmonton's leading citizens, accompanied them to the train platform to see them off. Before departing Edmonton, Winston told the *Bulletin* he was gratified at the reception he had received in Edmonton and hoped he would be able to return to western Canada again soon without another three decades having to pass.[24]

As the train proceeded south to Calgary and the foothills of the Rocky Mountains, Winston thought the landscape became more charming and beautiful. Calgary, which was then a growing city of 70,000, was a "busy hive," according to Winston.[25]

The original itinerary had planned for the Churchill party to spend the night of August 23–24 at Government House in Edmonton and depart the city at seven o'clock the next morning, with an arrival time in Calgary of mid–afternoon. This had been changed. At nine o'clock Friday morning, Winston's secretary called J.M. Miller, the city clerk for Calgary, to advise him of the changes. Now leaving Edmonton that night, the Churchills would arrive in Calgary on Saturday morning. The earlier arrival required a new program for the visit to be quickly arranged.

Despite the last-minute changes in the arrangements, Mayor Frederick Ernest Osborne of Calgary, members of the city council, and distinguished citizens were on hand on the morning of August 24 to welcome Winston to the city. The first visitors Winston received in the city aboard the *Mount Royal* were Professor Carlyle and A.J. Hacket. Carlyle was the manager of the E.P. Ranch that was owned by the Prince of Wales, while Hacket was a superintendent of the Canadian Pacific Railway. Carlyle told Winston that the Prince of Wales wished the visitors to stay at the ranch for the weekend.[26] Winston knew the Prince of Wales very well and later famously fought, without success, to preserve him as King during the abdication crisis. The visitor was quite pleased to accept the invitation to the ranch. He told Carlyle that after the hectic pace of travel and speeches over the previous two weeks, the beauty and quiet of the ranch would be delightful. This desire for some restful days was repeated to the newspapermen on the platform, with Winston remarking that after the four speeches he had planned to give in Canada had grown to ten, he was "looking forward to a quiet few days in the hills and valleys of southern Alberta." Winston continued that "one hears so much about the province, with its wheat fields, its oil resources and its mountain beauties. It does one good to get into the country and with such glorious skies overhead. I am sure I am going to enjoy every minute of my stay."[27]

"It is so fresh and beautiful out here," Winston remarked as he stepped off the *Mount Royal* at the CPR depot at 9:20 that morning. He was wearing a heather-colored suit with his "famous old grey hat" and, of course, smoking an enormous black cigar.

The cigar supply for the tour was of great concern to the *Calgary Daily Herald*. The newspaper reported that Winston had brought a whole trunkful of cheroots with him on the tour in the steadfast hope that a stockpile of several hundred would last until he reached home. Those who were supposed to be close in touch with the British statesman told the *Daily Herald* that the supply was dwindling, and he was being forced to give fewer and less imposing cigars to the friends he met. Winston's enjoyment of cigars was renowned. On one occasion when he was accused of smoking too much, he retorted, "If I had not smoked so much I might have been bad tempered at the wrong time."[28]

Mayor Osborne formally welcomed Winston to the city in a brief ceremony. An owner of a book and stationery store in the Old Herald Building on Centre Street, he had served two terms as a city alderman before being elected as the city's 24th mayor in 1927.

The mayor extended a welcome to the city, and the British statesman replied that he was pleased to be here and was looking forward to his tour of the oilfields and a quiet rest at the Prince of Wales' ranch. Winston was then introduced to the delegation of prominent Calgarians there to greet him, including Pat Burns; John H. McLeod, a production manager with the Royalite Oil Company; Manning Doherty, the former minister of agriculture in the Ontario government; L.W. Brockington, a Calgary lawyer; Inspector J.W. Spalding of the RCMP; John L. McFarland, president of a grain company; William Toole, a Calgary businessman; and several oilmen. Lieutenant-Colonel Dunbar, Brigadier-General D.M. Ormond, and A.C. Fraser from the Canadian Club were on hand, as was Major A.N. Martin of the Alberta Military Institute. The luncheon in Calgary would be jointly tendered by the Canadian Club, Board of Trade, Military Institute, and the City of Calgary.[29]

Also introduced to Winston by the mayor was a J. Stevens, who had been in the armored car with Winston in South Africa in 1900. Stevens had made it safely back to the British lines aboard the train, thanks to Winston's heroic efforts, while Winston was captured by the Boers.[30]

"I am very glad to meet you. You are the first man I have met who was on that train," Winston told Stevens.

After the introductions he walked across the platform and looked at the westward view towards the mountains.

"What a glorious day! I can just see the peaks of the Rockies from here. It must be wonderful to be in the hills today," Winston exclaimed. He then asked Osborne if the trip to the oilfields south of Calgary was to be taken as planned.

The Calgary mayor replied that they were ready to start for the oilfields at any minute. Winston was relieved and said, "They talked so much of forest fires last night that I did not know whether we would be able to go today."

Osborne explained that the shifting winds had shifted the fires, and the danger to Turner Valley and the ranchlands had passed. Winston replied, "I'm jolly glad to hear that."

As they prepared to leave the train station for the waiting automobiles, Winston was asked if he wished to travel in an open car or in an enclosed one. The visitor had a strong inclination on that question and answered, "I want to see every bit of the country. I've heard so much about this wonderful province of Alberta that I don't want to miss anything."

Warned that the open car in southern Alberta might be dusty, Winston took a "healthy puff" on his cigar and said he did not mind dust in the least. Burns volunteered to place an open car at Winston's disposal, who seemed "greatly pleased." With that decided, the party departed the train station and boarded the waiting motorcars. Some members of the welcoming committee joined the visit to the oilfields. Accompanying the Churchill party on the tour were Osborne, Burns, Brockington, McFarland, Toole, Doherty, and oilman William Stewart "Bill" Herron. John McLeod would lead the tour.[31]

Winston, Osborne, Burns, and McLeod rode together in one car, with the other members of the troupe and local citizens boarding the other motorcars. Reporters and photographers also joined the procession. Pat Burns was "one of Alberta's greatest ranchers and businessmen," having built a huge meat packing business in western Canada. He was one of the "Big Four," which referred to the four men who put up $25,000 each to finance the first Calgary Stampede in 1912.[32] In 1931 Burns would be appointed to the Senate of Canada.

Before the motor cars departed, a man stepped up to Winston's automobile and shook hands with the statesman. The man was originally from Manchester, England, and in his excitement he called Winston, "Mr. Baldwin."

"Very glad to meet you, but my name is not Baldwin," Winston said with a laugh.

The party drove south of Calgary to tour the oilfields and inspect the drilling and other operations in Turner Valley. These oilfields were the biggest oil-producing fields in the British Empire. The first, rather short-lived oil boom in the valley had started on May 14, 1914, when the well Dingman No. 1 hit at 2,718 feet. The second oil boom in the valley had started in 1924, with Royalite No. 4, located just north of the town of Turner Valley, making a strike. Within two years 34 companies were drilling in the valley's oilfields. Royalite No. 4 produced a sour gas that required processing to remove the hydrogen sulfide gas. As such, a scrubbing plant was built in 1925 in Turner Valley to generate the final "sweet" or clean gas. The plant was able to produce 60 million cubic feet of gas per day.[33]

Winston thought the oilfields were amazing. The valley was heavily dotted with 120-foot-high oil wells, each shaped like the Eiffel Tower, which bore down a mile through the limestone to force the oil under great pressure to the surface.[34]

Escorted by their hosts, the Churchills first went to Home No. 4 and Home No. 5, wells belonging to Home Oil, where Winston and the others watched the operations of drilling and bailing. They scrambled over the rigs and inspected the operation. The Churchills learned that the gas was so many degrees below zero when it reached the surface that all the pipes were covered with frost. At one of the Home Oil wells, Randolph and Herron were photographed writing their names on the frost-coated separators. Several other photographs were taken on the oilfields tour, including one of Winston, Randolph, and J.H. McLeod posing at a Home Oil well. Winston also examined the pipes which conveyed the oil from the Home Oil wells to the separators. The Imperial scrubbing plant in the oilfields was then visited before the party went on to inspect Royalite No. 4, which had hit at a depth of 3,740 feet. This well was one of the biggest producers in the valley, generating 21 million cubic feet of gas per day and 300 barrels of Naphtha that could be processed into gasoline. By 1926 the well was producing 217,000 barrels per year. Winston was most fascinated. The party then saw the operation of Royalite well No. 23. A photograph of the troupe with their local hosts shows them viewing the Smith Separators used in the processing of the gas.[35]

Throughout the inspection tour Winston closely questioned the officials escorting him around the oilfields, particularly Herron and McLeod, about how everything worked and was keenly interested in the potential of the Turner Valley oilfields. He found that the oilfields were developing rapidly. From Herron and McLeod, two pioneer oilmen of Turner Valley oil production, he also learned about the discovery of the fields and their early development.[36]

Most of the gas produced in the valley at the time, Winston learned, was being refined into petrol, with some sent through a pipeline to heat the city of Calgary. A 14-inch gas pipeline with a capacity of 75 million cubic feet per day had been built to Calgary in 1928 at a cost of $300,000. Even with this pipeline there was excess gas produced in the valley that exceeded the demand of the market in Calgary. No other pipelines had yet been built to pipe the gas to markets where it was needed. With excess production and no available market for the gas, the oil companies sold the oil and burned off the unneeded gas—or, as Winston put it, in the oilfields "far more demons have been loosed than can be harnessed." Burning or flaring the excess production proceeded at a rate of 200 million cubic feet per day in the winter months and 150 million cubic feet in the summer. Between 1924 and 1931, 260 billion cubic feet of natural gas were burned off. The loss of these millions of gallons of the valuable and finite product appalled Winston.[37]

The flares burning the excess production produced such heat that plants, such as wild strawberries, matured weeks early around the flare. The sky was so bright from the flaring that it was said Calgarians could read their newspapers at night. Many flares were concentrated in a small ravine that was known locally as "Hell's Half Acre," which had become a local tourist attraction. The visiting Englishmen observed the flaring, which Winston described as "pillars of flame" that were 80 or 90 feet high. These enormous fires gave the "landscape a truly satanic appearance."[38] In 1931 the Alberta government finally intervened to restrict the burning off of excess gas production.

The touring party drove to the Royalite Oil Company plant in Turner Valley for a luncheon. Roads in the valley had been quite poor, but by the late 1920s Royalite was improving the roads near the town of Turner Valley and its gas plant. Royalite was a major player in the Turner Valley oilfields and had been formed by the Imperial Oil Company. Luncheon at the Royalite plant was hosted by McLeod. The one-hour-long luncheon was informal, and the British visitors appeared to enjoy the affair. Winston was taken by the vision of the oilmen he met, later writing that they proposed bold schemes, such as saying, "Let us build a pipeline to heat Winnipeg; it is only 600 miles." The venture he was referring to was the proposal for Imperial Oil to build a pipeline from Turner Valley to Winnipeg at a cost of $50,000,000. Another such proposal was to build a gas pipeline to Moose Jaw, Saskatchewan. McLeod and Sam G. Coultis, the gas plant manager, would tour the Moose Jaw city council around Turner Valley a month after they met Winston as the proposal was being considered. By the time the Churchills had returned to England in two months, Winston noted that such ventures, both practical and impractical ones, had receded as possibilities.[39]

During the meal a reporter from the *High River Times* talked with Winston about old incidents from the Boer War when both men had been present at Winburg in the Orange Free State.[40] After the luncheon, Coultis showed the plant to the visitors and explained its operation. Coultis had been the man who drilled Royalite No. 4 that launched the second boom in the valley. Throughout the inspection of the plant, Winston "displayed a keen interest into the intricacies of the work carried on there."

That Winston was very interested in the operation of the oil wells and the plant is confirmed by Johnny's account of the visit to the oilfields. His uncle's questioning on how everything worked eventually became so detailed that his two hosts, probably Coultis and McLeod, were unable to answer. According to Johnny, they sent for a scientist from their laboratory to answer the questions being posed. The scientist soon looked astonished at Winston's knowledge and grasp of the subject. As the tour continued, the two gentlemen formerly leading the tour now followed behind Winston, it having been revealed that they did not know how their own plant worked.[41]

Winston was delighted with the visit to these oilfields that he had heard so much about. From what he had seen and learned he believed there were "unbound possibilities" both to the province of Alberta and the Empire in the oilfields. The *Calgary Daily Herald* reported these comments and editorialized that they hoped Winston would convey this information to British oil companies, who, they charged, had been apathetic in exploring Alberta oilfields. Although the newspaper's encouragement was not required, Winston was quite prepared to invest in the potential of the Turner Valley oilfields. In a letter to his wife written the next day he said he was considering buying a thousand-pound share in the oil companies if the answers to all of his enquiries were satisfactory. In doing so he would be ignoring the warning against over-optimism that was conveyed in a September 1929 *Saturday Night* article on the Alberta oilfields that such investments were still a "gamble."[42] Winston, however, in many aspects of his life was a gambler.

After the tour of the oilfields, the Churchills and their local hosts drove on roads covered with inches of deep black dust to the Prince of Wales Ranch. The Prince of Wales had arranged for the purchase of the ranch from Frank Bedingfeld during his 1919 tour of Canada that had been undertaken after the Armistice. It had cost $130,000. Named the E.P. Ranch, it was located on the Pekisko Creek in the forested foothills of Southern Alberta, with the majestic Rocky Mountains just to the west. The original cabin on the ranch had been renovated, expanded, and modernized into a comfortable dwelling. A kitchen, sitting room, and bedrooms had all been added. The Prince had already visited his ranch in 1923, 1924, and 1927. He saw the ranch as "a get-away" where he could walk, fish, shoot, and ride horses. With the Prince of Wales as its owner, the *Calgary Daily Herald* called the E.P. Ranch the "most famous property in Western Canada."[43]

The Prince of Wales had left the running of the ranch to his advisors. The manager of the ranch since 1919 had been Professor William Levi Carlyle. Before taking up his work on behalf of the Prince, the then 59-year-old Canadian had been an instructor at colleges in Canada and the United States, including three years as the Dean of Agriculture and director of the United States Experimental Station at the Oklahoma Agriculture and Mechanical College from 1914 to 1917. A leading figure in southern Alberta, Carlyle was also president of the Eden Valley Ranch at Pekisko, as well as vice-president of both the Alberta Horse Breeders' Association and the Alberta Cattle Breeders' Association. Beyond agricultural matters, he was also the president of Mohawk Bituminous Mines and a director of the Structure Oil & Gas Co. Under Carlyle, the 4,000-acre E.P. Ranch, which had 400 horses and 150 cattle when purchased in 1919, was a "centre of breeding excellence."[44]

Carlyle received the Churchills and invited the Calgarians who accompanied him to stay for supper. Over the meal a good chat was had about Calgary and southern Alberta. Winston and his new friends discussed the area's oil, agriculture, and connection to the Empire. The Calgarians told Winston that great development was going to take place there.

One of the men at the dinner was an old oilman who was a geologist and a pioneer in the oilfields. This man told Winston that he had studied the ground and was sure oil could be found, but he had been unable to raise the money for its development. He even offered Lord Cowdray, whose son was married to a Churchill cousin, a stake in the holdings for the price of $80,000. The offer was declined, and this oilfields pioneer had to scrape by for a year living on bread until he struck oil on his field. This field was now worth eighty million dollars. This pioneer told Winston that there were heaps of valleys in the foothills that had the same features that had first attracted his attention to his first oil finds.[45]

The oilman was Bill Herron, who was the "father of the petroleum industry in Alberta," as he had found and brought in the first well in Turner Valley when his Dingman well hit in 1914. He eventually had to sell his interests in the well and, with capital unavailable during the war, was forced to abandon the petroleum industry for a time and instead farm outside of Calgary. Herron was, however, experiencing his own personal boom in his fortunes again when he met Winston in 1929. The previous year his Okalta No. 1 had hit. This well was the "biggest discovery in Canadian history to that date."[46]

Herron entertained Winston with the legend of how he had cooked breakfast for potential investors over a gas seep at Sheep Creek almost twenty years before when he was trying to convince them to finance his operation. Winston was entertained by the story, and when Herron confessed it was just a legend and had never actually happened, the Englishman told him that such legends had their uses in politics as well.

The oilman, who was said to be lacking in social graces, complained to Winston that Turner Valley had not reached its potential because it had not received adequate capital from Canadian and British investors. Development was further hampered by provincial and federal government squabbles over natural resource jurisdiction, a lack of interest by the Canadian government in oil, and by the British and Canadian governments having betrayed Canadian independent oil companies to the American companies. Winston was said to have become greatly annoyed at Herron's frankness, but heard out his explanation of how the British concerns had lost interest in the Turner Valley oilfields and instead searched for oil in far off Persia and other places.

From his new companions Winston learned that it cost 40,000 pounds to sink a shaft in the hunt for oil. Those that were dry, of course, gave no return, but those that were a success gave a twenty-fold return. Winston wrote his wife that the towering oil wells were appearing all over the area, and with them came the possibility of newfound fortunes. Oil wells were even being drilled at opposite ends of the E.P. Ranch. Winston noted that should they "strike oil there is no reason why the Heir Apparent should not become a millionaire."[47]

The conversation became quite specific when McLeod told Winston that drilling by both Hargal Oil and Baltac Oil was practically certain to come into production in a few months. When these came into production, Winston believed shares in both companies could be expected to significantly increase in value.[48]

"I think I now understand how oil is produced and refined," Winston told Randolph and Johnny after dinner that evening.[49] He then gave a summary of all that he had learned that day and announced he would write a short article on the topic that night. Winston, according to his nephew, did indeed write the treatise. To Clementine he wrote that having learned the process in detail, he was now confident he could write a good, coherent piece about it.

Randolph was less impressed, most especially with the oilmen who had been their guests. After a day touring the "satanic" looking valley and meeting the wealthy oil magnates, Randolph said that it was depressing to see them "pigging up a beautiful valley to make their fortunes and then being quite incapable of spending their money."[50] He went on to denounce them to his father for their "lack of culture."

"Cultured people are merely the glittering scum which floats upon the deep river of production," Winston instantly retorted in a quote that Randolph thought was "damn good."

His father's riposte did not convince Randolph to think otherwise about Canada and culture, however. Although he liked Canada and Canadians, the youngest Churchill wrote in his diary, "There is little culture here, and the Canadians are crude and possess all the usual traits of a young nation." The people themselves, however, he did not consider "blatant or vulgar."[51]

That night the Churchills slept in the house on the ranch. Winston thought it was simple but still very nice. The next day, August 25, the weather was lovely, and they spent a "most peaceful Sunday in this wild place." In the morning the party went for a long ride on the ranch's ponies. They galloped up and down the foothills and obtained "wide views of the rolling fertile country." The ranch was set in a beautiful scene. Winston wrote that the "panorama of the Rocky Mountains rises along the Western horizon and endless serrated ridges reach to grey blue peaks forty miles away, five thousand feet above this place and nine above the sea."[52]

At the E.P. ranch that Sunday Winston began a letter to Clementine that was finished the next day. The letter was typed, so it is most likely that his private secretary for the Canadian tour left the private car in Calgary and came down to join them at the ranch. Winston vividly described his visits to Saskatchewan, Edmonton, and Calgary, as well as outlining his future travel plans. The California leg of the trip was falling into place, as the British Consul General for San Francisco would now meet them at Grants Pass. He was still intrigued by Churchill, Manitoba, and wrote that he was keen to arrange his return in such a manner that he could visit the port on Hudson's Bay. However, how this would be arranged he could not see at present. In fact, Winston would never visit Churchill, Manitoba, and twenty-five years later would in a radio broadcast from Ottawa in 1954 express his regret that one important place in Canada he had never visited was the port named after his illustrious ancestor.[53]

In his update to Clementine on Randolph, Winston wrote that their son was in "seventh Heaven and is looking extremely well."[54] He was sleeping ten hours each day, eating enormously, and at the E.P. ranch was riding as long and as often as he could.

The Churchill party spent a second night, Sunday night, at the Prince of Wales ranch and returned to Calgary on Monday morning, August 26, in time for the speech at noon. Arriving in the city with time to spare before they had to go to the venue, the party went aboard the *Mount Royal*. While on the private car, with two hours left before his speech, Winston finished his letter to Clementine.

The addition of Calgary to Winston's speeches had been made after he had arrived in Canada. On leaving England he had not planned to speak in the city. However, at the August

9 meeting of the executive of the Canadian Club of Calgary at the Empress Grill Room, the secretary, one J.W. Crawford, reported that he had had various interviews with Conservative party leader and friend of Lord Beaverbrook, Robert B. Bennett, in reference to Winston's upcoming visit to the city. The meeting minutes record that tentative arrangements were already being made for a speech. The executive appointed Crawford to represent the club's executive in meeting with other bodies to make arrangements for the entertainment of Winston in Calgary.[55]

The speech was to be made at a luncheon held in his honor at noon in the dining room at the Palliser Hotel. A 12-floor CPR hotel, the Palliser at that time in 1929 was Calgary's tallest building. Located at 133 9th Avenue, it was built in an "E" pattern and in Edwardian classical style.[56] The hotel was named after Captain John Palliser, who had led a British scientific expedition across the prairies in the late 1850s.

On the previous Thursday afternoon the 600 available tickets were placed on sale and had all sold within two hours. With people thronging the dining room and overflowing into the tea room and rotunda, about 750 people actually gathered to hear the address. Mayor Osborne said the capacity audience could have been many times larger had the facilities been available to accommodate greater numbers. A loud speaker system had been installed in the dining room so the guests could hear the speech with "ease," and arrangements had been made to broadcast it over CFAC, the *Daily Herald*'s radio station.[57]

The smoke from Winston's cigar was not out of place in the dining room of the Palliser Hotel that afternoon. In the 1920s Canadian Club meetings were clouded with smoke, including "pipe smoke, cigar smoke, cigarette smoke." Speakers commonly smoked before and after their speeches. The amount of smoke prompted a member of the Women's Canadian Club of Calgary to complain that she disliked listening to luncheon addresses "in a fog of rich Lataki."[58]

Mayor Osborne was presiding at the luncheon and began his remarks by again welcoming all four Churchills to the city. He thanked Winston for enlarging his schedule of speeches to include Calgary. Jack was included in the mayor's welcome, with Osborne saying in regard to his war service, "It is not for naught that the blood of the great Marlborough flows through the veins of the Churchill family." Lastly, Randolph and Johnny were given a welcome, with Osborne declaring, "And then we welcome two young men whose opportunities to add to the Churchill name and fame lies before them in the unknown future."[59]

For the formal introduction of Winston at the luncheon, Leonard Brockington was called upon for the honor. He was city solicitor for Calgary and had been in the party that toured the Englishmen around Turner Valley.[60] Considered by some to be Canada's greatest orator, Brockington proved his speaking ability by making his remarks in a "gracious and brilliant manner," for which he received warm applause.

There were several minutes of applause and cheering when Winston rose to speak. After it subsided he began his address. He covered the familiar topics. For Jack, Randolph, and Johnny it was now a speech they had heard several times. To the assembled audience and the Calgary newspaper writers, however, the speech was stirring and memorable. He received enthusiastic applause and laughter at his jibes throughout. The *Daily Herald* thought it a model of "lucidity and compactness." All those who heard the speech gained a "new conception of the remarkable qualities and virtues which have produced one of the most outstanding statesmen in the British Empire."[61]

Along with the now standard topics, he described Alberta's oil and mineral wealth. The immense development taking place in Turner Valley had been a surprise for him. Calgary, Winston said, had "proved a wonder and delight to me." He congratulated the city on its brilliant progress and said that this success was a sure sign of a great future for Calgary. With satisfaction he had witnessed good crops being grown, heard that farmers were getting good prices for their grain, and seen the great strides in oil production.[62]

After Winston had finished speaking, Osborne called on Arthur Meighen, who had been Canadian prime minister in 1920–21 and very briefly in 1926, for the task of thanking the speaker. Meighen would preside at Winston's speech in Toronto three years later on the 1932 lecture tour. In Calgary the former prime minister of Canada paid a "glowing tribute" to Winston. He thanked him not just on behalf of the Calgary audience but on behalf of the people of the Dominion for the speeches he had given all across the country. In the remarks that he otherwise considered congratulatory, Winston thought Meighen had clumsily quoted his old diatribe against the Conservative Party as a party of "cheap labour for the millionaire."[63]

Rather than hear further from Winston, Randolph replied to Meighen on behalf of his father, for which he received great applause. As part of his reply he said the "generation which is growing up in the Empire, today knows little of the horrors and suffering of the war, but it is learning of the sacrifices that were made." Randolph's short address was also praised in the local newspaper. It noted that despite being 18 years old, he spoke with assurance and demonstrated that he is "developing a strong bent for public life." Winston too thought his son's "rejoinder was excellent."[64]

Calgary's branch of the Canadian Club was well pleased with the entire luncheon. In the secretary's annual report, J.W. Crawford as secretary wrote that seven luncheon meetings had been held during the year. Of those, the "outstanding event" was the luncheon tendered to Winston.[65]

With the speech in Calgary, Winston completed his seventh major speech of the tour. For the next five days the Englishmen would relax in the Rocky Mountains. What he had seen in western Canada gave Winston great confidence in the future of three provinces. Manitoba, Saskatchewan, and Alberta were only at the beginning of their development, as each had only a small population. While mistakes would be made, disappointments suffered, and progress would be inconsistent (with occasional setbacks), Winston knew the ultimate outcome was certain. These three provinces possessed vast mineral and oil deposits, and great potential for the production of grain.[66]

Before leaving Calgary Winston acquired what became a treasured memento. A gift of a fine Stetson was given to him on behalf of the citizens of the city. Famous for his hats, he cherished this new addition. He would wear it on the remainder of the tour of North America and would keep it for the rest of his life. In his old age Winston would often like to wear it.

... 10 ...

# The Rocky Mountains, August 26–September 1

"Twenty Switzerlands rolled into one," was how Winston described the Rocky Mountains in a letter to Clementine.[1] Delighted with the mountains, he wrote in one of his articles on Canada that the "guide books and advertisements written in interested superlatives are surpassed by reality."[2]

To more thoroughly enjoy the beautiful scenery, the Churchills traveled by an open motorcar during the mountain portion of their tour. As John Burns, the brother of Pat Burns, loaned them his chauffeur and car for their visit to Banff, the *Mount Royal* was temporarily not required. The party left Calgary in the late afternoon or early evening on August 26 and drove the 80 miles to Banff, which they reached that night. This drive brought them gradually into the hills and mountains until they were finally completely enclosed.

After the whirl of travel and speeches across the country, Winston ordered a temporary halt at their hotel in Banff. For the next two nights the Churchills stayed at the majestic and gigantic Banff Springs Hotel, which first opened in 1888. This CPR hotel was the jewel in the company's chain of hotels. It has been called a "castle in the wilderness" and one of Canada's "architectural treasures," with its baronial-style great halls, colonnades, steep hipped roofs, peaked dormers, turrets, balconies, and bay windows.[3] Set against a backdrop of forests and mountains, the hotel sits above the Bow and Spray rivers and offers magnificent views. Winston thought the gigantic hotel was indeed "placed amidst very striking scenery."[4] It had every comfort, including an outdoor pool that was always kept at 90 degrees. A fire destroyed the north wing of the hotel in 1926, but the wing was rebuilt within two years, while at the same time the south wing was expanded. The spectacular hotel, with its attractions of golf, tennis, climbing, hot springs, walking and horse riding trails, attracted as guests royalty, politicians, aristocrats, wealthy Canadians and Americans, and Hollywood stars. The Churchills were not the first members of their family to stay at the Banff Springs Hotel, as Lord and Lady Randolph had stayed there during their world tour in 1894.

Winston, who pronounced himself exhausted after driving two 80-mile stretches that day, with a major speech sandwiched in between, went to bed at ten o'clock on August 26.

He did not wake until 7:30 the next morning. After all the traveling, the day would be one of leisure.

Early that morning Winston wrote another letter to Clementine, this despite having finished his previous letter to her only the day before. He missed his wife and told her that he wished all the time for her to be with him on the trip, as well as desiring the latest news from Chartwell.[5] Clementine would have enjoyed some of the days of the trip, Winston wrote, while others would have exhausted her. They had been traveling constantly for eight nights, "starting, stopping, packing, unpacking, scarcely ever two nights in any one bed except the train." The party had endured the "racket of trains, racket of motor, racket of people, racket of speeches!"[6]

"Never in my whole life have I been welcomed with so much genuine interest and admiration," Winston wrote as he described his wonderful reception in Canada from people of every political party and class. The "workmen in the streets, the girls who work the lifts, the ex-service men, the farmers, up to the highest functionaries have shown such unaffected pleasure to see me and shake hands that I am profoundly touched."[7]

The reception was such that Winston said he intended to interpret the British and Canadian peoples to each other and bring about an even closer association between Great Britain and Canada.

Winston found Canada quite appealing and wrote that with its immense development fortunes were to be made here. With only the one goal of the premiership still remaining for him, Winston predicted to Clementine that if Neville Chamberlain or someone else of his ilk were made Conservative party leader he would clear out of politics. If becoming prime minister were barred to him, Winston would "quit the dreary field for pastures new." He would try to make her and the children more comfortable. Winston did add in the letter that it was not yet time to make such a momentous decision.[8]

Since leaving Quebec City, the Churchill party had not had to pay any expenses as they traveled across Canada. Looking ahead for the rest of the tour, Winston foresaw only the cost of his current hotel and possibly a hotel in Vancouver as the only expenses for the next several weeks. It was amazing to be treated in this way. He had, however, given eight speeches already, with more to come, which could be considered as a "substantial offset" against the costs. So much so that Winston thought he could indeed "claim to have worked my passage."[9]

Winston closed the letter with an update full of praise for their son. Writing that he loved Randolph very much, Winston noted that he was becoming a very strong man and expected he would be tall and well-built. Randolph was said to speak very well, being "so dexterous, cool and finished." Their son slept ten or twelve hours a day, but Winston supposed the "deep oblivion" was required because he was growing at the same time.[10]

That morning the party enjoyed a swim in the pool and later went for a ride on a pack horse trail that wound along the Spray River. An automobile tour of points of interest in the district was also included in the day's activities.

While at the Banff Springs Hotel, Winston had his photograph taken by Harry Pollard, who worked for the hotel as well as Associated Screen News. The handling of these photographs created an almost heated exchange between Winston and the photographer. Baker, the private secretary, wrote to Pollard about the photographs. A response was sent by the photographer at Banff on September 11 on hotel stationery. The reply indicated the negatives had been destroyed as requested, with the others, being satisfactory, being issued as publicity. The photographs of Winston smoking a cigar became an issue. Nine days later Winston wrote to Pollard from Santa Barbara, California, saying he was surprised to see these photographs appearing in several newspapers. This despite Pollard having assured him the negatives had been destroyed. Winston went on to accept partial fault in the matter, as he had not written to Pollard as promised and thus said he could make no complaint.[11]

From the terrace of the hotel, Winston had his first try at painting on the tour. That afternoon he painted the famous view of the Bow Valley, with the Bow River and Fairholme range, as seen from one of the hotel's balconies.

Winston first started to paint in 1915. It was after he had been removed as first lord of the Admiralty over Gallipoli and was at his lowest ebb. Painting, however, came to his rescue.[12] That summer, while at a country retreat he was renting for weekends, Winston watched his sister-in-law Goonie painting. He eventually borrowed her painting equipment and tried for himself. Winston found that he loved painting. He later wrote in his work "Painting as a Pastime" that taking up painting when he was already past forty years old was an "astonishing and enriching experience." It became one of his great relaxations. His paintings were a "product of a man off duty, if not relaxed."[13] Late in life Winston commented that "if it weren't for painting, I couldn't live; I couldn't bear the strain of things." Winston was a "prodigious" painter. He painted whenever he had the opportunity. From 1915 to 1960 he produced more than 500 paintings, even though he only painted one picture, a view of the Atlas Mountains, during the Second World War. Contrary to his reputation that he did not like parting with his paintings, Winston gave away 100 of his works in his lifetime.[14]

Winston worked in oils and painted on canvas. Each of his paintings was said by the art critic Thomas Bodkin to have a dominant theme, whether a lake or a village, which was never obscured. While primarily interested in landscapes, Winston painted a wide range of subjects. He was said to have been bold in his choice of colors, and he painted without hesitation or inhibition. The paintings he created reflect an "obvious love of paint and brush."[15]

On some occasions Winston only painted after making a careful preparatory study of the scene to be painted, while other times he painted with only minimal appraisal of the scene and without a preliminary outline sketch or drawing. Given the limited time he

Winston Churchill, photographed with a cigar by Harry Pollard at Banff (Provincial Archives of Alberta).

had to paint at Banff, Winston probably worked quickly and plunged in without a lengthy preliminary study of the scene. In "Painting as a Pastime" Winston writes that when painting in the open air, as he would paint in Banff, the "sequences of actions is so rapid that the process of translating into and out of pigment may seem to be unconscious."[16]

In his essay on painting Winston linked painting and travel. By means of painting, the "vain racket of the tourist gives place to the calm enjoyment of the philosopher." The painter, he wrote, is "always on the look for some brilliant butterfly of a picture which can be caught and set up and carried safely home."[17] He would find three such "brilliant butterflies" in the Rocky Mountains.

The picture Winston painted on the terrace of the Banff Springs Hotel resides at Chartwell. It was painted on canvas board and is 14 inches by 20 inches. This painting had been wrongly entitled "In the Dolomites" for several years until a guide who volunteered at Chartwell visited Canada and recognized the scene being depicted in the painting. With this discovery, the painting was correctly retitled "The Bow River, Near Banff, Canada."[18]

The painting theme continued while at the hotel when Winston came upon Richard Jack, an Academician at the Royal Academy. Jack, who was also on holiday in Canada, was a well-known portrait painter who had painted the portraits of the King and Queen. With their common interest, Winston and Richard Jack spent some time together talking about painting.

From the Banff Springs Hotel Winston wrote to Schwab accepting his invitation to be the guest of honor at the American Iron and Steel Institute dinner in New York in late October, which would involve him having to make a speech. Having accepted the provision of a private car across the western United States, he was rather obligated to accept the invitation. He did, however, make his participation in the event contingent on his not having to cut his trip short and return to England to speak in a Parliamentary debate on Egypt. Winston was always following the latest political and international developments during his tour and was prepared, if he thought it necessary, to cancel the remaining part of the trip and return to England if events warranted.

After a very relaxing day on August 27, the Churchills began a 3-day, 300-mile motor tour in the mountains the following day.[19] Roads in the national park were all relatively new. The Banff–Lake Louise road had only opened in 1921, while the road the Englishmen would take on their first day of the motor tour, the Banff-Windermere road, had opened in 1924. The Banff-Windermere road ran through Kootenay National Park and provided access to Radium Hot Springs, the party's ultimate destination for the first day's drive. After being open five years, the Banff-Windermere road was modestly dotted with motor camps, bungalow camps, and one gas station at Vermilion Crossing, the spot where the road crossed the Vermilion River. The 90-mile highway was promoted to travelers as having majestic mountain scenery and being noteworthy for the "abundance and fearlessness of the wild life."[20]

In the open motor car Winston sat in the front with the chauffeur supplied by Burns, while Jack, Randolph, and Johnny sat behind. One of the anecdotes that Johnny recorded in his memoirs probably occurred at the start of this tour shortly after they had driven out of Banff. The day was "warm, the sky clear, and the scenery incredibly magnificent." After the motor car had only traveled a couple of miles, however, Winston yelled and let loose with a "rich stream of abuse."

"Stop the car! A 'wasp' is up my sleeve!" Winston shouted.

A wasp had managed to get into his jacket as his arm had been resting on the car door as they drove along. Only after the sleeve of the shirt was rolled up and the sting examined did Winston quiet down. To aid in his recovery and take his mind off the pain, the party took a stroll in the pine trees. Johnny thought the smell of the trees was wonderful but ruined by the ever-present smell of Winston's and Jack's cigars.[21]

The relatively new Banff-Windermere Highway was still primitive; at various places it was "little more than a narrow gravel track, with scarcely enough room to pass." It was "literally an avenue of trees," so much so that due to the tall trees it lacked a view for most of its length.[22] Winston enjoyed the trees. He once said that no one should cut down a tree without planting another, as "it is very much easier to cut down trees than to grow them." Winston also noted the autocamps that had been built alongside the highway to provide food, lodging, and gas to travelers.

On the highway the Churchills came around a turn in the road and came upon the first bears they saw on their trip. The bears were rather close, and the chauffeur stopped the open motor car alongside them. There were three bears—a mother and two large cubs. The female bear reared up on her hind legs, which was at first taken as an aggressive stance. The party soon determined she was not hostile but was rather begging for biscuits, as it was "accustomed to waylay travelers passing along this road." As they did not have any biscuits to give, the bear climbed onto the wooden rail on the side of the road and walked along it as on a tightrope, while her two cubs performed somersaults on the opposite bank, this entertainment being offered in return for food. Another car arrived which had biscuits, so the bears were then gently fed by hand and photographed.[23]

The encounter with the bears was important news. In his next letter to Clementine, Winston opened by announcing, "I have some news which will interest Mary." He then provided a long, detailed account of Banff's performing, but still entirely wild bears, which must have been thrilling to little Mary back in England.[24]

After driving down the Banff-Windermere Highway, the English tourists reached Radium Hot Springs. The springs, which had been used by Canada's First Nations before the arrival of the Europeans, had been expropriated from private ownership by the federal government in 1922 for addition to Kootenay National Park, which had been established on April 21, 1920. In 1911 the British medical journal *Lancet* had published a study of the spring waters that suggested it contained traces of radium. The park leased out lots around the springs on which several hotels and lodges for the visitors had been built. In 1927 a new bath house was built at the hot springs, and the following year the pool itself was enlarged.

The options available to the Churchills for accommodations that night at the hot springs were limited to the Radium Hot Springs Hotel, the bungalows operated by the Sinclair Hot Springs camp, or the government's motor campsite.[25] Most likely Winston preferred the comfort offered by the small hotel over the campsite or, as advertised to tourists, the "rustic bungalows."

Both that night and again the next morning the party bathed in the open-air swimming baths. Winston wrote that the radium-charged water bubbled out of the rocks at an unimaginably hot temperature. Each day 750,000 gallons of water poured out of the rocks and was caught in the large swimming bath. He felt it was about as hot as a really hot bath. While in the hot springs Winston "felt almost too languid to swim but afterwards it is refreshing."[26]

Randolph and Johnny quite enjoyed the springs and spent a great deal of time in the sulphur swimming bath. The pair swam, luxuriated, and dove in the hot springs and the regular swimming pool.

"How about a double acrobatic dive from the top board," Johnny suggested to Randolph at one point during their swimming in the pools. In what Johnny thought was a demonstration of his cousin's courage, Randolph agreed. He was utterly astonished. An acrobatic dive from thirty feet when you do not know how to do it was, in Johnny's opinion, more frightening than a parachute jump. In such diving, it is necessary for the diver to leave the board and control his balance in the air throughout the dive.

As his cousin was a beginner, Johnny chose a simple dive in which he lay on his back with his head at the edge of the board. He then raised his legs at right angles, with Randolph then placing his stomach on the soles of Johnny's feet. Looking down at the pool from Randolph's position, the long drop to the water must have seemed a terribly great distance, and he indeed asked for "a bit of encouragement" from his cousin.

"If you don't panic you will make it. Just keep your body straight and I will see that you enter the water all right," Johnny reassured him.

Johnny then did a backward roll over the end of the board that sent Randolph diving down to the water in a head first dive. Having turned in the air, Johnny followed after him feet first. They entered the water and completed the dive without injury and to great applause from their fathers, who had been watching intently.[27]

On the morning of August 29 Winston had a long-distance telephone conversation with James Richardson. This "little chat" was about business. Winston, as he earlier wrote Clementine, had decided to make some investments while in Canada and the United States. Having already sold another 1,200 copies of the *Aftermath* (worth 250 pounds) on the tour thus far, and with returns from other investments in England, Winston had some funds to invest. In the letter home Winston assured his wife that she did not have to worry about their finances. It was indeed good to save as much money as possible, but he was confident there were enough funds to cover all their needs.[28]

During the visit to Winnipeg ten days earlier, Richardson had volunteered his firm for any business the distinguished visitor may wish to transact while on his tour. Winston had decided to take advantage of this offer. Although he planned that the business he would do would be on a small scale, he thought it would be convenient to buy and sell using the Richardson firm while in North America. Already on August 27 Winston had directed that 2,000 pounds of his funds be sent to Richardson in Winnipeg as a credit in his account for the trading of shares. With the information he received from McLeod while in southern Alberta about the excellent prospects of Hargal Oil and Baltac Oil, he decided to invest in those companies. These investments were not being made on the properties themselves, as he had no means to judge their worth, but rather, as he said, on the "personality" of the businessmen who told him about the opportunity.[29] In accordance with long-distance telephone instructions from Winston, Richardson and Sons bought shares in Baltac Oil and in Hargal Oil on his behalf. One thousand shares of Baltac Oil were purchased at a price of $2.10 per share, and 2000 shares of Hargal Oil were likewise bought at $2.05 per share. During the long-distance call with Richardson, Winston requested shares in American Rolling Mills also be bought on his behalf. This investment was duly made.[30]

Beyond transacting financial affairs that morning, the Churchills also enjoyed another swim in Radium Hot Springs. After the swim they continued their driving tour. The destination for the day was Emerald Lake. The Englishmen may have retraced their steps back along the Banff-Windermere road and then driven west to Emerald Lake, or they might have taken a different route by driving along the provincial road, called the Columbia Valley Road, to Golden, British Columbia. From Golden the party could have driven east to Emerald Lake. Regardless of the road they took, the party enjoyed a fine drive. In the open air motorcar, as Winston wrote, they drove "along the sides of precipitous hills, foaming torrents, and magnificent gorges."[31] Leaving the highway and taking the Emerald Lake road, the party passed the popular tourist spot of the Natural Bridge. This was a barrier of rock that dams the Kicking Horse River.

At three o'clock that afternoon the Churchills reached Emerald Lake, located in Yoho National Park, a quite idyllic and beautiful location. Randolph described the small lake as being an "exquisite shade of turquoise," while his father said it had an "extraordinary colour more turquoise or Jade than Emerald. Its water is Opaque like Jade."[32] At Emerald Lake the party was surrounded on every side by wonderful mountains, as the lake lies under Mount Wapta, Mount Burgess, and Mount President.

The Canadian Pacific Railway had built and operated a chalet and an encampment of log bungalows at the lake. The party stayed the night at the bungalow encampment on one side of the lake. The bungalows were not entirely primitive, as they had hot water, electric light, and, as Winston reported, "every comfort."[33]

Emerald Lake was so beautiful and the colors so exquisite that Winston was inspired to unpack his painting supplies after they arrived and have his second bout of painting on the Canadian tour. He painted three pictures of the lake. Although Randolph thought they were quite good, the painter himself thought they failed to entirely convey the remarkable beauty of the scene.[34]

The quality of Winston's painting has been argued by critics. In this debate Winston as a painter may be a "victim of his own fame as a statesman."[35] Some critics are eager to call him no more than an amateur, while others see his paintings as the work of a devoted artist with real ability. In the 1920s one of his paintings was submitted to an exhibition of amateur works. All of the paintings in the show were submitted anonymously. One of the judges, Sir Oswald Birley, thought the work he submitted was "painted with great vigour," while another judge, Lord Duveen, said it must have been painted by a professional and therefore excluded from the exhibition.[36] In 1947 Winston's paintings were submitted under the name David Winter to the Royal Academy. Both of his paintings, *Winter Sunshine at Chartwell* and *The Loup River*, were accepted for the annual summer exhibition. Sir John Rothenstein, the retired director of the Tate Gallery, acknowledged in 1968 that because of Winston's achievements in other spheres, some have sought to call him a great painter while others have labeled him a dabbler. Rothenstein concluded that the "astonishing fact about Churchill the painter is that in spite of obstacles that would have prevented other men from painting at all, he painted a number of pictures of rare beauty."[37]

Winston, for his part, desired to be a great painter. While traveling in Aix-en-Provence on one occasion with his family and staff after the Second World War, he spent the afternoon painting. At dinner that night he told all assembled, "I have had a wonderful life, full of many achievements. Every ambition I've ever had has been fulfilled—save one."

"Oh, dear me, what is that?" Clementine asked.

"I am not a *great* painter," Winston replied as he looked slowly around at everyone at the table.

There was an embarrassed silence for several seconds until conversation moved on to other things.[38]

While his father painted, Randolph took a little boat out on the lake and sunbathed. Later the four members of the party rode horses. They might have taken a short ride, or taken the trail around the lake and over the Yoho Pass. It was either on this horse ride at Emerald Lake or the one the next day at Lake Louise that Jack, when riding ahead of the others, came upon a six-foot-high bear on the trail. This bear was much larger than the ones they had seen on the Banff-Windermere Highway. It was also much less accustomed to people. It reared up on its hind legs before turning and galloping off at "great speed," much to Jack's relief.[39]

On August 30 the Churchills motored through the Yoho Valley, with Lake Louise as their ultimate goal for the day. The scenery they encountered was magnificent.[40] Leaving Emerald Lake, they would have taken the highway east and passed by the town of Field. The party stopped to admire the great Takakkaw waterfalls. The beautiful falls were appreciated by Winston, who thought they leaped "like a mighty horsetail out of a narrow cleft in the mountain side large as a river, and *1,200 feet high*—a wonderful sight!" Winston actually slightly underestimated the size of the falls, as they were actually 1,500 feet high. From the falls the party returned to the highway and drove east through Kicking Horse Pass, the eastern entrance to Yoho National Park. This narrow pass was the original route taken through the mountains during the construction of the Canadian Pacific Railway. Having reentered Banff National Park, this time from the west, the party motored on, enjoying the scenery until they reached Lake Louise in the evening.

Winston was amazed by Lake Louise, which he thought was a "truly enchanting scene." It was a lake of "wide expanse surrounded by enormous precipices and with a wonderful line of snowclad peaks and glaciers in the centre." Of all the places Winston had visited before across four continents, the comforts and beauty of Lake Louise had "never been surpassed."[41]

Lake Louise, which is at an altitude of 5,000 feet, had been discovered by a CPR surveyor, Tom Wilson, and two Stoney Indian packers on August 21, 1882. The executives of the Canadian Pacific Railway knew that the stunning views of Lake Louise set against the surrounding mountains were worth a fortune. The railway first opened a hotel at Lake Louise in 1890, only to see it destroyed by fire three years later. They rebuilt and were soon advertising the Chateau Lake Louise as the "largest and most modern equipped chateau in the world."[42] The nine-storey and 400 room hotel was maintained by a staff of 425 and consisted of two wings, one a concrete Italianate villa wing with stucco walls, and the other designed more like a chateau. It had opulent interiors, a rotunda, lake view lounge, ballroom, tavern, billiard room, beauty parlor, barber shop, and swimming pool, as well as formal gardens and lawns and a putting green. This luxurious retreat, in 1929, was open only for the summer, with the season running from June 1 to September 30.[43]

With the Banff Springs Hotel and the Chateau Lake Louise in mind, Winston wrote in his newspaper articles about the large hotels in the parks that were "equipped with every sport or luxury that health can conceive or wealth command."[44] While Winston enjoyed luxury in all things, his traveling companion aboard the *Empress of Australia*, Leo Amery, was rather undecided. Amery had also been to the lake and was ready to acknowledge that the Chateau Lake Louise was a great hotel and the last word in comfort. As an outdoorsman and mountain climber, he could not, however, "help regretting the little log chalet."[45]

The natural beauty of Lake Louise had also attracted the attention of Hollywood studios. In 1928 the movie *Eternal Love*, starring Winston's friend John Barrymore, was filmed at the lake.

At the Chateau Lake Louise on the night of August 30, Winston attempted to get caught up on his correspondence. He wrote to Maurice Ashley about the Marlborough project. While he had not found the time to dictate a synopsis of Marlborough, he had been able to do some reading and at odd times a great deal of thinking about the enterprise. He also wrote to Thornton Butterworth regarding the payment of royalties that had accrued up to June 30. He was eager to receive these funds, as he saw many excellent investment opportunities in Canada which might not be available by the time he returned to England.[46]

Another letter he sent from Lake Louise was to James Richardson seeking his opinion on the value and prospects of the Calgary oilfields. He also told the Winnipeg stockbroker that 2,000 shares in Structure Oil & Gas Co. would be received in his account against a payment of $2,000. Professor Carlyle, who was a director in Structure Oil, had introduced him to this company. In Calgary, Carlyle and Fred A. Schultz, a financial broker and investment banker in the city's Lancaster Building, had presented Winston with a proposal that he invest in the company. This pitch also included adding Jack to the company's directors. Schultz praised Winston for buying shares in Structure Oil, writing to him on September 3, "Now, Mr. Churchill, to be quite frank with you, I liked your manner of fast action in accepting our proposition, showing that we Britishers can make up our minds in a hurry as well as the Yankees can."[47]

While Winston worked on his letters and financial matters, Johnny was enjoying, or at least trying to enjoy, the scenery. He remembered the beauty of the lake that evening, the "scent of the trees," and the "surrounding silence, so heavy that one could almost hear it."[48] The silence was only marred by Randolph, who was reciting from memory the lengthy definition of prostitution from Lecky's *History of European Morals*.

The first order of business for Winston on the morning of August 31 was to paint. The beauty of Lake Louise could not be missed. He recruited Johnny to assist him in the effort. That morning Winston loaded his painting gear into a boat and had his nephew row him around the lake so he could find a place where he could paint the lake and the mountains behind them. Upon finding a suitable spot, Winston ordered Johnny to leave him so that he could be alone to work, even though bears were said to prowl the surrounding forests. Johnny claimed he became "boatman-in-chief" on the lake as he rowed his uncle to several isolated spots around Lake Louise for him to paint different scenes. He was always relieved to arrive back at the appointed time and find that Winston had not been attacked by a bear. Rather than being mauled, his uncle would instead be sitting on a little stool wearing his Stetson and working hard on his painting. To protect his sensitive skin, most especially the top of his nose, from the sun, Winston would also wear a "piece of gauze tied round his nose with tapes."[49] Johnny reported that this peculiar "nose shield" was, of course, removed whenever photographers were present.

Winston thought the paintings he made that morning gave an idea of the coloring of the lake.[50] Two paintings of Lake Louise that Winston painted are currently housed at Chartwell. One is a 24-by-32-inch painting, and the other is a 14-by-20-inch work. The hours spent painting probably passed quickly for Winston. He wrote in "Painting as a Pastime" that two or three hours passed in a "flash" when painting.[51] The painter will forget all work and worries while painting. For Winston, the act of painting diverted, rested, and stimulated his mind.

A Churchillian horseback expedition to the glacier set out at 12 o'clock on August 31. Randolph wrote that his father looked "magnificent." On a pure white horse, Winston was wearing a Jodhpur riding suit of khaki and his ten-gallon hat, and carrying a "Malacca walking stick with gold knob."[52]

Pony trips to Victoria Glacier were advertised at the time as costing $2.50 and taking four hours. On horseback the party embarked on the trail through the forests and along high mountain tracks to the Plain of Six Glaciers.[53] At the teahouse at Lake Agnes, which was about 2,000 feet higher than the chalet, they stopped to eat. The teahouse, built by the CPR, was a two-storey stone building. Supplies for the teahouse could only be brought in to the isolated location on horseback.[54]

As they rested and ate a snack, chipmunks approached them in groups of two and three to eat crumbs out of their hands. The animals put their paws on their fingers and then sat up and ate the food in a sweet manner. Winston, who dubbed them "chumpwicks," thought the animal was about a quarter the size of the English squirrel and nicely marked on the side with black and yellow stripes.[55] It was a charming and lively animal that they believed could soon become tame.

After riding further up the trail, the Churchills stopped again, this time to have lunch about two o'clock that afternoon in a valley of stones. As they ate, further chipmunks appeared, as did three marmots. Looking rather like a beaver, this animal was described as being two to three feet in length, including tail. The marmots had iron grey and reddish auburn coloring, and a black tail. These animals, which Randolph thought rather tame, preyed on the party as they picnicked among the rocks.[56] Although entirely wild, the marmots allowed themselves to be fed by hand just like the chipmunks.

Winston was also interested in observing the butterfly species in the area. Among the ones he saw were the Camberwell Beauty, the Cloudy-Yellow, the larger Tortoise Shell, and several different kinds of Fritillaries. He expected to find a greater variety of butterflies as they started south on their tour.

Further riding along the mountain trails brought the Churchills to their destination, the Plain of Six Glaciers. All, save Jack, climbed all over the glaciers. Randolph thought his father displayed great energy and spirit in the effort.[57] Winston, Randolph, and Johnny walked across the largest of the glaciers up to the foot of the rock wall. The Plain of Six Glaciers captivated Winston. The mountains had precipices so sheer and silhouettes so jagged that they were far more impressive than anything he had seen in the Alps. The glacier was a "vast arctic cathedral surrounded by ice and walls of rock three or four thousand feet high. No more perfect Alpine scene exists than this though it is but two hours ride from a ritz hotel." With scenery of this sort, it was no surprise to Winston that Lake Louise was one of the most famous sites in North America.[58]

The original itinerary had the party departing from Lake Louise at 9:45 on the morning of August 31 for daylight travel through the Rockies and arriving at Sicamous shortly after six o'clock that evening. Sicamous was a popular stopover point for travelers who wanted to make the entire journey through the mountains in daylight and thus be able to take in the scenery. With so much to do at Lake Louise, however, the itinerary was changed. The

## 10. The Rocky Mountains, August 26–September 1

Churchills probably left Lake Louise late on August 31, boarding their private car at the train station, which was two miles from the chateau.

Winston had been impressed by the mountains. Of the sights he had visited he thought the grand scenery was the equal of anything in Switzerland.[59] He was already planning his next trip to Banff, which, unfortunately, never took place. After making this trip in 1929 he thought he knew the "ropes" and could plan a journey for Clementine and himself which would not be unduly fatiguing. He confided in his letter to his wife that he had wished for her to be with them at Emerald Lake and Lake Louise, and that he thought he must some day persuade her to come with him on a return visit.[60]

... 11 ...

# Vancouver and Victoria, September 1–6

September 1 found the Churchill party aboard the *Mount Royal* traveling west en route to Vancouver. This would be their last trip in the CPR's private car. Aboard the train that day Winston dictated a long letter to Clementine as the train traveled through the interior of British Columbia, following the course of the turbulent rivers. The original itinerary had specified "daylight travel" through the mountains, the Thompson Canyon, and the Fraser River Valley. The opportunity to view the landscape from the train was taken advantage of by the traveling party. Winston wrote home that as he was working on the letter, the train was at that moment running along the Fraser River, a "pretty and winding torrent of clear green water rolling like us down to the Pacific Ocean." That night the Churchills reached Vancouver. They had crossed Canada from Quebec on the St. Lawrence River to the "beautiful and luxuriant Pacific Coast."[1]

Throughout the tour the Churchills were kept well-stocked with newspapers and up to date about international events and local news. Randolph was amused by the newspaper articles he read about the demonstrations staged by the Doukhobors. At the end of August there was another outbreak of demonstrations by members of this Russian religious sect in which both males and females would remove their clothes and refuse to get dressed. At Nelson, British Columbia, on August 29, 150 protesters were arrested by police after refusing to get dressed. Randolph well-remembered reading about the Doukhobors and referred to them in his speech in Toronto two years later, saying he recalled, to the laughter of his audience, "those wild Russians you have here who go about with no clothes on. That seemed to me a very curious choice for your immigration authorities to make when they were selecting future citizens of Canada."[2]

Upon reaching the train station in Vancouver, the Churchills parted with their private rail car. The *Mount Royal* was not allowed to go beyond that city and take the party through the United States. It had to return east over the Canadian lines. The party would be temporarily without a private car of their own.

Winston Churchill, however, would enjoy the comfort of the *Mount Royal* again. In

1943 he arrived in Halifax by ship, bound for the Quebec Conference with Franklin Roosevelt. On his arrival in Canada he went aboard the same private car that had again been put at his disposal and strode down the corridor. Without hesitation he opened a certain door, looked inside, and turned to his daughter Mary, who was accompanying him, and said, "See here, Mary, this is my bedroom."[3] It was, of course, the same room that he had used 14 years earlier. The homecoming in 1943 was made complete by Winston recognizing and greeting by name the *Mount Royal*'s steward, George Grant, who had been with the private car in 1929. On this second trip in the *Mount Royal* Winston was carried to Quebec and then on to Washington, as well as to President Roosevelt's residence at Hyde Park.

During the stay in British Columbia's largest city back in 1929 the Churchills were booked into the Hotel Vancouver. The roof garden that topped the 490-room hotel had brilliant views, including that of the Strait of Georgia.

In Vancouver the Englishmen met William James Bingham, the chief of the Vancouver police, who would escort them everywhere they went during their stay. He was pronounced by Winston to be an extraordinary individual.[4] Bingham told the visitors the story of his adventures as police chief, which the British statesman relayed to his wife in detail. After 25 years with the Metropolitan Police he had retired with the rank of Inspector. Coming out to Canada, he had been appointed Chief Constable of the Vancouver police, against which accusations of corruption had been leveled. According to Winston's account, within three months Bingham had not only dismissed forty officers and cleaned up the city, but also arrested murderers and thieves at every turn. The remainder fled the district. Bingham was pronounced "omnipotent" by Winston, with the entire criminal element frightened of him. The Vancouver police chief's tenure would be cut short when he resigned in 1931 after one of the detectives who he had originally fired but then rehired was involved in further trouble.

In their conversations, Bingham told Winston that he could find a good job for Walter Thompson, the statesman's former bodyguard. Although Winston said he would write to Thompson to see if he was interested in coming out to Vancouver, the Scotland Yard man never emigrated to Canada. Instead, he remained in England and was called to serve Winston for many more years in the 1930s and during the war.

Bingham enthusiastically enforced the liquor laws of the province and was eager for even stricter laws to be enacted. His support for such controls did not prevent him from ensuring the Churchills were well-provided with liquor. Winston supposed this was "on the principal of not muzzling the ox."

With Bingham's knowledge of liquor laws, the party also discussed prohibition in the United States with him. They were looking ahead in their trip and asked him how best to ensure an adequate supply could be obtained, despite prohibition. Bingham replied that he would help them and make a telephone call to Seattle and have liquor put aboard their train in the city. Asked who would do this, Bingham replied, "The police!" He knew the chief of police at Seattle, who would happily assist them with the matter.[5]

On their first full day in Vancouver, which was September 2 and Labour Day in Canada, the Churchills were penciled in for several events at British Columbia's 60th provincial exhibition, which opened at nine o'clock that morning. These events included Winston officially opening the exhibition. To open the exhibition on schedule, the event organizers had to overcome a disastrous fire only seven weeks earlier. A fire on July 14 had destroyed several of the fair's buildings and caused $300,000 worth of damage. The Royal Agricultural and Industrial Society that organized the exhibition quickly arranged for the fair to proceed as scheduled, using the remaining building and seven huge white canvas tents that were erected on the site on the hills overlooking the Fraser River at Queens Park in New Westminster. The largest of these tents covered half an acre.[6]

Leaving the hotel, the party traveled the ten miles to the fairgrounds in nearby New Westminster. They arrived at the exhibition at 12:30 that afternoon. The six-day exhibition had tent pavilions devoted to industry, an auto show, agriculture, beef cattle, and dairy cattle, as well as 20 livestock barns and an art exhibit in the former banquet hall. A poultry exhibit was in one building, with a dog show nearby. Livestock being exhibited included 410 sheep, 250 hogs, goats, chicken, waterfowl, 350 cattle, and 150 head of horses, including Clydesdales and Belgians. Events scheduled for the exhibition included an outboard motor regatta on the Fraser River, Indian canoe races, and "Indian War Dances." Winston was scheduled to "face the ball" at the championship lacrosse match between Oshawa and New Westminster for the Mann Cup that was to start at 3:30 that afternoon. Attendance at the exhibition on the opening day was 40,000, making it one of the best days in the fair's history.[7]

The Churchills' events for the day started with attending a joint civic luncheon given for Winston at the Great Armouries building at Sixth Street and Queen's Avenue in New Westminster. The luncheon was arranged by Pacific Coast Terminals, the New Westminster city council, the Royal Agricultural and Industrial Society, and various New Westminster service organizations.[8] Tickets for the event that was set to begin at 12:45 p.m. had been sold at three local stores and were available at the door of the drill hall. Very few tickets must have been left for latecomers to purchase at the door, as the building was filled. After the luncheon part of the program was over, many people came in to fill in the aisles and the galleries. An estimated 700 people listened to the speech in a hall that was "finely decorated and the table arrangements for the great throng were very splendidly carried out." Winston sat next to the mayor of New Westminster, A. Wells Gray, who was presiding at the luncheon. At the time, Gray was serving as mayor of the city, a Liberal member of the British Columbia legislature, and president of the Union of British Columbia Municipalities all at the same time. The luncheon was associated with that morning's official opening of the Pacific Coast Terminals plant, which Winston did not attend. Several presentations were made, with recipients including at least two individuals who were not present to receive them.

While *The British Columbian* declared that "no more brilliant function has ever been staged in New Westminster," Randolph was in no way impressed by the event.[9] He thought the cold buffalo served at the lunch, which had been ushered in by a rendition of "Rule Britannia," was horrible. The presentations were interminable, as it seemed everyone present received an award, broken only by various gentlemen accepting trophies for those who were absent. The Queen of the May and her attendants received medals, but Randolph sniped that he could not understand why the May Queens were being recognized, since it was September. Two singers followed next, one a soprano and the other a tenor. Another round of singing "Rule Britannia" followed, as Winston then rose to speak after being introduced by Mayor Gray.

"I am glad to find myself again in Westminster. Perhaps many of you know that I have lived in Westminster most of my life," Winston said to laughter as he started his address.[10] He had been greeted with loud and sustained cheering after being introduced. Winston told the audience he was especially delighted to be present for the Diamond Jubilee of the exhibition and see the examples of the "citizens of the British Empire building up their own and the Empire's prosperity."

In the seven-minute speech, Winston said it had been one of his aspirations to visit British Columbia due to his friendship with the late Sir Richard McBride, who had championed the province. Unlike his son, Winston appreciated the playing of "Rule Britannia," as he told the audience that he had been welcomed by its playing when he came aboard British warships when he was first lord of the Admiralty.

Dr. James H. King, the minister of pensions and national health in William Lyon Mackenzie King's government, was to have spoken in reply. He could not, however, be present at the luncheon. In his place, his wife, Nellie King, spoke for a few minutes.

By the time the civic luncheon was over there was probably very little time before Winston was to be at the stand in front of the auto pavilion on the exhibition grounds for the official opening ceremony. The official opening began at half-past two that afternoon. A band played "Rule Britannia," or, as Randolph complained in his diary, it was more "Rule Britannia" and presentations.[11] As part of the opening ceremony, a group of veterans of the Great War that lived in the Lower Mainland of British Columbia paraded at attention in front of the stand. This guard of 46 veterans under Captain McNeil of Surrey were members of the Old Contemptibles Association of British Columbia. Escorted by Colonel A. Leslie Coote, Winston reviewed the double line formation. With Mayor Gray looking on, W.A. Anderson from the association then presented the visitor with a life membership in the association in the form of a life membership badge.[12]

Returning to the platform, Winston was presented with an "illuminated address" as a souvenir of his visit. The address that welcomed him to the city was presented and read to him on behalf of New Westminster by the city clerk, W.H. Keary. T.D. Trapp, president of the Royal Agricultural and Industrial Society, introduced Winston, who spoke for about 20 minutes in opening the exhibition. With an exhibition attendance of 40,000 that day, he estimated he had spoken to about 20,000 people. The speech was carried to all parts of the grounds over the loudspeaker system, and Winston remarked to the audience that it was the largest crowd he had ever addressed.[13]

In the speech Winston said it was his honor and privilege to come to British Columbia and, in reference to the fire, declared his admiration of the courage and resourcefulness of the exhibition organizers. The opening of the fair was the "culmination of a courage that does not know defeat." Perseverance in the face of such tremendous difficulties was declared to be a fine characteristic of the British race. Winston discussed Canada's great development over the past three decades and also quoted the line, "we stand on guard for thee," from what was then the unofficial Canadian national anthem. He assured the audience that if ever the occasion arose, the whole Empire would stand on guard for Canada like she had stood on guard for the Empire.

The audience was "thrilled" by Winston's "eloquent" speech, according to *The British Columbian*. It was a speech "bristling" with patriotism and references to the important role Canada played in the Empire, both in war and peace. The newspaper declared "fortune smiled" on the Royal Agricultural and Industrial Society when it was able to convince Winston to fit the exhibition into his schedule.[14]

After he finished his speech Winston received a great ovation. Many members of the audience pushed forward, including some who climbed onto the platform, to shake his hand. Besieged by well-wishers, Winston was obliged to sign a great number of autographs for his admirers. In a situation where the services of his Scotland Yard bodyguard would have been useful, Winston was mobbed by people slapping his back as he tried to make his way from the platform to the stadium. The crowd closed on him in such a manner that "he seemed to run the gauntlet. His departure constituted a scene of popular enthusiasm seldom, if ever, witnessed in Queens Park."

After a luncheon, two speeches, and a boisterous crowd, Winston and the other Churchills had reached their limit. Although it had been announced that he would make the official face off of the ball at the lacrosse match between the New Westminster Salmonbellies and the Oshawa Generals, the actual duty was performed in the end by Mayor Gray. The Churchills had already fled Queens Park.[15]

Safely away from the provincial exhibition, the English visitors spent the rest of the day in a more peaceful manner. Winston completed the letter to his wife that he started on the train the previous day by adding that he had just opened the exhibition and been presented with great demonstrations of loyalty and friendship. Time was also found for Winston to cable Vickers da Costa, instructing them to put 2,000 pounds in his account with Richardson and Sons.[16] While staying at the Hotel Vancouver, Winston received a visit from Captain Edgardo von Shroders, a Chilean navy commander whose ship was visiting the port of Vancouver. E.W. Dean, a Vancouver alderman, had come upon Von Shroders in the corridors of the hotel and learned that he had previously met Winston and wished to renew his acquaintance. Von Shroders had served as naval attaché at the Chilean legation in London 15 years earlier when Winston was first lord of the Admiralty. Dean and the Chilean navy officer thus went up to Winston's room and met the British statesman. An invitation was probably offered by the Chilean, which was later acted upon, for all of the visiting Englishmen to come aboard and inspect his ship.[17]

With the letter finished and other business attended to, the party drove to Grouse Mountain, which, at 4,000 feet, provided great views of Vancouver. According to one witness at the top of the mountain that day, Winston "jumped out of the car, opened the rear door, reaching in for his painting outfit, a large metal container, and without hesitation strode over to the flat rock." He either painted or sketched, reports differ, on the precipice. Bingham made himself useful by keeping well-wishers away so that the British statesman could work in peace. Observers recall Winston declaring the view from Grouse Mountain while he painted to be the "most beautiful he had ever seen." After painting, the party dined at the mountain chalet.[18]

A reception for Winston by the Vancouver mayor, William H. Malkin, might have been held this night. As he had been delayed on Grouse Mountain, Winston was reported to have arrived late and told his hosts, "I was afraid I might lose that light and colour. I wanted to get that exact colouring before it disappeared. You see, the way I do it, I just put on essentials and fill it in afterwards." Malkin, an English-born businessman and philanthropist, was in the middle of a two-year term as mayor of the city. Winston thought he was a first rate fellow.[19]

The following day, September 3, the Churchills made a motor trip inland out of Vancouver into the British Columbia interior to inspect the province's lumber industry with a visit to a logging camp. Forestry in Canada was an important economic sector, with forestry exports totaling $288,621,745 for the year of 1929. At 11 o'clock that morning the Churchills left the Hotel Vancouver. Smoking a cigar and wearing a brown soft felt hat, Winston boarded a motor car and was driven by Chief of Police Bingham to the main camp of Abernathy-Lougheed Logging Company at Port Haney.[20] This was a drive of about 30 miles. Nelson S. Lougheed, minister of public works at the provincial level, hosted their visit to the camp. Along with J.W. Abernathy, Lougheed had established the lumber company in 1905.

A demonstration of logging methods was put on for their benefit. It began with two men cutting down a 200-foot-high tree in about half an hour. Before the enormous tree was brought down, the Churchills were shown exactly what trees it would hit as well as miss as it fell to the ground. The tree fell exactly as predicted to the exact spot. A man known as a high-rigger next demonstrated his techniques. He put on a pair of steel spurs and tied himself to a 300-foot tree with a rope and began a quick climb. He cut off branches from the tree as he proceeded. The loggers intended to affix pulleys to this tree in order to assist in the cutting of other surrounding trees. One hundred eighty feet up the tree, the high-rigger, secured only by the rope around his waist, cut off the top of the tree. Randolph noted the top portion of the tree fell to the ground with a terrific crash. Winston thought the young man looked very small at the great distance in the air. Already having worries about the great height, he was horrified when the high-rigger volunteered to stand on his head on the top of the tree. As confirmed by Randolph's account, only Winston's firm protests prevented this frightening stunt.[21]

The high-rigger descended to the ground and then turned over his equipment so that Randolph could have a try. After putting on the spurs, belt, and rope, Randolph tried climbing a smaller tree. He found it rather easy and managed to climb a short way up. Despite his success, Randolph did not become overconfident, and he wrote in his diary that he doubted if he could have used the axe at that moment. Winston, a more neutral observer, said in a joking manner as he watched his son's efforts, "You will need *just a little* more practice, Randolph."

A luncheon was provided to the guests by the logging company, and the Churchill party also had the opportunity to see the damage wrought by the forest fires that had burned in the Haney area. Winston thoroughly enjoyed the visit to the logging camp but confessed that the "devastation of these beautiful trees was sad to see."

During the driving tour, Winston appreciated the scenery of British Columbia. Bingham recalled that throughout the day he would stop suddenly and look in all directions and say, "Simply grand." While driving across a bridge over the Pitt River, Bingham told the party about a famous sturgeon caught in the river and gave its weight. Winston replied with a humorous remark that all, save Bingham, who did not catch the joke, laughed at. Later Randolph told Bingham that his father had been joking. Bingham later found a photograph of the sturgeon in question, which gave the fish a greater weight than what he had told Winston. He sent the photograph to Winston's London address so that it would be awaiting him on his eventual return from North America.

That evening Winston spoke at a meeting sponsored by the National Council of Education held at the Vancouver Theatre. Every seat in the theater was occupied, and even though more room was found on the stage, hundreds still had to be turned away. "Waves of applause" greeted his arrival on the stage and brought him to the front of the platform, as he peered forward through the mask of footlights and "responded with a smile of greeting."

The *Vancouver Province* wrote there was "no mistaking Churchill when he marched to his place. His shining pate, his cutaway coat, wing collar, and cravat marked him the personality still called Britain's busy young man." Henry Herbert Stevens, a member of Parliament and former Conservative cabinet minister, introduced Winston in an address in which he noted the statesman's success in many areas and compared his biography of his father Lord Randolph Churchill to Boswell's *Life of Johnson*.[22] Like Winston's biography of his father, Randolph would write the first two volumes of his own father's life.

In the 55-minute speech, Winston opened with his refrain that he was traveling in search of truth and diversion, and covered the usual themes of naval disarmament, the Singapore naval base as a vital link with the Empire, Britain's strong position and need for peace, and Canada's progress. He also told his audience that Vancouver, with the gathering forces of a continent behind it, could not fail to find "greatness."

Recent international events on matters of great interest to Winston were commented on in the speech. In late August Snowden had reached an agreement on reparations after France's insistence on the Young Plan scheme had been dropped. Having managed to get his counterparts to "disgorge part of the spoils," Snowden had made minor concessions to reach a final agreement. Having fought and won, Snowden returned to a hero's welcome in Britain. Winston supported his successor as chancellor of the exchequer in his Vancouver speech, saying the ultimate conclusion of the conference was reasonable. No British government would have accepted the Young Plan, and Snowden quite properly opposed it. The final concessions made by Snowden to achieve the agreement were acceptable, as they involved an amount so small that they were not worth setting back the whole European resettlement. With the agreement at The Hague, Winston also believed it was time for a restatement of British policy on reparations that the United States would get as much from Britain as Britain got from her creditor-nations in Europe.[23]

Winston also discussed Egypt in Vancouver, but now in the context of the outbreak of violence in Palestine that had taken place in the past few days. Decrying the horrible massacres that had occurred, he predicted that even with troops and warships hurrying to the scene there would probably be more bloodshed before order could be restored. The British government would be supported in Parliament in their efforts to restore the situation in Palestine. Although he could see no reason why Arabs and Jews could not live side by side in peace, Winston left no doubt that "no British political party, Socialist, Conservative or Liberal, will repudiate undertakings made in time of war to the Zionist Movement."[24]

The trouble in Palestine was linked by Winston in thundering tones to the Labour government's plans for Egypt. "What an object-lesson! What a warning!" Should Britain abandon its responsibilities to minorities and foreigners in Egypt, the "scene of carnage which has disgraced Palestine will be reproduced on a far larger scale throughout the whole of the Nile Valley." Palestine would only be a terrible preview of what would happen if Britain withdrew from India or Egypt, Winston warned. He hoped that in light of the events in Palestine, the dreadful policy of British withdrawal from Egypt would be abandoned. The proposed withdrawal, Winston added, had probably been considered as a sign of weakness by the Arabs of Palestine.

The speech was concluded with the words, "Let us now go forward with confidence and courage to a brighter world than we in this generation have ever known."

J.G. Lister, chairman of the Vancouver committee of the National Council of Education, proposed the vote of thanks to Winston for his speech. Once again, Randolph stood in for his father in accepting the thanks. Calling himself the "youngest member" of the Churchill Troupe, Randolph told the audience that the older generation had fulfilled its duty, and it remained for the younger generation to carry out its work. He also said it was his pleasure and privilege to come to Canada and meet Canadians. One of the reporters wrote that Winston's eyes sparkled as his son spoke. As Winston left the platform at the end of the program he received a final cheer.[25]

As always, the reviews in the newspapers were laudatory. The *Vancouver Province* admired his "flashing and brilliant phrases," and observed that "his wit, his apt illustrations and ready delivery carried his audience with him from the time he stepped on the platform, and as he concluded, picturing the greater Empire of the future, he roused the assembly to a high pitch of patriotism." With his comments on recent developments, the *Province* said this was the most important speech Winston had given in Canada. It thought that "in London, in Paris, and in Washington his speech is being read anxiously today, for his words were freighted with criticism, praise, and revelation."[26]

The Bristol-born H.H. Stevens, the Canadian politician who had introduced Winston, did not have an opportunity to have a personal chat with the visitor. Instead, he wrote to Winston, saying the "brilliant" address in Vancouver had accomplished a great deal in bringing the separate portions of the Empire closer together. With his letter Stevens also forwarded Winston information about the potential of Canadian oilfields for British interests.[27]

A short time after the speech, late on the night of September 3, the Churchills were to sail aboard a ship for the provincial capital of Victoria. With time before they had to board their ship, the party visited the Chilean navy ship the *General Baquedano* that was berthed at the CPR pier in the port at Vancouver. The vessel was named after the general who led the Chilean army to victory in the War of the Pacific fought against Peru and Bolivia. A square-rigger with auxiliary power, this vessel was a training ship for Chilean naval midshipmen. It had a compliment of 335 men, of whom 39 were officers. The *Baquedano* was on a week-long visit to the city, having already called on several American west coast ports on its goodwill cruise along the Pacific coast. The Churchills were accompanied on the visit to the ship by the ever-present Chief of Police Bingham, as well as Herbert J. Morris, Chilean Consul in Vancouver, and Arturo Rios, who was Chilean Consul in Seattle and accompanying the ship to Vancouver. A salute of "God Save the King" was played by the ship's 20-piece band for Winston as he came aboard the vessel. The visitors were received by Captain Edgardo von Shroders of the *Baquedano* and Alderman E.W. Dean. Also aboard the ship was Alberto Complido, a representative of the Chilean Ministry for Foreign Trade. Winston inspected the 2,500-ton ship. It was 240 feet in length and had been refitted in 1923–24. As the party "recrossed the gangplank" after the visit, the ship's band again played the anthem. Captain Von Shroders said Winston's visit was the "highest honor" paid to his ship during its entire cruise of the Pacific.[28]

After the visit to the *General Baquedano* the Churchills bid farewell to Vancouver and boarded the luxurious SS *Princess Marguerite* for the four-and-a-half-hour crossing of the Straits of Juan de Fuca to Victoria on Vancouver Island. The ship sailed at midnight. Winston thought the voyage to Vancouver Island was marvelous, with the *Marguerite* a splendid ship passing through the "archipelago of delicious inlets."[29] Aboard the Victoria-bound ship were Lieutenant-Governor Robert Randolph Bruce and his niece Miss Helen Mackenzie, as well as Dr. James King and Nellie King.

Lieutenant-Governor Bruce would play host to the Churchill party in Victoria, as they were his guests at Government House. The 66-year-old Bruce had been born in Scotland and immigrated to Canada forty years before. Arriving with very little money to his name, Bruce had grown wealthy working as an engineer and in mining. Winston enjoyed the lieutenant-governor and considered him a grand Old Scotsman. The Kings were traveling to Victoria in order to attend the dinner at Government House to be held in Winston's honor. Winston had already met Nellie King before at the luncheon in New Westminster.

The Churchills would spend three days in the capital of British Columbia. With his only remaining speech in Canada to give in those three days, the remaining time would be spent touring the city and district. The commitment to give a speech in Victoria had only been given reluctantly. Winston was, however, looking forward to seeing the city, as he understood it was the "most English" place in Canada. After his visit, Winston agreed with favorable comparisons to England. With its sentiment, vegetation, and manners, Victoria was "English with a splendid climate thrown in."[30]

The Churchills disembarked with the other passengers from the *Princess Marguerite* at the Belleville Street docks in Victoria on the morning of September 4. Winston walked with Lieutenant-Governor Bruce briskly towards the official motor car awaiting them. Making allowances for the news cameramen, Winston paused for a moment before proceeding. Bruce then invited him to take a seat in the automobile.[31]

"After the King's representative," Winston protested, insisting Bruce take a seat first.

Once sorted out aboard the motorcar, the Churchills were driven to Government House. They stayed at the official residence for the duration of their time in the city and were entertained like visiting royalty by the lieutenant-governor. A Highland Piper even played them into and through dinner and parties that were held in their honor.

On their first day in Victoria, the lieutenant-governor escorted the party on a visit to the Parliament buildings. At the Parliament they were received on behalf of the government by Robert H. Pooley, the provincial attorney-general in the Conservative government and at the moment acting B.C. premier. During the tour of Parliament Winston visited the Provincial Archives, which were located in the Parliament building's Connaught Library. The provincial archivist, John Hoak, personally showed them the collections, and Winston spent a great deal of time studying the documents. He was most interested in the charts in the collection that had been made by Captain James Cook and the political letters of the Younger Pitt.[32]

As Winston expressed an interest in visiting the Naval Station at Esquimalt and the federal government dry-docks at Skinner's Cove, this was duly arranged. In the afternoon they set out with the lieutenant-governor on that expedition. They arrived at Esquimalt at 3:20 that afternoon for a forty-minute tour. At the dry-docks the party was met by Norman A. Yarrow, the managing director of Yarrows Limited, and two other company employees Edward W. Izard and B.D. Robinson. Yarrow was the son of a Clyde shipbuilding family who had been sent out by his father to manage the business in Victoria.

Allan Craig, the chief operator at the Skinner's Cove dry-dock, took charge of the party and led the tour. Winston was surprised by the size of the docks and that the facilities could handle the largest vessels afloat. They went down to the floor of the dock, inspected the gates, and looked through the pump house.

That evening a dinner was hosted by Bruce and Miss Mackenzie at Government House in honor of the Churchill party. The official residence was decorated for the event. On the tables were "great bowls of roses and tall mauve candles in silver holders, while the reception rooms were filled with golden chrysanthemums and bronze Helenium." Prominent among the guests were Lord and Lady Cromer. Also on a cross–Canada tour, Lord Cromer was the Lord Chamberlain to His Majesty's Household. Traveling with the Countess and members of their family, including Viscount Errington, Lady Rosemary Baring, and Lady Violet Baring, Cromer had arrived in Victoria on September 2.[33]

The guest list for the party was composed of the foremost residents of Victoria. These included James and Nellie King, the Very Reverend and Mrs. Cecil S. Quainton, attorney-general and Mrs. Pooley, Victoria lawyer Lindley Crease, and three of the province's leading jurists, James A. Macdonald, Archer Martin, and Albert E. McPhillips, accompanied by their spouses. Laura Dunsmuir was present for the party. She was the 71-year-old widow of James, a one-time premier and lieutenant-governor of the province, as well as the richest man in British Columbia. Also attending with his wife was the former lieutenant-general of Saskatchewan, Sir Richard Lake, who had retired to Victoria. Lake's brother, Percy, commanded a British army in Mesopotamia and in 1917 was appointed to a position in the Ministry of Munitions, then headed by Winston. Although Percy Lake had also retired to Victoria, it does not appear he met the British visitors in the city.[34]

The next morning, September 5, the Churchills rested at Government House, as Winston had to speak in a few hours. The Churchills and their hosts, Bruce and Mackenzie, went out into the grounds at Government House to have their photograph taken by Associated Screen News. Randolph and Johnny went over to the Crystal Garden where they were met by the manager, Alfred H. Cowlishaw, and then went for a swim in the pool.[35]

This was probably the last day Winston had the services of the private secretary loaned to him by the CPR. Having given up the *Mount Royal*, it is likely J.H. Baker remained in Winston's service and came over to Victoria with the Churchills. At some point on this day the British visitor wrote a letter to CPR vice-president Grant Hall thanking him for the arrangements the company had made on their behalf. The accommodations had made the trip across Canada comfortable and enjoyable. Winston also added that the services of the private secretary were satisfactory and helpful.[36] Baker then departed with the letter, which he hand-delivered to Hall.

Winston's final speech in Canada was at a luncheon held in his honor by the Canadian Club and the Victoria Branch of the National Council of Education on September 5. The luncheon was held at the Empress Hotel. This chateau-style hotel was named after Queen Victoria, the Empress of India, and had opened in January 1908. On the city's harbor, this CPR hotel was located at 721 Government Street. With 800 people attending, the meeting was the largest in the 25-year history of Victoria's Canadian Club. Three Victoria police officers, Inspector John T. Bolton and Constables Henry Jarvis and James Petterson, assisted with directing and marshalling the crowd.

At the luncheon, in Winston's opinion, were the elite of Victoria. Business, political, and civic leaders from all over Vancouver Island were in the audience, with many aldermen, reeves, and councilors from nearby municipalities also in attendance. At the 36-place head table Winston sat between Lieutenant-Governor Bruce and W.H.M. Haldane, the vice-president of the Canadian Club. Also at the table were Helen Mackenzie, Lord and Lady Cromer, several judges, attorney-general R.H. Pooley, Victoria mayor Herbert Anscomb,

U.S. Consul G.A. Bucklin, and four provincial cabinet ministers, William Atkinson, S.L. Howe, Frederick P. Burden, and William A. McKenzie. Also at the head table was Thomas Dufferin Pattullo, the leader of the opposition Liberal party who would win the premiership in 1933. The three other members of the Churchill party were also seated on the platform.[37]

As the guest of honor entered, the national anthem was played, followed by the audience singing "Rule Britannia" and "O Canada." Everywhere he went in British Columbia, Winston noted, he was met with "Rule Britannia" and an enthusiastic display of love for the British Empire.

Haldane, who as club president was presiding at the luncheon, introduced Winston. Rather than give a formal welcome, Haldane briefly spoke of the appreciation and pleasure felt for having their speaker with them that day. As he rose to speak, Winston was given a tremendous reception, the best he received in Canada. The audience stood, waved handkerchiefs and cheered. It was five minutes of cheering before he could start speaking. Throughout the hour-long speech there was one outburst of applause after another. Early in the speech Winston said that this was his final address on his "most memorable and thrilling journey" across Canada. A journey, he declared, that was ending quite fittingly in Victoria, a city where he was "reminded on every side of the small Island from which I started out. Your green lawns and sturdy oaks, and hearts as British as the oaks, all remind me of the mother country."

Although the address covered his standard topics—Singapore, Canada's development, Britain's strength, Egypt, naval disarmament and so forth—Randolph said it was different from the stock speech he had been giving. Beyond his usual topics, Winston also discussed the Pacific and spoke of Britain's long and important relationship with Japan. He said his confidence in the government and people of Japan had been strengthened by that country's conduct in both peace and war. On a local note, he discussed his visit to the Esquimalt drydock, which he said was a fine contribution to the strength of the Royal Navy. Another outburst of cheering followed the end of the speech, which the *Daily Colonist* called a "brilliant oration" and "masterly exposition." Randolph, who had, of course, listened to all of his speeches in Canada, thought this one was an "almost perfect example of his oratorical powers."[38]

The Very Reverend Quainton, chairman of the Victoria branch of the National Council of Education, and the dean and rector of Christ Church Cathedral in Victoria since 1917, then rose and made the vote of thanks. It was not a good speech. Randolph said the Rector rambled on for more than 15 minutes and made feeble attempts at humor. For his part, Winston thought Quainton was a "foolish cleric with Socialist leanings" who asked cheeky questions and went on unduly long.[39]

"I want to ask Mr. Churchill three questions," Quainton proclaimed. "If he ever becomes prime minister will he make me Archbishop of Canterbury? Does he intend to go into business with Lord Birkenhead? Is he still a member of the bricklayers union?"

After listening to the Rector, Randolph, who had not been planning to speak, "saw the opportunity to make a hit." He glanced at his father, who nodded his permission for his son to take his place. Randolph spoke for five minutes, during which time, according to his father, he turned the tables upon the dean. In response to the three questions, Randolph answered each humorously and "mildly twitted" Quainton. The audience, who the youngest Churchill said were so bored by the Rector that they would have been pleased with anything, roared with laughter. An ovation that rivaled that given his father followed Randolph's speech, and the newspapers called his answers "witty." Winston was impressed with the performance, thinking he could not have done any better himself. His son had demonstrated excellent tact in knowing how far to press his remarks while keeping the favor of the audience. Randolph believed the speech was the "greatest success I have ever had."[40]

Lord Cromer was also asked to speak. He said that he and his wife had enjoyed their visit to Victoria and, in regard to Winston's speech, recommended that everyone bear in mind what had been said, think it over, and greatly appreciate it.

Following the luncheon, Winston and the other Churchills posed for a photograph, which appeared in the *Victoria Daily Times*, with the Canadian Club executive and other guests. Seated in the front row were Lady Cromer, Pooley, Lieutenant-Governor Bruce, Haldane, Winston, and Miss Mackenzie, while standing behind were Lord Cromer, Dr. M.W. Thomas, Frank J. Sehl, Colonel W.R. Wilby, Herbert Pendray, A.D. King, John R. Bunn, Randolph, Mayor Anscomb, Johnny, F. McGregor, Jack, John Cochrane, and Kenneth Ferguson. From the luncheon the Churchill party visited Hatley Park, the beautiful Edwardian mansion and grounds built by the Dunsmuir family, and then went on to see the headquarters of the British Public Schools' Club in Victoria.

With their visiting over, the Churchills went on a fishing cruise for the rest of the afternoon. Norman Yarrow, whom they had met the previous day, took them and the lieutenant-governor out on his yacht *Cynthia*. They set out from the pilotage landing inside the breakwater at Ogden Point and spent most of the cruise fishing off the Dallas Shore. Aboard the *Cynthia* they fished for salmon. Jack, the avid fisherman, caught a ten-pounder, but no one else had any luck. Randolph had three fish hooked, but they escaped each time. Sensing his son's disappointment, Winston quipped, "'Tis better to have hooked and lost, than never hooked at all."[41]

Another party for the Churchills was hosted by the lieutenant-governor and his niece at Government House that evening. It commenced at 7:45 p.m. Attending were the Cromer party; the wife of the B.C. premier, Annie Tolmie; Pattullo; a provincial cabinet minister, R.L. Maitland; and other socially prominent figures in the city. Several members of the Dunsmuir family were in attendance, including Kathleen Humphreys and her husband Arthur Selden Humphreys. Kathleen, the prettiest of the Dunsmuir daughters, had met her husband in France, a major in the Army Service Corps, during the war when she was working in a soldiers' canteen. They were married in London in 1915 and returned to Victoria after the war, where Selden looked forward "to a life of leisure." He, however, agreed to serve as ADC to the lieutenant-governor of the province. This assignment ended in 1929. Kathleen, for her part, threw lavish parties with the glamour of the movie star she aspired to be. A year after the Churchills' visit Kathleen acted on her dream. Selden "joined the ranks of discarded husbands," as he was exiled to Shanghai with an allowance of 20 pounds per month, and Kathleen left for Hollywood for a failed attempt at movie stardom.[42]

As an avid fisherman, Jack would have much to talk about with Noel Money, who attended the party with his wife. Money was a former brigadier-general in the British Army who had retired to Vancouver Island primarily for the opportunities to fish the Campbell River's Chinook salmon. The author and fisherman Roderick Haig-Brown described Money as the "wisest and best fisherman I have ever known in British Columbia, and he was also probably the keenest."[43]

At Government House on the morning of September 6, Winston received an award from a local body. The Victoria branch of the Royal Society of St. George gave him an Honorary Life Membership in their organization for his distinguished service to the Empire. The Victoria branch president and vice-president, a W.H. Langley and Alderman John Harvey respectively, came to Government House to present the award. In accepting the honorary membership, Winston thanked the local branch for the honor and spoke of the "kindly feeling" he had felt throughout his Canadian tour.

Later in the morning the Churchill party, in the company of Lieutenant-Governor Bruce, went for a drive in their host's car over the Malahat Highway. They returned to Government House in time for lunch and then in the early afternoon visited Christ Church Cathedral. The Cathedral was under the deanship of Quainton, the silly cleric from the Canadian Club speech. Construction was underway at the cathedral, and the superintendent of the works, Fred Parfitt, recalling that Winston had a union card, said the masons would be very pleased if he would lay a stone. Winston immediately accepted the offer and climbed a ladder and went to work laying a stone in the cathedral's northwest tower, known as Bishop of London Tower. Remarking that the mortar was a "little stiff," Winston put in the stone with the level in a "true professional style." While at the cathedral, which would be consecrated a few weeks later on September 28, Winston signed the guestbook.[44]

The party next drove to Beacon Hill Park where Mayor Anscomb and Alderman Litchefield met them. A city park of 154 acres, Beacon Hill had recreation grounds, gardens, and wonderful views of the Olympic Mountains on the mainland across the Straits of Juan de Fuca. With the help of the local politicians, the party planted an English Hawthorn (May) tree in the "Mayor's Grove," which was near the park's Rupert Street entrance.

At 4:30 in the afternoon of September 6, Winston and the other Churchills departed Victoria for Seattle by CPR steamer.[45] After nearly a month of traveling, the Canadian leg of their North American tour was over. In this hectic holiday Winston had "been lunched, dined, and banqueted, and had repaid Canadian generosity by speaking on a seemingly endless variety of political topics at every available opportunity." Speaking at overflow meetings, Winston had won the goodwill of his audiences, and by granting so many interview requests, he had even won the goodwill of newspaper reporters.

Having already visited the major cities of eastern Canada in 1900–01, Winston devoted slightly more than a week to them on this tour. Eager to see new places, the party had spent just short of three weeks in western Canada. This suited Winston. He wrote that as they progressed west in their tour the country become more interesting. The new ground to cover and the appeal of these growing and newer cities gave him much to appreciate. On his earlier visit to Canada, Winston had heard doubts that the Dominion was too drawn out with physical barriers of forests and mountains to survive. The three decades of development convinced him, as he wrote in the *Daily Telegraph*, that Canada had established itself as an "economic, political and national unit." In his opinion, a "geographical abstraction had become a physical reality." Canada was destined to become a great country. It possessed abundant minerals, oil, cattle, and grain, as well as a "climate to breed a sturdy race."[46]

Randolph recorded three impressions of Canada in his diary. First, he was struck by the strong loyalty to England and the Empire, alongside a distinct dislike of the United States. Everywhere they went in Canada there were the "most marked signs of genuine sympathy and affection" for the Old Country. Second, he felt very much at home in Canada. Canadians possessed the same ideals and sentiments as England, and Randolph found them easy to make friends with. Last, Randolph was astonished by the rapid development. He predicted, like his father, the next quarter of a century would see the development of the north as the last 25 years had seen the developing of the West.[47] Both Randolph and Winston would return to Canada several more times in their lives, with the son next returning in 1931 and the father coming back to Canada again for his lecture tour in 1932.

... 12 ...

# Seattle to Napa Valley, September 6–9

"The lights of Seattle were Mr. Churchill's first glimpse of the United States in thirty years," the *Seattle Daily Times* reported incorrectly in their article on Winston's arrival in their city.[1] The reporter was quite unaware of the British statesman's brief visit to Niagara Falls three weeks earlier, where he saw the United States and indeed crossed into the country, stepping foot on American soil for the first time since 1901.

Winston admired the United States and "deeply cherished the blood link with America he possessed through his famously beautiful Yankee mother."[2] His having a British father and American mother prompted Harold Macmillan to describe Churchill as "half English aristocrat and half American gambler." From his first visit to the country he was impressed with it. During his 1895 visit he wrote his brother that "this is a very great country, my dear Jack."[3] The firsthand impressions he gained on visits to the United States, and the accompanying meetings with Americans, contributed to his knowledge of and feeling for the United States. Winston's "understanding of the United States … was to a large extent the product of his visits to the United States. They were important in his life. He got to know the country and many of its statesmen."[4] In this trip through the United States in 1929, Winston wanted to see the country, its industry, its scenery, and its leaders in the fields of politics, industry, and finance. He wanted to get to know America.

One thing which Winston knew from the outset that he would not admire about America or even wish to try to get to know at all was prohibition. By constitutional amendment, the making, selling, and transporting of alcohol was forbidden. This ban on alcohol, nicknamed the "noble experiment," had taken effect on January 17, 1920, and was to remain in place for a further four years after Winston's visit, until repealed in 1933.[5]

After the CPR steamer tied up at the Bell Street dock, the Churchills had a difficult time passing through American customs. Johnny claimed that the party had nothing to declare, save for Jack's 16-millimeter cine-camera and the rolls of film for the camera. Randolph, however, recorded in his diary that the party entered the United States prepared for prohibition. He claimed to be carrying on his person a big flask full of whiskey and a little one containing brandy, while two medicine bottles were also filled with liquor. If the contraband were discovered, it was planned that Winston would pay the fine and Randolph would get the publicity.[6]

Although the Chief of Customs, a man by the name of George D. Hubbard, and the British vice-consul came aboard the steamer to personally meet them, a rigorous examination by the customs officials was still conducted. Winston proffered diplomatic visas for himself and members of the party, and even a letter from Charles M. Dawes, the American ambassador to Great Britain, requesting normal customs procedures be waived. These documents did him no good. Ignoring the letter, the head customs officer closely examined every piece of the party's luggage; the contents were removed, scrutinized, and shoved back in. Dozens of questions were also asked of the travelers. Winston became quite angry, and Johnny thought he would "explode."[7]

"What are you looking for? I have already told you we have nothing to declare. The point of this letter from the ambassador is to assure you of my integrity," Winston shouted.

"We are looking for guns and ammunition," a customs officer replied.

"How many cigars?" was one of the questions that was asked.[8]

Despite the diplomatic visas and ambassador's letter, the party had to sit and wait as their luggage was thoroughly searched. Upon discovering that the party carried camera plates with them, they were told that normally they would be closely inspected to ensure they did not have anything of an obscene nature. On this occasion, however, the customs officers dispensed with this inspection as a "great favour." Additionally, Jack was required to "practically swear on the Bible that his camera was purely for private use and not for photographing military secrets."[9]

"Monstrous! Absolutely monstrous!" Winston seethed.

With the inspection over, Hubbard suddenly changed course and, after apologizing for the inconvenience, proceeded to invite the Englishmen for a drink! The offer was accepted. Johnny incorrectly remembered in his memoirs that the drink from two bottles of very good champagne took place in the man's office, while Randolph and Winston both wrote at the time that they were invited to a nearby hotel for the drink.[10]

Despite the annoyance, the Churchills emerged from their experience at customs with Randolph's flasks and medicine bottles safely intact. Having declined an offer from the Seattle Chamber of Commerce for Winston to speak to them, the visit to the city was brief, as the party planned from the outset to leave almost immediately for California by train. Winston and Randolph, however, were still met and photographed by the waiting newspaper reporters as they emerged from the dock.

"Do we see you now or on the train?" a young woman reporter from one of the local newspapers demanded to know from Randolph on the quay. That an interview would be given was apparently a foregone conclusion. For Randolph, however, an interview was given to the press as a favor rather than an obligation.[11]

Although Randolph thought the reporter was an "attractive young lady," he did not like this example of what he believed was the "pushing and assertive nature" of the American press. He snapped back, "I'm not sure if you see us at all."

Other than expressing regret that he could not spend more time in the city, Winston tried not to offer much comment to the Seattle newspapers. Specifically declining to comment on American prohibition, he allowed that prohibition would never work in Britain.

He said the "British have a deep-rooted prejudice against compulsion. British drinking is diminishing from champagne down to beer."[12] Even without prohibition, British drinking was declining each year, and as a result criminal convictions had been cut in half, he explained. During the five years he had been chancellor of the exchequer 3,000,000 pounds a year of tax revenue had been written off from liquor as a result of the decline in its consumption.

Comparing American prohibition with Britain's approach, he said, "We realize 100,000,000 pounds a year from our liquor taxes, which amount, I understand, you give to your bootleggers."[13]

A few other brief quotes on issues of the day were wrung from Winston, including a spirited reply about the Labour government in which he said, "I'm trying to get them out, you know." Perhaps as an appreciation of his providing him with the letter for the customs authorities, Winston commented positively on the work being done by Charles Dawes as the American ambassador to Great Britain.

One of the reporters thought Winston was "plainly bored" with the questions on world affairs and that his real concern was to find his south-bound train and get to bed. A compartment for the Churchills had been reserved on the Shasta Limited train that was to depart the city three hours after the arrival of the steamer.

As in earlier on the tour, an old comrade of Winston's came out to greet him on his arrival at Seattle. John McGill, who had lived in the city since 1910, had served with him in India and provided a thrilling account of their adventures to a newspaper. On September 16, 1897, the force of about 800 soldiers that McGill was part of was surrounded by 15,000 "wild tribesmen." The British entrenched themselves in a "Mohammeden graveyard," and Winston, a lieutenant in the 4th Hussars, galloped up to join them. Just as Winston reached them one of their men was hit. McGill and Winston lifted the wounded man onto the horse and led him to safety. Arming himself with a rifle, Winston fought with the entrenched British force for 48 hours, without food or water, until they were relieved by the Bengal Lancers.[14]

Before the party went to the train station they were driven to a local hotel by George Hubbard for the promised drinks. At the hotel they were personally entertained by the manager. Both Randolph and his father thought the iced beer they were served was excellent.[15] The chief of customs, for his part, did not have any himself. He explained to the visitors that the American government was not interested in the consumer but concentrated its enforcement efforts against the bootlegger. Randolph thought this was "rather lucky for us as the ultimate consumer is the only person in whom we are really interested."[16] Thus having a drink in the company of the Chief of Customs at Seattle was Winston's first experience with American prohibition. Possibly in case of future problems, Winston kept Hubbard's card with his papers.

At the train station the Churchills were again pursued for an interview by the pretty reporter from the pier. Winston answered her questions for about ten minutes. Randolph thought he was "rather captivated" by the young lady and, as a result, put up with it. During the interview the young lady turned to Randolph and asked him if he was going to marry an American woman. Not surprisingly, the younger Churchill was not amused. He replied that he did not intend to reveal his matrimonial plans to the press and walked away.[17]

For the trip south from Seattle to southern Oregon, where they would meet up with the British consul-general from San Francisco, the party would travel by train. On this leg they did not have a private car and had to travel, as Winston put it, "like the ordinary public."

Lacking a private rail car, as well as a steward and cook, was not too much of a hardship, and Winston noted that it was nonetheless "quite comfortable." As the night train was just pulling out of the station at Seattle at 11:45 p.m. Randolph was lying on his top berth in their compartment writing in his diary. His father, however, was unpacking and "swearing down below." At that point Randolph thought all of them were missing the comfort of the *Mount Royal*.[18]

Having thought prohibition silly from the outset, Winston's first experience with the enforcement of the law only served to confirm his opinion. While in the United States he would find it possible to continue to imbibe. Alcohol was found and consumed, but probably not at the same rate as normal at home in England or with the same ease of procurement. The ordeal of living under a prohibition regime was not as harsh as he had feared. At the end of the tour of the United States, Winston wrote that after two months of being subjected to prohibition he found the "effects upon my constitution very much less disturbing than I had expected."[19]

In his article "What I saw in America of Prohibition," Winston ridiculed it, calling it the "most amazing exhibition alike of the arrogance and of the impotence of a majority that the history of representative institutions can show." Prohibition in the United States was the inflicting of one individual's aversions onto everyone else. It had been brought about by wartime "hysteria" and electoral politics, and was prolonged by the inflexibility of the American. It was a "spectacle at once comic and pathetic."[20] Winston observed that millions of Americans who vote dry at the same time do not hesitate to consume alcoholic beverages as they wish. Americans, he said, were shocked with the growth of drunkenness and crime that occurred under prohibition, and disliked the interference of the government in their private lives so far as alcohol is concerned. Winston praised Canada for having a constitutional system that had allowed for prohibition to be repealed after their experiment with it had proved not to their liking. His remedy was to recognize both the imperfections of the citizens and respect the right of "personal liberty."[21]

While during the 1929 visit Winston found many Americans who supported prohibition, two years later when he returned for a lecture tour he could barely find anyone willing to defend it.[22] The biggest change in the United States between 1929 and 1932, Winston later observed, was in the opinion regarding prohibition.

After traveling for most of Saturday, September 7, aboard the train, the Churchills disembarked at five o'clock that afternoon at Grants Pass in southern Oregon. They left the Southern Pacific's Oregonian to meet the British consul and travel the rest of the way to San Francisco by automobile along the Redwood Highway. This plan was followed, perhaps, due to Bernard Baruch's advice that California was best seen by automobile. A local reporter observed that after Winston left the Pullman he was surrounded by his party and their "voluminous baggage." The British consul's "shiny new automobile" was waiting for them. It was driven by a chauffeur who had apparently refused to speak to the reporter and for his efforts was called an "uncommunicative driver" by Helen Reynolds, a reporter for a local newspaper.[23]

The "chauffeur" was not actually a professional driver but rather Gerald Campbell, who had been the British consul-general at San Francisco since 1922. Educated at Repton and Trinity College, Cambridge, the 55-year-old diplomat had previously been posted to Rio de Janeiro, the Belgian Congo, Venice, Addis Ababa, and Philadelphia. Campbell had already been in northern California for the past several days while assisting with the goodwill cruise of the *HMS Colombo*, then in port at Humboldt Bay. The previous day Campbell had given a talk at the lunch meeting of the Kiwanis Club at the Eureka Inn before coming up to Grants Pass to meet the distinguished visitors.[24]

As Campbell loaded the baggage on the motorcar's luggage rack, Winston "ruminated" over their next move on the trip. He was interrupted in his thoughts by the local reporter, who asked about war reparations and why the British Empire "didn't do something to the Arab Sheiks, Bedouin cutthroats and Bashi Bazouks" in Palestine. Winston declined the interview request, telling the reporter from the *Grants Pass Daily Courier*, "It is simply an outing. We came across Canada and then south, you see. I really do not know where we will stay tonight. We left the train here to go to San Francisco by automobile."[25]

Aside from the reporter, who filed a rather snippy article on their stop in the town, Winston also met, by complete coincidence, two prior acquaintances, Dr. Morton Smart and his wife Lilian, who were in the area on a fishing holiday. Dr. Smart would later be a surgeon to King George VI. The Smarts had been visiting with relatives at the Weasku Inn and came over to greet the Churchill party.[26]

With the luggage safely stowed on the motor car, Winston decided to immediately set off on the 600-mile automobile tour that would take them along the Redwood Highway and end at San Francisco. The party began by leaving Grants Pass for Crescent City that night. Over the next two days they would advance in stages of up to 250 miles and spend ten hours per day traveling. Winston thought these were long days, but was more concerned about everyone riding together in one motor car. Despite the vehicle being a large American car, Winston complained that there was not enough room and they were too cramped. Heeding the complaints, Campbell soon instructed one of the vice-consuls at San Francisco to bring up a second motor car.[27]

Despite prohibition, Campbell knew the priorities of his visitors and had procured a "meager supply of impeccable whiskey" for the automobile tour. This was duly finished before San Francisco, and he never thought of it again. However, 12 years later, during the Second World War, Campbell was summoned to Downing Street to meet Prime Minister Churchill. During the conflict Campbell served as high commissioner in Canada until 1941, director-general of the British Information Services in New York in 1941–42, and thereafter to 1945 as a minister at Washington. On the visit to Downing Street, Campbell was shown in to see Winston, and a butler was ordered to bring whisky and soda.

"I don't often do this at this time of day, but I remember the refreshment you offered me during that beautiful drive in California, and I want to return the compliment," Winston explained to his old traveling companion.[28]

For the next two nights the party stayed at two small hotels, first at the Lauff Hotel in Crescent City and then at the Van Hotel in Willits. As Winston described them, the hotels were simple and clean, with hot baths but no servants or alcohol. Even without servants, Winston assured Clementine that he had never been without what was necessary. All was eased, as Randolph was acting as an "unfailing Ganymede."[29]

Leaving Crescent City at about eight o'clock in the morning of September 8, the Churchills followed the highway that runs the length of California. As they drove south, Winston thought the road undulated and serpentined ceaselessly. Along the road were forests of fir trees that grew taller as they drove on. Only gradually did Winston realize the trees were becoming larger. On one occasion when they stopped to take stock of the forests, they were surprised by how small a car approaching around a bend 100 yards away appeared in comparison with the trees rising on either side of the road. Another hour of driving brought the party deeper into the tall trees. At that point Winston declared they were "in the heart of the Redwoods. There is no mistake about it this time."[30] Randolph noted the dimensions of the trees as about ten feet in diameter and 250 to 300 feet high, with an estimated age of anything between 1,500 years to 5,000 years.

To Winston, the road was merely an "aisle in a cathedral of trees." The huge Redwoods towered 200 feet "without leaf or twig to a tapering vault of sombre green and purple." Among the trees the daylight twinkled "through triangular and star-shaped openings." The trees were so close and dense that at one hundred yards the forest appeared to become "solid walls of timber." He found it amazing that so many trees could find the nourishment to grow and thrive in such a small area. On the ground below the trees there was "vivid green or yellow bloom and leafage." At the base of these giants, Winston thought, the "men look like ants and motor cars look like beetles."[31]

Randolph found the Redwoods as astonishing as his father. He specifically noted one tree in his diary that only had its first branch at 287 feet. He echoed his father's comparison to the great churches and wrote in his diary that the beautiful Redwoods were like the "great pillars of a cathedral."[32]

As they drove through the Redwoods, Winston was at length "declaiming to the trees." He changed subjects only long enough, possibly thinking of the recent outbreak in Palestine, to turn to the driver and say, "Campbell, has it ever occurred to you that God never blessed a nation which persecuted the Jews."[33]

Campbell remembered the quotation and recalled it to Winston during one of their meetings during the war. The then prime minister did not remember saying it but said that he had not changed his mind.

Traveling by motor car allowed Winston the opportunity to observe the seemingly constant flow of vehicles driving along the highway at speeds that rarely fell below forty miles an hour. He found that a great number of the motorists were couples in rather small cars who were traveling for fun. They thought nothing of driving thousands of miles. To serve the motorists, there were built every dozen or so miles along the road what Winston called rest camps, but he noted they were called motels in California. These motels provided plain but cheap lodging. The Californians staying in the cabins at the rest camps would enjoy themselves by singing together around the fire or by listening to the "ubiquitous wireless music."[34]

The Churchills reached Eureka in their cramped single motor car shortly before noon. They stopped for more than an hour at the town's Eureka Inn. The Inn captured Winston's interest, and he was seen closely studying the details of both the hotel's exterior and the lobby. F.W. Georgeson, publisher of the *Humboldt Standard*, met them on their arrival. Campbell had previously announced to the newspaper that Winston would be stopping in their city. Winston told the paper that he had trouble finding the words to express his impression of the Redwoods, but did say that the drive was "wholly delightful" and Eureka was a "pleasant city."[35] He proclaimed that he was enjoying this portion of his trip through the Redwood Empire more than any other part of his tour of the Pacific coast.

In Eureka the Churchills met Captain Claude C. Dobson, VC, DSO, the captain of the *HMS Colombo*. Dobson had received the Victoria Cross for leading a flotilla of coastal motor boats in the spectacular raid on Kronstadt on August 18, 1919, in which two Bolshevik battleships and one destroyer were sunk.[36] He had taken command of the *HMS Colombo*, a Royal Navy cruiser, in October 1927. The ship, with its crew of 394 men, was 450 feet in length and sported 6-inch guns, torpedo tubes, and anti-aircraft armaments. It had left Bermuda in January 1929 for a cruise of the Pacific coast and spent much of the summer in the waters off British Columbia. The *Colombo* had arrived in harbor at Humboldt Bay for a courtesy call on September 4. From there, scheduled to depart on September 10, the cruiser was to sail to Catalina Island.[37]

At Eureka the crowding problem aboard the one motor car was resolved. The vice-consul at San Francisco, Martin Watson, met them there with a second automobile. Watson was a young Oxford graduate from the same house, Christ Church, as Randolph and had joined the General Consular Service in 1928. San Francisco was his first assignment.[38] Watson drove up to Eureka with an open car he had managed to borrow. For the rest of the journey Campbell, Jack, and Johnny would travel in the one automobile, with Winston, Randolph, and Watson in the other. The next two days found Winston sitting alongside Watson, with Randolph in the rumble seat.

During the drive through the Redwood forests the party stopped at a restaurant which the owner claimed had the largest fireplace in the world. Randolph, Jack, and Johnny were prepared to accept the claim, as they had just seen that the Redwoods were the largest trees in the world. The fireplace was described by Johnny as "one of those monster Jacobean fireplaces with niches in which one could sit right close to the blaze."

"That is very interesting. But how do you know it is the world's largest fireplace?" Winston asked as he reflected on the claim.

"Well, many people come here, and so far no one has said that it isn't," the owner replied.

Johnny thought this explanation appeared to be satisfactory to his uncle.[39]

Now traveling in two motor cars, the party left Eureka and continued down the Redwood Highway. They drove for another twenty miles until they reached a "finger-point" sign for "The Big Tree." This tree at Bull Creek Flat was the largest tree in the state of California. Turning off the well-maintained highway, they drove for eight miles along a sandy track through a forest of huge Redwoods.[40] They jolted and bumped along in the motor cars until they reached Bull Creek Flat, where the party had lunch. They had driven 120 miles thus far that day. Discreetly left out of Winston's article on the visit to Bull Creek Flat but recorded in Randolph's diary, was the fact that after lunch the party bathed "au naturel" in the stream. Randolph described the water as wonderfully warm.[41]

The Churchills then inspected the "Big Tree." To reach the tree they gingerly walked across a fallen Redwood that formed a bridge over a river bed. The tree, in Winston's estimation, was about 380 to 400 feet high. At the Big Tree the party met several petty officers from the *HMS Colombo*, including G.D. Bear, P. Hammond, W.G. Massingham, and G. Goldthorpe. The naval officers were being entertained and shown around the district by a group of "hospitable Californians" composed of John W. Crockett, Frank Smith, Abraham L. Fraser, and Judge J.T. Fraser. With the naval officers and the locals, the Churchill party undertook the practice of joining hands to form a ring around the base of the giant tree. It took fifteen of them to reach around the tree that Randolph thought must have been 20 feet thick. This was even though they pressed themselves against the tree as they stretched out their arms to link together.[42]

From one of the men guiding the petty officers, Winston learned that the Big Tree was at least 4,000 years old. It had been growing the entire time and was still healthy and vital. Fires that periodically swept through the forests would burn the smaller trees and undergrowth but could not damage the great Redwoods. These trees could withstand nearly everything and recover. Winston wrote in his *Daily Telegraph* article devoted to California's natural beauty that the trees were already old "when the smoke of sacrifice arose from the Pantheon and camelopards bounded in the Flavian amphitheatre."[43] He thought these trees may well survive, save for the efforts of the timber companies, till Macaulay's traveler from New Zealand stands "upon a broken arch of London Bridge to sketch the ruins of St. Paul's." The Redwoods would grow, Winston concluded, as long as people allowed them to.[44]

All of the men at the tree were in good spirits and enjoying the occasion. After the group finished encircling the tree, there was chatting and picture taking. The photographs were taken by one of the Californians, Abraham Fraser. Winston specially requested that copies of the pictures be sent to him in care of the British consulate at San Francisco. The *Humboldt Standard* reported that of the entire group gathered in the forest grove, Winston was the "most active and full of life, nothing escaping his eye. He was high in his admiration for the whole country and in appreciation for the kindness shown him here."[45] After the visit to Bull Creek Flat, and having spent the greater part of the day in Humboldt County, the party drove on to Willits where they would spend the night at the Van Hotel.

The last day of their automobile tour of Northern California began with the Churchills departing their hotel about ten o'clock in the morning. Winston would later write that the road in California reminded him of the "Corniche roads in character and beauty of scenery." The roads in California were, however, much more crowded. The highway twisted and turned as it followed the coastline, with its mountains that were over a thousand feet high. He commented that with the "traffic, the precipices, the turns, the ups and downs, and the high speeds, the journey is not dull, and the scenery is splendid."[46]

From Eureka onwards Winston had noticed the first palms in the landscape, and as they drove on, the vegetation changed. The Redwoods were replaced by different types of trees, including oaks and other English-looking ones, and they drove past trout streams and rivers. With the summer, many of these bodies of water had been much reduced, with some mere small pools.[47]

After 100 miles of driving, aspects of the landscape became "Italian" in nature, as they had reached the "land of grapes." At the winery and country home of George de Latour at Beaulieu near Rutherford, California, the party stopped for lunch that afternoon. The party was the guests of De Latour and his wife. De Latour was a grand elderly Frenchman who was licensed to make wine by the government for sacramental purposes. Over a million gallons were stored in his factory. This, Winston pronounced, was a "goodly sight to see in this dry land."[48] They were joined at the excellent lunch, which included some of the sacramental wine, by their host's daughter and son-in-law, the Count and Countess Galcerand de Pins as well as the Count and Countess Francis de Pins, of France. Randolph made particular praise of both the wine and De Latour's very nice daughter, who had married a French count. The sacramental wine was a "sort of white wine" which was judged very good, while the 1825 brandy that was also served was considered similarly good. In the garden at the winery were "exquisite" butterflies and hummingbirds. Randolph also remembered that De Latour summed up California as "Fleurs sans odeur, femmes sans pudeur et hommes sans honneur," which translated as flowers without smell, women without modesty, and men without honor.[49]

A tour of De Latour's operation and store of wine followed the lunch. Winston wrote that it was an "immense wine factory," with the Californian wines stored in huge vats and barrels. From its stock of over a million gallons, the winery sold 200,000 each year. Their host told the Churchills that he was only permitted to sell his sacramental wine to priests, but they passed it along to their friends. Thus Randolph quipped in his diary that "Christ has come to the aid of Bacchus in a most wonderful way."[50] Another practice employed by De Latour to keep within the laws governing prohibition was to sell unfermented grape juice to individuals and then send along men later to ferment it.

Winston found these loopholes in the enforcement of prohibition to be silly and ridiculed them in a newspaper article. He wrote, "Fermented! Certainly! Do not be alarmed, dear Miss Anna, it is 'for sacramental purposes only.' The Constitution of the United States, the God of Israel, and the Pope—an august combination—protect, with the triple sanctions of Washington, Jerusalem and Rome, this inspiring scene."[51]

Proclaiming that he did not want to be "tantalized" too greatly by the winery, the Churchills soon departed southward. Fifty miles down the road they stopped again at an attractive inn whose advertising sign promised "Good Eats and Soft Drinks." On the inn's verandahs and porticos the party partook of the refreshments. Winston was served a glass of "near beer," which he thought was very good. This beverage was prepared by brewing old-world beer until all of the alcohol in excess of one percent was eliminated. The residue that remained when iced became an agreeable drink that was similar in appearance and taste to the real thing. Winston later gleefully informed his newspaper readers that distressing accidents sometimes happen in the brewing of the product. On one occasion the beverage was accidently released prematurely to "spread its maddening poison through countless happy homes." He added that safeguards were in place to prevent this from happening.[52]

By the time the Churchills had reached the restaurant, with its promise of "Good Eats and Soft Drinks," they had probably become acquainted with another American custom relating to beverages, in addition to prohibition. This was what Winston described as the universal American habit of drinking a huge amount of water. Any time, he found, you order in a cafeteria, drugstore, or anywhere else, the man behind the counter immediately sets a glass of iced water before you, as apparently it was "indispensable." Winston thought it "dangerous" to drink such quantities of this "bleak beverage," and that water was "surely a somewhat austere welcome for a hungry man."[53] The coffee in America was, however, considered commendable.

From his experience with American food on his trips to the United States, Winston would subsequently write that Americans of every class ate lighter foods than in England. He found that fruit, vegetables, and cereals played a larger part in the American diet, and that Americans ate more chicken than meat. Winston, for his part, declared himself a "beef-eater" who regularly had meat as part of his meals every day at home. One practice Winston also did not like was being given a slice of melon or grapefruit at the start of the midday and evening meals. Dessert should be eaten at the end of the meal, not the start.[54]

Winston was also bemused by the American drug store. First he could not understand why it was called a drug store, and then he observed that everything in that type of store was sold in small packages. It reminded him of cafes at French seaside resorts which also "gave a little for a lot."[55]

… 13 …

# San Francisco to San Simeon, September 9–16

On the evening of September 9 the Churchill party arrived in San Francisco. Winston had been dozing during the final leg of the drive and awoke to find himself on the ocean.[1] On either side of the automobile he could see only water. He had awoken while Watson was driving the motor car over the newly opened San Francisco Bay Toll Bridge. The bridge, Winston observed, was just feet above the waterline and illuminated its entire distance, while near its center were moveable spans to allow ships to pass through. Stretching 7.1 miles from Hayward on the mainland to San Mateo on the San Francisco peninsula, it was the longest highway bridge in the world. The bridge was just 27 feet from curb to curb, with a four-and-a-half-foot-high reinforced railing on either side. It had opened to traffic on March 2, 1929, having cost $7,500,000 to build.[2] Winston was enthralled by the bridge, calling it a "remarkable piece of engineering." Spending so much on building a bridge so that traffic, mostly pleasure traffic, could avoid lengthy detours or the delays involved in taking the ferry was, to him, further proof of the "wealth and enterprise of California."

The two motor cars had first driven to Berkeley, intending to call upon one of their local hosts, President W.W. Campbell of the University of California. Campbell was not home, being at the observatory on Mount Wilson when they called, so they continued via the San Francisco Bay Toll Bridge to the Burlingame home of William H. Crocker. Burlingame, which was about twenty miles south of San Francisco, was called a "rich man's suburb" by Winston.[3] Indeed, a travel guide called the area a "series of individual little mountains covered with great green oaks, a community of millionaires, where noble mansions stand within wild, parked estates."[4] As arranged by Bernard Baruch, Crocker would host the party as house guests for the duration of the San Francisco visit.

The 68-year-old Crocker was a very prominent San Francisco banker who had been called the "First Citizen of California." Inheriting a fortune made by his father in railways, he had been president of the Crocker First National Bank since 1893. His other businesses included the Crocker Securities Company, the Crocker Investment Company, and the Crocker Estate Company, while his directorships included such important companies as

Pacific Telephone and Telegraph, Pacific Gas and Electric, Mutual Life Insurance, and Metropolitan Life Insurance. Crocker had been prominent in rebuilding San Francisco after the earthquake and fire, and had been associated with the staging of the 1915 Panama-Pacific International Exposition in the city. Ethel Crocker had been married to William Crocker since 1886. A noted philanthropist, she had worked for the California Committee for Relief in Belgium during the war. Both of the Crockers were close friends of President Hoover and, indeed, there had been speculation William Crocker would be offered a position in the administration or an ambassadorship. Crocker, however, had not been interested in leaving California.[5]

Crocker and his wife lived at New Place in Burlingame. The residence had been designed by Lewis P. Hobart and been inspired by the Villa Clementine at Caen. At New Place, Crocker had a great collection of Chinese art, as well as famous paintings by Rousseau, Monet, and Millet. The surrounding estate was 700 acres and had woods, streams, an attractive lake, and gardens.[6] Winston thought New Place had a very pretty house and garden, as well as a fine swimming pool.[7] The Crockers were experienced at entertaining visiting British statesman as the previous year they had hosted Austen Chamberlain, then foreign secretary in Baldwin's cabinet, on his visit to San Francisco.

On their arrival at the Crocker mansion, the Churchills were warmly welcomed and entertained by their hosts quite informally at a dinner. There were only a few guests at the dinner, with the Crockers' daughter and son-in-law, a stock broker, and a few Hillsborough friends of the hosts in attendance. At the party Winston made friends with William Van Antwerp and his wife Edith, who had their own house in the suburb. The 61-year-old Van Antwerp had served in the navy in the Spanish-American War and in the Navy Intelligence Department during the Great War. After pursuing a career in the newspaper business as a publisher and editor, he became a stock broker in 1900. In 1912 Van Antwerp wrote *The Stock Exchange Within* and was hailed by many as a leading financier. In 1923 he became the local manager of E.F. Hutton in San Francisco and four years later was elevated to the resident partner.[8]

Winston found Van Antwerp to be a rather old-fashioned individual who was very pro-British and had read all his books. As Van Antwerp was an author and bibliophile, their conversation inevitably turned to books, with the stock broker recommending a book that came out of the experience of trench warfare. Van Antwerp had a copy of the book delivered to Winston at Burlingame the next morning. Winston and Van Antwerp also discussed the party's travel plans in California. Although the plans were still fluid, Van Antwerp offered to take on arranging for the party to visit Yosemite. He volunteered a motorcar, private rail car, or an airplane for use for the visit to the park, as Winston preferred. The two men also probably discussed investments, since by the time the party left California, Winston had taken up Van Antwerp's offer to arrange the visit to Yosemite as well as opened an account with the brokerage office. He thought that E.F. Hutton was the most well-informed financial institution about the stock market and that Van Antwerp would look after his money and manage it for the best chance of success. Winston was sure it would prove to be a smart decision.[9]

Winston was struck with the quality of men he met in the United States. During his trip across the country, and most especially later in the trip to New York, Winston met with many of the country's leading financiers, bankers, and industrialists. He was impressed with them as a group. In the United States, Winston observed, industry attracts the best men.

The young graduates from the universities go into business both to make money but also to play a part in the affairs of the country. The "prizes of American life are to be gained in business."[10]

At the dinner party at New Place, Winston was probably exposed to the American practice of a "repast" before the meal. After his travels in the United States, he would write how in that country the "guests arrive any time within half an hour of the nominal dinner hour, and stand about conversing, smoking cigarettes, and drinking cocktails." With prohibition, these cocktails could be of tomato juice, which Winston thought "admirable," or of liquor. Prohibition did not forbid Americans from drinking alcohol in their private homes from stocks they had already possessed before the restrictions came into effect. Winston was not a "devotee" of the cocktail, but concluded, "I must admit that this preliminary festival while the guests are arriving is most agreeable. The cocktails are supported by all sorts of dainty, tasty little dishes continually handed round upon trays or displayed upon tables."[11]

After traveling down the Pacific coast aboard a train and in a pair of motorcars, Winston was pleased to reach the comforts of Burlingame. Being responsible for their own packing for the previous few days, their clothes had become quite disordered. However, the good English footman in the employ of the Crockers set things right again. At Burlingame their clothes were properly washed and tidied.

The first full day in San Francisco, September 10, was spent mostly at leisure, relaxing on the Crocker estate. Randolph did not get up until eleven o'clock in the morning and then roamed around the garden. He thought it was beautiful and huge.[12] Randolph also thought the flowers in the garden disproved De Latour's claim from the previous day that California flowers were without odor. After enjoying the garden, Randolph went for a swim in the luxurious swimming pool on the grounds of the estate. This was the first swimming pool the Churchills encountered in the United States. Johnny, the most expert swimmer in the party, wrote in his memoirs of being taken aback by the number of swimming pools in the country, with even the smallest towns possessing one. The abundance of swimming pools, to Johnny's thinking, resulted in Americans being first-class swimmers. Probably referring to some of the men they met in California, he wrote that "when one meets a stock broker ... or any other type of sedentary-looking executive, he invariably turns out to be an expert diver."[13]

Lunch that day was just the four Churchills and the Crockers' daughter. This was either Ethel Mary, who had become Countess de Limur upon her marriage, or the Crockers' other daughter, the 32-year-old Helen. Randolph thought the daughter in question was a very charming woman. This was even though she talked in a well-informed fashion about stocks and shares, which Randolph confided in his diary that he did not find "very attractive" in a woman. During the lunch the Englishmen learned that the stock exchange in San Francisco opens at six o'clock in the morning in order to be in concert with New York. This early hour was pronounced "not my line at all" by Randolph. Winston likewise found the Crockers' daughter, and son-in-law as well, to be delightful. The couple made the travelers feel as if they would have liked them to stay much longer.[14]

While his son relaxed, Winston worked on his correspondence that had built up during the last few days of the tour. With Baker of the CPR returned to Montreal, Winston was without a private secretary of his own as his worked on his letters and papers. It is possible that Crocker loaned him one of his staff to assist him with his dictating. Beyond letters and cables home to England, and making arrangements for the rest of the tour, including a cable to McAdoo confirming their visit to Santa Barbara, Winston's attention again turned to his planned mammoth biography of the Duke of Marlborough. He prepared and sent off letters about the project to Rear-Admiral Dewar, Brigadier-General Sir James Edmonds, and Maurice Ashley.[15]

While in San Francisco, Winston telegraphed the 1,500-word article he had written on the recent crisis in Palestine to the *Sunday Times*. In the piece he repeated the same argument and even some of the same phrases he had used in his speech in Vancouver, condemning the murder of defenseless people, predicting such violence on a larger scale if the British withdrew from Egypt or India, and seeing no reason why the build-up of a Jewish national home in Palestine should be incompatible with the rights and claims of the Arabs. The article was published in the newspaper on September 22 and was later reprinted in the *Zionist Record*. For his literary effort Winston was paid 300 pounds.[16]

Other correspondence he sent from San Francisco included a letter to Clementine in which he said a full account of their travels would "take almost a volume." One message that was not sent was one of birthday wishes to his daughter Mary. Clementine had written Winston reminding him of Mary's birthday on September 15 and suggesting he send a cable to their daughter by September 12 to ensure it arrived in time. An orange cable envelope on her breakfast plate on her birthday, Clementine suggested, would be a source of immense pleasure.[17] The reminder reached Winston only in Santa Barbara, and without it, he was late with Mary's telegram.

In San Francisco Winston received an offer from Cyril Clemens, president of the Mark Twain Society, of an honorary vice-presidency in the society. Other honorary vice-presidents at the time included Prime Minister MacDonald and Chief Justice of the U.S. Supreme Court William Howard Taft, while the honorary president was the Italian leader Benito Mussolini. Winston met Mark Twain during his lecture tour to the United States in 1900–01. Twain, indeed, had introduced him at his December 12 lecture at the Waldorf-Astoria in New York, calling him a "blend of America and England which makes a perfect match."[18] Winston accepted the offer of the honorary office in the society in a letter dated September 12.

It had been planned for the Crockers to take the party on a motor tour of San Francisco on the afternoon of September 10, but the venture was cancelled, as Winston was too busy catching up on his private affairs. With his brother working, and the younger two Churchills roaming and playing on the estate, Jack spent some time shopping in San Francisco.[19]

That night Winston and the other members of the party were the guests of honor at a dinner given for them by Crocker at the Pacific Union Club, located in a "commodious brownstone mansion" at California and Manson streets in the Nob Hill district of the city. Membership in the club was restricted to just 100 members. It was one of San Francisco's most exclusive clubs, with its members composed of only the most wealthy and influential figures. In attendance at the private affair were the "important personages of city and state."[20]

After the dinner Winston and Jack returned to the Crocker mansion, but Randolph and Johnny had a much later night. It is likely the two younger members of the troupe did not attend the dinner at the Pacific Union Club. Either instead of or after the affair at Crocker's club, Randolph and Johnny that evening went to a dinner-dance party given by one Patsy Tobin at a big hotel in San Francisco. The party revealed that prohibition was a charade, in Randolph's opinion. They had cocktails in a private room upstairs at the hotel and then dined in the ballroom. Champagne—"plenty of it and very good"—was served in large silver canisters. Randolph reported that during the party he met a young married woman named Anita, who he thought was most striking. He made plans to go riding with her at nine o'clock the next morning. It was three o'clock in the morning before Randolph had reached the Crocker estate, wrote his diary entry, and finally went to sleep. Anita, alas, did not appear for the horse-riding date the next morning. Perhaps embellishing the story later in life, Randolph was said to have instead received a telegram from Anita inviting him to dinner at her house that evening. Arriving at the appointed hour of six o'clock he was surprised to find a hundred people present for a cocktail party, including Anita's husband.[21] As the Churchills' last night in San Francisco was spent at the Lick Observatory, the story of Anita's cocktail party was probably just a good anecdote.

Even without the mysterious Anita and her cocktail party, the Churchills' second day in San Francisco was a busy one. Among the day's activities was a visit to Seal Rocks. This sightseeing locale was one that Winston was most eager to see. He had written Crocker when first making arrangements for the visit to San Francisco of his interest in seeing the seals disport on Seal Rock. In advance of the party's arrival in the city, Crocker had told the press of Winston's wish to see the seals. The *San Francisco Examiner* reported that a friend of Winston, no doubt Crocker, said, "Of all the things he had read about San Francisco, Seal Rocks had clung most tenaciously to his imagination. It was the first thing he asked about."[22]

Despite the build-up, the visit to see Seal Rocks was a disappointment. The rocks were located at the north end of seven-mile-long Ocean Beach in San Francisco. Winston wrote that a special journey was made to see the renowned sea lions on the bay, but there were none to be seen. In place of the sea lions basking on the rocks, all that could be seen were some large and uninteresting birds. When Winston asked a bystander when the sea lions would make their appearance, the man replied in Italian. The reply was taken by the Englishman to mean eventually.[23]

A trip to one of the tallest building in San Francisco, the 26-storey Pacific Telephone and Telegraph Company building, was also included in the day's activities. Located on New Montgomery Street between Minna and Natoma streets, the building measured 453 feet tall from the sidewalk and had 280,000 square feet of space. The party went to the roof of the building to take in the view of the city and have photographs taken. Winston was impressed with the size of the gigantic building. He later wrote that the city (which he pointed out had been destroyed by the fire, not the earthquake) had risen "in quadrupled magnificence." The huge "forty-storey buildings tower above the lofty hog-backed promontory on which it is built." Although subject to frequent mists that blocked out the sunshine, the climate was nice and cool most of the year. Winston, however, overestimated the height of San Francisco's buildings at the time, as in 1929 the tallest one was only 31 floors.[24]

The chairman of Pacific Telephone and Telegraph, Horace Davis Pillsbury, escorted the traveling party on the visit to the building and invited Winston to telephone Clementine in England for a ten-minute conversation. Winston jumped at the opportunity to speak to his wife from the western coast of the United States. Despite the distance, he thought he could hear her about half as well as an ordinary London telephone conversation. After Winston spoke with Clementine, the children came to the telephone to talk to their father. As he spoke to his family he declared he could imagine them all collected around the telephone in the pantry. He was delighted to hear Clementine's voice and wished he could "have leaned forward and kissed your dear lips." Speaking so happily and clearly with his family in Kent from a distance of 7,000 miles caused Winston to ask in a *Daily Telegraph* article, "Why say the age of miracles is past?"[25]

Winston was quite grateful to Horace Pillsbury for sending him the photographs taken on the roof of the building and for the opportunity to have a telephone conversation with his wife and children after more than a month away from home. A week after the visit to San Francisco Winston wrote to Pillsbury that the party, after so long away, was "thrilled and cheered by the wonderful experience of talking to our family across the enormous distance of land and sea."[26] He added that Clementine, for her part, was quite overjoyed by the opportunity that Pillsbury provided them. As a souvenir of their visit to the building, Winston included with the letter to Pillsbury a copy of his latest volume of the *World Crisis*.

Consul-General Gerald Campbell hosted a luncheon in Winston's honor that day at the Bohemian Club, located at Post and Taylor streets. The Bohemian Club was open to those who had fashioned an achievement in art, science, and letters. Founded in 1872, it had 850 members. The club was "known everywhere as one of the truly great clubs of the world."[27] Among the one hundred guests were the long-serving mayor of San Francisco and future governor of California James Rolph, as well as the former United States senator from California James D. Phelan. Also at the luncheon was Winston's new friend from his first night in San Francisco, William Van Antwerp. Winston was very pleased with the dinner at the club and later wrote Crocker, who was a member and greatly devoted to the Bohemian Club, that he was impressed with the friendliness of the distinguished men he had met.[28]

At the luncheon a San Franciscan asked Winston whether he had difficulty sleeping during the "anxious days" of 1914.

"Difficult? Sleep? On, no. I just put my head on the pillow, said, 'Damn everybody,' and went off!" Winston replied.[29]

At this luncheon—the first official, or at least semi-official, function the Churchills attended in the United States—the problem of prohibition posed its difficulties in terms of refreshments. At such affairs it was impossible to organize wine with the meals. As Johnny described it, his father and uncle were normal men who liked the "simple habit of drinking to quench their thirst and supplement the enjoyment of food." Furthermore, they were not prepared to change their habits to suit prohibition. It was an even greater problem for Winston, who was usually called upon at these affairs for a few light after-dinner remarks. The statesman always contended that it was impossible to make a speech on iced water. A scheme was soon organized to supply each of the elder Churchills with something worthy of drinking at these functions. Randolph and Johnny, the latter of whom thought prohibition was a "lunatic experiment," carried hidden in their inside jacket pockets a "long thin metal flask of best brandy." The "innocent" looking youths would quickly drink their own coffee when it was served and then pour their respective father's coffee into their own cup. They would then refill Winston and Jack's cups from the flasks. All of this Johnny thought was "tricky business," as it also involved diverting the attention of the people sitting near them with conversation.[30]

After the luncheon Winston granted the *San Francisco Examiner* his first interview since arriving in the city. Previous interview requests had been denied, which had led the *Examiner* to complain that Winston was enjoying sightseeing and "dodging formal contacts," by which they meant interviews with the press.[31] Winston possibly chose to be interviewed by the *Examiner* because the paper belonged to William Randolph Hearst, who he would shortly visit at San Simeon.

Unlike in Canada, where he had granted most such requests, in the United States Winston would be much more grudging with the newspapers. As the Canadian leg of the tour had been an almost public trip, with speaking events, Winston had perhaps felt that he had to allow the interview requests. With the United States leg of the tour to be an entirely private visit, with no speaking events open to the general public, he perhaps felt no such obligation.

"Mr. Churchill wishes to see California first. He is keenly interested in California, of course, and desirous of meeting and talking with leaders of the state," Consul-General Campbell told the *San Francisco Chronicle* as he explained that Winston did not wish to be interviewed.[32]

In his two-hour-long chat with the *Examiner*'s reporter, Winston commented on, among other topics, the Labour government, Palestine, and prohibition. On the last topic he remarked that the voters in Britain would angrily throw out "quick as a wink" any government that attempted to impose it on his country.[33] Instead, Britain was solving its liquor problem with higher taxation and restricting hours during which drink could be obtained.

The Lick Observatory. A highlight of the trip for Winston Churchill was the evening spent watching the skies at the observatory (Library of Congress).

The *Examiner*'s representative concluded that Winston reflected a "feeling that the quandaries of the world, given time, can be reasonably coped with."

The party's trip that evening to the Lick Observatory was one of the highlights of the entire tour for Winston. He was awed by what he saw. So much so that he described it in detail in a letter to Clementine and devoted considerable space to the visit in one of his *Daily Telegraph* articles on California. The observatory was 26 miles east of San Jose and located on the 4,200-foot Mount Hamilton, part of the Diablo Mountain Range that formed the eastern boundary of the Santa Clara Valley.[34]

The visit to the Lick Observatory had been originally scheduled for the afternoon of September 11, but with the other activities had to be pushed back until the evening. After the luncheon at the Bohemian Club, the Churchills motored to the observatory. It was a journey of sixty miles to the observatory, which was a "broad, squat cupola." Their guide at the observatory was W.W. Campbell, a world renowned astronomer and director of the Lick Observatory, as well as president of the University of California. He had decided to become an astronomer after reading Newcomb's *Popular Astronomy*. First coming to the Lick Observatory as an unpaid volunteer in the summer of 1890, Campbell eventually became its director. He pioneered the use of the spectrograph to measure the speed of stars and discovered that most stars seen by the naked eye are not single stars but actually twin constellations. For his discoveries Campbell had been awarded medals by the Paris Academy of Sciences, the Royal Astronomical Society in London, and the National Academy of Sciences in Washington. Appointed president of the University of California in 1923, he officially remained the director of the observatory. By the time of the Churchills' visit, Campbell was nearing the end of his career. The following year he would retire from the university presidency and the Lick's directorship with failing health. Campbell's health would continue to decline to such an extent that on June 14, 1938, at the age of 76, apparently motivated by approaching blindness and aphasia, he would commit suicide by leaping to his death from the fourth floor window of his apartment.[35]

The Churchills were also accompanied on the visit by their San Francisco host William Crocker, who had probably arranged the visit to the observatory after the American diplomat Richard Tobin, one of Winston's many contacts, made the initial suggestion. Crocker was a friend of Campbell's and an enthusiastic supporter of the observatory. By 1929 he had financially backed ten solar eclipse expeditions that had been led by Campbell all over the globe, including to Spain, Sumatra, Egypt, Russia, and Labrador. Crocker and his wife had even gone on the expeditions to Washington in 1918 and Australia in 1922.[36]

Arriving at the observatory, the party dined with Campbell, associate director of the observatory Robert G. Aitken, and other members of the Lick senior staff. They might have dined at the director's house on Mount Hamilton, which was still occupied by Campbell, even though as university president he was unable to be in day-to-day charge of the observatory.

After the dinner the party went to the dome where the telescope was mounted and peered through a slit at the rapidly dimming sky. This telescope, Winston thought, was in some ways the best in the world. Everything in the great dome, from the roof, walls, floor, telescope, and dome itself, moved "silently and mysteriously on touching a button."[37] Winston was thrilled by the technology on display. He was always interested in science and would have his imagination fired by scientific developments such as the aircraft and tank. With his close friend Frederick Lindemann as his scientific advisor, Winston would pay close attention to the possibilities of science during the Second World War.

Conditions were excellent for viewing the heavens that night. It was a pleasant evening with a good atmosphere, which allowed use of the high magnifying power at the 36-inch refractor. Under Campbell's skilled direction, Winston and the others used the telescope to view the planets and stars. Assisting Campbell during the visit was Aitken and two other astronomers, William H. Wright and Joseph H. Moore. First the party was shown Saturn. To the "naked eye," Winston thought it looked like any other star, but when sitting on the ladder with his eye to the eye-piece of the telescope in the darkened observatory an object of "sublime beauty was disclosed." It astounded him. He had, of course, heard of the rings of Saturn but had "no conception of the perfectness and splendor of this orb." It was so wonderful that at first Winston thought he was seeing the reflection of the electric lights in the hall that someone had forgotten to turn off. He did not realize it was actually a "world 800,000,000 miles away." Winston was about to turn away from the telescope and ask for the light to be extinguished when he realized he was actually looking at Saturn. A picture postcard of Saturn was obtained for Clementine, but he thought it could in no way do justice to the glowing picture he had seen.[38]

Next Campbell and his team showed the visitors the moon, which was then in its first quarter. Winston was thrilled again. He wrote that the moon was extremely bright, and after a few minutes of looking at it he was almost rendered blind for a brief period. It was nearly dawn on the moon, and "all her great mountain tops were bathed in the light while deep violet shadows spread through the craters and valleys." Even though it was nearly a quarter million miles distant, it seemed like he could reach out and touch it. The powerful telescope, in fact, brought the moon "to within 800 miles of our eyes."[39]

The party stayed until very late at the observatory looking at the star cluster of Hercules, as well as "wonderful double stars which revolved around each other in pairs and look like the most brilliant diamonds you ever saw." As the dome rotated and the floor rose and fell, Winston was directed to look at the stars with just his eye and then look again through the telescope. Through the machine he saw the most incredible and beautiful stars.[40]

"You are looking at one of our best multiple stars. That faint speck you saw with the eye consists of these double twins, the stars in each pair revolving around the other pair!" Campbell explained to Winston.

In a letter to his wife recounting his visit, Winston supposed that he could write reams and reams about what he had seen, heard, and learned at the observatory, including the likelihood of there being "several million universes, each consisting of hundreds of millions of suns equipped with planets which again are attended by moons." He was distressed at the thought that these universes had not been brought to his attention before and hoped that "nothing had gone wrong with them."

As he was departing after spending several hours at the observatory gazing at the skies, Winston called himself "delighted" with the experience. It had been his cherished ambition for a long time to observe the heavens through the Lick's telescope. More philosophically, Winston told Clementine that "after contemplating the heavens for some hours one wonders why one worries about the Epping Division."[41]

It was quite late by the time the Churchills reached Burlingame. The morning newspaper, which was printed and published the evening before, was already available. Winston confessed to feeling relieved to read about the stock market and developments in British politics again after having spent the past hours considering the universes, suns, moons, comets, and meteoric streams, and the incomprehensible distances involved.

The Churchill party departed the Crocker estate on the afternoon of Thursday, September 12, bound by motorcar for Pebble Beach. In September 1930 the Crockers visited England and renewed their acquaintance with Austen Chamberlain and, most likely, Winston. The latter was always happy to return the hospitality of his American hosts.[42]

A few days after they left San Francisco, Jack took care to tidy up the financial end of the visit and sent Consul-General Gerald Campbell 16 dollars for expenses. Campbell used the funds to pay the luggage bills and applied the balance to the costs of forwarding telegrams on to the Churchills. Likewise, on learning a week out from San Francisco that his telephone bill had not been fully paid, Winston took pains to send $1 to make sure all expenses had been covered.

Another outstanding issue that was followed on Winston's behalf by Gerald Campbell was the fate of another Englishman. Campbell investigated and reported back to Winston on the situation of one Frederick W. Wilson, who had claimed a previous acquaintance with the statesman. The consul-general reported that Wilson had been jailed for presenting checks with insufficient funds.

The party was joined for the 125-mile journey to Pebble Beach by Edith Van Antwerp. At Pebble Beach they stayed at the magnificent villa that had been put at their disposal by Celia Tobin Clark, who was the sister of Tobin, the American minister to The Hague. This house was a seaside villa in an Italian style with a long loggia running along the length of the bay side of the structure. It had been designed by the renowned architect Arthur Brown, Jr. Brown had also designed Danvers House, the Van Antwerp's Burlingame house. The Van Antwerp's home was considered one of the finest Tudor houses in the United States. Van Antwerp, Clark, and Brown were all Burlingame neighbors. Edith Van Antwerp traveled with the English tourists to open up the house and stayed on to act as host and keep them company. Winston found her to be a most pleasant host, and they had a nice evening at the villa. While in Pebble Beach Winston was inspired enough by the beautiful scenery to take the time to paint a landscape of the view.[43]

On September 13, Winston wrote to Van Antwerp, returning another book which his new friend had sent to him and he had now finished reading. Winston recommended two books, *War Birds: Diary of an Unknown Aviator* and a German book titled *War*, for his friend to read. He also wrote that he had asked his book dealer to forward a copy of *Way of Revelation: A Novel of Five Years*, by Wilfrid Ewart, to Van Antwerp. Edith Van Antwerp would write Winston the next month that she was reading the book and quite enjoying it.

At Pebble Beach Winston was photographed wearing a cowboy hat, probably the one he received in Calgary. This picture ran in several newspapers in North America and back in Britain. The *Daily Express* had a great deal of fun with the photograph. Under the headline "Mr. Churchill's New Hat," the newspaper reported that Winston was wearing a "mighty sombrero, a rakish, dare-devil hat, which gives him the appearance of 'Two Gun Winston.'"[44]

Like elsewhere on the tour, Winston would have liked to have spent several days at Pebble Beach, but bound by their schedule they stayed only one night. On September 13 they pressed on and reached San Simeon, the villa of William Randolph Hearst, that evening. As they drove south, Winston had noticed a change in the terrain from that of northern California. South of San Francisco the country became "more like North Africa and the houses quite Moorish. The soil was sandier and the water, save for drinking of which there was plenty, more scarce."[45]

San Simeon was the legendary castle of William Randolph Hearst, who refused to call it a castle and always referred to it as the "ranch." The ranch encompassed 265,000 acres and had more than 50 miles of ocean front. The main house, La Casa Grande, sat atop a 2,000-foot-high mountain three miles from the Pacific Ocean. Hearst's mistress, the actor Marion Davies, thought San Simeon was an "awesome thing." She had seen Versailles and other palaces of Europe, but thought they could not compare with the Hearst Castle and the beauty of San Simeon, with its views of the mountains and ocean.[46]

At the time of Winston's visit to the United States in 1929, William Randolph Hearst was a mighty behemoth who dominated American journalism. His life would be immortalized on film in the 1941 movie *Citizen Kane* by Orson Welles. Beginning with the acquisition of the *San Francisco Examiner* in 1887, Hearst built a great newspaper empire. The Hearst newspapers were both notorious and successful with their "sensational" reporting and "lurid stories of violence, sex, and scandal of all kind."[47] Hearst dictated the editorial position of his newspapers and ensured that on the issues one line was followed in news coverage, editorials, and cartoons. He even wrote his own signed editorials, which ran in all of his newspapers.

William Randolph Hearst, newspaper magnate and the Churchills' host in California (Library of Congress).

William Randolph Hearst was an Anglophobe. While he disliked Europeans in general, he was monumentally and violently anti–British. In his editorials Hearst "poured scorn on the British, consistently belittling them and their rulers." With his newspapers reflecting his opinion, Hearst had been pro–German and opposed to America entering the Great War. Relenting after the United States joined the conflict, Hearst had immediately after its conclusion returned to an "almost unrelieved suspicion of the British and their designs." The anti–British tone was reflected in successive issues in the 1920s, with the Hearst Press being pro–Irish, opposed to the League of Nations, opposed to the Washington Treaty of 1921, opposed to a war debts settlement, and dismissive of British calls for an all-round cancellation. All plans to reduce or cancel the debts were vilified in the Hearst Press as plans "to plunder the American people."[48]

As an unsurprisingly fierce anti–British campaign was being conducted at that moment in the Hearst newspapers, there was some question among the traveling party about how they would be received and how Winston would get on with Hearst. Hearst and Winston had probably met before in 1928 but then only briefly. His articles, however, had been published in Hearst's *Cosmopolitan*.

Johnny was amazed by their arrival at the Hearst castle. He thought it was a "fantastic experience" that could only happen in America. The arrival and visit of the Churchills was treated as a "state occasion." Several miles from San Simeon the visitors' motorcars were met by a host of "private uniformed policemen" who formed up as outriders for the remainder of the journey. The motorcars, with their outrider escort, passed through the main entrance to the estate, which Johnny thought resembled a medieval castle. It had massive gates that slowly rose up like a portcullis, and the cars passed underneath. There was a five-mile drive from the main gate to La Casa Grande. Shortly after passing through the main entrance the cars bumped over a cattle grid. The necessity for the grid quickly became obvious, as the grounds of San Simeon were a "kind of private big game preserve." As they sped off towards the main house that stood atop a "pyramid mountain" in the distance, the cars passed through Hearst's private game preserve of wild animals which he had begun collecting in 1924. Johnny noted the buffalo, giraffe, and elephant, while Marion Davies recalled the animals also included lions, tigers, leopards, bears, spider monkeys, camels, deer, zebras, elk, emus, and ostriches. Raoul Walsh, the famous Hollywood director, believed the menagerie at San Simeon was as well stocked as a municipal zoo. Indeed, it was the largest private collection in the world. One story had it that on their arrival Winston's motorcars were delayed on the private road for over an hour by a stubborn giraffe that refused to move.[49]

Winston thought San Simeon was amazing. He had heard the house described as the "Monte Carlo Casino on the top of the rock of Gibraltar." It was, however, in Winston's opinion, better than that. Johnny also thought the house was incredible. The work on the main building had begun in 1919, and although Hearst moved into the castle in 1925, the work was never really finished. At San Simeon the newspaper magnate had a "compulsion to build and it seemed impossible for him to stop."[50]

The entrance to La Casa Grande was "like a Gothic cathedral," and the building had two Spanish "renaissance" towers, one of which was 137 feet and held 36 bronze carillon bells. In the main building there were 38 bedrooms, 14 sitting rooms, 31 bathrooms, two libraries, a billiard room, assembly hall, and a dining hall. Inside the house, Johnny noted, were copies of tapestries from Blenheim, copies of Greek and Roman statues, and a long refectory table taken from a European monastery. During the visit Johnny made a drawing of La Casa Grande, which he believed had been copied from a Spanish church, with a façade copied from an original in Morocco. Winston's nephew remembered the gardens as being laid out in an "open patio style," with interesting paths wandering through the trees. Periodically along the paths were marble statues. It was at San Simeon that Johnny first saw the statue of the Venus of Cyrene. Later he saw the original of this Greek work in the Neapolitan Museum in Rome. He thought almost nothing on the estate was completely American, and only the swimming pool seemed to have been an original not having been copied from anything.[51]

Rather than stay in the main castle, the Churchills were assigned one of the three guest houses, which Winston called the "little pagodas," built on the ranch.[52] These guest houses were heavily used, as Hearst regularly invited people for the weekend, including movie stars from Hollywood and other famous associates. The English visitors probably stayed in La Casa del Monte, The House of the Mountains, which was so-named for the views offered of the Santa Lucia Mountains from its windows. Finished in 1921, this guest house was on the hill near the main house. It had four bedrooms, four bathrooms, a vestibule, a living room, and was furnished with Persian carpets, Chinese and Persian urns, as well as desks, tables, and chairs that indicated "antiquity." The bedroom that Winston most likely slept in had a bed that had once belonged to Cardinal Richelieu. The bed was of "carved and gilt walnut; Lombardic, late sixteenth century." The headboard was "carved to simulate a canopy of fringed drapery, and in the center is a coat of arms of three fishes surmounted by a coronet and a bishop's hat."[53]

William Randolph Hearst's complicated personal arrangements were on display for the Churchills to see during the visit. The American, in Winston's phrase, operated two separate establishments. One consisted of his wife, the officially titled Mrs. Millicent Hearst, from whom he was estranged, and the other of his long-time mistress, the film star Marion Davies. Millicent Hearst, rather than Davies, was at San Simeon for the Englishmen's arrival. She had altered her plans in order to be there to receive them. Millicent Hearst had either chosen to be at the castle for the visit or, as Johnny supposed, had been summoned from New York to act as official hostess on this important occasion. In either case, with Mrs. Hearst present, Marion Davies had been exiled south to the palatial villa Hearst had built for her in Santa Monica.

Millicent Hearst had previously visited Winston and Clementine in England. At San Simeon she told Winston how pleased she had been with that visit and greatly praised Clementine. She even quoted some remarks Clementine had made about the Good Housekeeping Restaurant. Despite the awkwardness of Hearst's personal affairs, Winston got along very well with Millicent during the visit and found her very agreeable.[54]

Randolph too found Millicent Hearst charming. The other guests present at San Simeon on the party's arrival numbered 25. Unlike his pleasant appraisal of Millicent, Randolph thought the others were generally of poor quality. George Hearst, the eldest son of the newspaper magnate, was at the castle. Having been appointed publisher of the *San Francisco Examiner* the year before, the 25-year-old Hearst was named president of the *New York American* in 1929. Along with George Hearst was his wife, who he had eloped with when both were 18 years old. Randolph dismissed him as a "fat oaf" but was more taken with the wife, the former Blanche Louise Wilbur, who was described as "exquisite." The youngest Churchill's fascination with Hearst's young daughter-in-law would cause some anxious moments during the visit to San Simeon.[55] Among the others at the Hearst castle during their visit were friends of the Hearst family and journalists who had business with Hearst, including John Neylan, editor of Hearst's San Francisco newspaper and the great man's principal aide-de-camp. Neylan had previously revealed a noteworthy dislike of Britain to, among others, Consul-General Campbell.

Meals at San Simeon were taken in the main hall where the "enormous crowd" of people present would take a place at the European refectory table, sitting in "folding Dante chairs." Dinners were at nine o'clock. In a practice favored by Hearst, no one was introduced to anyone else. As a result, Johnny's neighbors at the monastic table could not tell him the names of any of the other guests. At the dinner after they had arrived, Randolph immediately became rather friendly with Blanche Hearst. He managed to get another guest, an elderly, annoying lawyer, to bet Blanche and himself against two identical cards turning up simultaneously when two decks of cards were gone through at the same time. Randolph won his bet. Both he and the Hearst daughter-in-law won 80 dollars each.[56]

Each night after dinner at San Simeon, Hearst and his guests watched talking films. The indoor theater at the castle had not yet been built, so the latest talkies were shown in a garden that had been outfitted with "full-sized cinematograph apparatus." This garden was just one of the dozen or more terraces on the grounds.[57]

On their first full day at San Simeon, Saturday September 14, Randolph rose about ten o'clock in the morning. The weather was perfect, with Randolph calling it the "most deliciously warm weather I have ever known." In the beautiful weather he began exploring the fantasyland William Randolph Hearst had created at San Simeon during nine years of construction. As he noted, the work was still in no way complete, as everywhere there were "workmen, motor lorries, and pneumatic drills." Despite his best efforts, Randolph estimated that that day he had been able to examine only one twentieth of the house and grounds. He though a great deal of false modesty was involved in calling this vast estate a ranch.[58]

The house at San Simeon was crammed full of European art. Randolph hazarded a guess of insurance value at sixteen million dollars and observed Hearst's wealth was 20 million dollars. Monasteries, palaces and castles throughout Europe, he wrote in his diary, had been and were at that moment being "ransacked for gems of one kind or another" to fill San Simeon.[59]

Randolph thought the house, with its white stone and two Moorish turrets, had the façade of a "great cathedral." He did not, however, like the large wooden roof, which he felt did not match the rest of the structure. Within La Casa Grande, Randolph was intrigued by a large 150-foot-long room in a "double cube" shape with a "magnificent oak roof" and was lit at night by 400 electric light bulbs. On that first full day at San Simeon Randolph also investigated a huge dining room built in a baronial fashion.[60] He did not have time to investigate the library that was upstairs in the house and considered equally remarkable. Randolph planned out an inspection of the library on the following day.

Despite the party's initial concerns, Winston was getting along quite cordially with Hearst. Both at San Simeon and later in Los Angeles the pair had many long discussions. During the conversations Winston was probably shown around San Simeon by his host, at which time he would have been introduced to the workers on the grounds. It was a Hearst habit to introduce his important visitors to his workers. The visitors were probably given a closer tour of Hearst's private game preserve. At its height the zoo had 60 species of grazing animals and 30 species of jungle animals on the 2,000 acres set aside for the preserve. The animals, some in cages, included musk oxen from Greenland, lions, tigers, polar bears, monkeys, birds, kangaroos, hundreds of zebras, ostriches, cheetahs, black panthers, elephants, and monkeys from Japan, Java, and India.[61]

Beyond the animals, Winston was interested in much smaller fare. As he had predicted back in the Rocky Mountains, more butterflies were indeed found further south. Winston loved butterflies. He wrote of them "gleaming, fluttering, settling for an instant with wings fully spread to the sun." As a child and youth he had enjoyed collecting butterflies during the summer; as a soldier in India he had sent home for equipment with which he managed to assemble a fine collection in Bangalore; and traveling in Uganda he had observed the most "glorious butterflies the colour of whose wings changed from the deepest russet brown to the most brilliant blue." After the Second World War, Winston would have a butterfly farm stock the grounds of Chartwell with butterflies.[62]

At San Simeon the butterflies were found in abundance. On one occasion two or three butterflies landed on Johnny's arm. These were large, brown, striped ones that he identified as Milkweeds. Animated by the discovery of these butterflies, Winston wanted to collect all the butterfly species in sight.[63] Johnny, less interested in the insect, refused.

In an entirely fanciful portion of his not altogether reliable autobiography, the great movie director Raoul Walsh claims to have been at San Simeon during the visit of the Churchill party. Walsh misplaces Winston's visit to California to 1933 rather than 1929 and claims that the British statesman was at San Simeon for a period of weeks rather than the five days he actually was there. He also claims a veritable who's who of famous people and celebrities dining alongside Winston and himself at the dining hall at San Simeon. Beyond Winston, the guests were said to include Douglas MacArthur, Howard Hughes, Somerset Maugham, J. Edgar Hoover, Will Rogers, John Barrymore, and many beautiful Hollywood actresses. While Hoover talked of capturing famous criminals, Winston and MacArthur were said to tell of the British navy exploits and memories of West Point, respectively.[64] As Winston, Randolph, and Johnny never mentioned meeting such a luminous gallery at San Simeon, many of whom can be placed elsewhere in September 1929, Walsh's memory can be safely discounted. Raoul Walsh probably did meet Winston in California in September 1929, but it was later in the month at the premiere of one of his films.

Even without the array of Hollywood actresses claimed by Raoul Walsh, both Randolph and Johnny enjoyed the social life at San Simeon. During their stay they were seen to be paying close attention to several of the women guests. This caused Winston some nervousness, as his son seemed to be getting on much too well with Hearst's daughter-in-law, Blanche. He did have some sympathy for his son, as he too thought George Hearst was "enormously fat," while the young Mrs. Hearst was a "pretty little woman."[65]

Randolph and Blanche spent a great deal of their time bathing in the sapphire swimming pool. This 104-foot outdoor pool had twice been rebuilt by Hearst. Called the Neptune Pool, it was lined with black and white marble, with marble colonnades from Italy ringing the ends of the pool. The two or three acres around the pool were at that time being likewise paved with the black and white marble. The surrounding gardens were filled with Greek and Roman statues.[66]

Together in the pool and elsewhere, Randolph and Blanche were, in Winston's words, the "pictures of youth and beauty." That his wife and the young guest were getting on so well caused George Hearst to become rather annoyed and required some watchfulness on the part of his mother. When Blanche departed San Simeon before the Churchills' visit was over, Winston confessed to Clementine that he felt quite relieved.[67] Hearst's daughter-in-law was perhaps the girl Randolph sneaked out with late one night at San Simeon, returning quite noisily at five o'clock in the morning.

As a friend of Randolph's recalled years later, an amused Winston was said to have told his son, "Randolph, don't you think you have been violating the rules of hospitality." In the end it did not matter too much, as George Hearst's marriage to Blanche ended in divorce, being merely the first of his seven marriages.[68]

Johnny remembered another occasion when he and Randolph made an "expedition in the night" at San Simeon. With Randolph in the lead, an error in navigation was made. The youngest member of the traveling party accidently led them stumbling into his own father's bedroom. This time Winston's remonstrance was not so good-natured. Woken up by his errant son, Winston was angry and blasted him a "withering reprimand." Johnny remembered that he and his cousin retreated, feeling "very sheepish and fed up."[69]

The reprimand only temporarily put a halt to matters. Late in the stay at San Simeon Winston was amused when one of the young ladies Randolph was interested in deserted him for Johnny after the latter had "plied her with romantic conversation under the stars."

"You know, I think it is just as well we are leaving soon because Johnny seems to be making unexpected progress!" Winston told his son. Despite the loss of the attention of that particular lady to Johnny, Randolph always claimed to his friends that he indeed successfully seduced a young woman amongst the splendor of the Hearst Castle.[70]

In what probably was a Hearst family anecdote, Winston was said to have painted a landscape while at San Simeon. As he was painting he sent a maid for supplies. The maid rushed by Hearst, who misheard what the maid had said and thought Winston was "fainting" and wanted some turpentine. An alarmed Hearst rushed to the terrace to find Winston painting and asking for turpentine to thin the oils. While his host started laughing, Winston merely continued to paint, unaware of the concern that had been raised. William Randolph Hearst, Jr., recalled that Winston spent a great deal of time considering the views of the landscape from different parts of the castle before he selected a location and started to paint.[71]

All through the visit to California, including at San Simeon, Winston continued to receive invitations for engagements at future stops on the American portion of the tour. Even at this late date the itinerary for the remainder of the trip was not fixed. At San Francisco Winston said that he was in California for pleasure and recreation, and did not know how long he would stay. With the travel plans still fluid, he received an invitation, as a result of Baruch's efforts, from the Utah Copper Mining Company to visit the copper mines and reduction plants near Salt Lake City. Other offers included dining at the Mile High Club in Denver, and one from Otto Kahn with details about a dinner in New York City. Winston had cabled Baruch several times from the west coast, as well as asked his friend to telephone him at San Simeon, as they tried to finalize the travel arrangements beyond California. Eventually it was worked out that Baruch would meet the Churchill party at Chicago. On September 19, Winston was finally able to cable Charles Piez, one of his proposed Chicago hosts, with his arrival details. Winston would also eventually accept Otto Kahn's invitation to dinner, asking only that he also extend an invitation to H.C. Vickers, who would be in New York at that time for a short holiday.[72]

A concern related to the travel itinerary had been added in Clementine's cable to Winston on September 13, the day after their 21st wedding anniversary. She cabled that the "Prof," Frederick Lindemann, was expressing concern for Randolph's career at Oxford if he did not return from North America in time for the new term.

On their last night at San Simeon Randolph visited with Millicent Hearst and recorded a remark she made that he thought demonstrated "even the nicest people out here suffer from megalomania and overweening pride." In reference to Arthur Brisbane, a Hearst writer and right-hand man, she said the "relationship between Voltaire and Frederick the Great is not unlike that between Brisbane and Mr. Hearst."[73]

… *14* …

# Los Angeles and Santa Barbara, September 17–21

On September 17 Winston and the rest of the party left San Simeon and were escorted, under the care of William Randolph Hearst, to Los Angeles. For the first few days in Los Angeles Hearst would continue to act as their host. The party traveled in a fleet of cars, again escorted by uniformed policemen on motorcycles through the game preserve and down to the coast road. For the six-hour ride from the Ranch to Los Angeles, Hearst and Winston rode together in the lead motor car, with Jack in the second, and Randolph and Johnny together in the third vehicle.[1]

Hearst would recount in remarks at a luncheon the next day that "I don't know exactly what to say," as during the previous day's car trip "I told him everything that I know anything about and a lot of things that I don't know anything about. I am sure he enjoyed the conversation, because he fell into the most peaceful and profound slumber and remained there."

"I hope to goodness there isn't going to be any talking at the luncheon tomorrow because I am looking forward to that as a pleasurable occasion," Winston later told Hearst, referring to the planned luncheon in Los Angeles.

"I don't think there will be much formal speaking and that anyhow I won't make a formal speech," Hearst reassured his guest. This seemed to relieve Winston, or so Hearst thought, as the British statesman was "comparatively cheerful after that." While ready to make some short remarks at the dinners given in his honor, Winston did not wish to have to make any "serious public utterances" while on his American holidays.[2]

At the luncheon Hearst would compare Winston's desire to avoid speaking engagements to that of the "man who did not take his wife abroad as he was going for pleasure." Randolph was amused by the comparison. Since Hearst had just left his wife at San Simeon and picked up with his mistress in Los Angeles, he thought the remark was "rather good value!"[3]

In Los Angeles Hearst did, in fact, switch over to the second establishment in his personal arrangements, that one being of his long-time mistress, the then 32-year-old Marion Davies. In this city, in Winston's words, William Randolph Hearst ran the film world, had another palace, and lived with his "unofficial wife" Marion Davies. Growing up on New

York City's West Side, Davies began her theatrical career at the age of 16 in a dancing role in a road show of *Chu Chin Chow*. A year later she was discovered by Ziegfeld and became a "Ziegfeld girl," appearing in the 1917 follies. Davies soon met Hearst, and became his mistress and companion. Hearst was determined to make her a movie star and founded Cosmopolitan Pictures in 1919 to produce her films. Davies appeared in several motion pictures, with her most popular being 1923's *Little Old New York*. She later admitted, "With me it was five percent talent and ninety-five percent publicity." All the Churchills found Marion Davies charming and a wonderful new host. Winston did not find Davies stunningly beautiful but thought her personality was attractive, with its "naive childlike" quality. Disagreeing with his uncle, Johnny remembered her as "blonde, blue-eyed, and fabulously attractive."[4]

Winston was indeed welcomed to Los Angeles by the motion picture industry in grand fashion, with a lavish luncheon given in his honor on a sound stage at the Metro-Goldwyn-Mayer Studios in Culver City on September 18. The reception was given jointly by Hearst and Louis B. Mayer, the head of the studio, and other film executives. Planning for the luncheon had been completed by September 17. The 150 to 200 guests included motion picture executives, actors from all of the Hollywood studios, elected officials, and civic leaders. The entertainment program at the luncheon had been arranged by Gus Edwards, a former star of the vaudeville stage. It had further been arranged for Fred Niblo to act as toastmaster. He was one of Metro-Goldwyn-Mayer's great directors, who had made such films as *Ben-Hur: A Tale of the Christ*, *Blood and Sun* with Rudolph Valentino, and *The Temptress* with Greta Garbo. A vaudeville star, he had twice performed in command performances before the British royal family. For his work at the luncheon Niblo would be praised as "easily our most polished and witty master of ceremonies."[5]

The luncheon, which began at 12:30 that afternoon, was considered a great success, with it called a "merry affair" and "possibly the most remarkable affair ever given" in Los Angeles. Sitting at the speaker's table were the English visitors, along with Mayer, Hearst, and Fred Niblo. Johnny looked very dapper for the affair, dressed in a white jacket, white shirt, and bowtie. Throughout the luncheon and program a crowd of photographers would take pictures of the head table. The audience was composed of those at the forefront of business, art, and motion pictures in Los Angeles, including stars of film, theater, and vaudeville. The nearly 190 people in attendance included such famous movie figures as Joan Crawford, Douglas Fairbanks, Jr., Basil Rathbone, Colleen Moore, Irving Thalberg, Ramon Novarro, Cecil B. DeMille, King Vidor, and, of course, Marion Davies. The Churchills met a number of the stars and producers during the luncheon; some they had heard of and others they had not. Randolph thought Davies was the most attractive of them all.[6]

A 20-piece orchestra played continuously throughout the lunch portion of the program, which was followed by the entertainment. The singers and actors booked for the entertainment portion performed on a stage that had been set up at the far end of the sound stage. The entertainment began with Lawrence Tibbetts, a famous baritone of the Metropolitan Opera Company, singing "On the Road to Mandalay." Tibbetts, as Randolph noted in his diary, was paid one thousand pounds a night in New York City. Miss Cecil Cunningham, a famous comedian, sang two songs which made the head table and audience "roar in laughter." An actor and comedian, Benny Rubin, performed next, with his "wise cracks" having as much success as Cunningham's songs. The vaudeville duo of Van and Schenck put on a sketch with some humorous songs before Lawrence Gray performed with Sammy Lee's chorus girls, who were wearing "peek-a-boo costumes." Gray's number was from the current Duncan Sisters motion picture. A light-hearted newspaper article on the entertainment reported that "in beauty and grace and choreographic skill" the MGM revue girls "made everyone sit up, and look, and look, and look, and look." Randolph apparently looked, as he thought the 25 girls in the chorus were "infinitely more attractive than the best in London." In his remarks at the luncheon Winston praised the performances as brilliant and that they "crowned" the feast, regretting only that it had all been too brief. Randolph also thought the performances were of a "high order" and "astounding."[7]

The speeches began with one by Clement C. Young, the governor of California. Young had, for the occasion, hurried to Los Angeles from the state capital as a guest of the MGM studio. While in the city, the governor also made two more speeches the following day and then attended the Los Angeles County Fair. After Young, Mayer spoke and then Hearst. As Hearst had reassured Winston during the drive from San Simeon, all of the speeches were "informal." Even so, Mayer spoke of the blood, ideals, and traditions that bound the United States and Britain, while Hearst called for understanding between the two countries in the hope of establishing peace in the world. This call for Anglo-American cooperation on the part of the newspaper baron was not entirely new. In an editorial earlier in 1929 Hearst had advocated cooperation of the English-speaking peoples of the world to maintain the peace both among themselves and in the world. This cooperation was not to be an offensive alliance. This call for cooperation did not prevent Hearst from maintaining his anti–British stance. Hearst's own newspaper, the *Los Angeles Examiner*, not surprisingly, praised their owner's speech, saying he had spoken in a "witty vein."[8]

In his own brief speech Winston expressed his regret at not having been in California before and saying he was a traveler on holiday. He quipped that after the last election result there was a noticeable feeling in some quarters that "I ought to have a holiday." He praised the work being done in motion pictures, along with broadcasting, as playing an essential part "in this great broadening of the joys and pleasures of life." After motoring many miles through California, Winston extolled the beauty, charm, scenery, and climate of the state. On the trip he had encountered, he declared, the "delightful, spacious hospitalities which it is the pride of California to offer. I have seen your big trees, your big men and I have seen with the eye of the mind your big future." He admitted only one painful "regret"—that he did not visit the state much sooner than he had. For his heartfelt tribute to California, Winston received prolonged applause.

Turning to international politics, Winston remarked on his joy upon entering the studio when he saw the American and British flags side by side. This was not just a symbol of the association of the two great peoples but also the secret of the "future of the world." These flags together represented the "peace and safety of the world."

Their duty, Winston continued, in this "new age" was to make a better world, "not for the few, but for the many, and not alone for the many, but ultimately for all or almost all."

The British statesman also took pains to declare that he was thrilled to have heard Hearst, who possessed such influence, say in his speech that the peace of the world could be best achieved by cooperation between their two countries.

A surprise had been arranged for Winston at the luncheon. Unbeknownst to him, the studio's electricians had hidden a microphone in the bouquet of flowers on the table in front of him in order to record every word of his speech "on the intricate studio sound device."

After Winston finished speaking, with the luncheon nearing its end, Niblo said that Winston's address was so brilliant that he would like to hear it again and the audience would like to hear it again—that is, if Mr. Churchill himself could bear to hear it again. At that moment, just two minutes after the Englishman had finished speaking, Winston's speech began playing from the loudspeaker that hung in the corner of the stage. Reports from the event said it was an "exact reproduction" that was "so wonderful, of such clear exactitude that it overwhelmed the listeners, and as in all periods of amazement everyone laughed." Randolph thought the recording was "absolutely perfect in tone and volume, and as clear as when he spoke himself!" Marion Davies remembered that Winston's lisp did not come through over the microphone. When they discussed it later, neither Winston nor Davies could figure it out, but the lisp just did not register over the loudspeaker. According to the *Los Angeles Times*, the novel experience of being recorded had left Winston speechless and members of his party spellbound.[9] This was probably the first time Winston's voice was recorded and the first time he heard such a recording of his own voice.

The gossip writer for the *Los Angeles Times*, Alma Whitaker, attended the event and raved about it in her column. She thought the company, entertainment, speeches, service, and food were all "above reproach." The motion picture people were in their "starry glory," while the other city notables present were "at their charming best." Whitaker also had praise for Jack, who she described as the "tall, aristocratic type, at once patrician and shy." Randolph and Johnny were thought to be "making a strenuous effort to look blasé, sitting next to world-famous beauties. Oh, but they had a good time!"[10]

After the program the Churchills were escorted on a lengthy tour of the MGM studios. As Winston loved films and was an enthusiastic filmgoer he was probably quite excited to visit the studio. The tour began with a "talking film" being shot of Winston, Hearst, and Mayer. They then visited several studios and watched scenes from various motion pictures being shot. Randolph noted that each studio had about six cameras in order to shoot the scene from every angle. He found it fascinating. On the tour the party learned that MGM had a staff of 40,000 and a payroll amounting to $17,000,000 per year.[11]

In Johnny's sometimes unreliable memoir he claims that after Mayer's studio tour it was suggested that the boys be entertained at the cinema while their fathers be further entertained by performances from the chorus girls. Needless to say, the two younger Churchills did not think that this was the right way round and quickly had the program switched. Their fathers went to the movies, and the boys were treated to further performances by the chorus girls.[12]

During one of his studio tours while in Los Angeles, Winston was asked whether he liked talking pictures over the silent movies. After hesitating for a moment he replied with a smile that he did not think the sound films had yet proved their worth. The sound pictures were, he said, "being carried along on the crest of one of your advertising waves. That is the difference between England and America. We are slow to embrace anything new, while you receive it with outstretched arms, whether it is any good or not. ... America is 'slogan mad.' On your radio I heard a song 'You're the cream in my coffee.' Visiting the studios, I discovered the Hollywood version of the song to be 'You're the scream in my Talkie.'"[13]

After the studio tour was completed, the party left Hearst's circle for a few days and motored to Santa Barbara, where they would spend two nights at the country home of William Gibbs McAdoo and his wife Eleanor. They arrived late that night. McAdoo had been secretary of the treasury in the Woodrow Wilson administration and had twice sought the Democratic Party nomination for president. Denied his bids for the highest office, McAdoo was back in California pursuing various business interests until he would win election as United States senator from the state in 1932. One of his latest business projects in 1929 was heading a new company, the Hawaii Airways Company, that was to provide daily air service using two tri-motor, 12-passenger Fokker airplanes between the three principal Hawaiian islands of Hawaii, Maui, and Kauai.[14]

Eleanor McAdoo, who was 26 years younger than her husband, was the second daughter of the former president of the United States Woodrow Wilson. As she was devoted to her father's liberalism and internationalism, the meeting with Winston might have been approached with some trepidation. The American president and Winston had met at the most five times, with Wilson intensely disliking him. He thought the British politician was a leading reactionary determined to sabotage his plans for a just peace. His opinion of Winston "consisted of aspersions on Churchill's character and disgust for his perceived principles and aims." In turn, Winston remarked that Wilson was a "man of fierce and deep resentments when his pride was offended or his purposes crossed." Despite his problems with Wilson, the visit with the president's daughter went well. Winston found Eleanor, in fact, to be delightful.[15]

The McAdoos welcomed the Churchills to their home located at the top of Las Alturas. From the top of this mountain superb views could be had of both the city of Santa Barbara and the Pacific Ocean. The house itself, in Winston's opinion, was modest but in "extremely good taste."[16]

Awaiting Winston on his arrival at the McAdoo house was a gift of flowers from the Santa Barbara American Legion Post No. 49. A Colonel Edward Olmsted, formerly chief of staff of the 44th Division, had left his card for Winston. On the back of the card Olmsted noted that he had served in Flanders and the Somme, and was an admirer of Winston's who wished the honor of paying his respects.

Having opened up their country home and ensured the Churchills' smooth arrival, the McAdoos placed the house at the disposal of their visitors and kindly disappeared to allow their guests to relax by themselves. Before they disappeared they made clear to the Englishmen that the house was at their disposal for the two days that were planned, or even two weeks if they had the time to spare. Left alone without commitments or hosts, Winston passed the next two days quite peacefully.[17]

The tourists probably found Santa Barbara's climate to be very pleasant. A travel guide wrote that Santa Barbara had a "climate of unrivaled healthfulness based on purity of air, absence of wind, great amount of sunshine, the small relative humidity, the very high winter and comfortably low summer temperature."[18]

With an accumulation of letters having developed, Winston obtained, probably through McAdoo, the services of a stenographer and started work on his correspondence. From Santa Barbara he wrote Clementine, saying that although he had been trying to keep his story of the trip up to date, with the continually moving it had proven to be difficult. Beyond the trip, he also detailed his "very great and extraordinary good fortune" that he had had in his financial affairs. Since having left cabinet office, Winston had assembled what he described as a "small fortune" of 21,825 pounds. This amount consisted of advances on his biography of Marlborough and his articles on the North American tour, royalties due him, payment for his other articles, and returns on his investments. Winston intended to use this money to "earn further profits in the future," including by speculating with Sir Harry McGowan, a British chemical industrialist, and with his usual firm of Vickers da Costa. Apart from these investments and maneuvers, Winston wrote Clementine that "there is money enough to make us comfortable and well-mounted in London this autumn." Having covered so many topics in his letter, Winston ended with, "I could write for hours—but must close now."[19]

While in Santa Barbara, Winston sent a package of letters and papers back to England, care of his secretary, Miss Cummings. He no longer needed the papers he sent while in North America and instructed his secretary to keep them for his return. Further instructions sent to Miss Cummings included for her to arrange for a copy of the *Way of Revelation* to be sent to Van Antwerp and for a painting table made by a man in Norfolk to be ordered and sent to Edith Van Antwerp as a gift. Winston also wrote to his host in the capital of British Columbia, R. Randolph Bruce, telling him that they had been touring and "whirling" since leaving Victoria. As thanks for the kindness Bruce had shown them, Winston had a copy of his own *Life of Lord Randolph Churchill* sent to him. A copy of this book was also sent to Crocker in return for his hospitality. Winston wrote his former host from Santa Barbara, saying he wished he could have stayed longer at Burlingame. Further in regard to books, Winston wrote Charles Scribner asking that a complete set of *The World Crisis* be bound up and ready for him on his arrival in New York, as he wished to give them to a friend. In respect to his literary affairs, he sent E.G. Rich at Curtis Brown a letter on the articles he would write about the tour of North America. Winston also received a cable from Thornton Butterworth that, as requested, 1,700 pounds had been paid into his account. It was money that he planned to invest in the stock market.

Other correspondence Winston tidied up at Santa Barbara was a letter of thanks sent to a Kilbec Gordon of Victoria for the poem he had written and sent to Winston entitled "Welcome Sir!" Winston also wrote to Mrs. R.A. Bray expressing his regret at not being able to meet her while in northern California.[20]

Beyond his papers and letters, Winston took the time to enjoy the McAdoo estate. At an early hour on September 19 he was already up and rambling through the orange, lemon, and avocado orchards of the grounds. He bombarded the gardeners with questions on the trees, particularly the orange and lemon trees, so much so that he "exhausted their knowledge in replies."[21]

While Winston admired the view of the Santa Barbara channel, the scene was not quite as brilliant as it should have been from atop the mountain.

"Is there much fog here?" Winston had asked as almost his first inquiry upon arriving at Santa Barbara. Although he was quite pleased when told that fog was unusual, the days he spent at the McAdoo house unfortunately proved to be cloudy. With fog hanging over the ocean most of the first full day there, the scenic view of the sea and Channel Islands was obscured.

William Randolph Hearst telephoned Winston at the McAdoo estate that morning to inquire when they would be returning to Los Angeles. He was pleased to learn that they would be back the next day and could lunch with him. Randolph thought that his father had won him over. As an indication of how seriously Hearst considered the MGM luncheon, his Los Angeles newspaper, the *Examiner*, gave it extensive coverage, with articles and photographs in that morning's edition, which the Churchills read in Santa Barbara. The speeches made at the luncheon were all printed in full in the newspaper.[22]

That afternoon the traveling party, save for Winston, who remained at the estate, made a driving tour around Santa Barbara and Montecito. They stopped to explore the mission at Santa Barbara. This mission was one of the best preserved of the Indian missions that had been built by the Spanish between San Diego and Sonoma. The Montecito Valley, which the party toured, lay between the mountains and the Pacific Ocean. A contemporary travel guide recorded that the valley had been "landscaped until it is one great beautiful garden." The travelers returned from their drive to have an early dinner and bedtime at the McAdoo home. While at Santa Barbara Winston relaxed by reading a biography of Brigham Young, of which he made significant progress. As he apparently did not finish the book, McAdoo sent him a copy of the *Life of Brigham Young* as a gift after Winston was in New York.[23]

On September 20 the Churchills made an early start, leaving Santa Barbara for their return to Los Angeles. They lunched with Hearst and Marion Davies at the Montmartre Café on Hollywood Boulevard, which Randolph said was the "luncheon haunt of the cinema world." At their table were P.G. Wodehouse and his daughter Leonora, the screen writer Donald Ogden Stuart, the silent film actress Virginia Valli, and four or five others.

Wodehouse was a British writer and humorist who enjoyed both critical and commercial success, and whose best known creations were the characters Jeeves and Wooster. Having traveled to Los Angeles for a short trip, he had become acquainted with Marion Davies, the only friend Wodehouse claimed he had really made thus far in Hollywood. She had invited him to her mansion on the beach in Santa Monica and made sure he was at the luncheon for Winston at the MGM studio. According to Wodehouse, this was the seventh time he had been introduced to Winston, but he could see that he "came upon him as a complete surprise once more." Wodehouse took this to mean that he must have one of those meaningless faces which make "no impression whatever on the beholder." Randolph had also met Wodehouse before and thought it great to see him again.[24] He felt the British writer was in excellent form.

There was much less chance of Winston meeting and recognizing Wodehouse after the Second World War, as during the conflict the British writer had remained in France after the German occupation and made five broadcasts on German radio. While others who broadcast for the Germans, such as John Amery, were later executed, Wodehouse—whose broadcasts were apparently considered humorous rather than treacherous—merely made sure to keep out of Britain for the last thirty years of his life. In regard to Wodehouse, Winston would suggest, "Let him go to Hell—as soon as there's a vacant passage."[25]

After visiting several movie studios that afternoon, the Churchills motored north from Los Angeles in the evening to Ocean House on the Beach Palisades Road in Santa Monica for a party that Marion Davies had organized in their honor. Davies' parties were thrown with such "panache" that they had become legendary. She loved to host parties, most especially fancy-dress and costume ones. Through their combined efforts, William Randolph Hearst and Davies ensured the Churchills would be entertained at a star-studded affair. As the party was being planned, Hearst had told Randolph and Johnny, "Draw up a list of all the film stars you would like to meet and I'll get them to come along for a banquet."[26]

With some knowledge of film stars, Johnny was able to draw up a lengthy list of the greatest actors and actresses in Hollywood. Randolph agreed to its composition, and the list was provided to Hearst, who used his influence to ensure all on the list indeed attended that party at Ocean House. The only star requested by the cousins that was not delivered by

Hearst was the ever remote Greta Garbo. Charlie Chaplin, the most famous star at the party, probably attended due to the convincing of Marion Davies. She was close friends with Chaplin. After a Dickensian childhood in London, Chaplin had built a long career as a comedian and filmmaker, and was declared by many to be the most famous man in the world, known to millions through his unforgettable performances as the "Little Tramp."

After arriving at Ocean House, the party swam in the heated Italian marble swimming pool and then dressed for dinner. Ocean House was the second Hearst abode, after San Simeon, that Winston referred to as a palace. It was a second palace to go along with his second wife. Ocean House was the "biggest and most opulent beach house in California." An impressed Winston would call it a palace on the ocean, while Randolph deemed it magnificent.[27]

It was a white Georgian-style mansion with 110 rooms, three stories, 37 fireplaces and 55 bedrooms. Hearst had spent seven million dollars on the construction and furnishing of Ocean House. Like San Simeon, the work on the structure did not spare money or time. A team of 75 wood carvers worked under the supervision of an architect for a year on the balustrades. Similar to the Hearst castle, the furnishings of entire rooms had been imported from European castles, mostly English, French, and Spanish, with little concern for continuity between rooms. While the ballroom's theme was a mid–18th century Italian palazzo, the main dining room, reception room, and drawing room, each 60 feet long, were in the baronial style, with their contents from Barton Hall in Ireland. In addition, the dining room had a "splendid antique Persian carpet of enormous dimensions," while the reception room held two grand pianos. A tavern that seated 50 was taken from an inn in Surrey that dated from 1560. In the dining room there were a dozen large full-length portraits of Marion Davies in her most famous film roles. Other rooms in the mansion included an art gallery, a powder room with Tiffany crystal chandeliers and walls paneled in gold leaf, and a library with a movie screen that rose from the floor. The mansion's bedrooms were all suites with their own sitting rooms, marble fireplaces, and bathrooms. Johnny particularly recalled the black marble bathrooms. The eighteen Ionic columns lining the length of the beach side of the house caused Davies' friend Charlie Chaplin to comment that it had "more columns than the Supreme Court building in Washington." On the grounds of Ocean House was a 110-foot swimming pool that separated the villa from the beach. It was lined with Italian marble and bridged by a Venetian marble bridge. The operation of Ocean House required a staff of 32 servants.[28]

Although Marion Davies asked the Churchills to consider Ocean House their own for the duration of their visit to Los Angeles, the party only stayed there for two nights. These were probably the night of the party and another night the next week after another party that stretched into the early morning. In her memoirs Davies recalls Winston as a "very good guest" who liked his Scotch and cigars, but incorrectly remembers the English group was in Los Angeles for three or four weeks and stayed at the beach house for the entire visit. Davies, who drank despite prohibition and, more importantly, despite Hearst being against it, found she shared a fondness for alcohol with Winston. One story had it that she led Winston around the mansion's 55 bathrooms to show him the gin and scotch she hid in the toilet tanks.[29]

The party on September 20 was a tremendous affair. The beach house was a "blaze of light and fragrance. Out-of-doors lamps swung with the soft ocean zephyrs, while indoors,

Marion Davies, the actress and Hearst's mistress, hosted the Churchills at one of her legendary parties during their visit to California (Library of Congress).

in the spacious dining room and the ballroom, clusters of blossoms formed the simple decorations." Music that evening was provided by Ray West's orchestra, and arias from Victor Herbert's light operas were also played. As the night progressed, more "rollicking numbers" were played, including several from the score of the film *Marianne*, a Davies picture released in 1929.[30]

The Churchills entered the party to find that Hearst had indeed assembled the promised stars and entertainers. Among the sixty glitterati were a host of beautiful actresses, including Pola Negri, Mary Brian, Billie Dove, Bessie Love, Bebe Daniels, Dorothy Mackaill, and Diane Ellis. Harold Lloyd, the great comedian-actor of the silent era, and Wallace Beery, famous for playing villains, were there to meet the Churchills. The most famous of all the guests was, without doubt, Charlie Chaplin. Johnny could not help but be impressed. In his memoirs he wrote that usually meeting a star means being presented to them. On this occasion it was the reverse. The Englishmen walked down the line of stars, shaking hands as each of the stars was presented to them.[31]

Chaplin was milling about with other guests when Winston arrived, accompanied by Hearst. Chaplin recalled the future prime minister standing apart, "Napoleon-like with his hand in his waistcoat," as he watched the dancing. He seemed lost and out of place, so Hearst waved Chaplin over and introduced him to the British statesman.[32]

At first Chaplin found Winston abrupt in manner. After Hearst left them they exchanged the usual small talk, and it was only when Winston started talking about Britain's new Labour government that Chaplin thought he brightened.

"What I don't understand is that in England the election of a socialist government does not alter the status of a King and Queen," Chaplin remarked.

"Of course not," Winston replied with a quick glance that Chaplin thought "humorously challenging."

"I thought socialists were opposed to a monarchy," Chaplin persisted.

"If you were in England we'd cut your head off for that remark," Winston countered with a laugh.

Among all the stars at the party, Johnny took the greatest liking to Mary Brian, who he described as a "sweet black-haired girl."[33] He, however, made little progress, as Brian's attentions at the party were focused on a young actor. Instead, Johnny enjoyed the evening in the company of Billie Dove, Bessie Love, and Bebe Daniels. The actress Dorothy Mackaill was found to be of great interest to both Randolph and Johnny as well. Marion Davies, both at the party and during the rest of the time they spent together in Los Angeles, was extremely kind to the two younger Churchills. She was, however, rather cautious. Both the cousins thought this was for the best, as a previous Hearst guest named Thomas Ince had died aboard the Hearst yacht in unexplained circumstances after supposedly paying too much attention to Davies.

Randolph had not immediately recognized Charlie Chaplin or Harold Lloyd, as they were missing their moustache and horn-rimmed spectacles, respectively. Lloyd was most famous for portraying his "glasses character" in such films as *Safety Last!* and *The Freshman*. So popular was his character that sales of the horn-rimmed glasses he wore experienced a boom. That Randolph did not recognize Lloyd was not unusual. Removing his glasses gave Lloyd "instant anonymity: his comic persona was built almost entirely on wearing them. Without glasses, he had, in effect, disguised himself." At the party Johnny found Lloyd to be disappointing, since he was rather ordinary off-screen, but did like the actor Wallace Beery who was known for his "tough guy" roles.[34]

The evening's entertainment was supplemented by the great stars in attendance at the party. Marion Davies persuaded Chaplin to join her in doing a series of impersonations. She did Sarah Bernhardt and Lillian Gish, while he played Napoleon, Uriah Heep, Henry Irving, John Barrymore as Hamlet, and many others. The Davies-Chaplin duo then performed a complicated dance, during which Johnny noticed that Charlie's feet were small enough to fit into Marion's shoes. Despite having worked a full day at the studio, Davies "danced and frolicked around" that evening for about an hour and a half. Hearst even joined in the entertaining. With his plump physique he performed a solo act in which he lurched his "enormous frame" around the room on wobbly legs to the rhythm of the band. Johnny thought it so funny that he added the performance to his own repertoire of party tricks.[35]

After their slow start, Winston and Chaplin got along famously at the party. They sat up talking until three in the morning, a sure sign of Winston's favor. Winston wanted Chaplin to take on the role of a young Napoleon as his next film; if Chaplin would do it, Winston promised to write the script.

"You must do it," Winston pressed, describing the opportunities the role presented for drama and comedy. "Think of its possibilities for humour. Napoleon in his bathtub arguing with his imperious brother who's all dressed up, bedecked in gold braid, and using this opportunity to place Napoleon in a position of inferiority. But Napoleon, in his rage, deliberately splashes water over his brother's fine uniform and he has to exit ignominiously from him. This is not alone clever psychology. It is action and fun!"

Randolph was thrilled with Charlie Chaplin. He thought him "absolutely superb" and felt he had "enchanted everyone." Chaplin, in turn, was impressed by Randolph's father, whom he thought dynamic with a "thirst for accomplishment" as well as a wonderful talker who could "rattle off brilliant epigrams."

In his memoirs, Raoul Walsh inaccurately but inevitably has himself attending the party at Ocean House with Winston. In Walsh's imaginative version the affair is transformed into a costume party for Hearst's birthday, which was marred by Walsh knocking out another guest who claimed to be a Romanian prince. The guests at Walsh's version of the party included William Powell, Gary Cooper, Howard Hughes, Gloria Swanson, and Carole Lombard. As Hearst's birthday was April 29, and no one else places any of these famous actors at the 1929 party, Walsh's account can be dismissed as a tad unreliable.[36]

During their visit to Los Angeles the party lunched on occasion with Marion Davies in her bungalow at the studio where she was working. Davies worked all day on her films and would bathe and entertain at Ocean House in the evenings. The first possible lunch the Churchills had with Davies at the studio was on September 21. Her bungalow at the studio was a "little Italian chapel sort of building, very elegant." At this bungalow Winston observed that Hearst directed his newspaper empire by telephone, badgering his "private chancellor of the exchequer—a harassed functionary who is constantly compelled to find money and threatens resignation daily."[37]

Although they would continue to see Marion Davies during the remainder of the trip to Los Angeles, the party at Ocean House and the lunches at the studio bungalows were probably the last times that the Churchills saw William Randolph Hearst on the trip to California. After almost a week in Hearst's company at San Simeon and Los Angeles, Winston thought him engrossing and found that he liked him. He provided a capsule description of Hearst as a "grave simple child—with no doubt a nasty temper—playing with the most costly toys. A vast income always overspent: Ceaseless building and collecting not very discriminating works of art: two magnificent establishments, two charming wives; complete indifference to public opinion, a strong liberal and democratic outlook, a 15 million daily circulation, oriental hospitalities, extreme personal courtesy (to us at any rate) and the appearance of a Quaker elder—or perhaps Mormon elder." Hearst, for his part, also liked Winston. He cabled Baruch that Winston was a "wonderful man and we had [a] delightful time together."[38]

Winston was pleased with how the meeting with Hearst went and thought it was a real success. Perhaps influenced by Winston's visit, the anti–British tone of Hearst's newspapers was at least temporarily lessened. The magnate's newspapers covered Winston's visit with Hearst in detail and reported their owner's statements about the need for cooperation between the United States and Britain as a means of assuring peace. Consul-General Campbell wrote to Winston at the end of September saying the visit had "produced wonderful and immediate results." With Hearst publically calling for friendly relations with Britain, Hearst newspaper editors had been told to drop the antagonism to British interests and adopt a friendly approach. Campbell described how Neylan, Hearst's close aide, had disavowed his prior dislike for Britain and had gone so far as to embrace Campbell at the opera and gush enthusiastically about Winston. Neylan said the visit had done a great deal of good which would continue into the future. However, this change in tone did not prove to be long lasting. Even as the Hearst press continued to call for cooperation among the English-speaking nations, the stridency in the anti–British tone returned. In October 1938 Hearst delivered a radio broadcast refuting Winston's call for the United States to join Britain and France against the dictators, saying that "English soft soap is again being poured over Uncle Sam's devoted head, lathered into his ears and eyes." Then, on September 4, 1939, days after the start of the Second World War, an editorial by Hearst was published in his newspapers saying that the United States must keep out of Europe's war.[39]

Lord Beaverbrook, who had helped arrange Winston's meeting with Hearst, wrote to his fellow newspaper magnate in October after the visit was over. Saying that he hoped Hearst had enjoyed the visit, Beaverbrook wrote, "He is good company. I am bound to say that I like him much better when he is down, than when he is up. At present he is down."[40] Beaverbrook continued that should the Conservatives come back into power again, Winston should be their leader. Too many Conservatives, however, mistrusted him. If Baldwin went, the Conservatives would replace him with Neville Chamberlain, who would be just as bad as Baldwin.

Winston and Hearst remained in contact with each other, as they occasionally exchanged greetings, including New Year's wishes. On Hearst's frequent visits to Great Britain (he owned St. Donat's castle in Wales), they often visited together. Davies was included on some of the visits to Britain and recalled in her memoirs visiting the Churchills at Chartwell. For several years through the mid–1930s, Hearst bought the rights to some of Winston's articles for syndication in his newspapers.

… 15 …

# Los Angeles and Catalina, September 21–26

After having been shown the top figures in Hollywood by William Randolph Hearst, Winston now moved into the orbit of Los Angeles' business and financial leaders. These men would host and entertain him for the remaining few days of his trip to the city. These "California swells," as Winston called them, were not part of the film world but involved in banking, finance, and industry. They did not know Hearst personally, but, as Winston observed, they regarded the newspaper magnate as the "Devil." The first time many of this circle had any contact with Hearst or the film world was when they attended the MGM luncheon given in Winston's honor. Impressed with how Hearst had spoken in friendly tones about Britain, the swells thought it proved Winston had been right to meet with Hearst and commended him for it.[1]

The main hosts of the Churchills were now Henry M. Robinson and James R. Page. Although Robinson was a host and organizer of the visit, he was most likely not in Los Angeles when Winston was there. He had been summoned back east and thus probably could not be present. Winston would have enjoyed meeting Robinson and had much to talk with him about, most especially on the issue of reparations. Having amassed a fortune as a lawyer, newspaper publisher, and banker, Robinson had been an American delegate to several international conferences, including the Paris Peace conference and the 1927 Economic Conference at Geneva. Although he had declined offers of cabinet positions from presidents Wilson, Harding, and Hoover, he had served as an American representative on the two Dawes Plan committees that worked on reparations schemes.[2]

Winston's other host was James Page, a prominent leader in business and civic matters in southern California as director of many leading business and financial firms. The 45-year-old had served in the United States army in the First World War and later organized an investment firm in Los Angeles. Having been vice-president of the First National Trust and Savings Bank, Page became president of the California Bank in 1929. His varied service included membership in the Greater Los Angeles Harbor Committee of 200 that was planning the development of the harbor.[3]

While in Los Angeles the party stayed, beyond their two sojourns to Ocean House, at the Biltmore Hotel, which was located at Fifth and Olive streets, across from Pershing Square and near the railway terminals. Built at a cost of $10 million, it opened on October 1, 1923, and was the "largest and grandest hotel west of Chicago." "Utterly sumptuous glory," was how the *Los Angeles Times* described the hotel when it opened, adding it had "luxury heaped upon luxury." Built as a modern example of Renaissance architecture, the hotel had a redbrick façade, arches, Ionic columns, marble fountain in the lobby, and cathedral style ceilings painted by Giovanni Battista Smeraldi. With 1,500 rooms in 1929, the hotel was called the "host of the coast." A swimming pool and private men's health club, which the Churchills may have used, were added in 1926. Winston, who was a discerning judge of luxury, called the Biltmore the "last word in hotels."[4]

The manager of the hotel during Winston's visit was Charles Baad. He had managed the hotel since its opening, after previously holding the same position at Los Angeles' Alexandra Hotel and the St. Francis in San Francisco.

Johnny loved the piano. His sister remembered that he seemed to play the piano constantly. Upon reaching hotels while touring in the United States, it was his practice, a pastime he probably continued at the Biltmore, to find the piano and enjoy some relaxation by playing. He played Wagner, Strauss waltzes, and Chopin. At that time he had not yet been able to master any Bach.[5]

James Page refused to allow the party to pay for anything while under his care. They had the "finest suite, an excellent valet-waiter—motor cars and every kind of liquor." With Page paying for everything, the Churchills had to practice "much self-effacement."[6]

In Los Angeles Winston met all of the leading men. In both his upcoming speech to the California Club and more informal talks he made to circles of ten to twelve at a time, he sought to explain England to them. Winston described "how splendid and tolerant" his country was, and how the Americans and British should work together. His audiences expressed approval of what he had to say.

Of the men Winston met in Los Angeles, he thought four or five were "very fine fellows indeed" and thought they, in turn, were "equally pleased with my companionship." The individual Winston took the greatest liking to was Andrew M. Chaffey, a Canadian-born, Australian-educated, naturalized American. An "early resident of Southern California," Chaffey had founded the American Savings Bank and, as bank president, started the practice of branch banking in the region. Winston wrote that Chaffey was "immensely rich and respected—a sincere lover of our country."[7]

Winston's introduction to Los Angeles' business and financial leaders began in earnest on the evening of September 21 when the Churchills were entertained at a dinner held by Page at his home at 354 South Windsor Boulevard in Los Angeles. Page was possibly joined at the affair by his wife Kate. After meeting famous motion picture stars and beautiful chorus girls, Page's party may have been a bit of a step down for the younger members of the traveling party, if they were, in fact, made to attend.[8]

Having been in Los Angeles for several days, Winston had learned and observed a great deal about the city. He found it very different from San Francisco. Both cities had populations exceeding one million, but while San Francisco stretched "to the heavens," Los Angeles was spread "widely over the level shores." With the city covering an area of about 410 square miles in the 1920s, Winston found Los Angeles to be spread out and the distances amazing.

He wrote, "You motor ten miles to luncheon in one direction and ten miles to dinner in another." He considered Los Angeles was a "gay and happy city, where everyone has room to live." On his visit he noticed an absence of "poverty and squalor." Rather, Los Angles was a city of "opulence" that at night was ablaze with electric lights and signs of every color. This city was a "carnival in fairyland!" Winston's description of Los Angeles was echoed in the twenties in one of the city's magazines that described the city at night as a "wonderland of light and in sheer extent the horizontal equivalent of vertical New York."[9]

In his *Daily Telegraph* article on Los Angeles Winston noted the city's two industries as being, of course, the motion picture industry and oil. Throughout the city he saw derricks used for the extraction of oil, even on the beaches and in the sea itself. Whereas the oil derricks he had seen in Alberta were veritable towers in order to reach the oil a mile below the surface, the derricks in Los Angeles were just fifty or sixty feet high. The derricks were clustered so thickly together on the hills south of the city that at a distance it looked like a forest. Winston learned about the organization of the oil industry and relayed to his readers that the oil industry was split into small holdings just yards away from each other. Each operator was "pumping away in mad haste" to ensure they were not beaten to the oil by their neighbor. While Winston doubted such a system could last for long, at present a great deal of oil was being produced cheaply, which left everyone, including the consumers, happy.[10]

On September 22 the Churchills went off in two groups for most of the day. Winston and Jack spent most of the day visiting the island of Catalina, while Randolph and Johnny gave the voyage a miss and spent their time looking around the Twentieth Century–Fox studio. Johnny thought tours of studios could become quite tedious, as they are all the same, with only the sets and actors differing. The people at Twentieth Century–Fox, he remembered, kept the boys' keenest interest by "parading a mass of lovely girls for our benefit."[11]

There were no lovely girls on parade for Winston and Jack, however, when they visited Catalina as the guests of Ben R. Meyer, a local banker who was chairman of the Union Bank and Trust Company. About 25 miles off the coast of Los Angeles, South Catalina Island is mountainous and very picturesque. The brothers sailed to the island aboard the motor yacht *Happy Days* that belonged to Colonel Ira C. Copley. The *Happy Days* had been completed two years before in 1927 at a cost of $500,000. Built in Kiel, Germany, the yacht was 200 feet in length, had a speed of 13 knots, and required a crew of 30. The commander of the yacht was Captain P.E. Hillman, who had previously commanded the Hamburg American liner *Cleveland*.[12]

Ira Copley, who had earned the title of Colonel from his service in the Illinois National Guard, had served six terms in the House of Representatives from 1911 to 1923. After building up a newspaper business in Illinois, Copley had expanded to enter the newspaper business in southern California only the previous year. Within a few months of launching his efforts in the state he had acquired 18 dailies in southern California.

Aboard the ship, along with the Churchills, was a who's who of Los Angeles, including James Page; Andrew Chaffey; Dr. Robert A. Millikan, a Caltech physicist and Nobel Laureate; Los Angeles surgeon Dr. Ernest Bryant; John B. Miller, president of the Southern California Edison Company; and a squad of powerful bank presidents, among whom were Joseph Sartori, G. Allan Hancock, and Richard Jewett Schweppe. Also aboard were the director of the Huntington Library, Max Ferrand; William May Garland, who had been instrumental in bringing the upcoming 1932 Olympics to Los Angeles and was in 1929 leading the preparations for the games; and the bank executive J. Benton Van Nuys, whose family once owned a ranch that covered most of the San Fernando Valley and for which the city of Van Nuys had been named. Lee A. Phillips of Los Angeles joined the trip later, as he sailed to the island on his own yacht and came aboard the *Happy Days* for dinner while it lay at anchor in Descanso Bay.[13]

The cruise aboard the *Happy Days* was very enjoyable for Winston, as Copley was used to entertaining famous people aboard the yacht and had the ship stocked with excellent brandy and cigars. Referring to the other yacht that Phillips had sailed out on, Winston passed on the opportunity to go aboard. He was happy where he was in the luxury of the *Happy Days*. Puffing on a cigar, he declined, saying in reference to the Phillips yacht, the "other might be a bore."[14]

Upon reaching the island, the party temporarily split up. Winston, Ben Meyer, and most likely the keen fisherman Jack went for a fishing trip on the ocean. With very little time to fish, about an hour, many in the party advised against going. As people go for long periods without catching a swordfish, they said it was useless to go out in the fishing boat that was at the ready. Winston ignored their advice and went anyways. The rest of the party took the opportunity to go aboard a glass-bottomed boat trip to view the submarine gardens, with its fish, brightly colored shells, mosses, ferns, and kelp.

Sailing aboard the fishing launch the U.R. No. 2, also called Sunbeam II and owned by Lee Phillips, Winston and his brother tried their luck in the waters off Catalina. Aboard the launch that was skippered by Monte Foster it took Winston only twenty minutes of fishing, using regulation tuna club tackle, to land a fish that would make news on two continents. He had hooked a Marlin Swordfish. A 20-minute struggle was needed to bring the fish in close enough for Captain Foster to gaff it and pull it onto the boat. With the catch of a Marlin, the fishing expedition was a success, and the launch retired back to the island. Catching a Marlin in so little time was some sort of a record for the waters around Catalina.

On this very brief fishing trip on the Pacific Ocean Winston had landed a 188-pound Marlin Swordfish. Upon landing at the pier at Catalina with his trophy, as the *Los Angeles Times* reported, there was "something of a stir" among the members of the Tuna Club, the big-game fishing club on the island. Some of these fishermen, the newspaper explained, had tried in vain for more than a decade to catch a Marlin. The *San Francisco Examiner* remarked, "Ordinary persons simply cannot hook Marlin swordfishes—unless they continue to try for at least fifteen or twenty years." Still wearing his fishing outfit, Winston happily posed for photographs, alongside Foster and Meyer, with his Marlin. Pictures of Winston with his trophy were transmitted worldwide and published in many American and British newspapers. Directions were issued after the photographs were taken for the Marlin to be shipped to the Biltmore in Los Angeles where the Churchills were staying.[15]

The *Manchester Guardian* humorously professed mock amazement at Winston's seeming success at anything he put his mind to. Referring to his landing the Swordfish, the newspaper wrote, "But what can you expect? When Mr. Churchill paints pictures the Royal Academy shakes in its shoes and Old Masters turn in their graves; when he goes brick-laying trade unions are plunged into fiercest strife and internal recriminations. When he goes fishing whales and swordfish fight for the honour of being hung on his hook, and if he went pigsticking the wildest and largest boars would hurl themselves at his lance." The publicity garnered from the landing of the Marlin caused the same newspaper to offer further comment that Winston was unable to keep out of the limelight. Even on a California holiday, "celebrity pursues and surrounds him."[16]

That evening, on their return from Catalina and the movie studio respectively, the Churchills dined with Charlie Chaplin at their suite at the Biltmore. Winston had previously invited him to dinner. The actor spent a delightful evening listening to Winston and Randolph pleasantly bantering about "inconsequential things." Chaplin was impressed with Randolph and could see Winston was proud of his son. The actor thought the youngest Churchill was "handsome" as well as "esurient for intellectual argument and had the criticism of intolerant youth."[17]

Winston and Chaplin enjoyed each other's company, despite their pronounced differences in political outlook. Winston was, of course, a British conservative, while Chaplin was on the left of the political spectrum. During conversations when they dined two years later in England, Chaplin and Winston occasionally lapsed into frosty political disagreement. At one dinner that Johnny attended he thought Chaplin delivered a soliloquy that was "pacifist and communist."[18] When another person at the dinner table suggested that Gandhi was a "menace" to the peace in India, Chaplin replied with conviction that "Gandhis or Lenins" do not start revolutions, but they are forced up by the masses and usually voice the want of a people.

"You should run for Parliament," Winston said with a laugh.

"No, sir, I prefer to be a motion picture actor these days," Chaplin replied. "However, I believe we should go with evolution to avoid revolution, and there's every evidence that the world needs a drastic change."[19]

On September 23 a luncheon was held in Winston's honor by his Los Angeles hosts, Henry Robinson and James Page, at the California Club, located at 455 South Hill. The 166-strong guest list at the luncheon was described as being composed of the "foremost men of the city." All of the men whom Winston had sailed with at Catalina the previous day were in attendance, as were others he had already met in California, including McAdoo and Consul-General Gerald Campbell. This meeting, in one newspaper's estimation, was of men who all already knew each other. In this group the guest of honor quickly became a friend of everyone. Flags of the United States and Great Britain were arranged in the room for the luncheon at the California Club, while colorful water lilies were set out on each table.[20]

Prior to the luncheon, Winston chatted with Andrew Chaffey, another sailing guest from the day before. In his speech at the luncheon he would refer to what Chaffey had told him just before the lunch about the "crimson thread of kinship that is precious" between the United States and Britain.

As the luncheon began, Page rose and proposed a toast "To the King." In turn, Winston stood and raised his glass, proposing "To the President of the United States." The toasts were made with glasses of fruit punch, which Winston must have found rather unworthy at the least. At this private luncheon, Winston made a speech. This was in line with his intention stated before he arrived to decline all speaking invitations in the United States save for those of a private nature. Introduced by Page, Winston lauded the "prosperity, enterprise and sunshine of Southern California." The main thrust of the remarks was of his hope for an accord between the English speaking peoples and his desire for cooperation between the United States and Great Britain. A unity of purpose between the two would carry both peoples forward to a "brighter world than has ever existed." He described the many common bonds between the two countries, including language, basic law, and literature. With his mother being American, he said it was important to him that the British and Americans should work closely together.[21]

Winston remarked that a falling out between Britain and the United States would ruin the possibilities of a better world. A disagreement between the two countries would not merely squander "all the moral and material wealth of the world, but would mean a return to barbarism."

In the address, Winston also returned to one of his points that he repeated in all of his Canadian speeches—that of Britain's condition. He defended his country's circumstance, saying its financial condition was healthy. In another holdover from his Canadian speeches he also pointed out Britain's desire for peace.

After Winston finished, Page called upon Randolph to speak to the luncheon. As Randolph acknowledged in his talk, this was the first time he had addressed an American audience. It would, of course, be the first of many such occasions, including his own lecture tour in 1931. The short speech by the youngest member of the traveling party, in which he expressed his thanks for the courtesies they had received in California, was applauded by the *Los Angeles Examiner* as having "all the aplomb of his father." Although he was praised in the newspaper and applauded by his audience, Randolph, nonetheless, thought the effort was quite poor.[22]

Winston would repeat his calls for Anglo-American cooperation in all his speeches given in the United States. By the time he spoke at the California Club he had already seen much enthusiasm for his call for friendship between the two countries. At the end of the tour of the United States he would declare himself struck by the kind feelings the Americans felt for the British Empire. A "wave of good will" on the part of the Americans, as well as recognition of how much the two countries had in common, was much in evidence on his trip. The good will originated with Americans and Brits having fought together in the Great War, when for the "first time for a hundred and fifty years the two kindred nations had history to write in common." The war established new ties between the countries, while the Irish settlement removed that "slow, virulent poison distilled against Great Britain for more than a century." Likewise the merging of the Anglo-Japanese alliance in the Four-Power Pact removed another source of suspicion from the relationship. The settlement of the debt was believed by Winston to have also created a positive reaction in America. All these issues had worked together to liberate the elements in the United States that have always been sympathetic to the British.[23]

As evidence of the good will, Winston pointed out the sympathy the American public showed for the King during his recent illness and by the way newspapers in the United States advocated close cooperation among the English-speaking countries. Twenty years before, the same newspapers would have merrily been "twisting the lion's tail." From his own visit Winston reported that the English traveler in America was received with customary politeness as well as great delight.

That night Johnny and Randolph ate dinner by themselves and then went to the theater, while Winston and Jack dined with William Gibbs McAdoo. This meal with McAdoo was the only entirely dry meal Winston had had thus far on his trip.[24]

On September 24, Charlie Chaplin hosted the Churchills at his studio at Sunset Boulevard and La Brea Avenue. Randolph thought the actor was a wonderful host and wrote that he was "too sweet for words." After first lunching together, Chaplin took his visitors on a tour of the studio where he was at work on his silent classic *City Lights*. He even performed a piano recital and sang English ballads for the entertainment of his fellow Englishmen, as well as acted his new film for them. After showing them around, Chaplin provided a private screening of his 1918 picture *Shoulder Arms*, one of his great movies, followed by the rushes for his current work, *City Lights*. At the studio it was Chaplin's habit to entertain his visitors by filming them, a practice he continued with the Churchills. Clips shot of these visitors were so distinctly uneventful that the actor probably could not help himself and started to perform. Another clip shows a rather self-conscious and wooden Winston walking beside an assured and relaxed Chaplin.[25]

During the tour and screening, Winston and Chaplin discussed the revolution that was engulfing Hollywood by the introduction of "talkies." Much of what they discussed Winston used in his article for the *Daily Telegraph*. In the piece on Hollywood Winston wrote of the great popularity of the talkies, even with their technical limitations and poor quality sound reproductions. Faced with the demand from the public for sound, all in Hollywood was radically transformed. The characters in films were now made to talk as well as act, while experts arrived at the studios with new apparatus for recording sound. Winston observed that new procedures were being put in place to make the talkies, which required not only darkness on the sound stage but silence as well. To that end, balloons were positioned above the studios to keep away noisy airplanes. In Hollywood Winston found only Chaplin had not been won over to the "talkies." While ready to acknowledge their popularity, he was unwilling to concede the demise of the silent film. *City Lights*, Winston thought, was to be Chaplin's attempt to prove silent film superior to talkies. Chaplin was ready to claim that "pantomime is the genius of drama, and that the imagination of the audience supplies better words than machinery can render, and prepared to vindicate the silent film by the glittering weapons of wit and pathos." In that regard, Winston predicted an easy victory for Chaplin and *City Lights*.[26]

The rushes from *City Lights* were followed by sequences of film from Chaplin's unpublished archives, which included scenes that were too embarrassing to be used. One such scene that Johnny vividly recalled in his memoirs was considered particularly unsuitable. It involved the harnessing of a horse-drawn fire engine.

"I wanted it done extremely rapidly," Chaplin explained to his guests. The actor and director found that putting a harness on a horse always took too much time. A solution, however, was thought of that involved filming the harness being taken off the horse—a quicker process—with the intention of just reversing the film. This solution worked perfectly—save for the fact that in the excitement of shooting the scene no one noticed the horse had, alas, relieved itself while being filmed. When the footage was reversed, as Johnny saw during the private screening, the horse's matter "leaped off the ground and all disappeared inside the animal with breath-taking exactitude."[27]

That evening the four Churchills and Charlie Chaplin joined the Marion Davies party at the premiere of *Cock-Eyed World* at Grauman's Chinese Theatre. The film starred Victor McLaglen and was directed by Raoul Walsh, who had already directed such classics as *The Thief of Baghdad* with Douglas Fairbanks. The members of the Davies group included the actresses Eleanor Boardman, Diane Ellis, and Juliette Compton. Hearst's Los Angeles newspaper dutifully reported the fashion worn by several of the ladies in the Davies party and wrote that Marion herself wore "white tulle made with a tight bodice and a flounced skirt and a wrap of pale rose velvet and white fox." Compton, who wore an ensemble of white velvet, would appear many years later in the film *That Hamilton Woman*, reputed to be Winston's favorite film.[28]

Randolph thought the premiere was an outstanding event. There were ten searchlights flashing in the street, and a huge crowd of film fans had gathered outside the theater for hours to watch the festivities. The entire film world seemed to have turned out, with the first nighters including such luminaries as Mary Astor, Loretta Young, Eric Von Stroheim, Cecil B. DeMille, and Basil Rathbone. Benny Rubin, who had performed for the Churchills at the MGM reception, was also at the premiere. Randolph even noted that they saw the Frenchman Georges Carpentier, the retired former boxing champion, who was in Los Angeles. The *Los Angeles Times* reported the film attracted one of the most brilliant audiences for a premiere yet that season. A microphone was set up to broadcast the remarks of the stars and makers of the movie over the radio as they arrived. All of the hoopla, however, did not prevent Randolph from loudly denouncing the film as the worst he had ever seen. The Los Angeles newspapers disagreed with Randolph's assessment and gave the picture positive reviews. Louella Parsons in the *Los Angeles Examiner* reported the first-night audience (Randolph aside, no doubt) laughed and loudly applauded the film.[29]

After the movie Marion Davies brought her group, Churchills and Chaplin included, to a "big party" for 300 people to mark the premiere held at the Blossom Room of the Roosevelt Hotel, located on Hollywood Boulevard. The dinner-dance that started at midnight was hosted by the director of *Cock-Eyed World*, Raoul Walsh. The Blossom Room had been decorated with colored lights and silver foliage. On some tables there were very large mulberry dahlias, American Beauty roses, and ferns, while on other tables rose trees in blossom were set out. Two orchestras played alternating numbers for dancing. Randolph mentioned that along with the dancing there was also sherry and champagne served openly, despite prohibition. Walsh also used the party to celebrate the 46th birthday of Winfield Sheehan, a film producer and studio executive. To mark the anniversary during the dessert course, scores of girls in dancing costumes, each carrying a cake with one candle, marched into the ballroom.[30]

At the movie premiere and party at the Roosevelt Hotel, Winston probably finally did meet Raoul Walsh. Like his extravagant claims of meeting Winston at San Simeon and Ocean House, Walsh describes further unlikely adventures with Winston in his autobiography. These include a trip to the Santa Anita race track and a visit to Walsh's ranch, where Winston was supposedly taken aback by the two-year-old lion kept as a house pet.[31]

Having spent a week in Hollywood, during which time he had met motion picture executives, film stars, watched silent pictures and talkies, toured studios, and attended a premiere, Winston pronounced Hollywood a "strange and amusing" place that sought to entertain the world.[32] This place had dozens of studios covering thousands of acres, and employing thousands of performers and technicians. A studio was a "Peter Pan township" where, "with magical quickness," sets for London, China, India, jungles, mountains, and every conceivable form of scenery were constructed. Twenty films were underway at once at a studio, Winston observed, and varied crowds stream around the lot, from South Sea Islanders to cowboys. To make the films, complicated photographic techniques are employed, while the studios themselves were "perfect installations for bridling light and sound." While "youthful beauty claims her indisputable rights" in Hollywood, Winston believed the film world was founded on personality and required "hard work, frugality and discipline."

Winston had become "great friends" with Chaplin during the visit to Los Angeles. Randolph and Johnny found him intriguing, while Winston thought anyone "could not help liking him." Writing to Clementine, Winston described the actor as a "marvelous comedian—bolshy in politics and delightful in conversation."[33] Chaplin was tremendously impressed with Winston and is reputed to have told a radio interview in 1961 that he had only met three geniuses in his life: Albert Einstein, Winston Churchill, and Clara Haskil.

Two years later Winston and Chaplin would renew their friendship when the actor came to England to premiere his now completed *City Lights*. Chaplin would twice visit Winston at Chartwell in 1931, on which occasions Jack, Randolph, and Johnny would also come and again meet the most famous actor in the world. Thereafter the great statesman and the great actor would remain friends, but from afar.[34]

The whereabouts of the Churchills on September 25 is slightly confused. It had originally been planned for the party to spend the day visiting San Diego, leaving Los Angeles at one o'clock in the morning aboard the Santa Fe train No. 78. After the day in San Diego it was planned for them to make the four-and-a-half-hour trip back to Los Angeles, arriving at 7:30 in the morning on September 26. The *San Diego Sun* even published a detailed article on the Churchills' visit to their city. It reported that the party spent the morning at Coronado and might visit the North Island before they departed back to Los Angeles. Winston was quoted as saying he was on vacation and did not want to delve into international affairs, while the newspaper reporter amused him by telling the British statesman that the swordfish off San Diego were just as big and three times as numerous near the Coronados.[35]

The *Los Angeles Examiner*, however, reported that the Churchills had changed their plans and cancelled the trip to San Diego in favor of remaining in Los Angeles for the day. Winston wrote Clementine from Los Angeles in a letter dated September 25 that makes no reference to San Diego. The *San Diego Sun* article to the contrary, it is most likely the Churchills spent the day in Los Angeles. While in Los Angeles, probably on September 25, Winston took Randolph to see a doctor, as he was concerned about his son's persistent cough and cold. Randolph's general health had not been helped by getting to bed quite late all week due to the film premiere and other engagements he attended. The doctor found that while the heart and lungs were good, Randolph had a very bad sinus condition and his tonsils were poor. The condition, however, was not urgent. Randolph could forgo treatment until he reached England, at which point he should seek out a specialist for a treatment that would last six or seven weeks.[36]

In the September 25 letter to Clementine, Winston wrote with news of the trip to Los Angeles and plans for the rest of the tour. Of Los Angeles, he commented that beyond swimming, their time in the city had been spent watching films and visiting studios to see them being made. Although enjoying himself, Winston wrote his wife that he "longed to be home."[37]

Winston explained their future travel plans and said that he intended to accelerate their journey and reach New York City in order to meet up with his friends Lord Birkenhead and Harry McGowan, who were sailing from there on October 9. Birkenhead and McGowan, along with Sir Laming Worthington-Evans, M.P., had arrived in the United States in mid–September to discuss business matters, including those of the Utility Power and Light Corporation, with American businessmen. Winston and Birkenhead had already arranged to dine together on the night before they sailed. The boys, Randolph and Johnny, would be going home on the same ocean liner as Birkenhead and McGowan, which would allow them to reach Oxford by October 14 or 15. Winston hoped this arrangement would meet with the "approval of the college authorities."

In an update on Randolph, Winston reported on what he had learned from their visit to the doctor and asked Clementine to cable him about who she advised to treat their son upon his return home. More positively, he wrote that Randolph was continuing to win "golden opinions from both sexes" and that his complexion was "almost perfect now." Winston added that he was trying to keep their son in order. Having received his wife's letter telling him of her new plan to travel to Italy with Diane, Winston wrote that he wished he knew what days she would be in the various Italian cities so that "one could conjure the scene in the mind." As it turned out, Clementine and Diana visited Florence, Perugia, and Assisi before arriving in Rome on October 16.

Near the end of September, while in Los Angeles, Winston completed his plunge into the stock market. On September 20 he had written James Richardson in Winnipeg directing him to retain the oil shares in Hargal and Baltac but transfer the remaining balance to Winston's account at Van Antwerp's firm in San Francisco. In doing business with the E.F. Hutton office in San Francisco, Winston bought and sold shares in such companies as Simmons, Montgomery Ward, Bethlehem Steel, and United Gas. Winston wrote Clementine that he had made 1,000 pounds speculating in the stock of the Simmons company. This furniture business had the slogan, which he quite liked, of "You can't go wrong on a Simmons mattress."[38]

Winston would write an article devoted to the stock market for the *Daily Telegraph* that was titled "Fever of Speculation in America."[39] In the United States he found that the entire population was dabbling in stocks. Millions from every part of the country eagerly pursued the quick return of the market. Maids, workmen of every class, chauffeurs, train conductors, railwaymen, and waiters all had their open accounts, as do quite often their wives. "Horseracing, baseball, football, every form of sport or gambling," he wrote, ceded its place to the stock market. While the British workman would bet on the turf, the American public concentrates on the stock markets. Winston found it was as easy to buy shares on margin as it was to buy tea, and easier to buy than a motorcar or gramophone on an installment plan. This mass participation in the stock market was to Winston a new innovation and something never even dreamed of before.

The Americans feverishly followed the rise and decline of their stocks. No pages of the newspaper, Winston wrote, were more "carefully printed, more eagerly and more earnestly studied" than those reporting on the stock markets. Transatlantic steamers had "floating migratory exchanges," while hotels had telephones and other equipment operated by expert clerks to allow for the minute-to-minute quotation of stock prices. Winston observed that in every hotel you can "go and sit and watch the figures being marked up on slates every few minutes."[40]

Winston's enthusiasm for the stock market was allowed to run wild while he was away from, as John Colville phrased it, Clementine's "sobering presence." Perhaps guessing what her opinion of betting on the market would be, Winston tried to reassure her from afar, explaining that his own feverish pursuit of the easy money was actually quite safe because he was being advised by a "very good man" in Van Antwerp and the firm of E.F. Hutton. This firm, he wrote, would "watch my small interests like a cat and mouse."[41]

On one of the days Winston was in Los Angeles, possibly September 25 or September 26, Winston and Jack made a visit to see the actor John Barrymore. Winston liked the Barrymore family and had, at least according to a Churchill legend, proposed marriage to John Barrymore's sister Ethel, who declined the offer. Winston and John Barrymore were great friends, and they spent a great deal of time together when the actor was playing Hamlet in London. It was only Winston that had saved that production. Barrymore thought Hamlet had opened so poorly in London that he might have quit after the first performance had he not received a note from Winston that "brightened matters considerably." Not wanting to let Winston down, Barrymore had successfully persevered with the role.[42]

Winston visited Barrymore on the set of the movie he was making, *The Man from Blankley's*, at the Warner Brothers Studio on Sunset Boulevard. He watched Barrymore as he filmed scenes for a comedy farce that was released in 1930. After they visited together and posed for photographs on the sound stage, Barrymore brought Winston over and introduced him with a flourish to Tiny Jones, a bit player who was acting in the production. Jones was left "completely aflutter" by the introduction. Jones, a 53-year-old lady from Wales, had confessed a desire to meet Winston when she had heard he would be coming to the set. Winston had to bend over to shake hands with the actress, who was only four-feet-five-inches and weighed 62 pounds. Barrymore and Winston also dined alone one night in Los Angeles, during which time they discussed the old days of John playing Hamlet and one occasion in which Barrymore, Winston, the Prince of Wales, and several members of Parliament were all together at the Whistler house. Shortly after Winston's visit, Barrymore suffered a recurrence of an ulcer but assured a friend that he "in nowise blamed Mr. Churchill's visit for this condition."[43]

During his visit to Los Angeles, Winston hosted a dinner as well as a luncheon for those among the "California swells" that he liked best. These two functions most likely took place late in his stay in the city, possibly on September 25 or 26, as his schedule for the other days was quite filled with studio tours and other functions. These business leaders whom Winston particularly liked and invited to dine were for the most part "British born and keenly pro–England." The dinner, as well as lunch, was hosted by Winston at the Biltmore, either in his suite or the restaurant, as he later wrote that it was only with difficulty that he managed to get the costs of the meals extracted from his bill so he could pay for them himself.[44]

The Churchills left Los Angeles for Yosemite on the night of September 26, having decided to accept William Van Antwerp's offer to arrange a visit to the park. A quaint scene took place when the party made their final farewells to Marion Davies for the last time in Los Angeles. In Hollywood Randolph and Johnny had adopted the custom of kissing a lady's hand on meeting them, as well as on saying good-bye. This practice was instituted in the thought it made for more "speedy headway" with the film stars. They were "surprised and delighted" when, after they said good-bye to Davies by kissing her hand, Winston outdid both of them by first raising his hat, bowing, and then too kissing her on the hand.[45]

... 16 ...

# Yosemite to Chicago, September 27–October 5, 1929

It was among the spectacular scenery of Yosemite Valley in the national park of the same name that the Churchills spent the day of September 27. Located on the western slope of the Sierra Nevada Mountains, Yosemite had been maintained by the National Park Service since 1916. With its rivers, waterfalls, cliffs, and majestic mountains, it is "unrivaled among beauty spots."[1]

The Churchills traveled by private rail car to Mariposa, California, where they disembarked and were met by William and Edith Van Antwerp, who had driven over from San Francisco to join them. While in Mariposa, before leaving for Yosemite, the party stopped to look at the county courthouse. The historic courthouse dated from 1854. Although the park had been open to motor cars since 1915, the Churchills and their Burlingame friends probably traveled into the valley over the Yosemite Valley Railroad. On the short rail trip, Winston regaled the Van Antwerps with his plan to write a biography of the Duke of Marlborough and all the "painstaking research involved in its production."[2]

The traveling party of Englishmen had been enlarged beyond the Van Antwerps at Yosemite, as it arrived with a new permanent member, who would join them for the rest of the tour. At some point during the last days in Los Angeles Lord Feversham had joined the party. He had not been mentioned as being with the party for any events they attended in Los Angeles, but in the newspaper report on their visit to Yosemite he was, for the first time, included as a member of the traveling group. Charles William Slingsby Duncombe, the third Earl of Feversham, was a 22-year-old who had been educated at Eton and succeeded to his father's titles in 1916 after he had been killed at the Battle of Delville Wood. With a passion for social work, Charles had become interested in the probation service. In 1925 he had started working as an assistant probation officer in Johannesburg under an assumed name, which he did for two years. Returning to Great Britain, he was horrified by the condition of the probation service and would work for its reform and improvement. A year after the trip to the United States, Feversham would become the president of the National Association of Probation Officers.[3] As Winston had pursued prison reform as home secretary, he and the Earl had a common interest.

Having Feversham join the Churchills for the remainder of the tour of the United States was not planned in advance, and he must have been a spur-of-the-moment addition to the group. There was no mention of the young Earl in any of Winston's correspondence from the planning of the trip or during the tour prior to departing Los Angeles. Winston would now regularly ask his hosts on the rest of the journey to extend an extra invitation to Feversham.

With Feversham having joined the troupe, Winston and the others enjoyed the beauty of Yosemite, especially liking the autumn colors. All five members of the party carried cameras during their exploration of the park and were seen to be photographing "everything right and left." The animal life they saw in the park was of great interest to them.

Mariposa County Courthouse. The courthouse was inspected by the Churchill party before their visit to Yosemite (Library of Congress).

The party had a picnic lunch at Inspiration Point, after which they spent the afternoon enjoying the views from Glacier Point. Winston was quite "carried away" by the magnificent scenery at the point. According to Van Antwerp, Winston thought that Yosemite Valley was unequaled by anything else in the United States, Canada, or England. The British statesman also mused to his companion that he would write a book on California upon returning home, with much of the proposed book devoted to Yosemite. Johnny was equally impressed with Yosemite, calling it the "broadest, longest, deepest and most remarkable valley in the world."[4]

William and Edith Van Antwerp left the Englishmen in the afternoon to start their drive back to San Francisco. It was probably Van Antwerp who played a part in one of Winston's anecdotes about the trip. Upon leaving California, as Winston remembered, a friend sent him a suitcase as a "parting gift." The good-sized suitcase was unlabeled and was placed in Winston's compartment "unostentatiously." Unfortunately, something had "gone wrong" with the contents of the suitcase, and a "very curious trickle had left its trail all along the station platform." No one, neither the railway porters nor other passengers, said a thing about it. Winston was quite relieved that, upon opening and inspecting the suitcase, it was found that only one bottle of alcohol had broken, and the remaining bottles were safely intact.[5]

The Englishmen traveled by train that night, while the Van Antwerps spent the night at the Hotel Tioga in Merced, California. While there, Van Antwerp gave an interview to the *Merced Sun-Star* in which he related Winston's impressions of Yosemite. The Burlingame couple hoped to see the Churchills in New York in October, but their plans changed and they did not come east as proposed.

"California is perfectly delightful. I have just spent a day in your Yosemite Park and I have never seen anything like it. I am now on my way to Chicago, where I am to deliver an address, but I will stop for a while in the Grand Canyon, and they tell me it is even more wonderful than anything I have seen before," Winston told the *Bakersfield Californian* during a forty-minute stop at Bakersfield on the morning of September 28. "It had been marvelous all the way, and I am sorry I have not more time to spend in California."[6]

Traveling in a private car attached to the *Navajo*, the travelers arrived at the Santa Fe station in Bakersfield at half-past nine o'clock in the morning. The reporter for the newspaper was "graciously" received by Winston and found him enjoying breakfast clad in a luxurious dressing robe and puffing on a big black cigar. Winston was relaxed and "totally oblivious" to anything, in the reporter's opinion, except for the wonders of the California climate, splendor of Yosemite, and anticipation of the Grand Canyon.

While ready to praise California, Winston did not want to commit himself on any political issues and declined to answer the questions the reporter attempted. When asked whether he thought the conference on naval parity between Ramsay MacDonald and Herbert Hoover would be successful, he only replied, "Indeed, I haven't heard the news recently in that matter."

"The American people would be interested in knowing your views on tariff matters," the reporter suggested.

"Ah, but that's your affair," Winston parried.

In a similar fashion, Winston did not comment on the Briand proposal for a United States of Europe, the question of diplomatic relations between Britain and Russia, and other topics he was asked about. He did add that he was grateful for the kindness he had received in California and had "never enjoyed anything quite so much."

While he ate breakfast and spoke to the reporter, Winston was handed a telegram, which he read carefully. He then passed it to the secretary who was in attendance on Winston with the remark, "Ah, that must have been yesterday's market!"

The *Navajo* left the Bakersfield train station at ten minutes after ten o'clock, with the Churchills aboard. Since leaving Los Angeles they had been traveling aboard the *Loretto*, the private car that had been loaned for their use by Charles M. Schwab. Johnny thought the car was an "elaborate affair," with bedrooms, bathrooms, a kitchen, drawing rooms, and an open air observation platform. This was actually the second private car Schwab had owned that had been called *Loretto*. He had ordered the present *Loretto* in 1917, which was manufactured at a cost of $150,000, after the first private car by that name had become outdated. It was "one of the most widely celebrated private cars of its time." The new *Loretto*, which was 83 feet in length and weighed 80 tons, had interiors of mahogany and a bathroom of Italian marble. One of the staterooms in the private car had seven mother-of-pearl buttons to summon the stewards.[7]

In describing traveling in private cars across North America, Winston would write of them as a "rare and costly luxury" that gave a "really joyous feeling." A private car was a "home from home. And what a sense of power and choice, to be able to stop where you would and for as long as you would, and to sleep on till you wished to get up, and to hook onto any train when satiated with the wonders of the Yosemite Valley, or the Grand Canyon, or the roar of Niagara, or the clack and clutter of the Chicago stockyards." On his next trip to the United States, in 1931–32 for a lecture tour, Winston investigated the hiring of a private car for the trip but found it far too costly.[8]

Further east, as they traveled across the California desert, the *Navajo* made a two-hour stop at Barstow. Here, which Winston termed an "oasis," they left the train for a bath in the hotel, the Casa Del Desierto. This hotel was one of many such establishments set up by a businessman named Fred Harvey, catering to rail travelers by offering fine dining and comfortable rooms. At the "nice and cool" hotel Winston wrote a letter to Clementine about his California trip. He wrote the note on the letterhead of the Casa del Monte he had from the visit to San Simeon, and in the letter remarked how the "enchanting" scene printed on the top of the letterhead contrasted with where they were now in the desert. Even though he had a private secretary aboard the *Loretto* he hand wrote the letter, as he had a few things to say—meaning his impressions of Hearst as a "grave simple child"—that would be "wiser not to dictate." Winston ended the letter in a hurry, writing that he would have to rush for the train, which is "just off."[9]

After three weeks in California, during which time he traveled the length of the state and visited its major cities, Winston thought it was beautiful. He, in fact, doubted that he had seen a place more beautiful.[10] Beyond its "undulating" countryside and mountain ranges, the state possessed "a smiling and varied fertility." He noted that the "forests, vineyards, orange groves, olives, and every other form of cultivation that the natives desire, crowns or clothes the sunbathed peaks and valleys." Winston would wax about the state's temperature, prosperity produced by agriculture, gold, oil, and film, abundance of food, pleasant dwellings, and absence of poverty, congestion, and heavy industry. He also recorded, on the part of Californians, an "unbounded hospitality, and a marked friendliness and respect towards Old England, her institutions, and Empire."

On Sunday, September 29, the Churchills visited the Grand Canyon. To do so they must have had the private car detached from the train in order for them to make the trip by the rail spur to the canyon. They were at the canyon at least by mid–morning, as Winston sent a telegram to Baruch from there that was stamped 10:30 a.m. As they toured the spot and took in the amazing views, Randolph and Johnny, out of "sheer devilry," played a stunt on their fathers. They stood on their heads near the canyon's edge, which caused the older Churchills to react in horror. Winston and Jack reacted to their daring "with a violent shout of alarm." Johnny thought their fathers always appeared to suffer from a form of vertigo when they saw someone doing a dangerous thing. In reality, the cousins were a safe distance from the edge, but it looked terrifying and was more than enough to scare their fathers. At the Grand Canyon the party learned a raft of statistics about the canyon being the longest, deepest, and widest. These statistics made an impression on Winston, and he listed the information on the back of the postcard of the Cathedral Steps sent to Clementine, including that the canyon was a mile deep. Postcards of the Grand Canyon were also sent to Sarah and Mary. Other postcards that were kept among Winston's possessions include the canyon from Pima Point, Hermit's Rest, Sunset from Mojave Point, cliffs on Hermit Trail, the fireplace at Hermit's Rest, and the stairs to Hermit's Rest.[11]

After the day spent at the Grand Canyon, the private car was hitched to the end of a train for the run to Chicago. This trip along the Santa Fe line into Chicago took the party out of Arizona and across New Mexico, Colorado, Kansas, and Missouri before entering Illinois. On the east-bound train Winston, as always, kept busy with his reading, writing, and stocks. He read *Meet General Grant* and made progress reading *The Tragic Era*. Both of these books had been given to him by William Gibbs McAdoo.

On the train trip from California to Chicago, Winston worked on an article that was due to a magazine publisher. Randolph later recalled that on that leg of the trip, perhaps while still in California, his father, despite the heat aboard the train, "shut himself up in his own small compartment and wrote an article."[12] Lacking a private secretary on the train, Winston spent two or three hours writing an article by hand, something he had not done in decades, as he preferred to dictate to a secretary. The article was probably on Sir John French, Lord Ypres, who was the first commander of the British Expeditionary Force during the Great War, as well as a friend of Winston's. After he was finished, Winston read the completed article to the rest of the party at dinner.

Randolph complimented his father on the piece. In reply, Winston remarked, "You know I hate to go to bed at night feeling I have done nothing useful in the day. It is the same feeling as if you have gone to bed without brushing your teeth."[13]

Winston's appetite for work and remarkable constitution was also reflected in the comments of the secretary who accompanied him on his 1932 lecture tour. One weekend on that tour Winston took a break at Bernard Baruch's large plantation in South Carolina. During the three days at the plantation he drafted articles for *Collier's* and a British newspaper, as well as dictated a "score of letters." That, the secretary remarked, was "Mr. Churchill's idea of a holiday."[14]

After reaching Chicago, Winston sent copies of the completed article on Ypres to Curtis Brown with instructions to post one copy to *Nash's*. The article was published in the January 1930 issue of *Nash's Pall Mall*. Another piece, on Trotsky, the Russian Bolshevik leader, that Winston had found time to write earlier on the trip was received by *Nash's* at the start of October. It was published by the magazine in December 1929.[15]

After his travels in the United States in 1929 and 1932, Winston was impressed with the size of the country and the American concept of distance. He marveled at it. In an article he wrote that Americans had a different concept of distance than the British.[16] In the United States a traveler thought as little of making a 14- or 15-hour rail journey as someone in Britain would think of making an hour-and-a-half journey. Winston wrote, "Even the mighty journey to California, from ocean to ocean, presents itself as quite an ordinary undertaking."

Traveling by railway in the United States for Winston was not tiring, even when he traveled day after day. In fact, he felt American trains were "extremely comfortable." On the trains in the United States, with their enormous rolling stock and steady pace, Winston felt a "sense of repose" he did not feel on Britain's "quick, tremulous, and comparatively light railways." While he always traveled by motorcar in Britain for any trip under four or five hours, in the United States Winston would happily travel by train. He would board the train and quickly settle down to work or reading.

As he traveled across Canada and the United States in the private rail cars, Winston listened to the latest stock quotes on the radio.[17] The progress of the Churchills aboard the train can be tracked in some manner by the cables that William Van Antwerp sent to Winston about the stock market. One of these cables was sent addressed to Winston aboard the private car attached to train number ten that was due at Danville, Kansas, at 11:44 a.m. on October 1. This message relayed that as heavy market liquidation was becoming "urgent," Van Antwerp had sold one hundred Simmons shares. The stockbroker also cabled that he would await Winston's telephone call, which they had arranged to be placed when the train reached Wellington, Missouri. Another Van Antwerp cable was sent to Newton, Kansas, for the train due at 3:45 p.m. that same day. The telegram updated Winston on the Simmons shares and concluded with a whimsical request for Jack's opinion about whether Van Antwerp and a "sedate old gentlemen" should go into the ministry.[18]

The traveling party arrived in Chicago for a four-day visit aboard the private car attached to the Santa Fe *Scout* at 10:30 in the morning on October 2. Arriving at the Dearborn Street train station, Winston was returning to a city he had visited, and at which made a speech, on his lecture tour 30 years before. On reaching Chicago, Randolph noted its reputation as being the world's most cosmopolitan city, with more Poles than Warsaw, more Jews than Jerusalem, and with enough Germans to rank as the third largest German city in the world.[19]

Awaiting Winston in Chicago was Bernard Baruch, his trusted American friend. At 59 years old, Baruch was six-feet-five-inches tall, with thick white hair. He had become wealthy as a Wall Street financier and had pursued public service in both official positions in the government as well as an unofficial advisor to American presidents, from Wilson to Johnson. Under President Wilson, whom Baruch idolized, he was chairman of the War Industries Board during the Great War and attended the Paris Peace Conference as a member of the United States Delegation.

In their respective positions in the First World War, Winston and Baruch had worked very well together and met in person for the first time in Paris during the peace conference. Baruch traveled to Europe each summer and always tried to spend a few days with Winston. Although occasionally disagreeing on various political and economic issues, Winston admired Baruch. He once told the American that the world would be fixed if he was allowed to run the politics and Baruch the economics. Years later, after the Second World War, Baruch called their friendship a "source of inspiration and pleasure which has grown more rewarding with each passing year." They would remain life-long friends.[20]

Randolph wrote in his diary that Baruch had bought a seat on the New York Stock Exchange for 100,000 pounds just to transact his own business and called him the "greatest speculator there has ever been." Baruch struck Randolph as a man of "great dignity and with a magnificent carriage and personality." Randolph and Johnny, and probably Jack, did not have to be introduced to Baruch, since they had met him previously on his trips to England, which included visits to Chartwell.[21]

Along with Baruch, welcoming the Englishmen to the city were their Chicago hosts, Donald McLennan and Charles M. Piez. Reporters from Chicago's newspapers were also there to greet Winston with questions on his arrival in the city. The *Daily Tribune*, *Herald and Examiner*, *Daily News*, and *Evening Post* all had journalists on hand, but all came away with less than they had hoped for. The reporters pounced on him as he stepped onto the platform from the private car, despite his protest that "I can't talk after three days on a train."[22]

In a brief interview with the reporters as he left the train station, Winston said he was on a vacation in America "so far as interviews on politics were concerned."[23] He most assuredly did not wish to speak on the issue of naval reductions with the Hoover-MacDonald discussions and maintained his policy of "good-natured avoidance" of questions on that topic. The *Herald and Examiner* said the visitor used "terse epigrams" to parry questions that ranged into political topics.

Asked about the statements on naval parity he had made in Canada, Winston declined to answer and insisted, "No politics." Likewise, when asked about what he would say in his scheduled speaking engagement at the Commercial Club while in the city, he replied, while tapping his light-colored cane, that since he would not know what he would talk about until he stood to speak, the topic "will come out when I make my speech."

Asked about what the English people thought of Chicago, Winston said, "Really, I can't say. I never asked them."

Bernard Baruch, the American financier and friend of Winston Churchill (Library of Congress).

More forthcoming on his visit to the city, Winston said he wanted to see the steel mills and the stockyards. He had come to Chicago for that purpose. Recalling his first visit to Chicago, he remembered, "I saw the stockyards when I was last here, thirty years ago, and I haven't forgotten them."

"Politics. Politics. You're always trying to get me to talk politics," Winston replied to questions on naval parity with readily apparent impatience. He was willing to go on the record that Ramsay MacDonald's visit to the United States was "very good."

The *Daily News* reporter thought Winston, who was wearing a tight-fitting gray business suit, looked the "picture of a healthy middle-aged man with apparently not a care in the world." He was "chuckling and smiling" as he walked along the train platform being questioned by the reporters. The statesman moved like a "spry youth."

Newspaper photographers took pictures of the party's arrival in Chicago, including ones with Feversham. Jack had the distinction of being described in the *Evening Post* as having a "sweeping Lord Kitchener mustache."[24]

From the train station the traveling party and their hosts took a cab to their hotel. During the visit to the city Winston and the others would be staying at the Drake Hotel, which was at the intersection of Lake Shore Drive and Michigan Avenue. The hotel originally had 800 rooms when it opened on New Year's Eve 1920. Built at a cost of ten million dollars, the builders of the 14-floor hotel had wanted a structure that "would inspire awe and emulation." A hotel brochure from 1920 boasted that it combined "all the pleasures of the most attractive summer resort with the comfort of a luxurious metropolitan hotel and the advantages of a great city." Winston was in good company in staying at the Drake. The British royal family, including the Prince of Wales in 1924, always stayed at the hotel when in Chicago, and for fifty years after it opened it remained the city's refuge for visiting kings, queens, diplomats, and entertainers.[25]

Upon entering the hotel, the English tourists were probably entertained by some animals, since throughout the 1920s the hotel's fountain court, also called the reception court, had "ducks and even baby alligators swimming in the fountain pond."[26]

Donald R. McLennan was the party's host in Chicago. He was a 46-year-old insurance broker who was president of Marsh & McLennan, a brokerage firm he had established in 1905. It had offices in twenty cities. McLennan was assisted as host of the party by Charles Piez, the 69-year-old president of the Chicago Link Belt Company. Born in Germany, he had started as an engineer in the firm in 1889 and risen to head the company.[27] During the World War, Piez had been vice chairman of the United States shipping board.

That afternoon the party, under the care of Baruch and their Chicago hosts, visited the stockyards where they were given a tour of a plant belonging to Armour and Company. This firm was a leading meatpacking company that, despite suffering financial difficulties earlier in the decade, would report sales of more than $900,000,000 for the fiscal year ending November 2, 1929.[28] Most likely the tour of the plant started, rather than ended, with a luncheon. At the meal the visitors were the guests of Philip D. Armour, the first vice-president of the firm, and other company officials. Winston, Armour, and Baruch were photographed together at lunch.

The factory, which Johnny thought a "gruesome spectacle," was huge.[29] A series of conveyor belts were organized in the factory for processing pigs, sheep, and bullocks with what he considered "terrifying efficiency."

"What you are about to see are the processes by which animals come to the factory alive and in a short space of time leave in the form of sausages or tins of meat," the guide for the tour of the Armour canning factory announced. With that, the tour began—whether the party, Johnny especially, wanted it or not. Standing in the middle of the factory, they were shown animals being brought in and slaughtered. The pigs squealed but the sheep were silent, which was compared by Johnny to "city workers trooping to their offices on a Monday morning." He did not like what he saw and recorded it in great detail in his memoirs more than three decades after the fact. The party watched as the animals were strung up by their hind legs on a hook, slaughtered, bled, and skinned until the "carcass was lowered on a conveyor belt in sections and meat was squirted like toothpaste out of a nozzle into an enormously long sausage skin." At the end of the visit Winston received as a gift a presentation box from the company officials. The box was filled with the parts of the animals which, not being edible, were used for other products. It contained soaps, creams, lipsticks, and other beauty aids. The visit might have been interesting for some members of the party, but not for Johnny. He did not enjoy eating meat for several days afterwards. The images also affected Winston. Many years later he would compare the German concentration camps to the slaughterhouses he had visited, writing that the Nazis "made human slaughter-pens like the Chicago stockyards."[30]

While in Chicago Randolph went to see a prize fight, along with other members of the traveling party. They probably attended the boxing card promoted by the former heavyweight champion Jack Dempsey on the evening of October 2 at the 14,000-seat Chicago Coliseum on South Wabash Avenue. The 7,260 spectators in attendance that night saw Jackie Fields defeat Vincent Dundee in an action-packed ten-round decision in the main event.[31] Some sources have placed Winston in attendance at the event, but his presence was not recorded in any of the newspaper reports on the night's boxing. Had Winston gone and been introduced to the famous Jack Dempsey, it is more than likely it would have been reported in the newspapers, complete with photographs of the pair meeting. It is more likely that Winston declined the invitation, as he disliked the sport and, in fact, thought it a "horrible business."[32]

At a dinner at Downing Street in 1950, Winston encouraged Edith Summerskill, a campaigner against boxing, in her efforts to get the sport outlawed. He told her, "They've invited me to their fights on many occasions but I always refuse to go. You carry on, you're sure to win."

Upon being told by Summerskill that supporters of the sport argued it developed courage and endurance, which were also needed in soldiers, Winston was unmoved. He said, "Absolute nonsense. Discipline and the cause make a good soldier and I can't see much of either in the squalid fights described in the newspapers."[33]

On October 3 a motorcar trip had been scheduled for the party to visit the Gary steel plants and the Insull power station at the Indiana-Illinois state line. Poor weather, or "typical English weather" as it was described by the *Gary Post-Tribune*, however, cancelled the plans for the visit to Gary, Indiana.[34] In Chicago, Winston had acquired a secretary, perhaps supplied by Baruch, to assist him. That day Winston's secretary completed some of his paperwork, including sending notes to Miss Hoffberg of Mount Vernon, New York, and Gerald Walker of New York City, who had requested Winston's autograph. In both cases Winston was pleased to provide his autograph. A society reporter for the *Herald Examiner* wrote of a private lunch that occurred during the visit to the city between Winston and actress Ethel Barrymore. This report was erroneous. The dinner did not take place, and the report was "quenched" by Ethel.

Instead of visiting Indiana that day, the party spent the day in Chicago, probably relaxing and seeing the sights. Winston did write to Curtis Brown, and, among other topics, asked for the money he was owed from *Cosmopolitan* for four articles he had written to be collected and forwarded to him. He intended to immediately put the money into the stock market to take advantage of the excellent opportunities he saw for investing in the United States.[35]

On October 4 Winston had two functions to attend. At midday he attended a luncheon with a small group of businessmen at the Chicago Club. That evening Winston went to a dinner in his honor at the Commercial Club, held at the Blackstone Hotel. The dinner for 300 people began at 7:30 p.m. Charles Piez was the president of the Commercial Club and introduced Winston to the audience. This was Winston's first speech in the United States that dealt with substantial issues rather than light remarks.[36]

The backdrop for the night's address was Prime Minister MacDonald's arrival in the United States that same day for an official visit with President Herbert Hoover. It was the first visit to America by a sitting British prime minister. Embarked upon to accelerate the recent improvement in relations between Britain and the United States, MacDonald's visit would be a great success. It would prove "decisive for the settlement of Anglo-American differences." He would receive a very warm welcome from the American public, and engage in friendly discussions with President Hoover and other American officials.[37]

In the Chicago speech Winston declared that Anglo-American friendship was the surest guarantee against future troubles that might arise and then largely reiterated the position on naval reductions that he had made in his speeches in Canada. Winston said the British had nothing to fear from American naval armaments, and he deplored an absurd agreement that involved meticulous comparisons of ships and naval guns. A new pact should put an end to all this, rather than encourage it. An agreement should not lead to "perpetually talking and arguing about warships and cannon and all the instrumentalities of war," which could create a rivalry rather than prevent it. A naval settlement should be based on the willing agreement of both countries, and avoid the jealousy and suspicion entailed in the two navies being constantly compared and analyzed. Repeating his opinion that such naval agreements lead to two navies built as replicas, Winston said the two countries each had their different needs and should maintain the navy necessary for its safety or for its influence. Winston foresaw that the two navies would not compete as rivals, but suggested the fleets be used together to maintain peace in the world. While a political opponent of Prime Minister MacDonald, Winston said he was pleased that Great Britain was being represented in the negotiations by "so experienced a statesman and so distinguished a man."[38]

On other aspects of international politics Winston declared his support for a reunion of the European family in a United States of Europe, especially if it reduced tariff barriers, consolidated credit, and led to a diminution of armies. However, if this new system led to a belligerent continental self-consciousness, Winston feared it might lead to new rivalries.

In the audience for the speech was Godfrey Haggard, the British consul-general in Chicago. He listened to the speech closely and sent a report to the Foreign Office. On the major issues, such as the naval question, Haggard thought the speech was "carefully limited." He concluded that Winston's speech "will have done good" among the Americans who had heard it.[39]

Colonel Robert B. McCormick, the powerful publisher of the *Chicago Tribune*, had planned to meet Winston during the visit and return the hospitality which the British statesman had shown him when he had been in London. The publisher was unable to do so, and instead sent his right-hand man, John T. McCutcheon, to meet Winston and the others. McCutcheon gave the tourists a tour of the Tribune Tower. The building had been built at a cost of eight-and-a-half million dollars and opened in July 1925. The gothic-style structure was 473 feet in height. Johnny recalled the building having a plain façade but a "strange accumulation of lumps projecting around the front door." These lumps, upon inspection, turned out to be stones, each with its own inscription underneath. The stones from the world's great sites, including the Great Wall of China, Taj Mahal, Coliseum, St. Paul's Cathedral, and the Houses of Parliament, had been brought to Chicago to form part of the wall. Johnny believed "only an American mind, surely, would think of making such a collection and displaying it in this way." A highlight of the tour had the party taken to the top of the building where they enjoyed the views of the lights of the city at night.[40]

By the time Winston had completed his visit to Chicago he had already seen a great deal of the American economy. After completing his entire tour he would write in the *Daily Telegraph* of the magnificent qualities of the structures of American industry.[41] In the vast territories of the United States a single integrated market for "production and distribution" was being created. While protected from outside competition by tariffs, within the country there was an entirely free exchange of products. The genius of American industry was the mass production of goods for their market of 120,000,000. Businesses in the United States would find a product that was needed or in demand and then make it on the largest possible scale. This, Winston thought, was the "secret of mammoth fortunes, of standards of living, and of practical convenience for millions already beyond all compare."

In the United States Winston had seen the confidence and grand plans of American industry, which he thought merited study by the British. The idea of slowly building a business was passé. In the United States huge ventures are planned from scratch. Planning on such a scale, Winston thought, was unknown in England since the factories established by the Ministry of Munitions under the conditions of the war. The scale of the United States market was so large and rich, however, that American businesses can function in that manner even in peacetime. Writing after he returned home, Winston thought that the potential of American industry was still merely at the beginning. He foresaw no limit to the prosperity of the United States.

After the speech to the Commercial Club and visit to the Tribune building, the movements of the Englishmen are not entirely clear. Some Chicago newspapers report the party was planning to leave the city on Friday night, while others say they were scheduled to leave the next day. Regardless of the departure time, on October 5 the party was traveling to New York City by train. On leaving Chicago they transferred from Schwab's train car to Baruch's private car for the journey further east. At half-past-ten o'clock that night the party had made much progress, as Winston sent a cable to Otto Kahn from Pittsburgh. The plans for Winston to make stops between Chicago and New York, with Detroit and Pittsburgh having been suggested when planning the trip, appear to have been dropped. The party probably went directly to New York.[42]

During the train trip east Baruch entertained his guests with the story of how he made his first fortune at the age of 26.[43] Along with some associates, he had engaged in speculation against a copper company, the process of which proved very tiring and nerve-wracking. As the speculation reached the crucial period, he arrived home to find a note from his orthodox Jewish mother saying, "I hope you will observe the Day of Atonement." Baruch followed his mother's wishes and telephoned his office to tell them he would not be coming in the next day and not to call him. He gave them instructions that if the market rose by more than five points they would have to clear out, but not to try to contact him.

"But Jehovah did not betray his servant," Winston cried with "tremendous anguish" as he listened to the story with great fascination.

"No sir," Baruch replied. "The stock broke forty points. Of course, if I'd been there we'd have taken our profits after ten points. As it was, all I had to do the following morning was to get down there and take the shirts off their backs. I found myself at the age of twenty-six, having made 700,000 dollars in a day."

On meeting up with Baruch, Winston happily recounted the tales of his journey as far as Chicago. Baruch cabled Hearst a few days later from New York that Winston is "full of the wonders of our country, the beauty of your home and your boundless delightful hospitality."[44]

On October 5, while on the train, Winston wrote to his private secretary in England commenting on British politics and remarking on the fascinating North American tour. They had been traveling almost every day now and had seen a great deal of the United States, meeting a huge number of people of all types in the process. For all the excitement of his tour, Winston did confess that he was looking forward to getting back to England and "sitting for a while after all this hurtling through space."[45]

… 17 …

# New York City, October 6–18

Winston and his party arrived in New York for the final stages of their trip on the morning of October 6. Upon arriving in the largest city in the United States, the nature of the tour would change. Randolph and Johnny would be leaving for home in three days time, and the trip would no longer be moving at a great pace and involve seeing new places. Instead, Winston would spend the next 12 days in New York until he departed for a trip south to Washington and Virginia. A great deal of his time would be devoted to arranging his business affairs with his publishers, including planning his future literary output. However, in typical Churchillian fashion, he would not and could not restrict himself to just mundane business affairs, but also dined with leading figures in finance and politics. Some of the details of Winston's activities undertaken in New York are difficult to trace, as they did not receive newspaper coverage, and Winston, pressed for his time, was negligent in writing to Clementine about what he was doing.[1]

Winston had originally accepted Percy Rockefeller's offer of accommodations for the party's stay in New York. This plan was changed while the party was in Chicago, and instead the traveling party stayed at the Savoy Plaza. This hotel was located at Fifth Avenue and Fifty-Eighth Street, and had opened on September 29, 1927. It had 31 floors and a total of 2,500 rooms. The president and managing director of the hotel since it opened was the French-born Henry Rost, who had worked in the hotel business in France and the United States. The hotel invoice indicates Winston and his party stayed at the hotel from October 6 until he left the city for Washington and Virginia on October 18. Also according to the invoice, Feversham stayed at the Savoy Plaza from October 9 to October 14. The Churchills occupied room numbers 1512, 1513, and 1514, while Feversham was in room 1509. Winston's apartment in the hotel initially cost $68 per day until Randolph and Johnny left, at which point it dropped to $51 a day. The invoice includes additional charges for telephone, newspapers, telephone long distance, postage, telegrams, valet, room service, messenger, and laundry. The bill for this first stay at the hotel, including Feversham in the party, was for $1,251.20, which appears to have been entirely or at least partly paid by Baruch, who issued a check for $828.16 towards the bill on October 19.[2]

Baruch also provided space for Winston to get his work done as it related to the business he had to carry out with his publishers. Throughout his stay in New York, Winston worked from Baruch's offices in the Equitable Building at 120 Broadway. This mammoth 40-storey skyscraper occupied an entire block and, at an assessed value of 31 million dollars, was the "most valuable plot of ground under single ownership in the world." Baruch must also have provided his guest with a secretary to help him with his papers. One secretary that worked for Winston in New York was a C.G. McDowell, who would receive a memento from Winston in return for his services.[3]

One of the reasons Winston had hurried to New York was to see his great friend Lord Birkenhead before he sailed on the *Berengaria*. Winston and Birkenhead, both then young members of Parliament, had been introduced by a common friend at the bar of the House of Commons in 1906. They quickly established a friendship that was the "truest and deepest in either of their lives." Clementine, however, disliked the influence Birkenhead had on her husband, as she thought he encouraged him to drink and gamble.[4]

Birkenhead was born Frederick Edwin Smith and was known as "F.E." He was handsome, brilliant, a great speaker, and extravagant in all of his habits, including spending money and drinking. One of England's great lawyers and an exceptional lord chancellor, Birkenhead had also been solicitor-general and attorney-general in the cabinet during the Great War, and secretary of state for India in the Baldwin cabinet. F.E. had been created a baron in 1919, advanced to Viscount in 1921 and then to an Earldom in 1922. He was "one of the most vivid personalities of the first third of the twentieth century, loved and loathed in equal measure by those who enjoyed the warmth of his friendship or suffered the sting of his tongue." By 1929, however, Birkenhead was past his prime and suffering the effects of his extravagant life. He would be dead within a year of the meeting in New York, dying on September 30, 1930.[5]

The two men, whose accomplishments included co-founding together the Other Club in 1911, were "subtly different" in character, "F.E. more reckless, Winston more volatile; F.E. more intellectual, Winston more emotional and instinctive; F.E.'s somber realism balanced by

Lord Birkenhead, a prominent British politician and friend of Winston Churchill (Library of Congress).

Winston's often impetuous romantic optimism." As Robert Rhodes James observed, Birkenhead, like other of Winston's closest friends, such as Beaverbrook, Bracken, and Duff Cooper, all shared a "marked tendency to the buccaneer."[6]

Birkenhead was Randolph's godfather. The younger Churchill had been brought up by Winston on "all the famous anecdotes illustrating his wit, brilliance and arrogance." Randolph admired his godfather and admitted that without his "learning or majestic command of language, I sought to emulate his style of polished repartee. It didn't work in my case." Johnny, for his part, thought Birkenhead "looked forbidding, but had twinkly eyes."[7]

On their first evening in New York, Winston's party, joined by Baruch, went to a dinner for Lord Birkenhead given by the publisher Conde Nast and his wife, Leslie, at their penthouse at 1040 Park Avenue. This party was the first large party given by the Nasts since their return to the city after spending the summer abroad. The more than 225 guests at the affair included some well-known performers from the stage as well as artists. The gathering was "almost entirely of the married set," with only a few younger people present. Although there were few people his age, Johnny at least had a very good time. Among the other guests were Fred Astaire, Gloria Swanson, and Kermit Roosevelt, the son of President Teddy Roosevelt. Kermit invited Winston to dinner while he was in New York, but it appears they were unable to arrange a mutually convenient date. Also present was P.G. Wodehouse, but it is not known if he actually met Winston at the party and was recognized by him.[8]

The evening's dinner was served in the ballroom, which had the walls and ceiling decorated with garlands of smilax that were illuminated with small electric light bulbs, as well as green streamers.[9] After the dinner there was dancing in the apartment's green-floored, glass-enclosed terrace. Many guests arrived after the dinner for the dancing. For the event, gardenia and rose bushes were arranged throughout the various rooms, while a fountain on which multi-colored lights were trained was set up in front of a huge mirror that was framed with flowers. Later in the evening a buffet dinner was served.

A society writer reported that Birkenhead enjoyed himself at the party, but that Winston having a nice time was "less apparent." A rumor was also recorded by the writer that while Birkenhead and Winston liked the "social rush," they would both greatly prefer to be "playing the great American game of poker."[10]

J. Leonard Replogle, a steel magnate, was at the party and was presented to Winston by Baruch. Replogle had been a steel administrator of the United States during the First World War and had been recently working on a project to modernize the steel industry of Great Britain. After the party Replogle would send the British statesman a five-page detailed report on the British steel industry, along with a request for a few minutes of Winston's time to talk about the subject.[11]

Also at the party was Adele Astaire, who captured Johnny's attention. Adele was the sister and dance partner of Fred Astaire. Johnny recalled that he could only dance well when he had a good partner, and that night he was partnered with Adele Astaire and danced splendidly. He so enjoyed her company that the next morning he called on her at her home. She was quite polite and invited him in to sit on the sofa. Johnny claimed that the situation was beginning to get "somewhat interesting" when the kitchen door burst open and an enormous servant stormed in. This man, he supposed, was Adele Astaire's "method of coping with amorous young men. Certainly it worked. I fled."[12]

Geraldine Sartain of the *New York World* probably telephoned Winston at his room at the Savoy Plaza at ten o'clock on Monday morning, October 7. For all her efforts, however, Sartain was unable to speak to the distinguished visitor. In New York Winston strictly abided by his pledge to avoid newspaper interviews. He gave his regrets to all interview requests, as he did "not wish to speak for publication." The key talks between Prime Minister MacDonald and President Hoover were then underway, and the British voters would most likely not have approved of Winston interfering with the talks by giving interviews against the direction of the naval disarmament negotiations. The dogged Sartain was alas refused an interview. She had waited at the hotel from two o'clock on Saturday afternoon until 8:30 on Sunday night but could not even meet Winston. For most of that time Winston had not yet even reached New York City. Sartain sent Winston a note asking him for an interview, saying she knew he was in America as a private citizen but appealing to him as a former newspaperman. Winston replied, praying to be excused.[13]

Randolph and Johnny enjoyed some of the night life of New York City on the evening of October 7, probably leaving their fathers behind. Night life was exciting in New York, with the city "notorious in the 1920s for its defiance of the dry laws and its more than 30,000 speakeasies and nightclubs." One Jim Smith took the two young men to a speakeasy called Tony's on Forty-ninth Street. This popular establishment was "known for its corded bar, white cotton tablecloths, inedible Italian food, and plentiful supplies of liquor of questionable quality served in coffee cups." Drinks in coffee cups at Tony's cost $1.25. While fashionable, with its regular crowd of actors, writers, and celebrities, Tony's was somewhat of a disappointment to the English visitors. Randolph thought it was the "mildest place" he had ever seen. It was "much more respectable than an English pub." It seemed most people at Tony's were just drinking lemonade. Randolph and Johnny had a half-bottle of champagne. The Lanson '21 was pronounced superior, but at eight dollars was about two-and-a-half times what would be paid in London.[14]

On October 8th Winston and his great friend the Earl of Birkenhead were the guests of honor at a luncheon of the prestigious Bond Club of New York, held at the Bankers' Club in the Equitable Building at 120 Broadway. The luncheon started at quarter-past-twelve that afternoon. A month before Winston arrived in New York City, Pierpont V. Davis, the president of the club, had extended him an invitation to be a guest of honor and speaker at a club luncheon. Davis was a wealthy investment banker and director of several companies. Winston declined the offer but ended up accepting an invitation to the guest table for the luncheon tendered for Birkenhead.[15]

In his speech to the luncheon Birkenhead observed that the United States and Great Britain were discharging their world-wide tasks in a "spirit of growing friendship." He discussed the recent disturbances in Palestine and pleaded for American understanding of the British responsibility for administering its territories in the Near and Far East.[16]

As expected, when Winston accepted the invitation to the guest table, he was called upon to supplement Birkenhead's remarks and said the British carried a great burden, but there was nothing in Birkenhead's speech that indicated it was a burden which they could not bear. Britain discharged these responsibilities not merely by force alone, but by moral force as well. He said that the mission being performed by Great Britain was for the benefit of the countries themselves, Britain, and the whole world. The support of the United States could not help but encourage Britain in its mission.

On October 9 Pierpont Davis wrote to Winston thanking him for addressing the club.

In what must have been agreed upon when they spoke together at the luncheon, Davis also dropped off that morning his copies of the first volume of the *World Crisis* and *The Aftermath* at Baruch's offices, as Winston had offered to autograph them. Within a day both books had been suitably inscribed and sent back to Davis.

On their last night in North America of the 1929 tour, Randolph and Johnny were the guests of honor at a dinner given for them by John Randolph Hearst and his wife Dorothy. The youngest son of William Randolph Hearst, John had married Dorothy in 1927 when he was 18 years old and she 19 years old. The dinner was held at the Central Park Casino. The casino was "one of the ritziest nightspots in Manhattan, where liquor flowed freely." The members of the dinner party included Genevieve Fox, Sophie Gay, Daisy Parsons, Eleanor Hutton, Richmond Hobson, and William Hollingsworth. After the dinner the Hearsts took their guests to the theater. Jack might have been at least mildly annoyed that in the *New York Sun*'s report of the party the cousins were misidentified as being Winston's two sons.[17]

Following the theater, Randolph and Johnny managed to separate themselves from the others, including Jim Smith, and went off to see Harlem. Despite all the talk he had heard of the district, Randolph found it "really very disappointing." They first went to the famous Cotton Club. As they had no ladies with them they found it quite difficult to get in. Once inside they found everyone very respectable. Randolph thought the cabaret was good and of "rather a sensual nature." They soon moved on to the "Nest Club" on 133rd Street, which was even harder to get into. It took some money to change hands before they were made club members and admitted. Randolph used the name of an unsuspecting fellow he knew by the name of Seymour in the process of being admitted. Although the proprietor of the "Nest" was a "most sinister man," Randolph found the club to be quite pedestrian. He did suspect, however, that there was more going on behind the scenes. Unlike the more respectable and influential Tony's and the Central Park Casino, going to the Nest Club presented a greater risk of landing in trouble, as the club had been padlocked for violations of the Volstead Act, the law enforcing prohibition, the year before.[18]

As hoped for by Clementine and the Prof, Randolph, along with Johnny, sailed for England on October 9 so that they could return to Oxford and pick up with their respective studies. Even leaving for home on that day they would still be two days late for the opening of the Oxford term. They sailed from New York on the ocean liner *Berengaria*. Also sailing on the ship were Lord Birkenhead, Sir Harry McGowan, and Sir Laming Worthington-Evans. Birkenhead and McGowan had been designated to look after the boys on the voyage. The article in the *New York Sun* reporting the ship's departure mistakenly listed Winston as being aboard the ship as well.[19]

No doubt still thinking a great deal of his son and nephew on the day of their departure, Winston took the time to send Randolph a Western Union radiogram wishing them all a good voyage. A further radiogram sent to Randolph aboard ship on October 14 asked how they were managing. Randolph and Johnny were, in fact, getting on quite well. Randolph wrote in his diary that the six days aboard the ship were "one long laugh." He thoroughly enjoyed Birkenhead's company, remarking "F.E. is in terrific form. I know no man who is more amusing company."[20]

Each day on the crossing Johnny and Randolph swam in the ship's pool, while Birkenhead and McGowan had a Turkish bath. Johnny had always thought a Turkish bath was a "rather desperate affair."[21] He was quite surprised, therefore, when on one occasion on the ship when he went to have a bath himself he saw "His Lordship and Sir Harry were sitting stark naked steaming their guts out, but each was smoking a fat cigar and each had a double whiskey and soda in his hand."

On the voyage Randolph and Johnny dined every night with Birkenhead at his table in the dining room. Also at the table were McGowan, who Johnny noted had the "typical face of a shrewd Scotsman." In addition at the table there were half a dozen hangers-on. Johnny noted their function was to say yes and play cards, in return for which they were able to enjoy the wit, company, cigars, and drink.

Each night after dinner Randolph and Birkenhead would form a pair for bridge and usually played against two wealthy American ladies. They almost always lost. Birkenhead played the game for stakes but carried Randolph, who could not afford such betting. Randolph could not decide "whether F.E. or I was the worse bridge player."[22]

After dinner and bridge, Randolph and Johnny would retire, "ostensibly to go to bed, but of course we wandered round the lounges and tried to have as much fun as we could." As the *Berengaria* neared England, Randolph became friends with a young 15-year-old Dutch girl who was traveling with her parents.

The *Berengaria* docked at Southampton on October 15. Randolph took the boat train to Waterloo, from where he motored to Chartwell for the night. Randolph would rejoin his studies in Oxford in 1929 but would soon quit without a degree in order to return to North America to make a lecture tour in 1931. Upon returning from the lecture tour he would work as a controversial and well-known journalist. Randolph would seek election to Parliament on several occasions in the 1930s before being elected unopposed as a Conservative in a by-election in 1940. During the war he served in the Middle East and parachuted into Yugoslavia to join a British mission to Tito's partisans. After losing his seat at the 1945 election, Randolph returned to journalism, as well as writing several books. He would complete the first two volumes of his father's official biography before his own death on June 6, 1968. Although Randolph's political writings as a journalist were often brilliant, his talents were overshadowed by his arrogant, argumentative, and infuriating personality. The relationship between Winston and Randolph, which enjoyed a golden period on the trip, later became filled with bitterness, and was marked by angry rows and bad feelings.

Johnny also returned to Oxford in 1929 and would eventually duly join his father's stock exchange firm of Vickers da Costa. Although he disliked the work and wanted to quit to be an artist, he was afraid to face his daunting father. After an unhappy eight months Johnny finally left the firm in 1931 and took a commission to paint a fresco for Chips Cannon for one hundred pounds. He studied at a series of art colleges and became a noted sculptor and painter of murals, portraits, and frescoes. Johnny undertook to paint the battles of the Duke of Marlborough on the walls of the summer house at Chartwell in 1935, as well as work on the temple at Blenheim, the palace of the dukes of Marlborough. He lived in Spain in the 1930s until the outbreak of the civil war when, along with his family, he had to be evacuated by the Royal Navy. Johnny served in the army during the war. By the 1950s he was a "bon viveur, and a celebrated figure in Chelsea." A prodigious drinker, Johnny was often in the newspaper gossip columns during that decade, continuing into the 1960s. He suffered a great deal of embarrassment in 1955 when he was arrested for being "drunk and disorderly" and using "insulting language." As his sister Clarissa was by that time married to the then-

British Prime Minister Anthony Eden, this incident received more public attention than would be normal. Married four times, Johnny died on June 23, 1992.[23]

In New York Winston was almost besieged by well-wishers and other people who wanted to meet him for various purposes. Some of them Winston was actually interested in meeting, while others he would put off and avoid. Among those he wished to make a few minutes for was a G. Alan Chidsey of Flushing, New York. Chidsey had sent Winston a note requesting that he be allowed to present Winston with a book his brother had written on Marlborough and possibly have him autograph a second copy for his brother. The book was *Marlborough, Portrait of a Conqueror* by Donald Barr Chidsey, which had just been published in 1929. The author of the book was at that moment in Paris, but his brother was invited to see Winston for a short visit. Winston was interested in seeing the book on Marlborough and was happy to autograph a second copy for the author.[24]

Another person Winston was at least tentatively interested in meeting was a Rodney Day of Philadelphia. Day had tried several times to call on Winston at his hotel on October 10, but had been told Winston was unavailable each time. He wrote to Winston the next day saying that they were related, as they had a common great grandfather by their respective mothers. Day wrote he would be happy to call at the hotel again if Winston cared "to talk five minutes with one of your American cousins." Winston's secretary replied with a letter on October 12 saying the Englishman was interested in hearing from Day on exactly how they were related. It is not recorded in Winston's papers whether Rodney Day did reply with an explanation of how they were related and whether a meeting with the "American cousin" took place.[25]

Owen D. Young dined with Winston Churchill in New York even though he had authored a reparations settlement plan that the British statesman disliked (Library of Congress).

Others who tried to meet with Winston included Louis Fischer, who had just completed a two-volume history of Soviet foreign affairs, which he offered to let the British statesman see, along with a request to ask him some questions. Another one besieging Winston's time was a man named Coghlam, who claimed to be late of the 4th Hussars. When unable to see Winston at the hotel, he sent a note up on the hotel letterhead asking to speak to him for a minute on a matter of personal importance.[26]

Louis Wiley, the business manager of the *New York Times*, sought to make Winston's visit to the city more enjoyable by having several clubs send the visitor a guest card. At Wiley's instigation the Advertising Club of New York, the Automobile Club of America, the Army and Navy Club, the Newspaper Club, and the Town Hall Club all sent him a courtesy card.[27]

While in New York that October, probably on a night before October 13, Winston had dinner with Owen D. Young. This was the Young that the Young Plan, which Winston so disliked, was named after. Despite their differences on the reparations scheme, the dinner and conversation must have gone well, as Young thought the evening was "marvelously entertaining." Young was the then chairman of General Electric and chairman of the Executive Committee of the Radio Corporation of America. He had been involved in the reparations issue as a member of the Dawes Committee in 1924 before chairing the committee that had negotiated the new reparations settlement earlier in 1929. During the dinner Young praised the work of Josiah Stamp, a British representative to the Dawes Committee and the Young Committee, and pointed out the unfair position Stamp had been placed in during the negotiations. Winston replied that he would ensure the record was corrected regarding Stamp. He also asked Young about the possibility of meeting Nelson Perkins, a Boston businessman and friend of Winston's, while in New York. Perkins, however, was away in the American South and unable to come to New York to meet his friend.[28]

On the night of October 10 Winston met with Charles Dana Gibson in the city. As Gibson, beyond being a famous American illustrator, was the controlling owner of *Life* magazine, the conversation between the two may have included talk of publishing and the arrangements Winston was making for selling his articles.[29] That same night Prime Minister MacDonald arrived in the city following his meeting with President Hoover in Washington. MacDonald would spend a few days in the city before departing on October 14 for his 11-day visit to Canada.

The charming MacDonald had overcome his being born illegitimately in 1866 to be elected to Parliament in 1906 and later elected leader of the socialist Labour party. Opposing British participation in the Great War, he had been defeated in the 1918 election. MacDonald quickly recovered from the loss to go on to win the British premiership, first for a brief tenure in 1924 and then for a second time in 1929. By the time he was prime minister, MacDonald's "dashing, matinee-idol good looks of his early manhood had given way to a statesmanlike, yet still romantic, gravitas, accentuated by greying hair and deeply etched lines on an expressive face."[30]

While in New York, MacDonald celebrated his 63rd birthday, which occurred on October 12. MacDonald was traveling with his 26-year-old daughter Ishbel, who acted as his hostess, as his wife had died in 1911. Ishbel gave her father his first present of the day after he rose that morning. At his hotel suite, which was in the Hotel Weylin, located at 40 East Fifty-fourth Street, MacDonald received between 500 and 600 messages of birthday congratulations. Winston delivered his own birthday greetings to the British prime minister, a man he would ridicule a few years later in a House of Commons debate as a "boneless wonder," in person that morning when he called upon MacDonald at the Hotel Weylin. He was ushered in to see the prime minister after a group of prominent Protestant churchmen departed. Just as he went in to the room, the hotel management presented the prime minister with a birthday cake that had 63 birthday candles. Winston and MacDonald, both smoking cigars, agreed to pose for a photograph with the cake as the prime minister prepared to cut it with a knife.[31]

"Don't point the knife at him," someone in the room called out to MacDonald as he faced toward Winston. Both men joined in the laughter. The photograph of Winston and MacDonald with the birthday cake was widely published in North America and Great Britain, including in the *Manchester Guardian* and the *Scotsman*.

Winston spent nearly an hour with MacDonald. Although upon leaving Winston assured the journalists accompanying the prime minister that the visit had "no political significance," it is likely that he talked politics with MacDonald in some manner, as Winston always discussed politics. He even discussed politics with David Lloyd George in the foyer of the church before his wedding in 1908. The innocent explanation that he was merely relaying his respects and birthday wishes to the prime minister was greeted with smiles by the British journalists, who were said to have played up his visit in their reports.[32]

Despite being opposed to most of the Labour government's policies, especially on the prospect of a naval reduction agreement with the United States, Winston thought MacDonald's mission to America was a triumph. Although no agreements were made or decisions reached, MacDonald's visit created a positive climate in which the important discussions could take place.[33] Winston noted that the United States was pleased with MacDonald, as "New York turned out in scores of thousands to receive its visitor. The English-Speaking Union reveled; Washington was delighted; and the Senate purred."

Only suspicion about MacDonald's political ideology, Winston thought, marred American enthusiasm for him. He confided to his readers that he had been asked privately many times whether it was true that the prime minister was a socialist. This was, he told his readers with some satisfaction, because in the United States Socialism was considered a "very wicked thing" and "altogether un–American." Socialism was barred from elected

Prime Minister Ramsay MacDonald and his daughter Ishbel arrived in the United States during the Churchills' tour (Library of Congress).

office, disdained by "decent society," ignored by the newspapers, ridiculed by the workers, and set upon with their "batons" by the police. Winston added that the Socialist candidate in American presidential elections usually waged their campaigns from jail.

In his *Daily Telegraph* article Winston warned that despite the successful visit of the prime minister and American goodwill toward Britain, there were still very difficult problems to be overcome in resolving the question of naval parity. However, Winston thought the time had come for an honest exchange of views on the issues involved. He was confident that if the countries both tried to understand each other's views, the Anglo-American relationship would emerge unharmed. To help his readers understand the naval argument between Great Britain and the United States, Winston wrote two articles for the *Daily Telegraph*. The first, titled "The Naval Understanding," was published on November 25, and the second, titled "Fleets of Britain and America," ran in the newspaper in January 1930.

The triumphant visit of MacDonald resulted in the agreement to hold the London Naval Conference in early 1930. At this conference the British and Americans would reach a settlement on cruiser parity, with the Americans holding an advantage in a heavier type of cruiser and the British holding an advantage in cruiser tonnage. Agreement would also be reached on destroyers and submarines. The conference ended the Anglo-American naval disagreements and created the opportunity for new understanding between the two countries.[34]

After visiting with the British prime minister in the morning, it is likely Winston, along with Jack, spent the rest of that weekend at Roslyn, Long Island, the guests of Amy Guest. She was the daughter of Henry Phipps, a wealthy Pittsburgh financier and partner of Andrew Carnegie, and she had married Winston and Jack's cousin Frederick E. Guest, M.P., in 1905. Marrying the heiress to such a fortune—Amy's father would die in 1930 with an estate of almost three million dollars, and her mother would die four years later, leaving an estate of over fourteen-and-a-half million—dramatically improved Freddie Guest's finances. Winston and Freddie were very close until the latter's death in 1937, with Guest following his cousin first out of the Conservative Party to the Liberals and then back to the Conservatives. As a controversial member of Parliament, Guest was a "cunning backroom fixer" deeply involved in the scandals surrounding the selling of honors in the 1920s. He was dismissed by his critics as an aristocratic sportsman, playboy, and snob. By 1929 Amy Guest was living in the United States apart from her husband, who remained in England.[35]

Winston and Jack were guests of Amy Guest at her great estate of Templeton, one of the most beautiful properties on Long Island. Originally called White Eagle until renamed by Guest, the estate was part of the fashionable Wheatley Hills colony and was surrounded by the properties of many of America's leading financiers, including Marshall Field, J. Pierpont Morgan, and Otto H. Kahn. She had bought the manor in 1921 at auction for a bid of $470,000, despite the property being valued at over a million-and-a-half dollars. The estate of 260 park-like acres extended along the Hempstead Turnpike and had a "stately" mansion that was built of brick, with white marble trimmings, in the Georgian style. The interior of the building had been designed by Charles of London, who had "scoured England" for antiques and treasures to adorn the mansion. The woodland park around the mansion was laid out with lawns, gardens, a private lake, native trees, roadways, pathways, and a private golf course.[36]

Guest knew many of the leaders of the social, political, and financial fields during her life. With a keen interest in promoting women in aviation, she had been a financial backer and owner of the airplane in which Amelia Earhart made her 1928 flight across the Atlantic Ocean, becoming the first woman to fly the ocean. Guest had hoped to make the flight herself but had been dissuaded by her family. Upon hearing of Earhart's plans, Guest had promptly offered the use of her plane. After Earhart made the voyage, a happy Guest was quoted as saying, "Now she has fulfilled completely my old dream of a woman duplicating the solo ocean crossing which only one man has ever accomplished."[37]

While staying at Templeton that weekend, Winston likely motored over to Locust Valley, also on Long Island, on Sunday afternoon to see John W. Davis and his wife. Davis was then a Wall Street lawyer making $400,000 a year, having previously served in the House of Representatives for West Virginia, been solicitor-general of the United States under Woodrow Wilson, ambassador to the Court of St. James's after the Great War, and the Democratic candidate who lost to Calvin Coolidge in a landslide defeat in the 1924 presidential election. While in London as the American ambassador, Davis and his wife Ellen, a "classic Anglo-American beauty with golden hair, blue eyes, and perfect, if severely chiseled features," had met Winston and Clementine many times. They had met on matters of state as well as socially. As ambassador, Davis described Winston in his diary as a man of "intense physical restlessness" who talks well and "sustains his reputation as a man of brains, however erratic he may have proved himself." Winston's nature, Davis thought, was that of an "adventurer."[38]

The Locust Valley estate owned by John W. Davis paled in comparison to Templeton. The small estate of five acres of land was bought by Davis in 1923, along with the house, servants' cottage, and some outbuildings. It was named Mattopan by Davis, which was said to be an Indian word meaning "I sit down." The house was eventually expanded to 16 rooms and, in keeping with Davis' love of England, had a living room that was "reminiscent" of an English house.[39]

Returning to New York after the weekend, Winston continued to complete his business arrangements and dine with select financial and political leaders. Through the month of October, while in the city, he settled a number of literary contracts. The most pressing was completing the arrangements for the articles on the North American trip. To this end he met with E.G. Rich at Curtis Brown, as well as with John Wheeler from the Bell Syndicate at Baruch's office, probably on October 8. It was agreed that Winston would try to have the first two articles finished before he left for home at the end of the month. The series of articles could begin being published in mid–November. Winston said he would produce two to three articles a week and finish writing the pieces before the Christmas holidays.[40]

Also through Curtis Brown, Winston negotiated with the *Saturday Evening Post* for six articles on topics to be mutually agreed upon. The articles were to be 3,000–4,000 words in length, with the first two delivered by Winston by the end of February 1930 and the last four by the end of the following month. While Curtis Brown worked with the *Saturday Evening Post*, Winston used the literary agent Paul Reynolds to deal with *Collier's* on his behalf. Reynolds, who was at 599 5th Avenue, was recommended to the British statesman as an agent who gets "very big prices." Working with this agent proved useful, as Winston thought the contract reached with *Collier's* for six articles on the "Crucial Crises of the War" was satisfactory. Adding to the work requiring Winston's attention were two articles due to the magazine by December 1929, with the other four due by the end of January. Additionally, late in October Winston also tried to arrange to meet Ray Long of *Cosmopolitan*.[41]

In New York Winston also planned to meet and have a productive talk with Charles Scribner, the vice-president of the publishing house founded by his father. The firm was set to publish the four-volume biography of Marlborough in the United States.

The success of his efforts at arranging his publishing affairs was made evident by the October 17 cable Winston sent to Clementine that noted he had arranged for 22 articles, all maturing before June 1930, at the usual rate. The articles he had contracted for while in New York were worth around 40,000 pounds. In November he noted in another correspondence that by the end of the year he would receive 900 pounds for two Ray Long articles and 450 pounds for two Bell Syndicate articles. In the first quarter of 1930 he would get 450 pounds for a *Saturday Evening Post* article and a further 2,160 pounds for six articles for *Collier's*. He would then still have outstanding 12 *Strand* articles and five other articles for the *Saturday Evening Post*.[42]

Since leaving California, Winston had continued speculating in the stock market—a market that was rather "confused and disorganized." Share values were falling, but the market would occasionally rally. In this rough market Winston was closely monitoring his investments. Cables were regularly sent to Van Antwerp in San Francisco, Richardson in Winnipeg, Bernau at the Lloyd's Bank, Pall Mall in London, and even to McGowan aboard the *Berengaria*. In mid–October he cabled MacLeod in Alberta requesting information about Hargal and Baltac, while he also cabled Richardson about the significant decline of the stock in these companies. Hargal shares were off from $2.05 to $1.45, while Baltac shares were down from $2.10 to $1.26. Winston, however, remained confident. He guessed the considerable decline in the oil companies was the result of the problems in the American market. Even as the stock market remained unstable, Winston continued to invest in stock, including buying shares in American Smelting and Refining through Van Antwerp, as well as shares in Sherwood Starr Gold Mining Company. American Smelting may have been recommended to Winston by Baruch, who was heavily invested in its stock. Winston's faith in the stock market was probably encouraged by Baruch. On October 21, in response to another friend's request for advice on whether to buy or sell, the American financier recommended standing pat.[43]

In his second week in New York Winston tried to make arrangements to call upon Percy Rockefeller, either Tuesday or Wednesday.[44] Norman Toerge, senior partner in the New York City brokerage firm of Toerge and Schiffer, had attended Winston's speech to the Bond Club and entirely admired it. Although Winston's schedule in New York was filled with lunches and dinners, he invited Toerge to come by his hotel one evening.

Across the United States and then in New York, Winston had met many wealthy and powerful men. He would later observe in his newspaper articles that in his view the "old antagonism between the millions and the millionaire had become obsolete."[45] That multimillionaires presiding over businesses could provide what the American population wanted far better than a great number of small producers was, he thought, widely understood. To support this view he pointed out that the electorate had reduced taxation on the "well-to-do, the rich, and the very rich." In America the young do not want to ruin the millionaire, they want to be one. The American capitalist "advances under the banner of 'High wages, enough leisure to spend them in, and better times for all'; and the masses follow, confident that in one way or the other they will all win through." Winston's contention that the old rivalries were obsolete, and that the masses had confidence in the millionaires, would be severely tested in the Great Depression that was about to engulf the United States.

Bernard Baruch, Winston's New York host, asked him if there was anyone he would like to meet while in the city. Winston replied that he would like to see the American politician Al Smith, a former governor of New York and the 1928 Democratic nominee for president. The failed presidential campaign had been closely followed by Winston, as he had been in complete agreement with Smith's policy of repealing prohibition. He even came up with a slogan for Smith of "All for Al and Al for All."[46] Smith, who had been dubbed the "Happy Warrior" by Franklin Roosevelt, had been attacked in the campaign for his Catholic faith.

Baruch set about trying to arrange matters, but the only day that all three men—Winston, Smith, and Baruch himself—were available for dinner was on October 15. On that night Smith was scheduled to speak at a rally at Tammany Hall.[47] Smith accepted the invitation to dinner with the understanding that he would have to leave early. The dinner was probably held at Baruch's home at 1055 Fifth Avenue. On the night of the dinner Smith stayed until the last possible moment and then excused himself, explaining where he had to go.

"Would it [be] possible for us to come too?" Winston asked, to which Smith readily agreed.

The rally at Tammany Hall was a joint campaign event for two local politicians seeking reelection, Controller Charles W. Berry and Aldermanic President Joseph V. Mckee. The event was described in the *New York Times* as an "old-fashioned Tammany rally," with Alfred E. Smith and current New York mayor Jimmy Walker speaking and "furnishing the heavy artillery." It was the first campaign event in the new Tammany Hall at East 17th Street at Union Square. Although rain prevented any crowds from gathering outside the building, the hall itself was filled with 2,500 people.[48]

Smith arrived with his guests and led them onto the stage. Smith took his place in the front beside his daughter Emily, while Baruch and Winston sat down in the second row of chairs behind the speakers. Winston would view the proceedings with keen interest from this place on the edge of the platform.

Before the speeches began, a motion picture was shown that illustrated all of the achievements of the Walker administration. During the film a band in the gallery played to provide musical entertainment. After the film there were speeches by most of the Tammany candidates for all of the judicial and county offices. As Al Smith was called upon to address the audience as one of the two featured speakers, Winston joined the enthusiastic reception. Smith's daughter could hear applause and "Hear! Hear!" coming from the British guest seated behind her.[49] The great demonstration Smith received proved his continuing popularity with the "Tammany rank and file," despite his loss in the presidential election the previous year. The *New York Evening Post*, however, was unimpressed with the speech. They thought it was hardly "impassioned" or "inspirational."[50] After the meeting ended, a cord of disharmony was struck when Smith refused the requests of the newspaper photographers to pose for a picture with Mayor Walker.

Not surprisingly, the journalists sought out Winston's opinion on the rally he had just observed. In an article called "Winston Churchill Sees Tammany Tiger in Fight," the *Evening Post* quoted the statesman as saying, "It was all very nice, very interesting and much like our meetings in England. But, on the other side, we are constantly interrupted by derisive questions from the audience. We mull them over and answer them at leisure."[51]

After the rally Al Smith introduced Winston to his wife and daughter and several mem-

Al Smith, the 1928 Democratic candidate for president, brought Winston Churchill to a rally at Tammany Hall (Library of Congress).

bers of Tammany before suggesting they adjourn to the Biltmore Hotel at Madison Avenue and 43rd Street. Smith's daughter remembered it was late before the "fascinating evening" ended. During the evening, Winston pointed out that the British political system had the great advantage over the American one in that the defeated leader in the election remained in the House of Commons as a member of the minority. He was thus able to continue to represent the views of his supporters. Under the United States system there was no role for the losing candidate to "carry forward all the prestige and allegiances he has gathered in a nationwide campaign." Smith, a defeated presidential candidate himself, agreed with his British guest. As Winston remembered, Smith spoke on the topic a mere seven months after Hoover's inauguration, with some emotion. He told Winston that he had even made the same point himself, suggesting that the candidate finishing second in the presidential election be sent to the United States Senate as a senator at large for the duration of the winner's four-year term.[52]

Almost exactly eighteen years later Winston recorded a speech in London that was played for the Al Smith memorial dinner in New York on October 14, 1947. In the recorded remarks Winston recalled meeting Smith and said he was a "man of the highest quality of brain and heart."

Winston's appearance at a Democratic campaign rally provided the Republicans with an opportunity to make light of their opponents. The Republican candidate for mayor, F.H. La Guardia, attacked Mayor Walker as an "English fop" and a "Paris gigolo" at a rally at Bryant Hall a couple of weeks later. La Guardia proclaimed that Al Smith was going back to the "political scrapheap," and that he would not be surprised if he went over to England, as "you saw Al and Winston Churchill paling together and saw Al settling down." Although the "English fop" handily won reelection in 1929, La Guardia would finally win the office of mayor in 1933. Winston's attendance at the rally also attracted the interest of Wheeler of the Bell Syndicate, who was inspired to write to him at the Savoy Plaza suggesting he write an article on American politicians, Tammany, and political campaigns.[53]

The following night, October 16, Winston and Jack dined with their cousin William Travers Jerome at eight o'clock in the evening at the Union Club, located at Fifth Avenue and Fifty-first Street. Established in 1836, the club was among the most exclusive in New York City. The prestigious club had 1,400 members. The 70-year-old Jerome was one of their cousins on their mother's side. Jerome had been twice elected district attorney in New York City (in 1901 and 1905) but, deterred by the "squalor and indignity" of the city's politics, never sought political office after finishing his second term in 1909. He successfully practiced law with the firm Jerome, Rand & Kresel. Winston had met Jerome in the 1920s on the latter's trips to Europe. Winston greatly admired his cousin and later said that he had followed Jerome's career and believed that his cousin "might have gone on to the Presidency had he wished to pay the price." At the dinner the Churchill brothers and Jerome were most likely joined for the meal by John W. Davis.[54]

On the night of October 17 Winston and Jack were guests at a dinner hosted by Otto Kahn at his "resplendent mansion" at 1100 Fifth Avenue. The host for the evening was described by his biographer as an "appealing figure" with silvery white hair and mustache, a "gentle smile" as his normal expression, and a slight German accent reflecting his German birth. A fabulously wealthy financier, Kahn was "one of New York's best-dressed men." Winston may previously have met Kahn in England.[55]

The five-storey Kahn mansion at the northeast corner of Fifth Avenue and Ninety-first

Street was in the Italian high renaissance style and had been completed in 1918. The mansion on the southeast corner of that intersection had once been owned by Andrew Carnegie. Guests arriving at the main entrance to the Kahn mansion were greeted by one of the footmen who were on duty both night and day. The footman would escort the visitors to the elevator for admission to the mansion.

At Winston's special request, Kahn had also invited Feversham and Horace Cecil Vickers, the founder and senior partner of Vickers da Costa, to the affair. Vickers was staying at the Ambassador Hotel on his visit to New York. Upon leaving England, Clementine had entrusted Vickers with a letter for Winston. The dinner at Kahn's home was an informal affair to which many of the most prominent figures in finance and industry had been invited. While enjoying the conversation with the businessmen, Winston possibly met Kahn's wife, Addie, and might have had a chance to view their collection of paintings that included Rembrandt's *Portrait of a Young Student*. In February 1931 Kahn would invite and host Clementine and Randolph, who were both in the United States, at his villa in Palm Beach.[56]

A great many of the social gatherings Winston attended in the United States were hosted by businessmen. This prompted him to later write that, unlike in Europe, the "social life of the United States is built around business."[57] In America it was the businessmen who led society and gave the parties to which the other professions were invited. Businessmen competed against each other, but also played together in their clubs and organizations. In the comradeship of the social scene, much business was accomplished. Winston observed that many major business deals were made at the golf club, country club, or over dinner. While anyone in the United States could go into business and make a fortune, it was pleasant and practical to be elected to the golf club and join the social circle. These connections would be useful in business, especially during difficult times.

After Kahn's dinner party, Winston, accompanied by Feversham, went to Pennsylvania Station in New York to board the train for Washington. Probably entering the station at the main entrance at Seventh Avenue and 32nd Street, they went to their waiting train car on one of the station's 11 platforms. Jack was not recorded as participating in any of the events in Washington and appears to have stayed behind in New York while his brother dashed to the American capital. Winston's visit to the White House to meet President Hoover had been scheduled for October 18. The original plan had been to leave New York, visit the White House, and make a tour of Virginia. Winston had not planned to return to New York for six or seven days. However, Millicent Hearst had arranged a party in Winston's honor on the evening of October 18. Winston did not wish to upset her plans, aside from the obligatory request to tender an extra invitation to Feversham, and it was, of course, impossible to reschedule the meeting with the American president.[58] With these two conflicting commitments, Winston rearranged his travel plans. He would now travel overnight to Washington, spend the day in the American capital, and then return to New York in time that night for Hearst's party. Once the party was over he would re-board the train and travel overnight to Virginia to start his tour of that state. At the end of the tour of Virginia, Winston would stop again in Washington, this time for a longer stay.

Again traveling aboard the *Loretto*, Schwab's private car, Winston was scheduled to leave New York at 12:35 in the morning of October 18. For the trip, the railway car was attached to Train No. 103. The train reached the American capital at five minutes after six o'clock that same morning.[59]

Ronald Ian Campbell, the counselor and chargé d'affaires at the British embassy, was responsible for Winston's progress in Washington in the absence of the British Ambassador, Sir Esme Howard, who was on a six-week trip in the West Indies. Winston had cabled that he would like to talk to Campbell before the interview with the president and invited him to his railway car at 11:30 that morning.[60] Escorted by Campbell, Winston and Feversham went to the White House, where they were officially presented to Hoover by the British diplomat. For the meeting Winston dressed formally, complete with top hat and cane. President Hoover was not the first American president Winston had called on. Previously he had met William McKinley in Washington; Theodore Roosevelt, while he was still New York governor; and Woodrow Wilson, as well as a future president, Franklin Roosevelt, in London in 1918.

Although Hoover's daily calendar was quite light that day, with only meetings with the Washington correspondents and Winston penciled in, it is likely the meeting was a brief, formal affair. Winston called on Hoover to pay his respects rather than engage in detailed talks or make momentous decisions like he would during his White House meetings with President Roosevelt during the Second World War. President Hoover would have had little interest in negotiating with or even hearing the opinions of an opposition member of the British House of Commons right after holding talks with the sitting British prime minister. Further discounting the meeting being anything but a quick affair were the sharp words Winston had had for Hoover during the Great War. As first lord of the Admiralty, he had lashed out at Hoover's organizing of a relief effort for German-occupied Europe, calling him a "son of a bitch for his callous disregard of British military interests."[61] After calling upon Hoover, Winston posed for a photograph with Campbell and Feversham outside the White House.

While the meeting with President Hoover was merely a formal call, Winston had the opportunity for more in-depth discussions with a distinguished group Campbell had assembled to have luncheon at 1:15 that afternoon with the British visitor. From the White House, the party, Feversham included, went to Campbell's "charming little house" at 1830 Jefferson Place in Washington for the lunch party. Campbell was in the middle of moving from his apartment at 100 Massachusetts Avenue to the house at Jefferson Place and had to hurry to have the home ready for entertaining. The guests at the lunch to meet Winston included half of the members of Hoover's ten-man cabinet: Secretary of State Henry L. Stimson, Secretary of the Treasury Andrew W. Mellon, Secretary of the Navy Charles Francis Adams, Secretary of Commerce Robert Patterson Lamont, and Secretary of Labor James J. Davis. The remaining guests were the United States senator from Kansas, Arthur Capper, along with the minister of the Irish Free States, Michael MacWhite, and the first secretary of the Canadian legation Hume Wrong. The first secretary of the legation attended in the absence from Washington of Vincent Massey, the Canadian minister to Washington. Massey and Winston had exchanged cables and hoped to meet for lunch or dinner when Winston made his return visit to Washington, by which time Massey would be back. Likewise, at the lunch Stimson invited Winston to have dinner with him when he returned to Washington in a few days time. During the lunch at Campbell's house Winston spoke with Capper, the former two-term Republican governor of Kansas and current senator from that state. Being from Kansas and a strong supporter of agriculture, Capper probably talked to Winston about wheat. At least that was their topic of conversation when they met in the 1940s when Winston was again in Washington and Capper was still a serving senator.[62]

Winston Churchill outside the White House after calling on President Hoover (Library of Congress).

With his tight schedule to keep, Winston left Washington aboard the *Loretto* at three o'clock that afternoon attached to Train No. 144. After passing through Baltimore, where he cabled Baruch, Winston and Feversham arrived back in New York at five minutes to eight o'clock that night. That day Winston continued to watch the stock market, with its recent weakness, and cabled specific instructions to his agent, care of Baruch, that 200 Simmons shares should be sold through E.F. Hutton and Vickers da Costa if the price rebounded. Also, 100 shares of Montgomery Ward should be sold if the price climbed back to 1.04 dollars per share. Winston was concerned about his Montgomery Ward investment because the value of those shares had fallen steadily since September.

From Pennsylvania Station, Winston and Feversham probably went directly to Millicent Hearst's home on Riverside Drive for the party given for the British statesman. Riverside Drive ran along the western shore of Manhattan, with only the small Riverside Park between the street and the Hudson River.

Jack rejoined his brother at the Hearst party. The 57 guests included the Astors, Vanderbilts, and Conde Nasts. Dinner was served at a "long flower-banked table" in the Tapestry Room. Later in the evening there was dancing, with music provided by the orchestras of Rudy Vallee and Coleman. During the evening a showing was given of a specially prepared motion picture news reel composed of footage showing some of the dinner's guests at important events of the past. Millicent Hearst thought the party had gone well, as she cabled her husband in California the next day that the event was "very successful. You should have been here for it."[63]

After departing Hearst's home, Winston, Jack, and Feversham returned to the private train car for an overnight trip that would take them to Virginia to begin a brief tour of the American South.

... 18 ...

# Virginia, Washington, and Pennsylvania, October 19–23

The Virginia that Winston traveled in for two days in 1929 was, as he noted, the Virginia of the Civil War. On arriving in Virginia he found that he breathed a "different air" and was in "another country." The twentieth century had been exchanged for the nineteenth. In passing into the South they had "crossed the mysterious boundary which separates the present from the past. More than that, we have crossed the frontiers which divide victory from defeat. We are in the rebel capital." Winston's Virginia in 1929 had been "beaten down, trampled upon, disinherited, impoverished, riven asunder and flung aside while Northern wealth and power and progress strode on to Empire! And yet it had to be. Hardly even would the adherents of the lost cause wish it otherwise."[1]

The tourists were traveling to Virginia primarily to tour the battlefields of the American Civil War. Winston was fascinated by the history of the United States and "deeply stirred by the history of the Civil War," so much so that he disproportionately devoted four chapters to it in the *Great Democracies* volume of his *History of the English Speaking Peoples*. His knowledge of the war's battles was such that his wartime private secretary, John Colville, witnessed American generals listening "openmouthed" to his account of Gettysburg, a battlefield Winston toured in 1932.[2]

The party arrived at the Broad-Street train station in Richmond, the capital of Virginia, at 20 minutes past 11 o'clock on the morning of October 19. Originally they had been scheduled to arrive in Richmond from Washington shortly before nine o'clock that morning, but with the change in plans to accommodate Millicent Hearst the arrival had been pushed back. The planning of the trip to Virginia had been initiated by Baruch, who had asked Admiral Cary T. Grayson to take the party in hand. The admiral was a native of Culpepper, Virginia, and had been the personal physician to three presidents, Theodore Roosevelt, William Howard Taft, and Woodrow Wilson. Winston had met Grayson previously when the doctor accompanied Wilson to Europe for the Paris Peace Conference. Grayson had arrived in Richmond by motorcar the previous night in advance of his guests. It had also been arranged that Virginia governor Harry Flood Byrd would receive Winston's party as overnight guests in the executive mansion.[3]

Stepping off the private car, the Englishmen were welcomed to the state by the aforementioned Admiral Grayson, as well as a committee composed of John Stewart Bryan and Dr. Douglas S. Freeman, both of *The Richmond News Leader*; Eppa Hunton, Jr., the president of the Richmond, Fredericksburg, and Potomac Railway; and other prominent citizens of Richmond.

Baruch had promised to arrange for Winston to be conducted over the battlefields by someone who knew the battles. He was as good as his word. For the visit Dr. Douglas Southall Freeman, the leading authority on Robert E. Lee and Confederate military history, would lead the tour of the Civil War historic sites and battlefields. Beyond being an expert on the war, Freeman was also experienced at guiding visiting dignitaries, as he had previously escorted David Lloyd George over the battlefields in 1923 and had been Ferdinand Foch's guide during the French general's visit to Richmond in 1921.[4]

Since 1915 Freeman had been the editor of the *News Leader*. That same year he had started work on his mammoth biography of General Robert E. Lee. By 1929 Freeman had completed a great deal of the study. It would not be finished, however, until 1933. When finally completed, the biography would amount to more than a million words published in four volumes, for which the author would receive the Pulitzer Prize. Winston would read the biography and write Freeman, praising the work and expressing the wish that they could meet again.[5] Beyond an interest in the American Civil War, Winston and Freeman shared the same publisher in Charles Scribner's Sons, as well as a unique sleep schedule. While Winston would work late into the night, Freeman managed the demands of being a newspaper editor and historian by getting up very early in the morning. Eventually Freeman would establish a habit of waking up and starting his day at 2:30 in the morning after getting just six hours of sleep.[6]

Winston told those who received him at the train station that his arrival in Richmond was the realization of a long-cherished desire to visit the capital of the Southern Confederacy.

"Excellent weather," was Winston's response when asked for his first impression of Richmond.[7]

For the day of touring in ideal weather, Winston was dressed in a "jaunty sack suit of brown," with green golf shirt, bow tie, black hat, and cane. As always, he was puffing a long cigar. The *News Leader* reported he was "looking youthful and enthusiastic" on his arrival in the city.[8]

After being welcomed at the train station, the party was immediately "whisked" off on their tour. From noon until that night the travelers would follow in the footsteps of the Confederate generals Lee, Jackson, Stuart, Longstreet, and Early. They first went to the Battle Abbey. At the abbey they viewed the Charles Hoffbauer paintings of Confederate leaders and battles. Winston liked the abbey and paintings, remarking, "These vivid pictures by Hoffbauer are intensely interesting." While in Richmond, Winston also saw the Parliament buildings where Lee received his commission.[9]

Guided by Dr. Freeman, who Winston thought possessed a thorough knowledge of the Civil War, the party was conducted across the historic battlefields of the Seven Day's fighting that occurred around Richmond. Winston was thrilled and inspired by what he saw and learned. He filled a *Daily Telegraph* article on Virginia with the details of the bloody struggles that occurred on the battlefields he tramped over that day. They began touring the battlefields of Mechanicsville, Beaver Dam Creek, and Gaines' Mills, where days of fierce fighting took place between Union General George McClellan and Robert E. Lee. After that round of fighting, McClellan, in what Winston thought a quite daring move, severed himself from his base and marched his 80,000 men down the peninsula to establish a new base on the James River. Following Lee's maneuvers, the traveling party hurried back almost to Richmond and then on to inspect the battlefields of Frazier's Farm and Malvern Hill, where the Confederates attempted to intercept McClellan's force as it toiled along a single road. As they drove from point to point, the expert Freeman told the visitors the story of the battles in vivid detail.[10] In his telling the story of the battlefields he walked that day, Winston rode and fought with Lee rather than McClellan; when Winston wrote "we" it was always referring to Lee, Virginia, and the South.

Admiral Cary T. Grayson, physician to three American presidents and Winston Churchill's host in Virginia (Library of Congress).

It had been planned for the party to return to Richmond and have lunch at the Governor's mansion at half-past-two o'clock that afternoon. That event was probably dropped from the itinerary due to the late arrival in Richmond. The day of touring was, however, broken by a "brilliant tea" at the home of Mrs. Richard Crane in Westover Hills.

Winston was surprised by the traces of the Civil War that could still be seen in 1929, ranging from buildings scarred by shot, woods crisscrossed by trenches and rifle pits, and trees full of bullets. With a "tattered rebel flag" still flying at the War Museum in Richmond, Winston guessed that "if you could read men's hearts, you would find that they, too, bear the marks."[11]

The day concluded with a dinner for the three English visitors and 22 guests at the home of John Stewart Bryan, the refined publisher of a Richmond newspaper. That night the Englishmen were the guests of Governor Byrd at the executive mansion. This mansion had been used by Jefferson Davis when he was president of the Confederacy. Winston made a great impression on his hosts during the one-night stay at the mansion—so much so that the one-night visit was remembered by the Byrd family's recounting as lasting ten days. They may have been mistakenly recalling another visitor, or perhaps one day of entertaining the demanding Winston felt like ten. Governor Byrd was joined as host by his wife Anne Douglas

Beverly Byrd, his son Harry F. Byrd, Jr., and at least one of his nephews. The then Virginia governor, who would go on to be a United States senator, was quite unlike Winston in several of his personal habits. Byrd did not smoke and was a "near teetotaler" who even prohibited the serving of alcohol at his daughter's wedding in 1936.[12] However, for his English visitor, Byrd procured brandy from John Stewart Bryan so that Winston could imbibe.

Harry Byrd, Jr., who would also go on to be a United States senator after his father, later recalled episodes from the visit. The younger Byrd and an older cousin first saw Winston when he came down the stairs at the mansion. Both of the young boys were dressed in their formal clothes, and Winston, thinking they were members of the household staff, asked the cousin to go and buy him a newspaper. The Byrd cousin dutifully fulfilled the assignment and was rewarded with a quarter tip for his efforts. The cousin kept the quarter as a souvenir for the rest of his life.[13]

Governor Harry F. Byrd of Virginia hosted the Churchill party at the governor's mansion—with some difficulty (Library of Congress).

Although Anne Byrd, as wife of the governor, had acted as hostess to many visitors to the executive mansion, such as Lady Astor and Charles Lindbergh, her patience was tried by Winston. Of all her guests, the cigar-smoking, alcohol-drinking, and self-absorbed Winston held the distinction of being called by Anne Byrd the "worst house guest I ever had." Her son recalled that at a formal meal given for Winston at which a main course of Virginia ham was served, the Englishman asked for mustard. Anne Byrd sent to the kitchen for mustard, only to be told there was none. Telling Winston the unfortunate news, she offered, in no way expecting him to accept, that someone could be sent to the store to buy mustard. To her great surprise, Winston replied that yes he would like someone to go to the store. Harry Byrd, Jr., was thus sent to the store while Anne politely "slowed the dinner down to a snail's pace" until the mustard arrived. The trials of Anne were further added to by Winston's specifying what time he wanted his meals and supervising the menu. Even beyond that, the Byrd family recalled that Winston was remembered to have walked around the mansion dressed in his underwear.[14]

While Governor Byrd liked Winston, his wife was not impressed. As Winston was leaving the next day, she told her husband, "Don't you ever invite that man here again!" Harry

Byrd, Jr., would see Winston again in 1951 when he and his wife were guests of Winston at the Parliament buildings in London.[15]

After departing the executive mansion, Winston's traveling party left Richmond on the morning of October 20 in Admiral Grayson's motorcar. They then drove sixty miles north along the highway to Fredericksburg.

Both Fredericksburg and the surrounding region had seen heavy fighting during the Civil War. Winston discovered that south of the Rappahannock the war's battlefields ran into each other, as "Fredericksburg and Chancellorsville are overlaid by the Wilderness and Spotsylvania." The old battle lines and trenches, as well as monuments for the "dead commanders and shot-torn regiments," became interspersed. On these battlefields, Winston speculated, more soldiers had died in an area of equal size than anywhere else save for Ypres and Verdun."[16]

The visit to the city was not announced locally until shortly before the party arrived in the early afternoon. On arrival the party took a room at the Princess Anne Hotel, where they refreshed and had lunch. That hotel had also been visited by David Lloyd George. Upon being informed of the previous visit of his friend, Winston laughed and said he hoped his visit would be similarly recalled. As had been arranged in advance, the party was met in Fredericksburg by the former state senator C. O'Conor Goolrick, who remained with them until they left for Washington that evening. At the invitation of Goolrick, a George W. Perry also joined the party.[17]

Under the tutelage of their local hosts, the tourists finished lunch and started a tour of the battlefields and other local sites. They first visited Marye's Heights, which formed part of the Confederate lines during the Battle of Fredericksburg. Winston discovered that almost all the historical points on the battlefields were furnished with markers that had descriptive accounts of the events that had taken place.[18] At his request, the motorcar stopped at the foot of the hill, and the party left the car to walk up the heights. Winston was not satisfied with merely driving the battlefields; to fully understand the events that had occurred there, he felt you must see and cover the ground in person. In his personal inspection he was surprised to find the Chickahominy River was just a woodland stream, and the White Oak Swamp was a mere undergrowth with some puddles. Having fought in modern wars which measured the battlefield in miles, Winston had trouble adjusting to the Civil War in which battles were fought at a range of a few hundred yards.

As an illustration of how real the Civil War was in 1929, during the tour one of the local guides told the visitors that his father, who was then living in Richmond (with a good memory, despite his age), had been wounded on one of the nearby battlefields.

Perry tried to lead the party to the Bloody Angle, which had been a salient in the Spotsylvania lines. However, the rough trails though the heavily wooded area were so convoluted that they had to stop to ask for directions at a farmhouse. A farmer came out to meet the motorcar and, after telling them they should have turned off the high road a half-mile back, ended up volunteering to come with them to show the way.

As they bumped along in Grayson's motorcar, the farmer pointed out the features of the battlefield, with which he seemed to be very familiar. Winston engaged the local in a conversation and learned that he had lived there all his life and had been eight years old at the time of the battle.

With the farmer an actual witness to the events, Winston eagerly asked him to tell them exactly what he remembered. In reply, the farmer described his memories of how one morning soldiers arrived at their farm in a swarm, and his father was told to leave, as there was going to be a battle. The family fled aboard a wagon as the cannons began firing. After three or four days they returned to find their farmhouse in ruins and a thousand dead soldiers lying in the field. The battle had taken everything they owned, and they had nothing left. They were so hungry that they scavenged broken biscuits from among the dead soldiers, but the farmer was scolded by his father for trying to take the boots off a dead soldier.

Reaching the salient, the motorcar stopped and the party alighted to make a closer observation. Winston took in the ground as he walked through a wood of small oak, beech, and maple trees, and studied the trenches around the spot. He was very interested in this part of the battlefield.

"Here is the Angle. Here is where the dead lay thickest. In this trench they were piled in heaps, both sides together, blue and grey," the farmer recounted. He then showed them a small gully where he remembered the water ran red with blood, as it was raining heavily at the time.

At the Bloody Angle a small boy appeared with a basketful of bullets and regimental badges gathered from the terrible battlefield. The traveling party took some of the artifacts offered by the boy.

From Bloody Angle the tour continued driving along the Brock Road and passed a number of points of interest, including the monument marking the spot where General Alexander Hayes was killed. After touring the sites of the Wilderness fighting, the tourists returned to Fredericksburg, passing Charlottesville and Salem Church where they stopped to inspect the sites. A further stop was made at the monument where General Stonewall Jackson was mortally wounded in 1863.

The battlefields were very real for Winston that day. Seeing the cemeteries for the Union and Confederate dead, and the remaining signs of the old trenches and battle lines, had revived the "past with strange potency."

The party, no doubt meaning Winston, was reported in the local newspaper to have "expressed deep interest in the history of the battlefields and displayed a remarkable knowledge of facts, including troop movements, positions of various commands and other details in connection with the various battles."

The *Free Lance Star* also quoted the travelers as saying they were greatly pleased with the visit to Virginia. It was more like England than any other part of the United States they had visited. They further said they were delighted with the weather they had had, which was far superior to English weather.[19]

Winston long remembered the battlefields of Virginia and the tour provided by Freeman. In a 1946 address to the General Assembly of Virginia he recalled visiting the battlefields in Virginia and being guided by Freeman, who was in the audience for the speech. Winston then praised his former guide's literary works as contributing not only to the "fame of the South but to the whole strength of the undissoluable union."[20]

That evening the party drove with Grayson in his automobile the remaining distance to Washington. In a *Daily Telegraph* article Winston noted the progress he had observed in Virginia, with new industries coming into the state, the population rapidly increasing, roads lacing towns together, skyscrapers being built, land values rising, and old inhabitants getting rich.[21] He recorded that Virginians were taking this "very coolly." They felt that while it would be wonderful to be "prosperous," they had, in fact, managed all right before with their quiet life and culture. This growth and advancement might actually overwhelm them. Winston quoted them as believing, "We were knocked out of the world seventy years ago. We are not so very keen on going back. It may be progress, but it is Yankee progress."

Winston in his article considered both the constitutional amendment declaring prohibition and the Fifteenth Amendment allowing Blacks and Whites to vote on equal terms to have been similarly based on "intolerant idealism" and not having followed "commonsense procedure."[22] While conceding the North had the fine motive of abolishing slavery, Winston observed the Fifteenth Amendment had been rendered null by the use of many ploys and violence in its imposition. The "Southern negroes" had equal political rights according to the constitution, but he wrote that for the past two generations it was clearly understood that they were not allowed to exercise them.

Winston's second visit to the American capital on the 1929 tour probably stretched over two nights, with him arriving late on October 20 and departing the city on October 22. During the return visit to Washington Winston stayed at the Carlton Hotel with the other members of his party. Baruch joined the traveling party in the American capital, having arranged for a tea at the house of Dr. Adolph Caspar Miller at five o'clock on the afternoon of Monday, October 21. Miller was a member of the Federal Reserve Board, having been named to the board when it was originally established by President Wilson in 1914. At the tea Winston met the members of the Federal Reserve that were available to come. Miller, a former professor of economics, had written much on the field, including a 1925 article which he may have discussed at the tea with the former chancellor of the exchequer entitled "Restoration of British Gold Standard: What It Means." The social event might have been joined as well by Secretary of State Stimson, who had issued his own conflicting invitation for Winston to dine with him that same night. Winston had attempted to rectify the conflict by inviting Stimson to the Miller's tea. Even if they did not see each other at that event, Winston and Stimson were to meet each other when the American secretary of state came to London in 1930 for the London Naval Conference. Winston and Clementine would host Stimson and his wife at dinner in their home at 113 Eaton Square on February 12, 1930.[23]

Winston met further powerful American politicians at a reception held for him the next day at the United States Capitol Building. The luncheon was arranged by Arkansas senator James T. Robinson, who had been informed of Winston's visit by Baruch. Robinson, a former member of the House of Representatives and briefly governor of his state, was the Senate Minority Leader. He had been on the losing ticket with Al Smith as the vice-presidential nominee in the 1928 presidential election. Robinson, who was notorious for his temper, had once been banned from the Chevy Chase Country Club for fighting. Robinson and his wife Billie had traveled to Europe on at least two occasions earlier in the decade, meeting and becoming friends with Winston on these trips.[24]

The party, which included Baruch, Feversham, and Ronald Ian Campbell from the British embassy arrived at the capital and assembled in the President's Room at the Senate. They then went to the informal luncheon in Winston's honor held in the Minority Conference Room. The luncheon was scheduled to begin at one o'clock on the afternoon of October 21. Among the politicians attending was the sitting vice-president of the United States Charles Curtis. A former member of the House of Representatives, a senator from Kansas, and a senate majority leader, he had been elected with Hoover in the 1928 election. Curtis was, however, not close to President Hoover and played an insignificant role in the administration. As vice-president he was deemed a "dismal failure."²⁵

Winston probably discussed naval disarmament and the planned London Naval Conference with the American politicians, most especially with Robinson. That very day it had been announced that Stimson, Senator Robinson, and another senator, Reed of Pennsylvania, would go to London as the American delegation to the conference. Robinson, although an Anglophile, had nonetheless been firm on reparations and war debts. In London for the conference Robinson and his wife would again meet socially with Winston and Clementine. At the Capital Building Winston was photographed with Baruch, Robinson, and Curtis.²⁶

On October 22 Winston and Baruch traveled by train to dine and spend the night with Joseph Widener at his great estate of Lynnewood Hall at Elkins Park outside of Philadelphia.²⁷ Jack and Feversham came on later to join them after dinner, but then returned to Philadelphia for the night, leaving Winston and Baruch to remain with Widener. That Jack and Feversham went back to Philadelphia for the night was certainly not due to there not being enough room at Lynnewood Hall. The 110-room hall, designed by Horace Trumbauer, had more than enough room for the travelers, with 18 bedrooms on the second floor and two bachelor bedrooms on the ground floor.²⁸

Joseph E. Widener was the son of P.A.B. Widener, who started as butcher's boy and became a great tycoon and one of the richest men in America. P.A.B. Widener commissioned the building of Lynnewood Hall, which passed to his son Joseph on his death, his other son

**Lynnewood Hall at Elkins Park, where Winston Churchill was hosted by Joseph Widener for a night (Library of Congress).**

and one grandson having perished on the ill-fated maiden voyage of the Titanic in 1912. The magnificent hall, which had a Corinthian portico with six columns, was set on a 36-acre park with landscaped grounds and enclosed by a seven-foot-high iron fence.[29]

Aside from his involvement in horse racing, which included his owning the race track at Belmont Park, Joseph Widener was best known for possessing "one of the greatest private collections of art treasures in the world."[30] The collection included porcelain, French engravings of the eighteenth century, tapestries, and paintings. Among the tapestries was *The Triumph of Christ*, called the "greatest of all tapestries." It had been woven in Brussels around 1500 and was also known as the *Mazarin Tapestry*, since it had once been owned by French Cardinal Mazarin. Other tapestries in the collection included *Christ and the Woman*, *The Dreams of Rinaldo*, *The Garden at Gethsemane*, and *The Crucifixion*.[31]

The paintings in this collection, which was housed at Lynnewood Hall, was valued in the 1940s at between 15 and 50 million dollars. With at least 14 paintings by the artist, the Widener collection was also the world's greatest Rembrandt collection. Winston, no doubt, spent a great deal of time at the hall viewing and enjoying the works of the great masters in the Widener collection. In the First Gallery, located on the second floor of the hall, were paintings by El Greco, Titian, Romney, Cuyp, Jan Lys, and Gainsborough. Proceeding to the Second Gallery, called the Rembrandt Room, Winston would have seen the works by Rembrandt and other Dutch painters. The Rembrandts in the collection included *Study of an Old Man*, *Head of St. Matthew*, *The Apostle Paul*, and *Portrait of Himself*. Two paintings by Jan Vermeer—*A Woman Weighing Gold* and *Young Girl with a Flute*—were also in the Rembrandt Room.[32]

Two Rembrandts hanging in the room, *A Gentleman with High Hat and Gloves in Right Hand* and *A Lady with Ostrich Feather Fan in Right Hand*, were accompanied by a fascinating story that would have appealed to the guests. These two Rembrandts had been owned in Petrograd by the Youssoupoff family and were smuggled out of Russia after the Revolution. In 1921 Widener had inspected the paintings in London and bought them from Prince Felix Youssoupoff for about 200,000 British pounds. A few years later Youssoupoff tried to buy back the paintings, claiming their contract of sale allowed him to repurchase them for the original price plus interest. Widener refused, saying there had been no such agreement. At this point Youssoupoff sued. The case dragged through the courts until it was resolved in 1927 in favor of Widener, who was allowed to keep the Rembrandts.[33] The American art collector may have been at the very least a little concerned about drawing the ire of Youssoupoff, the Russian prince being world famous as the murderer of Rasputin. Not only did he lead the assassins, but he poisoned and personally shot their victim.

Between the Rembrandt Room and the Van Dyck Gallery was hung Bellini's *Feast of the Gods*. In the Van Dyck Gallery Winston would have seen six paintings by Anton Van Dyck and two more by Titian. In the other rooms of Lynnewood Hall were paintings by Raphael, Edouard Manet, John Constable, Renoir, Degas, and Rubens.[34]

After just a single night at Lynnewood Hall, the traveling party reassembled on October 23 and journeyed from Philadelphia to Bethlehem, Pennsylvania. Baruch, however, would forgo that leg of the trip. Winston, Jack, and Feversham arrived in the city that morning aboard the *Loretto* for a tour of the plant of the Bethlehem Steel Company. For the plant tour the Englishmen were joined by Winston's friend J. Leonard Replogle. They were met in Bethlehem by H. Edgar Lewis, executive vice-president of Bethlehem Steel, and other company officials.

The steel works at Bethlehem comprised three plants that stretched three-and-a-quarter miles along the south bank of the Lehigh River and occupied 820 acres. A further 1,680 acres were owned in the area by the company for use in operation of the plants. The Bethlehem Steel plant in the 1920s operated seven blast furnaces, 34 open hearth furnaces, three Bessemer converters, and two electric furnaces. There were iron, steel, and brass foundries, as well as an electric steel foundry and an ingot mould foundry. The plant had treatment and fabricating shops; rolling mills; and drop, press, and hammer forges; as well as an armor plate plant, and coke and coke by-product plant.[35]

Various parts of the plant were toured before Winston's party was provided a lunch with the company executives in the private dining room at the plant. The story of Bethlehem Steel impressed Winston. Founded by a private citizen, the company had been built up to such a point that in 1928 it produced as much steel as the entire British steel industry. Winston found that nearly all of the men who ran the factory had first started out as regular workers. Following lunch, the remainder of the plant tour was conducted.[36]

As first lord of the Admiralty and minister of munitions, Winston had inspected plants in Britain, and, based on his experience, the first question that came to his mind on his visit to the steel plant was where were all the workers. They walked into a huge, almost deserted hall that was 300 or 400 yards in length and filled with machinery. It was working at full capacity but with few workmen visible. Winston noted that scattered small groups of men operated sets of levers to control the working of the plant, while other workers made adjustments or performed special tasks. The impression he took away was of "men using machinery rather than machines using men!"

At the steel plant Winston believed he observed the foundations of American mass production at work. In all possible cases the plant used the horse-power of machinery in place of man-power. Further, the plant brought all types of heavy steel products together in one location. Orders could be entirely completed at the one plant without unnecessary transportation costs or dislocation of the workforce.

The fields outside the plants were, however, crammed with the motorcars belonging to the workmen. The works at Bethlehem Steel were so vast that even with the workshops that Winston thought empty, the plant still employed 12,000 to 14,000 workers. In total, the tourists learned, the company employed 70,000 workers, with very few being paid less than five pounds a week or being a member of a trade union. As they inspected the plant, Winston's hosts told them they had very few problems with the workers. The company paid high wages to ensure the active cooperation of their workforce. While the executives managed the plant, they could not actually sack any of the workers for poor performance. Any disciplinary incidents that arose were handled by the independent workman's committee, who were quite often rather strict. The steel plant executives further explained that their company could not afford the labor problems they had in England because they lacked that country's natural advantages in distance, where everything was nearby and the finished product sold to markets a short distance away. Bethlehem Steel, on the other hand, had to import part of its ore from Chile and bring in the remainder 600 miles by rail, with its coal brought in from 400 miles. Their finished output then had to be distributed all over the United States by train.

Told by Winston that they could not compete with British steel makers in a neutral market that was equal distance from each of their shores, the hosts conceded that this was true. They, however, were not at the moment interested in exports and happily made steel for the United States. It was a market that they had all to themselves and their American competitors.

After the tour the Englishmen returned to New York, still traveling aboard the *Loretto*. In his newspaper article, Winston said he wondered on the train why the British could not have a few great centers of steel production that built a finished product through every stage to completion with a work force paid high wages to secure their cooperation. He could only wonder what could be achieved in Britain if they combined their own inherent advantages and strengths with the American methods of production and labor peace.

... 19 ...

# New York, October 23–29

Winston, Jack, and Feversham returned to the Savoy Plaza on October 23. The two brothers would stay at the hotel for the remainder of their visit to the city, while Feversham would stay in Room 1509 until October 26. Feversham's room was billed at a rate of $9 per day. Upon reaching the Savoy Plaza, Winston cabled James Richardson in Winnipeg for information on his stocks in Hargal and Baltac. He was continuing to avidly follow his investments.[1]

One man Winston did not meet in the United States in 1929, despite spending three weeks in New York City that October, was the then governor of the state, Franklin Roosevelt. This was in spite of the efforts of Baruch, who invited the governor to a dinner he was giving for Winston late in the month, before the visitor sailed for England. Henry Morgenthau, a friend and confident of Roosevelt, wrote to Winston on October 23 indicating that Roosevelt would not be in the city on October 28 or 29 and was thus unable to meet the visiting statesman.[2]

Winston and Morgenthau already knew each other, having previously met when Morgenthau was traveling in England. They had dined together on at least two occasions in 1922. Morgenthau remembered Winston at one of the dinners as talking "with delightful freedom for hours, and I enjoyed the conversation thoroughly." On Winston's behalf, Morgenthau had talked to Charles Schwab and New York Police Commissioner Grover Whalen about night life to be seen in New York, with an eye to something that would be attractive for Winston. Wallace told Morgenthau that some of the night clubs might be worthwhile, but no police protection would be necessary for that. Schwab told Morgenthau to come to the dinner on October 25 and the two would then discuss going out to see the New York night life. Morgenthau also enclosed a copy of his latest book, *I Was Sent to Athens*, with his letter to Winston. The British statesman was more interested in the book than he was in the night life. He cabled his thanks for the book but said, "Let us discard night life."[3]

October 24, 1929, was "Black Thursday." After rising weakness and instability during the month, the stock market dramatically crashed as a "tidal wave of selling" hit the New York Stock Exchange when it opened that day. As the day proceeded, millions of shares were sold as prices collapsed. The market that Winston had heavily invested in since arriving in August saw hundreds of millions of dollars disappear from the value of the shares. A newspaper report that evening called it the "wildest break ever recorded" in the financial history of the United States.[4]

With the stock market crashing, there were scenes of "wild excitement" on the streets of New York's financial district. A "weird roar" emanating from the trading floor could be heard outside on Broad Street. As the news spread of the ongoing collapse on the trading floor, the traffic became choked on Broad and Wall Streets as 10,000 people jammed the steps of the Sub-Treasury building, window ledges, and sidewalks. A "great pool of humanity" formed in front of the exchange. Police reserves had to be sent in to keep order, as "rumor after rumor" and "report after report" circulated. Wild rumors of suicides, robberies, fights, failures, and other assorted calamities spread. Extra editions of the newspapers were printed with the headline "Panic."[5]

After two hours of trading, the chaos on the trading floor peaked at 11:30 that morning. Drawn by the news of a "mad market," a record number of more than 700 people jammed the visitors' gallery in two hours to get a glimpse of the frantic scenes. The noise from the floor was a "composite shout from a thousand throats of traders on the stock exchange floor. It was like unorganized rooting at a great football game, save that it never rose and ebbed but continued hour after hour unwaning." The lines four deep filled the stairway to the gallery almost all the way down to the street.[6]

**A crowd outside the New York Stock Exchange following the crash (Library of Congress).**

At the height of the panic, after having an early lunch with Baruch, Winston strolled into the middle of the chaos, as he "happened to be walking down Wall Street." He was recognized by a complete stranger and invited into the gallery of the stock exchange. Unlike other reports, Winston remembered watching a spectacle that was composed and orderly. He did not remember the noise but instead observed that the 1,200 members of the exchange, who had each paid 100,000 pounds for their membership, were "walking to and fro like a slow-motion picture of a disturbed ant heap." They were trying to sell huge numbers of securities at a fraction of the old prices but could not find anyone to buy.[7]

With so many people in the gallery, the exchange officials ordered the Broad Street gallery closed at 12:30 that afternoon. The people in the gallery were asked to leave. Winston was still present when the gallery was closed, but did not mind. He declared he had "seen enough." By the end of trading that day 16,383,700 shares would have been sold, and a total share value of ten billion dollars was lost from the New York Stock exchange.[8] Worse, however, was yet to come.

Later that autumn afternoon, which he thought was bright and clear, Winston looked out at the city from a window in one of the city's skyscrapers, possibly his hotel room or Baruch's offices at the Equitable Building. The scene out the window, as compared to the "helpless liquidation" of the trading floor, gave him confidence that the terrible financial disaster would pass. While the stock market was collapsing, Winston watched the many ships, from tugs to ocean liners, on the Hudson and North rivers as they arrived and departed from the vast docks. Further east he could see the cities and factories of New Jersey, which continued to pour out "clouds of smoke and steam," while directly below him, the streets around the city's huge buildings were "swarming with human life."[9]

From his skyscraper on "Black Thursday" Winston recalled that a "gentleman cast himself down fifteen storeys and was dashed to pieces." The incident caused a great uproar and brought the arrival of the fire department to the scene. He added that quite a number of people seemed to have thrown themselves to their deaths on that day. Whether anyone actually committed suicide by jumping from the skyscrapers on "Black Thursday" is a controversial question. Winston's report of the gentleman casting himself to his death could be said to be similar to his claim in a House of Commons debate that the inventor of the guillotine was eventually executed by his own invention. When he made this assertion, another member of Parliament yelled out that it was not true, to which Winston retorted that it should have been. If it is not true that desperate men plunged to their death on that terrible day, thus adding to the drama of the unfolding disaster, Winston could retort in a similar fashion that if it was untrue it indeed should have been.

In his article on speculation in America, Winston wrote of the crash as when "suddenly, the earth trembled." The small stockholders who had feverishly played the market now "ruthlessly sold out" as they let all their investments go and tried to keep their homes and make do with the old car for another year.

Although he had seen the value of his shares nearly ruined, Winston endured the terrible blow to his finances and continued with his trip. He was encouraged by his American financial friends to adopt an optimistic outlook about the market. Baruch reacted quite calmly to the unfolding events, in Winston's observation, while Van Antwerp cabled him on October 25 that "yesterday's debacle laid the foundation for a constructive advance which will probably extend well into next year." He said that his best judgment was to buy 200 additional shares in a stock Winston had inquired about. On Saturday, however, the San Francisco stock broker qualified his previously stated confidence by cabling that there could be a period of readjustment before the advance resumes.[10]

On October 25, Winston went as planned to the annual meeting of the American Iron and Steel Institute at the Hotel Commodore, a 28-storey hotel at 42nd Street and Lexington Avenue. Charles Schwab was president of the institute, in addition to his duties as chairman of the Bethlehem Steel Corporation. The morning and afternoon sessions had presentations on such technical topics as "Waste Prevention and Salvage as Applied to the Steel Industry" and "Thermit Welding and the Steel Mill." Schwab tried to be positive, despite the previous day's momentous events, noting humorously in his welcome that morning that "there may be the smile of uncertainty upon the faces of a few who thought last week they were very rich and not quite so rich this week."[11]

The institute's dinner on Friday evening was attended by Winston and his party. In gratitude for the kindness shown him by Schwab, the British statesman had agreed to make the second of his two major speeches on the United States leg of his tour. The audience of 2,000 at the Hotel Commodore was easily far larger than that for the previous major speech in Chicago.[12] A week prior to the event Winston had cabled Schwab asking him to also invite Feversham, Travers Jerome, and John W. Davis.

Despite providing the private car that brought the traveling party from California to Chicago and carried them on the swing through Virginia and Pennsylvania, it appears that the dinner on October 25 was the first meeting between Winston and Schwab on the 1929 tour. Schwab was a 67-year-old steel magnate who had been a leader in the industry as chairman of the Bethlehem Steel Corporation for the previous 26 years. He was the "most powerful, successful, charismatic, and for a time one of the wealthiest of the great industrialists of the Gilded Age." He built up the world's second ranking steel company and headed the "biggest industrial enterprise on earth."[13]

During the war Schwab met

Charles M. Schwab, president of the Bethlehem Steel company, put his private rail car at Winston Churchill's disposal for the American leg of the tour (Library of Congress).

Winston in England and arranged to supply Britain with war materials, including 50,000 rounds of ammunition a day. More dramatically, Schwab arranged for 20 submarines for the Royal Navy to be built in the United States but shipped in sections to Montreal for final assembly in order to avoid breaking American neutrality laws. By November 1914, Bethlehem Steel was filling British orders worth fifty million dollars. Winston believed it was a gigantic task that Schwab had completed in an amazing fashion. Later, as director-general of the Emergency Fleet Corporation, Schwab oversaw the building of 495 ships in 16 months.

Schwab acted as toastmaster at the dinner and opened proceedings by declaring they had distinguished guests with them that evening, and that it was an "English night for the American Iron and Steel Institute." He then proposed a toast to "His Majesty, the King of England" and then a second toast to the President of the United States. Referring to Winston, Schwab said he was speaking with a great deal of reluctance, as he was in the presence of the "polished orator who is to follow me." Schwab pointed out that Winston was "not accustomed to the language and methods of speech which I have used to you mill men—the language I think you understand best."[14]

In the remarks he made to the institute, Schwab said he saw no reason why the present industrial prosperity could not continue as long as the balance between production and consumption was maintained.

"In my long association with the steel industry I have never known it to enjoy a greater stability or more promising outlook than it does today," Schwab told the attendees. He added humorously, in a remark Winston quite enjoyed, "I may well have said in addressing you, 'My friends and Former Millionaires.'"

The 2,000 guests at the dinner enjoyed the quip, as did Winston, who long remembered it. Despite his apparent cheerfulness, Schwab was indeed a "former millionaire." He would later confide to an acquaintance that he had once had a fortune of 40 million dollars, but most of it had been lost in the stock market crash. Schwab never recovered his fortune and died in 1939, with his liabilities outweighing his assets by more than 300,000 dollars.[15]

In introducing Winston, Schwab recalled they had met during the World War, and of all the "great statesmen, officers and executives during that period I never met any man who displayed more energy and more ability to make decisions promptly and get things done. There developed in me a very high regard and great admiration for this man."

In his speech, Winston called for understanding between the United States and Great Britain, as the world was dependent "almost entirely in the immediate future on the cooperation and development of the English-speaking countries." On the naval question, he spoke of his countrymen's desire for a settlement and his own desire that Britain and the United States should be for "all time equal on the seas." Reaching such a settlement and removing the differences between the two countries would require understanding and tolerance on the part of both the British and Americans. Winston said both countries should be strong, as he did not want to see the good people disarmed and all the "evil people" heavily equipped for war. During the speech he was interrupted by laughter when he made a slip and referred to the 45 states that make up the United States. He also paid tribute to Schwab, Baruch, and Replogle for their services in the last war. At the end of his remarks, Winston sat down to cheers while the audience rose to applaud.[16]

"Gentlemen, we have heard, as I told you, the polished oratory of a great statesman and administrator," Schwab declared as he thanked Winston for his speech.

The next speaker that evening was Sir Frederick Mills, the chairman of the Ebbw Vale Steel Company. Mills thanked the institute for the honorary membership they had bestowed upon him and poked good-natured fun at Winston. He said that the honorary membership was a "great convenience" because "after the many years of the administration of my friend, the last speaker, we have little funds left with which to pay any subscriptions at all." Mills finished speaking at ten minutes to ten o'clock that evening, and Schwab called on John W. Davis for a speech before he closed the proceedings. Davis would also suffer financially due to the crash over the coming years, since his salary as a Wall Street lawyer would be reduced significantly.

In the wake of the stock market crash, Winston recounted in his newspaper article that he was surprised to hear the common refrain from the captains of industry of the importance of maintaining high wages.[17] It was explained to him that without good wages the public would not be able to buy the goods being produced, and without people buying their goods they were doomed to fail. Maintaining good wages would ensure that the economy would recover. While he did not know whether it would work, Winston thought this approach should be considered by Europeans.

With only days to go before he left for England, Winston was eager to be getting home. He wished both to see his family as well as get back to British politics. On October 25 he cabled Clementine that all was well, but he was looking forward to November 5, the day he was scheduled to arrive home. During the month of October, in the face of his approaching return to the House of Commons, Winston's mind had become more focused on politics. He cabled Stanley Baldwin and David Lloyd George about postponing the Egyptian and Russian debates, and followed that up with a letter to the Liberal leader.[18]

Winston and Jack originally planned to spend much of the last weekend of their trip in Connecticut, most likely staying with Mrs. Rockefeller at Greenwich.[19] In reference to their host for the weekend, Winston only refers to her as "Mrs. Rockefeller." While there were several different Rockefellers living in the extremely wealthy enclave of Greenwich, it is most likely that their host was Elsie Rockefeller, living on Lake Avenue, the widow of William Goodsell Rockefeller and sister-in-law of Percy Rockefeller.

Having again been loaned Schwab's private car, they planned to start from New York's Central Station at about eleven o'clock Saturday morning and have lunch on board the train. Joining them on the train for the short trip was, most likely, Amy Guest and her party. Together they would detrain at Stamford, presumably to make an initial short visit to Mrs. Rockefeller at Greenwich before proceeding on to New Haven for the Army-Yale football game that afternoon. The game Winston and Jack watched, along with 80,000 spectators, in the Yale Bowl was an exciting affair. The favored Army jumped out to a 13–0 lead before Yale, led by their quarterback Albic Booth, stormed back to win by a score of 21–13. Demonstrating Winston's ability to focus on more than one thing at a time, while watching football he also discussed his literary plans with Charles Scribner, who appears to have been at the game with him. While the college football game was underway, Winston thought of writing his multi-volume work, *A History of the English-Speaking Peoples*, after being asked if he had ever thought of writing a history of the British Empire. Although Scribner's would eventually decide to pass on the project, the four volumes would appear in the 1950s after being delayed by the war and other literary initiatives. After the game was over Winston and Jack probably returned to Greenwich for dinner.[20]

Returning to New York, the travelers had two busy days before going aboard their ship for the return Trans-Atlantic crossing. Winston was invited for lunch by Millicent Hearst, either at her Riverside Drive home or the Colony Restaurant on Thursday afternoon, October 31. As he was already planning to sail by that date, Winston asked if it would be possible to have tea on either Monday or Tuesday afternoon of that week. Arrangements were probably made to cancel the later date, and Winston had luncheon with Millicent Hearst early in the week.[21]

The stock market suffered a terrible day on Monday, October 28. After some optimism at the outset, the market experienced a disastrous day of trading. More than 9,000,000 shares were traded as the *Times* general stocks average fell 29 points, the worst single-day loss in the history of the New York Stock Exchange. That evening Bernard Baruch hosted a dinner party for Winston at his mansion at 1055 Fifth Avenue. Just over two years later Winston, in New York at the outset of his planned lecture tour, was knocked down on Fifth Avenue in a collision with an automobile driven by Mario Constasino. Severely injured, the start of the lecture had to be delayed into 1932 as Winston recuperated first in a New York hospital and then in the Bahamas.[22]

Guests for the Baruch affair that evening were the elite of the financial world. They included Charlie Mitchell, president of National City Bank; Albert Wiggin, chairman of Chase National Bank; Charles Schwab; John D. Ryan, president of Anaconda Copper; Eugene Meyer, a millionaire banker and financier; and Thomas Lamont, the senior partner at J.P. Morgan. Also attending were the Swope brothers: Gerard, the president of General Electric; and Herbert, Baruch's friend and former editor of the *New York World*. At the dinner Mitchell made a toast, similar to Schwab's at the steel institute dinner, to "my fellow former millionaires." Among such high-powered financiers and industrialists the stock market was the topic of the evening. The mood was hopeful, with much discussion of concrete plans to save the market. Herbert Swope wrote a friend that the general consensus of those present was that investors who could withstand the pressure would surely reap substantial profits when the market recovered, as the share prices were now so far undervalued. The meeting of these major figures talked that evening about making money again instead of losing it, and most agreed the stock market was going to change for the better.[23]

That evening may have been the last meeting of Winston and Baruch on the 1929 trip. The British statesman appreciated all Baruch had done to organize the tour and would cable him from the ship as he sailed from New York: "Many thoughts about your kindness and friendship to me and the wonderful tour you planned for us." In turn, for all of Baruch's work to make his American trip a success, he would plan and host a week-long visit for Baruch to England in August in 1930. During this visit Winston showed his American friend Chartwell, the battleships at Portsmouth, Blenheim Palace, Salisbury Plain, and Oxford, as well as introducing him to all his friends.[24]

## ... 20 ...

# The Return to England, October 29–November 5

Winston and Jack's second-to-last day in North America on the trip was October 29, 1929, known to history as "Black Tuesday." The stock market suffered savage losses throughout the day of panicked trading. In one half-hour period that morning, stocks lost $2,000,000,000 in value, while for the day more than 16 million stocks were traded, with losses of ten billion dollars.[1] The certain recovery Winston had heard about at Baruch's dinner the night before had proven to be terribly inaccurate.

The stock market collapse in the last days of October was a financial disaster for Winston. His investments were wiped out. The Baltac stock he had bought for $2.10 a share was down nearly 80 percent and closed at $0.45 a share on "Black Tuesday." Likewise, Montgomery Ward shares were off 57 percent from mid–September after that day's trading, while the Simmons share had fallen over 60 percent during that same period. One estimate is that he lost over 10,000 pounds in the crash.[2] The amount is likely higher. In California he had written, with a tabulated estimate, that he had earned 21,825 pounds from book royalties, advances on the Marlborough biography, and his articles since leaving the cabinet in May 1929. On the trip Winston had Thornton Butterworth and Curtis Brown quickly forward him the money he was owed so it could be invested. This small fortune was largely gone. Winston, accused so often of being a reckless gambler in politics, had gambled on the stock market and lost.

Winston admitted in his article on speculation that the public, including such feverish investors as himself, had been warned many times about speculation.[3] The Federal Reserve had denounced it, and Andrew Mellon had declared the position of the market to be unsafe. The warnings "fell upon ears deaf to unwelcome tidings." He stoically concluded that the "American public have certainly been cleaned out, but they cannot say that they have been hoodwinked."

Once back in England, Winston would remain optimistic about the collapse that had struck the United States stock market, an optimism he was supported in by Baruch, who cabled him as early as mid–November 1929, at the outset of the Great Depression, that the "financial storm definitely passed."[4] In the *Daily Telegraph* Winston would optimistically write that the American system had allowed the brokers "to weather, with scarcely a shipwreck, the greatest financial hurricane that ever blew." American methods were established not to prevent the onset of such crises, but to survive them. With their "unshakable faith in a golden future," Americans assumed good days were surely coming. Blunders would be repaired, hideous losses made good, and ruins rebuilt. Winston shared the belief in America's future prosperity. He argued that with its Constitution and an abhorrence of Socialism, the United States had nothing to fear. With its great and diffused wealth, vast size, seven million college students, leadership in science, abundant food, industrial ventures of a huge scale, and high wages alongside a growing number of millionaires, Winston was sure that in the United States "All will be well."

Only slowly would Winston comprehend that the crash on Wall Street was an "economic blizzard" that would have devastating consequences worldwide. It would also eventually turn Britain, in his words, into "one vast soup kitchen."[5]

After spending the day in New York, Winston dined with some friends on the night of "Black Tuesday." It was the final engagement of his three-month tour. After dining, Winston and Jack, having checked out of the Savoy Plaza, bid their friends farewell, went to the harbor, and boarded the *Berengaria* to sleep aboard the ship that night.[6]

Lord Feversham remained behind in the United States for a few more weeks. He went back to southern California, where he visited the W.K. Kellogg Arabian horse ranch near Pomona. From the ranch Feversham bought a three-year-old pure-blooded Arabian stallion named Shelif which he arranged to have shipped to England. Following after the newly purchased stallion, he returned to London on December 4. Feversham would continue his work in social welfare, especially for the improvement of the British probation service. His efforts would produce results, with the establishment of a full-time probation service for every court in the country in 1936. Feversham would serve with distinction in the Yorkshire Hussars during the Second World War and die in 1963 at the age of 56.[7]

The *Berengaria* of the Cunard Line was scheduled to sail from Pier 54 of the North River Piers on the morning of October 30. A group of newspaper reporters came aboard the ship that morning to try to speak to Winston before the ship departed. He was, however, nowhere to be seen. He was asleep in his cabin as the *Berengaria* made ready to sail.

"He is asleep and he can't be disturbed, and anyway he's already been interviewed 42 times," Jack brusquely told the journalists, referring to the number of times he had spoken to the press during the previous three months in North America.[8]

In case the journalists were not put off by Jack, two stewards stood guard outside of Winston's cabin as well. The cabin for the trans–Atlantic voyage was one of the ship's huge first-class rooms. Winston and Jack were among the 240 first-class passengers making the crossing.

The 52,226–ton *Berengaria* sailed at nine o'clock in the morning from New York, bound for Southampton.[9] Winston's three-month visit to Canada and the United States was over. It had been a tremendous success. He had thoroughly enjoyed himself and had fun. Beyond that, he had seen and learned about the two countries, and met the men in charge,

*Opposite*: The *Berengaria* of the Cunard Line carried Winston and Jack Churchill on their return voyage to England from New York (Library of Congress).

both politically and financially, of the respective countries' destinies. In Canada he had seen the great political, social, and economic expansion that had occurred in the thirty years since his previous trip. He was sure of her having a wonderful future. In the United States he had heard the "hum of Chicago, the rattle of Wall Street, the roar of New York." He had seen the "tranquil prosperity of California" and felt himself in the "domain of history" in Virginia. In Canada, Winston had received an enthusiastic welcome, his speeches being greeted with fervent patriotism and excitement. The farther west he traveled in Canada, the more keen the sentiment for England became. Similarly, in the United States his message of the need for Anglo-American cooperation had been appreciatively received in all quarters.[10]

On the seven-day crossing of the Atlantic Ocean, Winston, apart from taking Turkish baths, spent most of his time in his cabin. With the contracts for articles completed in New York, Winston probably worked hard on them during the voyage. He also read, most probably including the biography of Brigham Young that had been given to him by William Gibbs McAdoo. Winston did appear at a fancy dress ball held one night aboard the *Berengaria*. At this affair a small lottery was organized on what hat Winston would wear to the ball. He came in wearing a little red fez that was "perched saucily on the top of his head." No one won the lottery, and the money had to be returned. While voyaging on the North Atlantic Ocean, Winston received the honor of being elected the Lord Rector of Edinburgh University.[11]

Winston would remember the men and women he had visited in Canada and the United States, and remain in contact with them. In 1933, on the publication of a volume of his massive biography of the Duke of Marlborough, he sent copies of the book to Crocker, Admiral Grayson, Senator Robinson, Schwab, Baruch, Millicent Hearst, McAdoo, and the Van Antwerps. William Van Antwerp would write, expressing his appreciation for the gift, and say that a photograph of Winston hung in their library along with one of Randolph taken at Pebble Beach. Both were close to their copy of the *World Crisis*. "On many an evening we lift our glasses to you both," Van Antwerp would write.[12]

The *Berengaria* docked at Southampton on November 5. On disembarking, Winston told a journalist he had traveled about 18,000 miles and had had a "thoroughly enjoyable time."[13]

After the three-month trip to North America, Jack resumed work at his firm at the Stock Exchange in England. He remained close to his brother for the remaining years of his life, and he was often present in the gallery of the House of Commons for the important moments. After his wife Goonie died in 1941 and he was bombed out of his own house, Jack went to live with his brother, then prime minister, at 10 Downing Street. He often accompanied Winston on trips around Britain but did not go on any of the overseas war-time trips. Jack died on February 23, 1947, at his home in London, with Winston and Johnny in close attendance.[14]

After arriving at Southampton, Winston took the next train for London. He was met at Waterloo station by Clementine to whom he immediately "blurted" out that he had lost a fortune in the stock market crash. The losses "cast a shadow over his otherwise joyful return home to Clementine and Chartwell." Having sustained such a financial setback, even if he still had the contracts for articles and the book on Marlborough, Winston and Clementine were forced to stay at the Goring Hotel off of Grosvenor Gardens or in furnished houses for a few months at a time for the next couple of years until matters were put right. They managed to keep Chartwell, but it was not really open during this period.[15]

From Waterloo Winston hurried to the House of Commons to make his first appearance in the chamber since July. He was cheered from both sides as he entered the House and was smiling as he sat down in the opposition front benches beside Stanley Baldwin. Winston and Baldwin exchanged friendly greetings.[16]

Despite the cheery reunion with Baldwin, the stage was already set for Winston to quit the Conservative front bench and be thrown into the political wilderness. On October 31, while he was aboard the *Berengaria*, the Irwin declaration had been issued, which stated that the ultimate goal of India's constitutional progress was the obtaining of dominion status. It was over India that Winston first broke with the Conservatives. By the time he completed his lecture tour of Canada and the United States in 1932, he would be politically isolated. Winston, however, was far from finished. He would next return to North America in 1941 for the conference with President Franklin D. Roosevelt in the waters off Newfoundland. By then he had been turned to as Britain's prime minister and war leader during his country's darkest hour.

# Chapter Notes

## Chapter 1

1. *The Scotsman*, August 5, 1929.
2. Amery Papers, AMEL 7/23.
3. *Southern Daily Echo*, August 5, 1929.
4. Ibid.

## Chapter 2

1. *Ottawa Journal*, August 14, 1929.
2. Richard Langworth, ed., *Churchill by Himself: The Definitive Collection of Quotations* (New York: PublicAffairs, 2008), 516.
3. R. Crosby Kemper III, ed., *Winston Churchill: Resolution, Defiance, Magnanimity, Good Will* (Columbia: University of Missouri Press, 1996), 150–151.
4. Philip Williamson, "'Safety First': Baldwin, the Conservative Party, and the 1929 General Election," *The Historical Journal* 25, no. 2 (1982): 409.
5. John Barnes and David Nicolson, eds., *The Leo Amery Diaries Volume I: 1896–1929* (London: Hutchinson, 1980), 596.
6. Ronald I. Cohen, *Bibliography of the Writings of Sir Winston Churchill Volume II* (New York: Thoemmes, 2006), 1389.
7. Sir Winston Churchill Papers, CHAR 1/206.
8. Sir Winston Churchill Papers, CHAR1/205.
9. Beaverbrook Papers. BBK/C/86.
10. Martin Gilbert, *Churchill and the Great Republic* (New York: Free Press, 2005), 23.
11. Martin Gilbert, *Winston S. Churchill, Volume V 1922–1939: The Prophet of Truth* (Boston, Houghton Mifflin, 1977), 344.
12. Sir Winston Churchill Papers, CHAR 8/227.
13. Cohen, 1358–59.
14. CHAR 1/206 Randolph Churchill, *Twenty-One Years* (London: Weidenfeld and Nicolson, 1965), 75.
15. Langworth, 324; Bernard M. Baruch, *Baruch: The Public Years* (New York: Holt, Rinehart and Winston, 1960), 121–123.
16. Sir Winston Churchill Papers, CHAR 1/205.
17. Sir Winston Churchill Papers, CHAR 1/206.
18. Ibid.
19. Ibid.
20. Ibid.
21. Ibid.
22. Ibid.
23. Ibid; Beaverbrook Papers BBK/C/86.
24. Sir Winston Churchill Papers, CHAR 1/206.
25. Ibid.
26. Ibid.
27. Ibid.
28. Ibid.
29. *Ottawa Evening Citizen*, August 10, 1929; David Dilks, *The Great Dominion: Winston Churchill in Canada, 1900–1954* (Toronto: Thomas Allen, 2005), 61.
30. Sir Winston Churchill Papers, CHAR 1/205.
31. Sir Winston Churchill Papers, CHAR 1/206.
32. *The Times* (August 3, 1929); CHAR 1/205 Gilbert, *Winston S. Churchill, Volume V: 1922–1939*, 334.
33. Cate Haste, ed., *Clarissa Eden, a Memoir: From Churchill to Eden* (London: Weidenfeld and Nicolson, 2007), xiii.
34. John Colville, *Winston Churchill and His Inner Circle* (New York, Wyndham Books, 1981), 32; Robert H. Pilpel, *Churchill in America, 1895–1961: An Affectionate Portrait* (New York: Harcourt Brace Jovanovich, 1976), 78–79.
35. Peregrine Churchill and Julian Mitchell, *Jennie, Lady Randolph Churchill: A Portrait with Letters* (New York: St. Martin's Press, 1974), 210–211; Celia Lee and John Lee, *The Churchills: A Family Portrait* (New York: Palgrave MacMillan, 2010), 201; *The Times*, February 25, 1947.
36. Haste, 5.
37. Martin Gilbert, *Winston S. Churchill, Volume V, Part 2 Documents: The Wilderness Years 1929–1935* (Boston: Houghton Mifflin, 1981), 32.

38. Ibid., 40.
39. Ibid., 50.
40. Roy Jenkins, *Churchill: A Biography* (New York: Farrar, Straus and Giroux, 2001), 354.
41. Sir Winston Churchill Papers, CHAR 1/206.
42. Anita Leslie, *Randolph: The Biography of Winston Churchill's Son* (New York: Beaufort, 1985), 12; Colville, 35.
43. Pilpel, 78.
44. Leslie, *Randolph: The Biography of Winston Churchill's Son*, 13.
45. Ibid., 14.
46. Colville, 35.
47. Winston S. Churchill, *His Father's Son: The Life of Randolph Churchill* (London: Weidenfeld and Nicolson, 1996), 45–48.
48. Sir Winston Churchill Papers, CHAR 1/207.
49. *The Independent*, July 9, 1992.
50. Ibid.
51. Pilpel, 78.
52. John Churchill, *A Churchill Canvas* (Boston: Little Brown 1962), 74–75.
53. *The Independent*, July 9, 1992.
54. Haste, 3.
55. Randolph Churchill, *Twenty-One Years*; John Churchill, 79.
56. *The Independent*, July 9, 1992.
57. Robert Rhodes James, *Victor Cazalet: A Portrait* (London: Hamish Hamilton, 1976), 129.

## Chapter 3

1. Robert D. Turner, *The Pacific Empresses: An Illustrated History of Canadian Pacific Railway's Empress Liners on the Pacific Ocean* (Victoria, B.C.: Sono Nis Press, 1981), 128.
2. *Seventh Annual Round the World Cruise, Empress of Australia* (Canadian Pacific, 1929), 66.
3. Gilbert, *Documents*, 37.
4. *The Times*, November 7, 1940.
5. David Laurence Jones, *See This World Before the Next: Cruising with CPR Steamships in the Twenties and Thirties* (Calgary: Fifth House, 2004), 25.
6. *Montreal Herald*, August 9, 1929; *Toronto Daily Star*, August 3, 1929.
7. David Faber, *Speaking for England: Leo, Julian and John Amery—The Tragedy of a Political Family* (New York: Free Press, 2005), 53.
8. Lynne Olson, *Troublesome Young Men: The Rebels Who Brought Churchill to Power and Helped Save England* (New York: Farrar, Straus and Giroux), 114; *New York Times*, September 17, 1955.
9. Robert Rhodes James, *Churchill: A Study in Failure, 1900–1939* (New York: World Publishing Company, 1970), 328.
10. Winston Churchill, *My Early Life* (New York: Touchstone, 1996), 17–18.
11. L.S. Amery, *Days of Fresh Air: Being Reminiscences of Outdoor Life* (London: Jarrolds, 1939), 21.
12. Deborah Lavin, 'Amery, Leopold Charles Maurice Stennett (1873–1955),' Oxford Dictionary of National Biography, Oxford University Press, 2004; online, May 2012.
13. L.S. Amery, *My Political Life, Volume Two: War and Peace, 1914–1929* (London: Hutchison, 1953), 490.
14. John Barnes, 598.
15. Amery Papers, AMEL 7/23.
16. David Dilks, 39.
17. Amery Papers, AMEL 7/23.
18. Randolph Churchill, *Twenty-One Years*, 73.
19. Gilbert, *Documents*, 40.
20. Ibid., 38.
21. Gilbert, *Winston S. Churchill, Volume V: 1922–1939*, 338.
22. Ibid., 337. David Carlton, *MacDonald Versus Henderson: The Foreign Policy of the Second Labour Government* (New York: Humanities Press, 1970), 168.
23. Amery Papers, AMEL 7/23.
24. Ibid.
25. Ibid.
26. Ibid.
27. Gilbert, *Documents*, 45.
28. Randolph Churchill, *Twenty-One Years*, 73.
29. Gilbert, *Documents*, 37.
30. Ibid., 40.
31. Ibid., 39.
32. Ibid., 40.
33. Amery Papers, AMEL 7/23.
34. Peter Mansfield, *The British in Egypt* (New York: Holt, Rinehart, and Winston, 1971), 249.
35. Randolph Churchill, *Twenty-One Years*, 74.
36. Amery Papers, AMEL 7/23.
37. L.S. Amery, *Days of Fresh Air*, 141–142.
38. Randolph Churchill, *Twenty-One Years*, 74.
39. Gilbert, *Documents*, 38.
40. Ibid., 37; John Churchill, 79; *New York Times*, April 16, 1928.
41. Gilbert, *Documents*, 39.
42. *Quebec Chronicle-Telegraph*, August 9, 1929.
43. *Montreal Daily Star*, August 10, 1929.
44. *Montreal Gazette*, August 10, 1929.
45. *Quebec Chronicle-Telegraph*, August 12, 1929.
46. *Montreal Daily Star*, August 10, 1929.
47. Winston Churchill, "World's Greatest Grain Emporium," *Daily Telegraph*, January 6, 1930, 8.
48. John Churchill, 79.

## Chapter 4

1. *Manitoba Free Press*, August 19, 1929; *Toronto Telegram*, August 16, 1929.
2. *Saturday Night*, 1929.
3. K.C. Wheare, *The Statute of Westminster and Dominion Status* (London: Oxford University Press, 1942), 40; *The Canada Year Book 1930* (Ottawa: Acland, 1930), xxvvi.
4. Winston Churchill, "World's Greatest Grain Emporium," 8.
5. *Quebec Chronicle-Telegraph*, August 10, 1929.
6. *Toronto Daily Star*, August 10, 1929.
7. Ibid.
8. L.S. Amery, *My Political Life, Volume Three: The*

*Unforgiving Years, 1929-1940* (London: Hutchinson, 1955), 103-104.
9. Barbara Chisholm, *Castles of the North: Canada's Grand Hotels* (Toronto: Lynx Images, 2001), 130-132.
10. Gilbert, *Documents*, 43.
11. Sir Winston Churchill Papers, CHAR 1/207.
12. Randolph Churchill, *Twenty-One Years*, 75.
13. Francois Kersaudy, *Churchill and De Gaulle* (London: Collins, 1981), 32; Gilbert and Martin, *Winston S. Churchill, Volume III: The Challenge of War, 1914-1916* (Boston: Houghton Mifflin, 1971), 278.
14. Sir Winston Churchill Papers, CHAR 1/207.
15. Ibid.; Gilbert, *Documents*, 44; Baruch Papers.
16. *Toronto Daily Star*, August 12, 1929.
17. *Quebec Chronicle-Telegraph*, August 12, 1929.
18. C.P. Stacey, *Quebec, 1759: The Siege and the Battle* (New York, St. Martin's Press, 1959), vii.
19. John Churchill, 80.
20. Winston Churchill, "World's Greatest Grain Emporium," 8.
21. Gilbert, *Documents*, 43; Winston Churchill, "World's Greatest Grain Emporium," 8.
22. William D. Middleton, *The Bridge at Quebec* (Bloomington: Indiana University Press, 2001), 171.
23. Gilbert, *Documents*, 43; Andre Charbonneau, Yvon Desloges, and Marc Lafrance, *Quebec, the Fortified City: From the 17th to the 19th Century* (Ottawa: Parks Canada, 1982), 195.
24. Winston Churchill, "World's Greatest Grain Emporium," 8.
25. John Churchill, 80-81.
26. *Montreal Gazette*, August 12, 1929; *Quebec Chronicle-Telegraph*, August 12, 1929.
27. Gilbert, *Documents*, 44.
28. *Montreal Gazette*, August 12, 1929; Gilbert, *Documents*, 45.
29. Gilbert, *Documents*, 43.
30. R.H. Hubbard, *Ample Mansions: The Viceregal Residences of the Canadian Provinces* (Ottawa: University of Ottawa Press, 1989), 38-40.
31. Gilbert, *Documents*, 43; *Montreal Gazette*, August 13, 1929; *New York Times*, April 12, 1938.
32. *Quebec Chronicle-Telegraph*, August 12, 1929; Gilbert, *Documents*, 44.
33. Gilbert, *Documents*, 44.
34. Randolph Churchill, *Twenty-One Years*, 75.
35. *Montreal Daily Star*, August 13, 1929.
36. *Toronto Globe and Mail*, August 17, 1929.
37. *Quebec Chronicle-Telegraph*, August 12, 1929.
38. Randolph Churchill, *Twenty-One Years*, 75.
39. CPR Archives JAS 961210.
40. Walter Graebner, *My Dear Churchill* (Cambridge, MA: Houghton Mifflin, 1965) 48.

## Chapter 5

1. Gilbert, *Documents*, 46; Randolph Churchill, *Twenty-One Years*, 75.
2. Gilbert, *Documents*, 46.
3. Phyllis Moir, *I Was Winston Churchill's Private Secretary* (New York: Wilfred Funk, 1941), 74.

4. Graebner, 64.
5. Gilbert, *Documents*, 46.
6. Moir, 40.
7. Charles Eade, ed., *Churchill by His Contemporaries* (London: Reprint Society, 1955), 156.
8. Elizabeth Nel, *Mr. Churchill's Secretary* (New York: Coward-McCann, 1958), 33.
9. Gilbert, *Documents*, 46.
10. Ibid.
11. *Toronto Daily Star*, August 13, 1929.
12. *Montreal Gazette*, August 13, 1929.
13. Chisholm, 155-160.
14. David T. Leary, "Winston S. Churchill in California," *California History* (Winter 2001/2002): 163.
15. Randolph Churchill, *Twenty-One Years*, 75; Gilbert, *Documents*, 45.
16. Martin Gilbert, Daun Van Ee, and Allen Packwood, *Churchill and the Great Republic* (Washington: Library of Congress, 2004), 10.
17. H.C. Allen, *Great Britain and the United States: A History of Anglo-American Relations, 1783-1952* (London: Oldhams, 1954), 757-758.
18. Carlton, 53; Bruce Kent, *The Spoils of War: The Politics, Economics, and Diplomacy of Reparations 1918-1932* (Oxford: Clarendon Press, 1989), 307.
19. *Montreal Daily Star*, August 14, 1929.
20. *Montreal Herald*, August 13, 1929; *Montreal Gazette*, August 14, 1929.
21. *Montreal Daily Star*, August 13, 1929.
22. Ibid.
23. *Montreal Gazette*, August 14, 1929.
24. *Montreal Herald*, August 13, 1929; *Montreal Gazette*, August 14, 1929; *Montreal Herald*, August 14, 1929; *Montreal Daily Star*, August 14, 1929; *Montreal Daily Star*, August 13, 1929.
25. Robert Rhodes James, ed., *Winston S. Churchill: His Complete Speeches* (New York: Chelsea House Publishers, 1974), 4674.
26. Eade, 231.
27. Gilbert, *Documents*, 51.
28. *Ottawa Evening Citizen*, August 13, 1929.
29. *Ottawa Evening Citizen*, August 14, 1929.
30. Randolph Churchill, *Winston S. Churchill, Volume I: Youth, 1874-1900* (Boston: Houghton Mifflin, 1966), 527.
31. *Ottawa Journal*, August 14, 1929.
32. *Ottawa Evening Citizen*, August 14, 1929.
33. D.A. Low, "Thomas, Freeman Freeman-, First Marquess of Willingdon (1866-1941)," *Oxford Dictionary of National Biography* (Oxford University Press, 2004); online edition.
34. R.H. Hubbard, *Rideau Hall: An Illustrated History of Government House, Ottawa, from Victorian Times to the Present Day* (Montreal: McGill-Queens University Press, 1977), 161-163.
35. *William Lyon Mackenzie King Diaries*, online edition.
36. Ibid.
37. Randolph Churchill, *Twenty-One Years*, 76.
38. *Montreal Daily Star*, August 14, 1929; *Montreal Gazette*, August 14, 1929.

39. *Ottawa Evening Journal*, August 14, 1926; *Ottawa Evening Journal*, August 15, 1926.
40. R. MacGregor Dawson, *William Lyon Mackenzie King: A Political Biography, 1874–1923* (Toronto: University of Toronto Press, 1958), 418–419; H. Blair Neatby, *William Lyon Mackenzie King, 1924–1932: The Lonely Heights* (Toronto: University of Toronto Press, 1963), 272.
41. Dawson, 201–202.
42. Dilks, 36–37.
43. Ibid., 37.
44. Edwina von Baeyer, *Garden of Dreams: Kingsmere and Mackenzie King* (Toronto: Dundurn, 1990), 11; Neatby, 201.
45. Von Bayer, 112.
46. Ibid., 13.
47. Kemper, 195; Robin Fedden, *Churchill at Chartwell* (London: Pergamon Press, 1969), 7.
48. Randolph Churchill, *Twenty-One Years*, 76.
49. Lita-Rose Betcherman, *Ernest Lapointe: Mackenzie King's Great Quebec Lieutenant* (Toronto: University of Toronto Press, 2002), 74.
50. John Swettenham, *McNaughton, Volume I: 1887–1939* (Toronto: Ryerson Press, 1968), 55.
51. *William Lyon Mackenzie King Diaries*, online edition.
52. Gilbert, *Documents*, 50; Von Bayer, 138.
53. *William Lyon Mackenzie King Diaries*, online edition.
54. Gilbert, *Documents*, 50.
55. *William Lyon Mackenzie King Diaries*, online edition.
56. Randolph Churchill, *Twenty-One Years*, 76, 81.
57. Ibid., 76.
58. Gilbert, *Documents*, 50.
59. *Ottawa Evening Citizen*, August 10, 1929; *Ottawa Evening Citizen*, August 16, 1929; *Ottawa Journal*, August 16, 1929.
60. Allen, 728.
61. Stephen Roskill, *Naval Policy Between the Wars, Volume I: The Period of Anglo-American Antagonism, 1919–1929* (New York: Walker, 1968), 20; Carlton, 101–105; Allen, 746; John W. Wheeler-Bennett, *Disarmament and Security Since Locarno, 1925–1931* (New York: Howard Fertig, 1973), 136.
62. *Ottawa Evening Citizen*, August 16, 1929.
63. *Montreal Gazette*, August 16, 1929; *Ottawa Evening Citizen*, August 16, 1929.
64. *Ottawa Evening Citizen*, August 16, 1929; *Ottawa Journal*, August 16, 1929.
65. *The London Times*, July 22, 1929.
66. *William Lyon Mackenzie King Diaries*, online edition.
67. *Parliament Buildings: Les Edifices du Parlement* (Ottawa: House of Commons, 1980), 1–2.
68. Ibid., 12.
69. *William Lyon Mackenzie King Diaries*, online edition.
70. *Parliament Buildings*, 38; *Ottawa Evening Citizen*, August 16, 1929.
71. Gilbert, *Documents*, 50.
72. Ibid., 49; John Churchill, 81–82.
73. *William Lyon Mackenzie King Diaries*, online edition.
74. Gilbert, *Documents*, 49–50.
75. Dilks, 33.
76. *Ottawa Evening Citizen*, August 16, 1929.
77. John Churchill, 81; Randolph Churchill, *Twenty-One Years*, 77.
78. *Ottawa Evening Citizen*, August 16, 1929.
79. *William Lyon Mackenzie King Diaries*, online edition.

## Chapter 6

1. *Toronto Daily Star*, August 16, 1929; *Toronto Telegram*, August 16, 1929; Randolph Churchill, *Twenty-One Years*, 77.
2. *Toronto Globe and Mail*, 1.
3. *Toronto Daily Star*, August 16, 1929; *Toronto Telegram*, August 16, 1929.
4. *Toronto Telegram*, August 16, 1929; Randolph Churchill, *Twenty-One Years*, 77.
5. Hubbard, *Ample Mansions*, 123–124.
6. Gilbert, *Documents*, 50.
7. Chisholm, 187–190.
8. *Toronto Globe and Mail*, August 17, 1929; *Toronto Telegram*, August 16, 1929; CHAR 1/207.
9. Ian Hamill, *The Strategic Illusion: The Singapore Strategy and the Defense of Australia and New Zealand, 1919–1942* (Singapore: Singapore University Press, 1981), 217.
10. *Toronto Telegram*, August 16, 1929.
11. Michael Bliss, *A Canadian Millionaire: The Life and Business Times of Sir Joseph Flavelle, Bart., 1858–1939* (Toronto: Macmillan, 1978), 289.
12. *Toronto Telegram*, August 16, 1929; *Toronto Telegram*, August 17, 1929; *Toronto Globe and Mail*, August 17, 1929; James, *Winston S. Churchill: His Complete Speeches*, 4670–4671.
13. *Toronto Telegram*, August 17, 1929; *Toronto Globe and Mail*, August 17, 1929; Dilks, 76; *Saturday Night*, August 24, 1929.
14. Gilbert, *Documents*, 51.
15. *Toronto Telegram*, August 17, 1929.
16. *Toronto Globe and Mail*, August 17, 1929; *Hamilton Spectator*, August 17, 1929.
17. *Niagara Falls Evening Review*, August 17, 1929; *Niagara Falls Gazette*, August 17, 1929; *Toronto Telegram*, August 19, 1929; *Hamilton Spectator*, August 17, 1929.
18. Dilks, 78; *Kenora Miner and News*, August 21, 1929.
19. Sir Winston Churchill Papers, CHAR 1/207.
20. *New York Times*, March 26, 1916.
21. *Niagara Falls Evening Review*, August 17, 1929; *Niagara Falls Gazette*, August 17, 1929; *Toronto Telegram*, August 19, 1929.
22. *New York Times*, August 18, 1929; *Niagara Falls Gazette*, August 17, 1929.
23. *Niagara Falls Gazette*, August 17, 1929.
24. *Hamilton Herald*, August 17, 1929.

25. Winston Churchill, "World's Greatest Grain Emporium," 8.
26. *Toronto Telegram*, August 17, 1929.
27. Eade, 240-248.
28. Gilbert, Martin, "Churchill and Canada," *Proceedings of the International Churchill Societies 1988-89*.
29. Brian Roberts, *Randolph: A Study of Churchill's Son* (London: Hamish Hamilton, 1984), 52; *Toronto Daily Star*, August 19, 1929.

## Chapter 7

1. Winston Churchill, "World's Greatest Grain Emporium," 8.
2. Ibid.
3. Ibid.
4. Ibid.; *New York Times*, October 22, 1933.
5. Winston Churchill, "World's Greatest Grain Emporium," 8.
6. *Port Arthur News-Chronicle*, August 19, 1929; *Fort William Daily Times-Journal*, August 19, 1929.
7. Winston Churchill, "World's Greatest Grain Emporium," 8.
8. *The Canada Year Book 1930* (Ottawa: F.A. Acland, 1930), xxvii.
9. *Fort William Daily Times-Journal*, August 19, 1929.
10. Graebner, 29; Kemper, 112.
11. Winston Churchill, "World's Greatest Grain Emporium," 8.
12. Sir Winston Churchill Papers, CHAR 1/207.
13. *Winnipeg Evening Tribune*, August 19, 1929.
14. Winston Churchill, "World's Greatest Grain Emporium," 8.
15. *Winnipeg Evening Tribune*, August 19, 1929.
16. Winston Churchill, "World's Greatest Grain Emporium," 8.
17. *Manitoba Free Press*, August 20, 1929.
18. *Winnipeg Evening Tribune*, August 19, 1929.
19. Sir Winston Churchill Papers, CHAR 1/207.
20. *Winnipeg Evening Tribune*, August 21, 1929; Shirley Render, *Double Cross: The Inside Story of James A. Richardson and Canadian Airways* (Toronto: Douglas & McIntyre, 1999), 4-5.
21. Allan Levine, *The Exchange: 100 Years of Trading Grain in Winnipeg* (Winnipeg: Peguis Publishers, 1987), 3-4.
22. Ibid., 114.
23. Sir Winston Churchill Papers, CHAR 1/207.
24. Randolph Churchill, *Twenty-One Years*, 83.
25. *Winnipeg Evening Tribune*, August 21, 1929.
26. Sir Winston Churchill Papers, CHAR 1/207 *Manitoba Free Press*, August 20, 1929; *Manitoba Free Press*, August 21, 1929; Reinhold Kromer and Tom Mitchell, *When the State Trembled: How A.J. Andrews and the Citizens' Committee Broke the Winnipeg General Strike* (Toronto: University of Toronto Press, 2010), 7.
27. *Kenora Miner and News*, August 21, 1929.
28. Sir Winston Churchill Papers, CHAR 1/207.
29. Sir Winston Churchill Papers, CHAR 1/207 *Manitoba Free Press*, August 21, 1929.
30. *Manitoba Free Press*, August 21, 1929.
31. Sir Winston Churchill Papers, CHAR 1/211.
32. Sir Winston Churchill Papers, CHAR 1/207.
33. Ibid.
34. *Manitoba Free Press*, August 21, 1929; *Winnipeg Evening Tribune*, August 20, 1929; *Manitoba Free Press*, August 22, 1929.
35. *Manitoba Free Press*, August 21, 1929; *Manitoba Free Press*, August 22, 1929; *Winnipeg Evening Tribune*, August 21, 1929.
36. John Kendle, *John Bracken: A Political Biography* (Toronto: University of Toronto Press, 1979); Sir Winston Churchill Papers, CHAR 1/211.
37. *Manitoba Free Press*, August 21, 1929; *Winnipeg Evening Tribune*, August 21, 1929.
38. *Manitoba Free Press*, August 22, 1929.
39. Ibid.
40. *Winnipeg Evening Tribune*, August 21, 1929.
41. Ibid.
42. Ibid.
43. *Manitoba Free Press*, August 21, 1929.
44. *Winnipeg Evening Tribune*, August 21, 1929.
45. Ibid.; *Manitoba Free Press*, August 21, 1929; *Manitoba Free Press*, August 22, 1929;
46. *Winnipeg Evening Tribune*, August 21, 1929.
47. *Ottawa Journal*, August 20, 1929.
48. *Ottawa Journal*, August 23, 1929; *Calgary Daily Herald*, August 23, 1929.
49. Winston Churchill, "World's Greatest Grain Emporium," 8.

## Chapter 8

1. Winston Churchill, "Across Canada to the Pacific," *Daily Telegraph*, January 13, 1930, 8.
2. *Regina Morning Leader*, August 22, 1929.
3. Sir Winston Churchill Papers, CHAR 1/207.
4. *Regina Morning Leader*, August 22, 1929.
5. *Regina Morning Leader*, August 21, 1929.
6. *Saskatoon Star-Phoenix*, August 21, 1929; *Regina Morning Leader*, August 22, 1929.
7. Garth Pugh,, ed., *"A Tower of Attraction": An Illustrated History of Government House, Regina, Saskatchewan* (Regina: Government House Historical Society, 1991), 56.
8. Ibid., 86; Shirley Render, *No Place for a Lady: The Story of Canadian Women Pilots, 1928-1992* (Winnipeg: Portage & Main Press, 1992), 361.
9. Chisholm, 219-220.
10. *Regina Morning Leader*, August 21, 1929; *Regina Morning Leader*, August 22, 1929.
11. *Regina Morning Leader*, August 22, 1929.
12. Ibid.; *Saskatoon Star-Phoenix*, August 22, 1929.
13. Sir Winston Churchill Papers, CHAR 1/207.
14. *Regina Morning Leader*, August 22, 1929; *Regina Morning Leader*, August 23, 1929; CHAR 1/207.
15. *Regina Morning Leader*, August 22, 1929.
16. Pugh, 88; Norman Ward and David Smith, *Jimmy Gardiner: Relentless Liberal* (Toronto: University of Toronto Press, 1990), 104-105.
17. Sir Winston Churchill Papers, CHAR 1/207.

18. Gordon Barnhart, ed., *Saskatchewan Premiers of the Twentieth Century* (Regina: Canadian Plains Research Center, 2004), 100.
19. *Regina Morning Leader*, August 23, 1929.
20. *Saskatoon Star-Phoenix*, August 22, 1929.
21. *New York Times*, March 24, 1945.
22. Winston Churchill, "Across Canada to the Pacific," 8.
23. *Saskatoon Star-Phoenix*, August 23, 1929.
24. Winston Churchill, "Across Canada to the Pacific," 8; Sir Winston Churchill Papers, CHAR 1/207.
25. Ibid.
26. Sir Winston Churchill Papers, CHAR 1/207.
27. *Saskatoon Star-Phoenix*, August 23, 1929; Sir Winston Churchill Papers, CHAR 1/207.
28. *Saskatoon Star-Phoenix*, August 23, 1929.
29. Winston Churchill, "Across Canada to the Pacific," 8.
30. Sir Winston Churchill Papers, CHAR 1/207.
31. Ibid.
32. *Edmonton Journal*, August 23, 1929.
33. Ibid.
34. Sir Winston Churchill Papers, CHAR 1/207.

## Chapter 9

1. *Edmonton Journal*, August 23, 1929.
2. Ibid.
3. Hubbard, *Ample Mansions*, 193.
4. Sir Winston Churchill Papers, CHAR 1/207.
5. *The Times*, December 21, 1973.
6. *Edmonton Journal*, August 23, 1929.
7. *Edmonton Journal*, August 22, 1929.
8. Chisholm, 242.
9. *Edmonton Bulletin*, August 24, 1929.
10. *Edmonton Bulletin*, August 23, 1929.
11. Ibid.; *Edmonton Bulletin*, August 24, 1929; *Edmonton Journal*, August 23, 1929; *Edmonton Journal*, August 24, 1929.
12. Sir Winston Churchill Papers, CHAR 1/207.
13. *Peterborough Examiner*, August 31, 2007.
14. Sir Winston Churchill Papers, CHAR 1/207.
15. Winston Churchill, "Across Canada to the Pacific," 8.
16. Sir Winston Churchill Papers, CHAR 1/207.
17. Winston Churchill, "Across Canada to the Pacific," 8.
18. *Edmonton Bulletin*, August 24, 1929.
19. David J. Hall, "Brett, Robert George," *Dictionary of Canadian Biography*.
20. Paul Stanway, *Alberta in the 20th Century: A Journalistic History of the Province* (Edmonton: CanMedia Inc., 2005), 166–167.
21. Sir Winston Churchill Papers, CHAR 1/207.
22. *Edmonton Journal*, August 24, 1929.
23. Winston Churchill, "Across Canada to the Pacific," 8.
24. *Edmonton Journal*, August 24, 1929.
25. Winston Churchill, "Across Canada to the Pacific," 8.
26. Sir Winston Churchill Papers, CHAR 1/207.
27. *Edmonton Journal*, August 24, 1929; *Calgary Daily Herald*, August 24, 1929.
28. *Calgary Daily Herald*, August 24, 1929; Chris Wrigley, *Winston Churchill: A Biographical Companion* (Santa Barbara: ABC-Clio, 2002), 130–131.
29. *Calgary Daily Herald*, August 24, 1929; Canadian Club papers, Glenbow Museum.
30. *Calgary Daily Herald*, August 24, 1929.
31. *Calgary Daily Herald*, August 26, 1929.
32. Susan Warrender, *Alberta Titans: From Rags to Riches During Alberta's Pioneer Days* (Canmore, Alberta: Altitude Publishing, 2003), 37–40.
33. Frank Dabbs, *Branded by the Wind: The Life and Times of Bill Herron* (Calgary: Herron, 2001), 108–109; David A. Finch, *Hell's Half Acre: Early Days in the Great Alberta Oil Patch* (Surrey, B.C.: Heritage House, 2005), 25–30; *Calgary Daily Herald*, August 26, 1929.
34. Winston Churchill, "Across Canada to the Pacific," 8; Sir Winston Churchill Papers, CHAR 1/207.
35. CHAR 1/207 *Calgary Daily Herald*, August 26, 1929; Earle Gray, *The Great Canadian Oil Patch: The Petroleum Era from Birth to Peak* (Edmonton: JuneWarren Publishing, 2004), 83; Stanway, 138–139.
36. *Calgary Daily Herald*, August 26, 1929; Sir Winston Churchill Papers, CHAR 1/207.
37. Sir Winston Churchill Papers, CHAR 1/207 Finch, 98, 102; Winston Churchill, "Across Canada to the Pacific," 8.
38. Sir Winston Churchill Papers, CHAR 1/207 Finch, 98, 102; Winston Churchill, "Across Canada to the Pacific," 8; Gilbert, *Documents*, 57.
39. Winston Churchill, "Across Canada to the Pacific," 8; Finch, 101.
40. *High River Times*, August 29, 1929.
41. John Churchill, 82.
42. *Calgary Daily Herald*, August 26, 1929; Sir Winston Churchill Papers, CHAR 1/207 *Saturday Night*, September 7, 1929.
43. Sir Winston Churchill Papers, CHAR 1/207 Simon M. Evans, *Prince Charming Goes West: The Story of the E.P. Ranch* (Calgary: University of Calgary Press, 1993), 23–26, 71.
44. Gilbert, *Documents*, 57; Sir Winston Churchill Papers, CHAR 1/211 Evans, 87.
45. Gilbert, *Documents*, 57; Sir Winston Churchill Papers, CHAR 1/207.
46. Dabbs, 108–109.
47. Sir Winston Churchill Papers, CHAR 1/207.
48. Sir Winston Churchill Papers, CHAR 1/211.
49. John Churchill, 82.
50. Randolph Churchill, *Twenty-One Years*, 77.
51. Ibid, 80.
52. Sir Winston Churchill Papers, CHAR 1/207.
53. Langworth, 157.
54. Sir Winston Churchill Papers, CHAR 1/207.
55. Canadian Club papers, Glenbow Museum.
56. Chisholm, 233–234.
57. *Calgary Daily Herald*, August 24, 1929; *Calgary Daily Herald*, August 26, 1929.
58. Canadian Club papers, Glenbow Museum.

59. *Calgary Daily Herald*, August 26, 1929
60. Edward M. Bredin, "Leonard M. Brockington: Calgary's Silver-tongued Orator," *Alberta History* 56, no. 1 (Winter 2008): 23+.
61. *Calgary Daily Herald*, August 27, 1929.
62. *Calgary Daily Herald*, August 26, 1929
63. Gilbert, *Documents*, 62.
64. *Calgary Daily Herald*, August 26, 1929; *Calgary Daily Herald*, August 27, 1929; Gilbert, *Documents*, 62.
65. Canadian Club papers, Glenbow Museum.
66. Winston Churchill, "Across Canada to the Pacific," 8.

## Chapter 10

1. Sir Winston Churchill Papers, CHAR 1/207.
2. Winston Churchill, "Across Canada to the Pacific," 8.
3. Christine Barnes, *Great Lodges of the Canadian Rockies* (Bend, Oregon: W.W. West, 1999), 22.
4. Sir Winston Churchill Papers, CHAR 1/207.
5. Gilbert, *Documents*, 61–62.
6. Ibid., 61.
7. Ibid.
8. Ibid.
9. Ibid.
10. Ibid., 62.
11. Sir Winston Churchill Papers, CHAR 1/207.
12. Winston Churchill, *Painting as a Pastime* (New York: Whittelsey House, 1950), 16.
13. David Coombs, *Churchill, His Paintings: A Catalog* (New York: World Publishing, 1967), 12.
14. Kemper, 222–232.
15. Ibid., 222–232; Mary Soames, *Winston Churchill: His Life as a Painter* (London: Collins, 1990), 14.
16. Winston Churchill, *Painting as a Pastime*, 29.
17. Ibid., 31–32.
18. Derek Lukin Johnston, "Paintings: Banff's Bunkers," *Finest Hour* 59 (Summer 1988): 18.
19. Sir Winston Churchill Papers, CHAR 1/207.
20. M.B. Williams, *Kootenay National Park and the Banff Windermere Highway* (Ottawa: F.A. Acland, 1929), 33.
21. John Churchill, 82.
22. Dale Zieroth, *Nipika: A Story of Radium Hot Springs* (Hull, Quebec: Minister of Supply and Services Canada, 1978), 27.
23. Sir Winston Churchill Papers, CHAR 1/207.
24. Ibid.
25. Williams, 37.
26. Sir Winston Churchill Papers, CHAR 1/207.
27. John Churchill, 83.
28. Sir Winston Churchill Papers, CHAR 1/207.
29. Sir Winston Churchill Papers, CHAR 1/211.
30. Ibid.
31. Sir Winston Churchill Papers, CHAR 1/207.
32. Randolph Churchill, *Twenty-One Years*, 77; Sir Winston Churchill Papers, CHAR 1/207.
33. Sir Winston Churchill Papers, CHAR 1/207.
34. Randolph Churchill, *Twenty-One Years*, 77; Sir Winston Churchill Papers, CHAR 1/207.
35. Coombs, *Churchill His Paintings: A Catalog*, 12.
36. Ibid., 13.
37. David Coombs and Minnie S. Churchill, *Sir Winston Churchill, His Life and His Paintings* (Philadelphia: Running Press, 2004), 219.
38. Graebner, 83.
39. Sir Winston Churchill Papers, CHAR 1/207.
40. Ibid.
41. Ibid.
42. Christine Barnes, 44.
43. H. Armstrong Roberts, *Resorts in the Canadian Pacific Rockies* (np, Canadian Pacific Railway, 1924), 7.
44. Winston Churchill, "Across Canada to the Pacific," 8.
45. Chisholm, 48.
46. Gilbert, *Documents*, 64.
47. Sir Winston Churchill Papers, CHAR 1/211.
48. John Churchill, 83.
49. Ibid., 83
50. Sir Winston Churchill Papers, CHAR 1/207.
51. Winston Churchill, *Painting as a Pastime*, 31.
52. Randolph Churchill, *Twenty-One Years*, 78.
53. Sir Winston Churchill Papers, CHAR 1/207.
54. Roger Patillo, *Lake Louise at Its Best: An Affectionate Look at Life at Lake Louise by One Who Knew It Well* (Aldergrove, B.C.: Amberlea Press, 2000), 150.
55. Sir Winston Churchill Papers, CHAR 1/207.
56. Randolph Churchill, *Twenty-One Years*, 78; Sir Winston Churchill Papers, CHAR 1/207.
57. Randolph Churchill, *Twenty-One Years*, 78.
58. Sir Winston Churchill Papers, CHAR 1/207.
59. Winston Churchill, "Across Canada to the Pacific," 8.
60. Sir Winston Churchill Papers, CHAR 1/207.

## Chapter 11

1. Sir Winston Churchill Papers, CHAR 1/207 Winston Churchill, "Across Canada to the Pacific," 8.
2. *New York Times*, August 31, 1929.
3. *Canadian Pacific Bulletin*, October 5, 1943.
4. Gilbert, *Documents*, 78.
5. Randolph Churchill, *Twenty-One Years*, 82.
6. *Vancouver Sunday Province*, September 1, 1929; *Vancouver Province*, September 3, 1929; *Vancouver Sun*, September 3, 1929.
7. *Vancouver Province*, September 2, 1929; *Vancouver Province*, September 3, 1929; *British Columbian*, September 3, 1929; *British Columbian*, August 31, 1929.
8. *Vancouver Province*, September 2, 1929; *Vancouver Sun*, September 5, 1929; *British Columbian*, September 3, 1929.
9. *British Columbian*, September 3, 1929; Randolph Churchill, *Twenty-One Years*, 78.
10. *Vancouver Province*, September 2, 1929.
11. Randolph Churchill, *Twenty-One Years*, 78.
12. *Vancouver Sun*, September 3, 1929; *Vancouver Province*, September 3, 1929; *British Columbian*, September 3, 1929.
13. *British Columbian*, September 3, 1929; Vancou-

ver Province, September 3, 1929; *Vancouver Province,* September 2, 1929; Randolph Churchill, *Twenty-One Years,* 78.
14. *British Columbian,* September 3, 1929.
15. Randolph Churchill, *Twenty-One Years,* 79.
16. Sir Winston Churchill Papers, CHAR 1/207 Sir Winston Churchill Papers, CHAR 1/211.
17. Gilbert, *Documents,* 70; Vancouver City Archives.
18. Vancouver City Archives.
19. Gilbert, *Documents,* 78.
20. *Vancouver Sun,* September 3, 1929.
21. Gilbert, *Documents,* 77–78; Randolph Churchill, *Twenty-One Years,* 79; Vancouver City Archives.
22. *Vancouver Province,* September 3, 1929.
23. Ibid.; James, *Winston S. Churchill: His Complete Speeches,* 4672–4673.
24. *Vancouver Province,* September 3, 1929.
25. Ibid.; *Vancouver Sun,* September 4, 1929.
26. *Vancouver Province,* September 3, 1929.
27. Sir Winston Churchill Papers, CHAR 1/207.
28. *Vancouver Sun,* September 3, 1929; *Vancouver Province,* September 1, 1929; *Vancouver Province,* September 2, 1929; *Vancouver Province,* September 3, 1929; *Vancouver Sun,* September 5, 1929.
29. Gilbert, *Documents,* 79.
30. Ibid., 79; Sir Winston Churchill Papers, CHAR 1/207.
31. *Victoria Daily Times,* September 5, 1929.
32. Ibid.; *Victoria Daily Colonist,* September 5, 1929.
33. *Victoria Daily Colonist,* September 4, 1929; *Victoria Daily Colonist,* September 5, 1929; *Victoria Daily Colonist,* September 6, 1929.
34. Terry, Reksten, *The Dunsmuir Saga* (Vancouver: Douglas & McIntyre, 1991), 211–212; *The Times,* November 20, 1940; *The Times,* April 29, 1950.
35. *Victoria Daily Times,* September 5, 1929.
36. Sir Winston Churchill Papers, CHAR 1/207.
37. *Victoria Daily Colonist,* September 6, 1929; Gilbert, *Documents,* 79; *Victoria Daily Times,* September 5, 1929.
38. Randolph Churchill, *Twenty-One Years,* 79–80; *Victoria Daily Colonist,* September 6, 1929.
39. Randolph Churchill, *Twenty-One Years,* 80; Gilbert, *Documents,* 79.
40. Gilbert, *Documents,* 79; Randolph Churchill, *Twenty-One Years,* 80.
41. Randolph Churchill, *Twenty-One Years,* 80.
42. *Victoria Daily Colonist,* September 6, 1929; Reksten, 251–252.
43. Roderick L. Haig-Brown, *A River Never Sleeps* (New York: William Morrow, 1946), 156; Trey Combs, *Steelhead: Fly Fishing* (Guilford, CT: Lyons Press, 1999), 211–212.
44. *Victoria Times Colonist,* January 23, 2005; *Victoria Daily Colonist,* September 7, 1929.
45. *Victoria Daily Colonist,* September 7, 1929.
46. Gilbert, *Documents,* 77; Winston Churchill, "Across Canada to the Pacific," 8.
47. Randolph Churchill, *Twenty-One Years,* 81–82.

## Chapter 12

1. *Seattle Daily Times,* September 7, 1929.
2. Gilbert, *Churchill and the Great Republic,* 7.
3. Randolph Churchill, *Winston S. Churchill: Youth, 1874–1900,* 258.
4. John Chettle, "Winston Churchill in America," *Smithsonian* (April 2011): 80.
5. Michael A. Lerner, *Dry Manhattan: Prohibition in New York City* (Cambridge, MA.: Harvard University Press, 2007), 1–2.
6. Randolph Churchill, *Twenty-One Years,* 82.
7. John Churchill, 83.
8. Randolph Churchill, *Twenty-One Years,* 83.
9. John Churchill, 84.
10. Ibid., 86; Randolph Churchill, *Twenty-One Years,* 83.
11. Randolph Churchill, *Twenty-One Years,* 83.
12. *Victoria Daily Times,* September 7, 1929.
13. *Seattle Daily Times,* September 7, 1929.
14. *Victoria Daily Colonist,* September 7, 1929.
15. Randolph Churchill, *Twenty-One Years,* 83; Gilbert, *Documents,* 82.
16. Randolph Churchill, *Twenty-One Years,* 83.
17. Ibid., 83.
18. Ibid., 80; Gilbert, *Documents,* 82.
19. Winston Churchill, "Peter Pan Township of Films," *Daily Telegraph,* December 30, 1929, 8.
20. Winston Churchill, "What I Saw in America of Prohibition," *Daily Telegraph,* December 2, 1929, 10.
21. Ibid., 10.
22. Winston Churchill, "The Shattered Cause of Temperance," *Collier's* (August 13, 1932): 20–21, 48–49.
23. *Rogue River Courier and Oregon Observer,* September 13, 1929.
24. Gerald Campbell, *Of True Experience* (New York: Dodd, Mead, 1947), 59; *Humboldt Standard,* September 6, 1929.
25. *Rogue River Courier and Oregon Observer,* September 13, 1929.
26. Ibid.
27. Gilbert, *Documents,* 73, 82.
28. Campbell, 159–160.
29. Gilbert, *Documents,* 82.
30. Winston Churchill, "Nature's Panorama in California," *Daily Telegraph,* December 23, 1929, 8.
31. Ibid.
32. Randolph Churchill, *Twenty-One Years,* 84.
33. Campbell, 59.
34. Winston Churchill, "Peter Pan Township of Films," 8.
35. *Humboldt Standard,* September 9, 1929; *Humboldt Standard,* September 4, 1929; *Humboldt Standard,* September 10, 1929.
36. John Smythe, *The Victoria Cross, 1856–1964* (London: Frederick Muller, 1965), 150; *The Times,* August 22, 1919.
37. *Humboldt Standard,* September 4, 1929.
38. Gilbert, *Documents,* 73.
39. John Churchill, 87.

40. Winston Churchill, "Nature's Panorama in California," 8.
41. Randolph Churchill, *Twenty-One Years*, 84.
42. Gilbert, *Documents*, 82; *Humboldt Standard*, September 4, 1929; *Humboldt Standard*, September 9, 1929; Randolph Churchill, *Twenty-One Years*, 84.
43. Winston Churchill, "Nature's Panorama in California," 8.
44. Ibid., 8.
45. *Humboldt Standard*, September 9, 1929.
46. Winston Churchill, "Peter Pan Township of Films," 8.
47. Winston Churchill, "Nature's Panorama in California," 8.
48. Sir Winston Churchill Papers, CHAR 1/207.
49. *San Francisco Examiner*, September 10, 1929; Randolph Churchill, *Twenty-One Years*, 84–85.
50. Randolph Churchill, *Twenty-One Years*, 85.
51. Winston Churchill, "Peter Pan Township of Films," 8.
52. Ibid.
53. Winston Churchill, "Land of Corn and Lobsters," *Collier's* (August 5, 1933): 16–17, 45.
54. Ibid.: 259–260.
55. *Los Angeles Times*, November 10, 1929.

## *Chapter 13*

1. Winston Churchill, "Peter Pan Township of Films," 8.
2. *New York Times*, February 5, 1929; *San Francisco Bay Toll-Bridge, the Longest Bridge in the World: Souvenir Program, March 2, 1929*, 5.
3. Sir Winston Churchill Papers, CHAR 1/207.
4. *Rand McNally Guide to San Francisco, Oakland, Berkeley, and Environs of the Bay Cities* (New York: Rand McNally, 1927), 183.
5. David Warren Ryder, *"Great Citizen": A Biography of William H. Crocker* (San Francisco: Historical Publications, 1962), 151, 155; *New York Times*, July 23, 1934; *Los Angeles Times*, July 25, 1934.
6. Porter Garnett, *Stately Homes of California* (Boston: Little, Brown, 1915), 6–11.
7. Sir Winston Churchill Papers, CHAR 1/207.
8. *San Francisco Examiner*, September 10, 1929; *San Francisco Chronicle*, September 10, 1929; *New York Times*, February 18, 1938.
9. Gilbert, *Documents*, 98.
10. Winston Churchill, "Industrial Conditions in America," *Daily Telegraph*, February 3, 1930, 8.
11. Winston Churchill, "Land of Corn and Lobsters," 16–17, 45.
12. Randolph Churchill, *Twenty-One Years*, 85.
13. John Churchill, 95.
14. Randolph Churchill, *Twenty-One Years*, 85; Sir Winston Churchill Papers, CHAR 1/207.
15. Gilbert, *Documents*, 75–77; Sir Winston Churchill Papers, CHAR 1/207.
16. Gilbert, *Documents*, 86; Cohen, 1357; Winston Churchill, "The Palestine Crisis," *Sunday Times*, September 22, 1929, 16.
17. Gilbert, *Documents*, 65.
18. Sir Winston Churchill Papers, CHAR 1/207 *New York Times*, December 13, 1900.
19. *San Francisco Chronicle*, September 11, 1929.
20. *Rand McNally Guide to San Francisco*, 99; *San Francisco Examiner*, September 11, 1929; *San Francisco Chronicle*, September 11, 1929.
21. Randolph Churchill, *Twenty-One Years*, 85–86; Leslie, *Randolph: The Biography of Winston's Churchill's Son*, 17–18.
22. *San Francisco Examiner*, September 10, 1929.
23. Winston Churchill, "Peter Pan Township of Films," 8.
24. Ibid.; *Rand McNally Guide to San Francisco*, 13; Sir Winston Churchill Papers, CHAR 1/207 Leary, 167.
25. Winston Churchill, "Nature's Panorama in California," 8; Gilbert, *Documents*, 85.
26. Sir Winston Churchill Papers, CHAR 1/207.
27. *Rand McNally Guide to San Francisco*, 96.
28. *San Francisco Examiner*, September 12, 1929; Sir Winston Churchill Papers, CHAR 1/207.
29. Campbell, 160.
30. John Churchill, 86; Bill Alder, *The Churchill Wit* (New York: Coward-McCann, 1965), 49.
31. *San Francisco Examiner*, September 10, 1929.
32. *San Francisco Chronicle*, September 10, 1929.
33. *San Francisco Examiner*, September 12, 1929.
34. Donald E. Osterbrock, John R. Gustafson, and W.J. Shiloh Unruh, *Eye on the Sky: Lick Observatory's First Century* (Berkeley: University of California Press, 1988), 13; *Rand McNally Guide to San Francisco*, 181.
35. Sir Winston Churchill Papers, CHAR 1/207 *San Jose Mercury Herald*, September 12, 1929; *Los Angeles Times*, June 15, 1938; Osterbrock, 131.
36. Ryder, 170.
37. Winston Churchill, "Nature's Panorama in California," 8; Sir Winston Churchill Papers, CHAR 1/207.
38. Sir Winston Churchill Papers, CHAR 1/207 Winston Churchill, "Nature's Panorama in California," 8; *San Jose Mercury Herald*, September 12, 1929; Osterbrock, 198.
39. Sir Winston Churchill Papers, CHAR 1/207.
40. Winston Churchill, "Nature's Panorama in California," 8; Sir Winston Churchill Papers, CHAR 1/207 *San Jose Mercury Herald*, September 12, 1929.
41. Sir Winston Churchill Papers, CHAR 1/207 *San Jose Mercury Herald*, September 12, 1929.
42. Robert C. Self, ed., *The Austen Chamberlain Diary Letters: The Correspondence of Sir Austen Chamberlain with His Sisters Hilda and Ida, 1916-1937* (Cambridge: Cambridge University Press, 1995), 353; *San Francisco Examiner*, September 13, 1929.
43. Sir Winston Churchill Papers, CHAR 1/207 Jeffrey T. Tilman, *Arthur Brown Jr., Progressive Classicist* (New York: W.W. Norton, 2006), 111–113; Randolph Churchill, and Helmut Gernsheim, eds., *Churchill: His Life in Photographs* (Murray Hill, New York: Rinehart, 1955), 71.
44. *Daily Express*, October 2, 1929.

45. Sir Winston Churchill Papers, CHAR 1/207 Winston Churchill, "Peter Pan Township of Films," 8.
46. Ken Murray, *The Golden Days of San Simeon* (Garden City, New York: Doubleday, 1971), 2; Marion Davies, *The Times We Had: Life with William Randolph Hearst* (New York: Bobbs-Merrill, 1975), 45.
47. Ian Mugridge, *The View from Xanadu: William Randolph Hearst and United States Foreign Policy* (Montreal: McGill-Queen's University Press, 1995), 23.
48. Mugridge, 30, 43; Ferdinand Lundberg, *Imperial Hearst: A Social Biography* (Westport, CT: Greenwood, 1970), 90–91.
49. John Churchill, 88; Murray, 25–26.
50. Gilbert, *Documents*, 87; Murray, 14.
51. John Churchill, 88; Murray, 110.
52. Gilbert, *Documents*, 87.
53. Murray, 107–108.
54. Gilbert, *Documents*, 87; John Churchill, 88.
55. Randolph Churchill, *Twenty-One Years*, 86; *New York Times*, January 27, 1972; Gilbert, *Documents*, 88.
56. Gilbert, *Documents*, 88; John Churchill, 89; Randolph Churchill, *Twenty-One Years*, 86; Murray, 63.
57. David Nasaw, *The Chief: The Life of William Randolph Hearst* (New York: Houghton Mifflin, 2000), 418.
58. Randolph Churchill, *Twenty-One Years*, 86–87.
59. Ibid., 87.
60. Ibid., 86.
61. John Churchill, 89; Sir Winston Churchill Papers, CHAR 1/207 Nasaw, 375; Murray, 54–57.
62. Langworth, 534; Randolph Churchill, *Winston S. Churchill: Youth, 1874–1900*, 90, 284; L. Hush Newman, "Butterflies to Chartwell," *Finest Hour* 89 (Winter 1995/96): 34- 39.
63. John Churchill, 89.
64. Raoul Walsh, *Each Man in His Time: The Life Story of a Director* (New York: Farrar, Straus, and Giroux, 1974), 266.
65. Gilbert, *Documents*, 88; John Churchill, 89.
66. Gilbert, *Documents*, 88; Murray, 1, 104.
67. Gilbert, *Documents*, 88.
68. C.L. Sulzberger, *A Long Row of Candles, Memories and Diaries, 1934–1954* (New York: Macmillan, 1969), 751; *New York Times*, January 27, 1972.
69. John Churchill, 89.
70. Roberts, *Randolph: A Study of Churchill's Son*, 57.
71. William Randolph Hearst, Jr. and Jack Casserly, *The Hearsts: Father and Son* (Niwot, CO: Roberts Rinehart Publishers, 1991), 82.
72. *Los Angeles Times*, September 15, 1929; Sir Winston Churchill Papers, CHAR 1/207 Baruch Papers.
73. Randolph Churchill, *Twenty-One Years*, 87.

## Chapter 14

1. John Churchill, 90.
2. *Time*, September 30, 1929; *Los Angeles Examiner*, September 19, 1929; Sir Winston Churchill Papers, CHAR 1/207.
3. Randolph Churchill, *Twenty-One Years*, 88.
4. Gilbert, *Documents*, 88, 96–97; *Los Angeles Times*, September 23, 1961; John Churchill, 88; Fred Lawrence Guiles, *Marion Davies: A Biography* (New York: McGraw-Hill, 1972), 60–66.
5. *Los Angeles Times*, September 18, 1929; *Los Angeles Times*, September 29, 1929; *Los Angeles Times*, November 12, 1948.
6. Randolph Churchill, *Twenty-One Years*, 88; *Los Angeles Examiner*, September 19, 1929.
7. Randolph Churchill, *Twenty-One Years*, 88; *Los Angeles Examiner*, September 19, 1929; *Los Angeles Times*, September 19, 1929; *Time*, September 30, 1929.
8. *Selections from the Writings and Speeches of William Randolph Hearst* (San Francisco: privately published, 1948), 195; *Los Angeles Examiner*, September 19, 1929.
9. *Los Angeles Times*, September 19, 1929; Randolph Churchill, *Twenty-One Years*, 87; Davies, 136; *Los Angeles Examiner*, September 19, 1929.
10. *Los Angeles Times*, September 29, 1929.
11. Randolph Churchill, *Twenty-One Years*, 87.
12. John Churchill, 91–92.
13. *Los Angeles Times*, October 27, 1929.
14. *Los Angeles Examiner*, September 20, 1929; *Los Angeles Times*, September 19, 1929; *Santa Barbara Morning Post*, September 20, 1929; *New York Times*, July 2, 1929; William G. McAdoo, *Crowded Years: The Reminiscences of William G. McAdoo* (Boston: Houghton Mifflin, 1931).
15. Markku Routsila, "Churchill and Wilson," *Finest Hour* 92 (Autumn 1996): 18–23; Gilbert, *Documents*, 88.
16. *Los Angeles Examiner*, September 20, 1929; *Santa Barbara Morning Post*, September 20, 1929; Gilbert, *Documents*, 88.
17. Sir Winston Churchill Papers, CHAR 1/207.
18. *Rand McNally Guide to Los Angeles and Environs* (New York: Rand McNally, 1925), 138.
19. Gilbert, *Documents*, 86–87.
20. Sir Winston Churchill Papers, CHAR 1/207 Sir Winston Churchill Papers, CHAR 8/226.
21. *Santa Barbara Morning Post*, September 20, 1929; *Los Angeles Examiner*, September 20, 1929.
22. *Los Angeles Examiner*, September 19, 1929; Randolph Churchill, *Twenty-One Years*, 88.
23. *Santa Barbara Morning Post*, September 20, 1929; *Los Angeles Examiner*, September 20 1929; *Rand McNally Guide to Los Angeles*, 142; Sir Winston Churchill Papers, CHAR 1/208 Sir Winston Churchill Papers, CHAR 1/207.
24. Randolph Churchill, *Twenty-One Years*, 89; David A. Jasen, *P.G. Wodehouse: A Portrait of a Master* (New York: Mason & Lipscomb, 1974), 118–119.
25. Langworth, 379.
26. David Wallace, *Lost Hollywood* (New York: LA Weekly Books, 2001), 88; Anne Edwards, "Marion Davies Ocean House: The Santa Monica Palace Ruled by Hearst's Mistress," *Architectural Digest: The International Magazine of Fine Interior Digest* 51, no. 4 (April 1994): 277; John Churchill, 90.
27. Wallace, 86; Gilbert, *Documents*, 97; Randolph Churchill, *Twenty-One Years*, 89.

28. Wallace, 86–90; Edwards, 170–175, 277–278; John Churchill, 90.
29. Davies, 136–137; Wallace, 89.
30. *San Francisco Examiner*, September 22, 1929.
31. Randolph Churchill, *Twenty-One Years*, 89; John Churchill, 91.
32. Charlie Chaplin, *My Autobiography* (New York: Simon and Schuster, 1964), 339–340.
33. John Churchill, 91.
34. Ibid., 91; Randolph Churchill, *Twenty-One Years*, 89; Tom Dardis, *Harold Lloyd: The Man on the Clock* (New York: Penguin, 1983), 172.
35. Randolph Churchill, *Twenty-One Years*, 90; John Churchill, 91.
36. Walsh, 270–272.
37. Gilbert, *Documents*, 97.
38. Ibid., 96; Hearst Papers.
39. Baruch Papers; Sir Winston Churchill Papers, CHAR 1/207 *The Scotsman*, September 28, 1929; *The Times*, October 24, 1938; *Selections from the Writings and Speeches of William Randolph Hearst*, 219.
40. Beaverbrook Papers, BBK/B/103.

## Chapter 15

1. Gilbert, *Documents*, 97–98.
2. *Los Angeles Examiner*, September 22, 1929; *Los Angeles Examiner*, September 24, 1929; *Los Angeles Times*, November 4, 1937.
3. *Los Angeles Times*, July 22, 1962.
4. *Los Angeles Examiner*, September 22, 1929; Margaret Leslie Davis, *The Los Angeles Biltmore: The Host of the Coast* (Los Angeles: The Regal Biltmore Hotel, 1998); Gilbert, *Documents*, 97.
5. John Churchill, 95; Haste, 8
6. Gilbert, *Documents*, 97.
7. *New York Times*, July 17, 1941; Gilbert, *Documents*, 98.
8. *Los Angeles Examiner*, September 22, 1929.
9. Winston Churchill, "Peter Pan Township of Films," 8; Davis, *The Los Angeles Biltmore*, 18.
10. Winston Churchill, "Peter Pan Township of Films," 8.
11. John Churchill, 92.
12. *San Francisco Examiner*, September 23, 1929; *New York Times*, March 8, 1957; *New York Times*, April 9, 1927; *New York Times*, June 15, 1927.
13. *New York Times*, September 27, 1948; *New York Times*, June 8, 1929; *New York Times*, September 3, 1962; *Los Angeles Times*, September 23, 1929; Leary, 171.
14. Walter S.J. Swanson, *The Thin Gold Watch: A Personal History of the Newspaper Copleys* (La Jolla, CA: The Copley Press, 1970), 164.
15. *Los Angeles Times*, September 23, 1929; *New York Times*, September 23, 1929; Gilbert, *Churchill and the Great Republic*, 35; Gilbert, *Documents*, 98.
16. *Manchester Guardian*, September 24, 1929.
17. Chaplin, *My Autobiography*, 340.
18. John Churchill, 133.
19. Charles Chaplin, "A Comedian Sees the World," *Woman's Home Companion* 60, no. 10 (October 1933): 28.
20. *San Francisco Examiner*, September 24, 1929; *Los Angeles Examiner*, September 24, 1929; *Los Angeles Examiner*, September 22, 1929; *Los Angeles Times*, September 24, 1929.
21. *San Francisco Examiner*, September 24, 1929; *Los Angeles Times*, September 24, 1929; *Los Angeles Examiner*, September 24, 1929.
22. Randolph Churchill, *Twenty-One Years*, 90; *Los Angeles Times*, September 24, 1929; *Los Angeles Examiner*, September 24, 1929.
23. Winston Churchill, "Public Prayers for Our King," *Daily Telegraph*, November 18, 1929, 10.
24. Randolph Churchill, *Twenty-One Years*, 90.
25. Ibid, 90; Gilbert, *Documents*, 97; *Los Angeles Examiner*, September 26, 1929; John Churchill, 92–93; *Cleveland Plain Dealer*, October 13, 1929; *Unknown Chaplin*.
26. Winston Churchill, "Peter Pan Township of Films," 8; Gilbert, *Documents*, 97.
27. John Churchill, 92–93.
28. *Los Angeles Times*, September 24, 1929; Randolph Churchill, *Twenty-One Years*, 90; *Los Angeles Examiner*, September 25, 1929.
29. Randolph Churchill, *Twenty-One Years*, 90; *Los Angeles Times*, September 25, 1929; *Los Angeles Times*, September 29, 1929.
30. Randolph Churchill, *Twenty-One Years*, 90; *Los Angeles Times*, September 29, 1929; Davies, 136.
31. Walsh, 272–274.
32. Winston Churchill, "Peter Pan Township of Films," 8.
33. Gilbert, *Documents*, 97.
34. Bradley P. Tolppanen, "Churchill and Chaplin," *Finest Hour* 142 (Spring 2009): 16–21.
35. *Los Angeles Examiner*, September 25, 1929; *San Diego Sun*, September 25, 1929.
36. Randolph Churchill, *Twenty-One Years*, 90; Gilbert, *Documents*, 96.
37. Sir Winston Churchill Papers, CHAR 1/207 Gilbert, *Documents*, 96.
38. Gilbert, *Documents*, 95.
39. Winston Churchill, "Fever of Speculation in America," *Daily Telegraph*, December 9, 1929, 10.
40. Ibid., 10; Gilbert, *Documents*, 95.
41. Gilbert, *Documents*, 95; Colville, 114.
42. Gene Fowler, *Good Night, Sweet Prince: The Life and Times of John Barrymore* (New York: Viking, 1944), 223.
43. Ibid., 332; *Atlanta Constitution*, November 3, 1929; John Kobler, *Damned in Paradise: The Life of John Barrymore* (New York: Atheneum, 1977), 256; *Chicago Daily Tribune*, October 6, 1929.
44. Gilbert, *Documents*, 98.
45. John Churchill, 93.

## Chapter 16

1. Robert Scharff, ed., *Yosemite National Park* (New York: David McKay, 1967), 1.

2. Sir Winston Churchill Papers, CHAR 1/207 *Merced Sun-Star*, September 28, 1929; Gilbert, *Documents*, 683; *San Francisco Chronicle*, September 28, 1929.
3. *The Times*, September 6, 1963.
4. *Mariposa Gazette*, October 4, 1929; *Merced Sun-Star*, September 28, 1929; John Churchill, 93.
5. Winston Churchill, "Land of Corn and Lobsters," 16–17, 45.
6. *Bakersfield Californian*, September 28, 1929.
7. John Churchill, 93; Lucius Beebe, *Mansions on Rails: The Folklore of the Private Railway Car* (Berkeley: Howell-North, 1959), 305.
8. Winston Churchill, "Land of Corn and Lobsters," 16–17, 45.
9. Sir Winston Churchill Papers, CHAR 1/209 Gilbert, *Documents*, 96–98.
10. Winston Churchill, "Nature's Panorama in California," 8.
11. *Coconino Sun*, October 4, 1929; John Churchill, 93–94; Sir Winston Churchill Papers, CHAR 1/209.
12. Winston S. Churchill, *His Father's Son*, 62.
13. Ibid., 62.
14. Moir, 113.
15. Cohen, 1367; Sir Winston Churchill Papers, CHAR 8/225B.
16. Winston Churchill, "Land of Corn and Lobsters," 16–17, 45.
17. William K. Klingaman, *1929: The Year of the Great Crash* (New York: Harper & Row, 1989), 224.
18. Sir Winston Churchill Papers, CHAR 1/211.
19. Randolph Churchill, *Twenty-One Years*, 91; *Chicago Daily Herald*, October 3, 1929; *Chicago Daily News*, October 2, 1929.
20. Jordan A. Schwarz, *The Speculator: Bernard M. Baruch in Washington, 1917–1965* (Chapel Hill: University of North Carolina Press, 1981), 545; James Marchant, ed., *Winston Spencer Churchill: Servant of Crown and Commonwealth* (London: Cassell, 1954), 162–170.
21. Winston S. Churchill, *His Father's Son*, 35; Randolph Churchill, *Twenty-One Years*, 91.
22. *Chicago Herald and Examiner*, October 3, 1929; *Chicago Evening Post*, October 2, 1929; *Chicago Daily News*, October 2, 1929.
23. *Chicago Evening Post*, October 2, 1929; *Chicago Daily Tribune*, October 3, 1929.
24. *Chicago Evening Post*, October 2, 1929.
25. *Chicago Daily News*, October 2, 1929; Robert V. Allegrini, *Chicago's Grand Hotels: The Palmer House Hilton, the Drake, and the Hilton Chicago* (Chicago: Arcadia, 2005), 57.
26. Allegrini, 66.
27. Gilbert, *Documents*, 99.
28. *1929 Financial Report of Armour and Company* (1930); *Chicago Herald and Examiner*, October 3, 1929.
29. John Churchill, 94.
30. Gilbert, *Churchill and the Great Republic*, 119.
31. *Chicago Daily Tribune*, October 3, 1929.
32. *Irish Times*, April 10, 1967.
33. Edith Summerskill, *A Woman's World* (London: Heinemann, 1967), 138–139.

34. *Gary Post-Tribune*, October 3, 1929.
35. Sir Winston Churchill Papers, CHAR 1/207 128; Philip P. Larson, "Encounters with Chicago," *Finest Hour* 118 (Spring 2003): 30–35; Sir Winston Churchill Papers, CHAR 8/225B.
36. *Chicago Daily Tribune*, October 3, 1929; *Chicago Daily Tribune*, October 5, 1929.
37. William Starr Myers, *The Foreign Policies of Herbert Hoover, 1929–1933* (New York: Charles Scribner's Sons, 1940), 60; Carlton, 114; B.J.C., McKercher, "'A Certain Irritation': The White House, the State Department, and the Desire for a Naval Settlement with Great Britain, 1927–1930," *Diplomatic History* 31, no. 5 (November 2007): 861.
38. *New York Times*, October 5, 1929; *Chicago Evening Post*, October 5, 1929; *Chicago Daily News*, October 5, 1929.
39. Gilbert, *Documents*, 101.
40. *Chicago Daily Tribune*, July 6, 1925; John Churchill, 94; Larson, 32–33.
41. Winston Churchill, "Vastness of America's Industry," *Daily Telegraph*, January 27, 1930, 10.
42. *Chicago Herald and Examiner*, October 3, 1929; Randolph Churchill, *Twenty-One Years*, 91; Kahn Papers.
43. Randolph Churchill, *Twenty-One Years*, 91–92.
44. Hearst Papers.
45. Gilbert, *Documents*, 100.

## Chapter 17

1. Sir Winston Churchill Papers, CHAR 1/208.
2. *New York Evening Post*, October 9, 1929; *New York Times*, April 30, 1954; Baruch Papers.
3. Sir Winston Churchill Papers, CHAR 1/208 Sir Winston Churchill Papers, CHAR 1/211 *Rand McNally Guide to New York City and Environs* (New York: Rand McNally, 1929), 33; Gilbert, *Documents*, 101.
4. John Campbell, *F.E. Smith: First Earl of Birkenhead* (London: Jonathan Cape, 1983), 143, 203.
5. Campbell, *F.E. Smith*, 112; John Campbell, "Smith, Frederick Edwin, First Earl of Birkenhead (1872–1930)," *Oxford Dictionary of National Biography* (Oxford University Press, 2004), online edition.
6. Campbell, *F.E. Smith*, 263; Kemper, 132.
7. Randolph Churchill, *Twenty-One Years*, 93–94; John Churchill, 96–97.
8. *New York Post*, October 7, 1929; CHAR 1/208.
9. *New York Times*, October 7, 1929.
10. *Chicago Daily Tribune*, October 13, 1929.
11. Sir Winston Churchill Papers, CHAR 1/208.
12. John Churchill, 96.
13. Sir Winston Churchill Papers, CHAR 1/207 Sir Winston Churchill Papers, CHAR 1/208.
14. Lerner, 127; Randolph Churchill, *Twenty-One Years*, 92–93.
15. Sir Winston Churchill Papers, CHAR 1/207 *New York Times*, February 7, 1965.
16. *Chicago Daily Tribune*, October 9, 1929; *New York Times*, October 9, 1929.
17. *New York Sun*, October 9, 1929; Lerner, 168.

18. Randolph Churchill, *Twenty-One Years*, 93; Lerner, 223.
19. Randolph Churchill, *Twenty-One Years*, 93; John Churchill, 96; *New York Sun*, October 9, 1929.
20. CHAR 1/208 Randolph Churchill, *Twenty-One Years*, 95; Winston S. Churchill, *His Father's Son*, 63.
21. John Churchill, 96–97.
22. Randolph Churchill, *Twenty-One Years*, 93–94.
23. *The Times*, June 25, 1992; *The Independent*, July 9, 1992.
24. Sir Winston Churchill Papers, CHAR 1/208.
25. Ibid.
26. Ibid.
27. Sir Winston Churchill Papers, CHAR 1/207.
28. Klingaman, 252; Josephine Young Case, *Owen Young and American Enterprise: A Biography* (Boston: David R. Godine, 1982), 468.
29. *New York Times*, December 24, 1944.
30. David Marquand, "MacDonald, (James) Ramsay (1866–1937)," *Oxford Dictionary of National Biography* (Oxford University Press, 2004), online edition.
31. *New York Times*, October 13, 1929; *Chicago Daily Tribune*, October 13, 1929.
32. *New York Telegram*, October 12, 1929.
33. Winston Churchill, "Public Prayers for Our King," 10.
34. Allen, 749; F.S. Northedge, *The Troubled Giant: Britain Among the Great Powers, 1916–1939* (New York: Frederick A. Praeger, 1966), 346; Roskill, 20.
35. G. R. Searle, "Guest, Frederick Edward (1875–1937)," *Oxford Dictionary of National Biography* (Oxford University Press, 2004), online edition; *New York Times*, October 8, 1959.
36. *New York Times*, October 2, 1921; *New York Times*, April 24, 1921, 7; Robert B. Mackay, Stanley Linduall, and Carol Traynor, *AIA Architectural Guide to Nassau and Suffolk Counties, Long Island* (New York: Dover Publications, 1992), 38.
37. *New York Times*, May 22, 1932.
38. William H. Harbaugh, *Lawyer's Lawyer: The Life of John W. Davis* (New York: Oxford University Press, 1978), 82; Julia Davis and Dolores A. Fleming, eds., *The Ambassadorial Diary of John W. Davis: The Court of St. James's 1918–1921* (Morgontown, WV: West Virginia University Press, 1993), 151.
39. Harbaugh, 385–390.
40. Sir Winston Churchill Papers, CHAR 8/225B.
41. Sir Winston Churchill Papers, CHAR 8/228 CHUR 4/1 CHAR 8/225B; CHAR 1/208.
42. Sir Winston Churchill Papers, CHAR 1/211 CHAR 1/208 Mary Soames, *Clementine Churchill: The Biography of a Marriage* (Boston: Houghton Mifflin, 1979), 283.
43. Sir Winston Churchill Papers, CHAR 1/211 Klingaman, 259.
44. Sir Winston Churchill Papers, CHAR 1/208.
45. Winston Churchill, "Vastness of America's Industry," 10.
46. Kay Halle, *Winston Churchill on America and Britain: A Selection of His Thoughts on Anglo-American Relations* (New York: Walker, 1970), 161.
47. Emily Smith Warner and Hawthorne Daniel, *The Happy Warrior: A Biography of My Father Alfred E. Smith* (Garden City, NY: Doubleday, 1956), 245.
48. *New York Times*, October 16, 1929; *New York Evening Post*, October 16, 1929.
49. Smith Warner, 245.
50. *New York Evening Post*, October 16, 1929.
51. Ibid.
52. Smith Warner, 246; Halle, 161.
53. *New York Times*, October 28, 1929; CHAR 8/225B.
54. Richard O'Connor, *Courtroom Warrior: The Combative Career of William Travers Jerome* (Boston: Little, Brown, 1963), 119; Sir Winston Churchill Papers, CHAR 1/208.
55. Klingaman, 253; John Kobler, *Otto the Magnificent: The Life of Otto Kahn* (New York: Charles Scribner's Sons, 1988), 4; Kahn Papers.
56. Sir Winston Churchill Papers, CHAR 1/208 Mary Soames, ed., *Winston and Clementine: The Personal Letters of the Churchills* (New York: Houghton Mifflin, 2001), 352–353; Kahn Papers.
57. Winston Churchill, "Industrial Conditions in America," 8.
58. Sir Winston Churchill Papers, CHAR 1/208.
59. Ibid.
60. Ibid.; Randolph Churchill, *Winston S. Churchill: Youth, 1874–1900*, 524.
61 Klingaman, 18.
62. *Washington Post*, October 15, 1929; *Washington Post*, October 19, 1929; Sir Winston Churchill Papers, CHAR 1/208 Homer E. Socolofsky, *Arthur Capper: Publisher, Politician, and Philanthropist* (Lawrence, KS: University of Kansas Press, 1962), 217.
63. *New York Times*, October 19, 1929; Hearst Papers.

## Chapter 18

1. Winston Churchill, "Old Battlefields of Virginia," *Daily Telegraph*, December 16, 1929, 10.
2. Kemper, 123.
3. *Richmond Times-Dispatch*, October 19, 1929; Sir Winston Churchill Papers, CHAR 1/206 *New York Times*, February 15, 1938; *Richmond News-Leader*, October 19, 1929; *Fredericksburg Free Lance Star*, October 21, 1929.
4. *Richmond Times-Dispatch*, October 19, 1929; Henry F. Byrd Jr., *The Churchill I Knew* (Winchester, VA: Farmers and Merchants National Bank, 1965), 2; David E. Johnson, *Douglas Southall Freeman* (Gretna, LA: Pelican Publishing, 2002), 145.
5. Johnson, 168.
6. Ibid., 224.
7. *Richmond Times-Dispatch*, October 19, 1929.
8. *Richmond News-Leader*, October 19, 1929.
9. Winston Churchill, "Old Battlefields of Virginia," 10; *Richmond News-Leader*, October 19, 1929.
10. CHAR 8/228 Winston Churchill, "Old Battlefields of Virginia," 10; *Richmond Times-Dispatch*, October 19, 1929.

11. Winston Churchill, "Old Battlefields of Virginia," 10.
12. *Richmond Times-Dispatch*, October 19, 1929; Ronald L. Heinemann, *Harry Byrd of Virginia* (Charlottesville: University Press of Virginia, 1996), 109; Byrd, 2.
13. Celia Sandys, *Chasing Churchill: The Travels of Winston Churchill* (New York: Carroll and Graf, 2003), 96.
14. Heinemann, 109; Byrd, 3; *New York Times*, August 26, 1964; Sandys, 97.
15. Sandys, 97; Byrd, 2.
16. Winston Churchill, "Old Battlefields of Virginia," 10.
17 *Fredericksburg Free Lance Star*, October 21, 1929.
18. Winston Churchill, "Old Battlefields of Virginia," 10.
19. *Fredericksburg Free Lance Star*, October 21, 1929.
20. James, *Winston S. Churchill: His Complete Speeches*, 7294–7295.
21. Winston Churchill, "Old Battlefields of Virginia," 10.
22. Winston Churchill, "What I Saw in America of Prohibition," 10.
23. Washington Herald, October 23, 1929; *New York Times*, February 12, 1953; Baruch Papers.
24. Cecil Edward Weller, Jr., *Joe T. Robinson: Always a Loyal Democrat* (Fayetteville: University of Arkansas Press, 1998), xiii.
25. Mark O. Hatfield, *Vice Presidents of the United States, 1789–1993* (Washington: United States Government Printing Office, 1997), 373–381.
26. *Washington Post*, October 22, 1929; Weller, 126–128.
27. Baruch Papers.
28. Michael C. Kathrens, *American Splendor: The Residential Architecture of Horace Trumbauer* (New York: Acanthus Press, 2002), 62–71.
29. Frederick Platt, "Horace Trumauer's Mansions in Elkins Park," *Bulletin of the Historical Society of Montgomery County, Pennsylvania* 30, no. 4 (Spring 1997): 252–299; Kathrens, 62–71.
30. *New York Times*, October 27, 1943.
31. George Henry McCall, *The Joseph Widener Collection Tapestries at Lynnewood Hall, Elkins Park, Pennsylvania* (Philadelphia: privately published, 1932), 6–7.
32. *New York Times*, October 27, 1943; *Time*, November 3, 1924; *Paintings in the Collection of Joseph Widener at Lynnewood Hall* (Elkins, PA: privately published, 1931); Kathrens, 70–71.
33. *New York Times*, January 29, 1927.
34. Kathrens, 71.
35. *Visit to the Bethlehem Plant of Bethlehem Steel Company* (Bethlehem, PA: Bethlehem Steel Co., 1923), 2–3.
36. Winston Churchill, "Industrial Conditions in America," 8; *Bethlehem Globe Times*, October 23, 1929.

## Chapter 19

1. Baruch Papers; Sir Winston Churchill Papers, CHAR 1/208.

2. Sir Winston Churchill Papers, CHAR 1/208 Baruch Papers.
3. Henry Morgenthau and French Strother, *I Was Sent to Athens* (Garden City, NY: Doubleday, Doran, 1929), 45; Sir Winston Churchill Papers, CHAR 1/208.
4. *New York Evening Post*, October 24, 1929.
5. *New York Telegram*, October 24, 1929; *New York Times*, October 25, 1929.
6. Ibid.; *Washington Post*, October 25, 1929.
7. Klingaman, 265; Winston Churchill, "Fever of Speculation in America," 10.
8. *New York Telegram*, October 24, 1929; *New York Times*, October 25, 1929; Gordon Thomas and Max Morgan-Witts, *The Day the Bubble Burst: A Social History of the Wall Street Crash of 1929* (Garden City, NY: Doubleday, 1979), 399.
9. Winston Churchill, "Fever of Speculation in America," 10.
10. Sir Winston Churchill Papers, CHAR 1/211 James, *Victor Cazalet*, 129.
11. *Year Book of the American Iron and Steel Institute 1929* (New York: American Iron and Steel Institute, 1930), 293.
12. *New York Times*, October 26, 1929.
13. Gilbert, *Documents*, 29; Kenneth Warren, *Industrial Genius: The Working Life of Charles Michael Schwab* (Pittsburgh: University of Pittsburgh Press, 2007), xii.
14. *Year Book of the American Iron and Steel Institute 1929*, 241.
15. Robert Hessen, *Steel Titan: The Life of Charles M. Schwab* (New York: Oxford University Press, 1975), 303.
16. *New York Times*, October 26, 1929; *Chicago Daily Tribune*, October 27, 1929.
17. Winston Churchill, "Vastness of America's Industry," 10.
18. Sir Winston Churchill Papers, CHAR 1/208 Gilbert, *Documents*, 101.
19. Sir Winston Churchill Papers, CHAR 1/208.
20. Ibid.; Moir, 168; *New York Times*, October 27, 1929; Matthew J. Bruccoli, ed., *Dictionary of Literary Biography Documentary Series, Volume 16, The House of Scribner, 1905–1930* (Detroit: Gale, 1997), online.
21. Sir Winston Churchill Papers, CHAR 1/208.
22. Bradley Tolppanen, "The Accidental Churchill," *The Churchillian* 3, no. 4 (Winter 2012): 6–13.
23. Klingaman, 279; Baruch Papers; James Grant, *Bernard M. Baruch: The Adventures of a Wall Street Legend* (New York: Simon and Schuster, 1983), 239–240.
24. Gilbert, *Documents*, 176.

## Chapter 20

1. Thomas, 392–399.
2. Soames, *Winston and Clementine: The Personal Letters of the Churchills*, 349; *New York Times*, October 31, 1929.
3. Winston Churchill, "Fever of Speculation in America," 10.
4. Baruch Papers.
5. Klingaman, 332.

6. Sir Winston Churchill Papers, CHAR 1/208.
7. *New York Times*, November 15, 1929; *The Times*, December 4, 1929; *The Times*, September 6, 1963.
8. *New York Times*, October 31, 1929; *Hartford Courant*, October 31, 1929.
9. *New York Sun*, October 29, 1929.
10. James, *Winston S. Churchill: His Complete Speeches*, 4673; Winston Churchill, "Public Prayers for Our King," 10; Winston Churchill, "Old Battlefields of Virginia," 10.
11. *New York Times*, November 4, 1929; *The Scotsman*, November 6, 1929.
12. Gilbert, *Documents*, 683.
13. *The Scotsman*, November 6, 1929.
14. *The Times*, February 25, 1947.
15. Soames, *Winston and Clementine: The Personal Letters of the Churchills*, 349; Mary Soames, *Winston Churchill: His Life as a Painter*, 76.
16. *The Scotsman*, November 6, 1929.

# Bibliography

## Primary Sources

### Sir Winston Churchill Papers, Churchill College, Cambridge

Files consulted: CHAR 1/205 CHAR 1/206 CHAR 1/207 CHAR 1/208 CHAR 1/209 CHAR 1/211 CHAR 8/225 CHAR 8/226 CHAR 8/227 CHAR 8/228 CHUR 4/1

### Other Private Papers

Bernard Baruch Papers, Seeley G. Mudd Manuscript Library, Princeton University.
Canadian Club papers, Glenbow Museum, Calgary.
Canadian Pacific Archives, Montreal.
Joseph T. Robinson Papers, University of Arkansas.
Leo Amery Papers, Churchill College, Cambridge.
Lord Beaverbrook Papers, Parliamentary Archives, London.
Otto Kahn Papers, Princeton University Library.
Vancouver City Archives.
William Lyon Mackenzie King Diaries. Web. 2012.
William Randolph Hearst Papers, Bancroft Library, University of California, Berkeley, CA.

### Articles by Winston Churchill

Churchill, Winston. "Across Canada to the Pacific." *Daily Telegraph*, 13 January, 1930.
\_\_\_\_\_. "Fever of Speculation in America." *Daily Telegraph*, 9 December, 1929.
\_\_\_\_\_. "Fleets of Britain and America." *Daily Telegraph*, 20 January, 1930.
\_\_\_\_\_. "Industrial Conditions in America." *Daily Telegraph*, 3 February, 1930.
\_\_\_\_\_. "Land of Corn and Lobsters." *Collier's*, August 5, 1933.
\_\_\_\_\_. "Nature's Panorama in California." *Daily Telegraph*, 23 December,1929.
\_\_\_\_\_. "The Naval Misunderstanding." *Daily Telegraph*, 25 November, 1929.
\_\_\_\_\_. "Old Battlefields of Virginia." *Daily Telegraph*, 16 December, 1929.
\_\_\_\_\_. "The Palestine Crisis." *Sunday Times*. 22 September, 1929.
\_\_\_\_\_. "Peter Pan Township of the Films." *Daily Telegraph*, 30 December, 1929.
\_\_\_\_\_. "Public Prayers for Our King." *Daily Telegraph*, 18 November, 1929.
\_\_\_\_\_. "Vastness of America's Industry." *Daily Telegraph*, 27 January, 1930.
\_\_\_\_\_. "What I Saw in America of Prohibition." *Daily Telegraph*, 2 December, 1929.
\_\_\_\_\_. "World's Greatest Grain Emporium." *Daily Telegraph*, 6 January, 1930.

### Books by Winston Churchill

Churchill, Winston. *A History of the English-Speaking Peoples. Volume IV: The Great Democracies*. New York: Bantam, 1963.
\_\_\_\_\_. *My Early Life 1874–1904*. New York: Touchstone Book, 1996.
\_\_\_\_\_. *Painting as a Pastime*. New York: Whittelsey House, 1950.
\_\_\_\_\_. *World Crisis*. New York: Charles Scribner's Sons, 1923–1931. 5 volumes.

### Newspapers and Magazines

*Atlanta Constitution*
*Bakersfield Californian*
Bethlehem (PA) Globe Times
*British Columbian* (BC)
*Calgary Daily Herald*
*Canadian Pacific Bulletin* (QC)
Chicago Daily News
Chicago Daily Tribune
Chicago Evening Post
Chicago Herald and Examiner

Cleveland Plain Dealer
Coconino (AZ) Sun
Daily Express (UK)
Edmonton Bulletin
Edmonton Journal
Evening Standard (UK)
Fort William Daily Times-Journal (Thunder Bay, ON)
Fredericksburg (VA) Free Lance-Star
Gary (IN) Post-Tribune
Grants Pass (OR) Daily Courier
Hamilton (TX) Herald
Hamilton (ON) Spectator
Hartford Courant
High River (AB) Times
Humboldt (NE) Standard
Independent (UK)
Irish Times
Kenora (ON) Miner and News
London Times
Los Angeles Examiner
Los Angeles Times
Manchester Guardian
Manitoba Free Press
Mariposa (CA) Gazette
Merced (CA) Sun-Star
Montreal Daily Star
Montreal Gazette
Montreal Herald
New York Evening Post
New York Sun
New York Telegram
New York Times
Niagara Falls Evening Review
Niagara Falls Gazette
Ottawa Evening Citizen
Ottawa Journal
Peterborough (ON) Examiner
Port Arthur (TX) News-Chronicle
Quebec Chronicle-Telegraph
Regina (SK) Morning-Leader
Richmond News Leader
Richmond Times-Dispatch
Rogue River Courier and Oregon Observer
San Diego Sun
San Francisco Chronicle
San Francisco Examiner
San Jose Mercury Herald
Santa Barbara Morning Press
Saskatoon Leader-Post
Saskatoon Star-Phoenix
Saturday Night (ON)
Scotsman
Seattle Daily Times
Southern Daily Echo (UK)
Sunday Times (UK)
Time
Toronto Daily Star
Toronto Globe and Mail
Toronto Telegram
Vancouver Province
Vancouver Sun
Victoria (BC) Daily Colonist
Victoria (BC) Daily Times
Wall Street Journal
Washington Herald
Washington Post
Winnipeg Evening Tribune

## Published Speeches, Documents, and Memoirs

Addresses Delivered Before the Canadian Club of Toronto. Volume XXVIII Season of 1929–30. Toronto: Warwich Bros. and Rutter, 1930.

Amery, L. S. In the Rain and the Sun. London: Hutchinson, 1946.

_____. Days of Fresh Air: Being Reminiscences of Outdoor Life. London: Jarrolds, 1939.

_____. My Political Life, Volume Two: War and Peace, 1914–1929. London: Hutchinson, 1953.

_____. My Political Life, Volume Three: The Unforgiving Years, 1929–1940. London: Hutchinson, 1955.

Barnes, John, and David Nicolson, eds. The Leo Amery Diaries, Volume I: 1896–1929. London: Hutchinson, 1980.

Barrymore, Ethel. Memoirs: An Autobiography. New York: Harper, 1955.

Baruch, Bernard M. Baruch: The Public Years. New York: Holt, Rinehart and Winston, 1960.

Byrd, Henry F. Jr. The Churchill I Knew. Winchester, VA: Farmers and Merchants National Bank, 1965.

Campbell, Sir Gerald. Of True Experience. New York: Dodd, Mead, 1947.

Chaplin, Charles. "A Comedian Sees the World." Woman's Home Companion, October 1933.

Chaplin, Charlie. My Autobiography. New York: Simon and Schuster, 1964.

Churchill, John Spencer. A Churchill Canvas. Boston: Little, Brown, 1962.

Churchill, Randolph. Twenty-One Years. London: Weidenfeld and Nicolson, 1965.

Currelly, Charles Trick. I Brought the Ages Home. Toronto: Ryerson Press, 1967.

Davies, Marion. The Times We Had: Life with William Randolph Hearst. New York: Bobbs-Merrill, 1975.

Davis, Julia, and Dolores A. Fleming, eds. The Ambassadorial Diary of John W. Davis: The Court of St. James's 1918–1921. Morgontown, WV: West Virginia University Press, 1993.

Gilbert, Martin. Winston S. Churchill, Volume V, Part 2 Documents: The Wilderness Years 1929-1935. Boston: Houghton Mifflin, 1981.

Graebner, Walter. My Dear Churchill. Cambridge, MA: Houghton Mifflin, 1965.

Haste, Cate, ed. A Memoir: From Churchill to Eden. London: Weidenfeld & Nicolson, 2007.

Hearst, William Randolph, Jr., and Jack Casserly. The Hearsts: Father and Son. Niwot, CO: Roberts Rinehart Publishers, 1991.

James, Robert Rhodes, ed. Winston S. Churchill: His Complete Speeches. New York: Chelsea House Publishers, 1974. 8 volumes.

McAdoo, William G. *Crowded Years: The Reminiscences of William G. McAdoo*, Boston: Houghton Mifflin, 1931.

Moir, Phyllis. *I Was Winston Churchill's Private Secretary*. New York: Wilfred Funk, 1941.

Nel, Elizabeth. *Mr. Churchill's Secretary*. New York: Coward-McCann, 1958.

*Selections from the Writings and Speeches of William Randolph Hearst*. San Francisco: privately published, 1948.

Self, Robert C., ed. *The Austen Chamberlain Diary Letters: The Correspondence of Sir Austen Chamberlain with his Sisters Hilda and Ida, 1916–1937*. Cambridge: Cambridge University Press, 1995.

Smith Warner, Emily, and Hawthorne Daniel. *The Happy Warrior: A Biography of My Father Alfred E. Smith*. Garden City, NY: Doubleday, 1956.

Soames, Mary, ed. *Winston and Clementine: The Personal Letters of the Churchills*. New York: Houghton Mifflin, 2001.

Sulzberger, C.L. *A Long Row of Candles, Memories and Diaries, 1934–1954*. New York: Macmillan, 1969.

Summerskill, Edith. *A Woman's World*. London: Heinemann, 1967.

Walsh, Raoul. *Each Man in His Time: The Life Story of a Director*. New York: Farrar, Straus, and Giroux, 1974.

## Secondary Sources

Alder, Bill. *The Churchill Wit*. New York: Coward-McCann, 1965.

Allegrini, Robert V. *Chicago's Grand Hotels: The Palmer House Hilton, the Drake, and the Hilton Chicago*. Chicago: Arcadia, 2005.

Allen, H.C. *Great Britain and the United States: A History of Anglo-American Relations, 1783- 1952*. London: Oldhams, 1954.

Barnes, Christine. *Great Lodges of the Canadian Rockies*. Bend, OR: W.W. West, 1999.

Barnhart, Gordon, ed. *Saskatchewan Premiers of the Twentieth Century*. Regina: Canadian Plains Research Center, 2004.

Beebe, Lucius. *Mansions on Rails: The Folklore of the Private Railway Car*. Berkeley: Howell-North, 1959.

Best, Geoffrey. *Churchill: A Study in Greatness*. London: Hambledon, 2001.

Betcherman, Lita-Rose. *Ernest Lapointe: Mackenzie King's Great Quebec Lieutenant*. Toronto: University of Toronto Press, 2002.

Bliss, Michael. *A Canadian Millionaire: The Life and Business Times of Sir Joseph Flavelle, Bart., 1858–1939*. Toronto: Macmillan, 1978.

Bredin, Edward M. "Leonard M. Brockington: Calgary's Silver-tongued Orator." *Alberta History* 56, no. 1 (Winter 2008): 23+.

Brennnan, Brian. *Alberta Originals: Stories of Albertans Who Made a Difference*. Calgary: Fifth House, 2001.

Bruccoli, Matthew J. (ed.) *Dictionary of Literary Biography Documentary Series, Volume 16, The House of Scribner, 1905–1930*. Detroit: Gale, 1997. Web. 2012.

Burton, Brian K. *Extraordinary Circumstances: The Seven Days Battles*. Bloomington: Indiana University Press, 2001.

Campbell, John. *F.E. Smith: First Earl of Birkenhead*. London: Jonathan Cape, 1983.

*The Canada Year Book 1930*. Ottawa: F.A. Acland, 1930.

Carlton, David. *MacDonald versus Henderson: The Foreign Policy of the Second Labour Government*. New York: Humanities Press, 1970.

Case, Josephine Young. *Owen Young and American Enterprise: A Biography*. Boston: David R. Godine, 1982.

Charbonneau, Andre, Yvon Desloges, and Marc Lafrance. *Quebec: The Fortified City from the 17th to the 19th Century*. Ottawa: Parks Canada, 1982.

Chettle, John H. "Winston Churchill in America." *Smithsonian*, April 2001.

Chisholm, Barbara. *Castles of the North: Canada's Grand Hotels*. Toronto: Lynx Images, 2001.

Cohen, Ronald I. *Bibliography of the Writings of Sir Winston Churchill*. New York: Thoemmes, 2006. 3 volumes.

Churchill, Peregrine, and Julian Mitchell. *Jennie, Lady Randolph Churchill: A Portrait with Letters*. New York: St. Martin's Press, 1974.

Churchill, Randolph S. *Winston S. Churchill, Volume I: Youth 1874–1900*. Boston: Houghton Mifflin, 1966.

———. *Winston S. Churchill, Volume II: Young Statesman 1901–1914*. Boston: Houghton Mifflin, 1967.

Churchill, Randolph, and Helmut Gernsheim, eds. *Churchill: His Life in Photographs*. Murray Hill, New York: Rinehart, 1955.

Churchill, Winston S. *His Father's Son: The Life of Randolph Churchill*. London: Weidenfeld and Nicolson, 1996.

Colville, John. *Winston Churchill and His Inner Circle*. New York: Wyndham Books, 1981.

Combs, Trey. *Steelhead: Fly Fishing*. Guilford, CT: Lyons Press, 1999.

Coombs, David. *Churchill, His Paintings: A Catalog Compiled by David Coombs*. New York: World Publishing, 1967.

Coombs, David, and Minnie S. Churchill. *Sir Winston Churchill, His Life and His Paintings*. Philadelphia: Running Press, 2004.

Crowsfield, Peter. *The British in Egypt*. New York: Holt, Rinehart, and Winston, 1971.

Dabbs, Frank. *Branded by the Wind: The Life and Times of Bill Herron*. Calgary: Herron, 2001.

Dardis, Tom. *Harold Lloyd: The Man on the Clock*. New York: Penguin, 1983.

Davis, Margaret Leslie. *The Los Angeles Biltmore: The Host of the Coast*. Los Angeles: The Regal Biltmore Hotel, 1998.

Dawson, R. MacGregor. *William Lyon Mackenzie King: A Political Biography, 1874–1923*. Toronto: University of Toronto Press, 1958.

*Dictionary of Canadian Biography*. Web. 2012.

Dilks, David. *"The Great Dominion": Winston Churchill in Canada, 1900–1954*. Toronto: Thomas Allen, 2005.

Donaldson, Frances. *P.G. Wodehouse: A Biography*. New York: Alfred Knopf, 1982.

Eade, Charles, ed. *Churchill by His Contemporaries*. London: Reprint Society, 1955.

Edwards, Anne. "Marion Davies Ocean House: The Santa Monica Palace Ruled by Hearst's Mistress." *Architectural Digest: The International Magazine of Fine Interior Digest* 51, no. 4 (April 1994): 170–175, 277–278.

Evans, Simon M. *Prince Charming Goes West: The Story of the E.P. Ranch*. Calgary: University of Calgary Press, 1993.

Faber, David. *Speaking for England: Leo, Julian and John Emery—The Tragedy of a Political Family*. New York: Free Press, 2005.

Fedden, Robin. *Churchill at Chartwell*. London: Pergamon Press, 1969.

Finch, David A. *Hell's Half Acre: Early Days in the Great Alberta Oil Patch*. Surrey, B.C.: Heritage House, 2005.

Fowler, Gene. *Good Night, Sweet Prince: The Life and Times of John Barrymore*. New York: Viking, 1944.

Garnett, Porter. *Stately Homes of California*. Boston: Little, Brown, 1915.

Gilbert, Martin. *Churchill: A Life*. Toronto: Minerva, 1993.

\_\_\_\_\_. *Churchill and America*. New York: Free Press, 2005.

\_\_\_\_\_. "Churchill and Canada." *Proceedings of the International Churchill Societies 1988–89*. Web.

\_\_\_\_\_. *Winston S. Churchill, Volume III: The Challenge of War, 1914–1916*. Boston: Houghton Mifflin, 1971.

\_\_\_\_\_. *Winston S. Churchill, Volume V: 1922–1939, the Prophet of Truth*. Boston: Houghton Mifflin, 1977.

Gilbert, Martin, Daun Van Ee, and Allen Packwood. *Churchill and the Great Republic*. Washington: Library of Congress, 2004.

Grant, James. *Bernard M. Baruch: The Adventures of a Wall Street Legend*. New York: Simon and Schuster, 1983.

Gray, Earle. *The Great Canadian Oil Patch: The Petroleum Era from Birth to Peak*. Edmonton: JuneWarren Publishing, 2004.

Guiles, Fred Lawrence. *Marion Davies: A Biography*. New York: McGraw-Hill, 1972.

Haig-Brown, Roderick L. *A River Never Sleeps*. New York: William Morrow, 1946.

Halle, Kay (ed). *Randolph Churchill: The Young Unpretender*. London: Heinemann, 1971.

Halle, Kay. *Winston Churchill on America and Britain: A Selection of His Thoughts on Anglo-American Relations*. New York: Walker, 1970.

Hamill, Ian. *The Strategic Illusion: The Singapore Strategy and the Defence of Australia and New Zealand, 1919–1942*. Singapore: Singapore University Press, 1981.

Harbaugh, William H. *Lawyer's Lawyer: The Life of John W. Davis*. New York: Oxford University Press, 1978.

Hatfield, Mark O. *Vice Presidents of the United States, 1789–1993*. Washington: United States Government Printing Office, 1997.

Heinemann, Ronald L. *Harry Byrd of Virginia*. Charlottesville: University Press of Virginia, 1996.

Hessen, Robert. *Steel Titan: The Life of Charles M. Schwab*. New York: Oxford University Press, 1975.

Hubbard, R.H. *Ample Mansions: The Viceregal Residences of the Canadian Provinces*. Ottawa: University of Ottawa Press, 1989.

\_\_\_\_\_. *Rideau Hall: An Illustrated History of Government House, Ottawa, from Victorian Times to the Present Day*. Montreal: McGill-Queens University Press, 1977.

James, Robert Rhodes. *Churchill: A Study in Failure, 1900–1934*. New York: The World Publishing Company, 1970.

\_\_\_\_\_. *Victor Cazalet: A Portrait*. London: Hamish Hamilton, 1976.

Jasen, David A. *P.G. Wodehouse: A Portrait of a Master*. New York: Mason & Lipscomb, 1974.

Jenkins, Roy. *Churchill: A Biography*. New York: Farrar, Straus and Giroux, 2001.

Johnson, David E. *Douglas Southall Freeman*. Gretna, LA: Pelican Publishing, 2002.

Johnston, Derek Lukin. "Paintings: Banff's Bunkers." *Finest Hour* 59 (Spring 1988): 18.

Jones, David Laurence. *See This World Before the Next: Cruising with CPR Steamships in the Twenties and Thirties*. Calgary: Fifth House, 2004.

Kathrens, Michael C. *American Splendor: The Residential Architecture of Horace Trumbauer*. New York: Acanthus Press, 2002.

Kemper, R. Crosby III (ed.) *Winston Churchill: Resolution, Defiance, Magnanimity, Good Will*. Columbia: University of Missouri Press, 1996.

Kendle, John. *John Bracken: A Political Biography*. Toronto: University of Toronto Press, 1979.

Kent, Bruce. *The Spoils of War: The Politics, Economics, and Diplomacy of Reparations 1918-1932*. Oxford: Clarendon Press, 1989.

Kersaudy, Francois. *Churchill and De Gaulle*. London: Collins, 1981.

Klingaman, William K. *1929: The Year of the Great Crash*. New York: Harper & Row, 1989.

Kobler, John. *Damned in Paradise: The Life of John Barrymore*. New York: Atheneum, 1977.

\_\_\_\_\_. *Otto the Magnificent: The Life of Otto Kahn*. New York: Charles Scribner's Sons, 1988.

Kromer, Reinhold, and Tom Mitchell. *When the State Trembled: How A.J. Andrews and the Citizens' Committee Broke the Winnipeg General Strike*. Toronto: University of Toronto Press, 2010.

Langworth, Richard, ed. *Churchill by Himself: The Definitive Collection of Quotations*. New York: Public Affairs, 2008.

Larson, Philip P. "Encounters with Chicago." *Finest Hour* 118 (Spring 2003): 30–35.

Lavery, Brian. *Churchill Goes to War*. Annapolis, MD: Naval Institute Press, 2007.

Leary, David T. "Winston S. Churchill in California." *California History* (Winter 2001/2002): 163–175 and 238–239.

Lee, Celia, and John Lee. *The Churchills: A Family Portrait*. New York: Palgrave Macmillan, 2010.

Lerner, Michael A. *Dry Manhattan: Prohibition in New*

York City. Cambridge, MA: Harvard University Press, 2007.

Leslie, Anita. *Randolph: The Biography of Winston Churchill's Son*. New York: Beaufort Books, 1985.

Leslie, Jean. *Past and Present: People, Places, and Events in Calgary*. Calgary: Century Calgary Publications, 1975.

Levine, Allan. *The Exchange: 100 Years of Trading Grain in Winnipeg*. Winnipeg: Peguis Publishers, 1987.

Lundberg, Ferdinand. *Imperial Hearst: A Social Biography*. Westport, CT: Greenwood, 1970.

Mackay, Robert B., Stanley Linduall, and Carol Traynor. *AIA Architectural Guide to Nassau and Suffolk Counties, Long Island*. New York: Dover Publications, 1992.

Marchant, James, ed. *Winston Spencer Churchill: Servant of Crown and Commonwealth*. London: Cassell, 1954.

Marquis, Albert Nelson, ed. *Who's Who in America, Volume 15, 1928-1929*. Chicago: A.N. Marquis Company, 1928.

Marsh, James, ed. *Canadian Encyclopedia*. Edmonton: Hurtig Publishers, 1985.

Matter, William D. *If It Takes All Summer: The Battle of Spotsylvania*. Chapel Hill: University of North Carolina Press, 1988.

McCall, George Henry. *The Joseph Widener Collection Tapestries at Lynnewood Hall, Elkins Park, Pennsylvania*. Philadelphia: privately published, 1932.

McKercher, B. J. C. "'A Certain Irritation': The White House, the State Department, and the Desire for a Naval Settlement with Great Britain, 1927-1930." *Diplomatic History* 31, no. 5 (November 2007): 829-863.

McKercher, B.J.C., and Lawrence Aronsen, eds. *The North Atlantic Triangle in a Changing World: Anglo-American-Canadian Relations, 1902-1956*. Toronto: University of Toronto Press, 1996.

Middleton, William D. *The Bridge at Quebec*. Bloomington: Indiana University Press, 2001.

Moore, Christopher. *The British Columbia Court of Appeal: The First Hundred Years, 1910- 2010*. Vancouver: University of British Columbia Press, 2010.

Morgenthau, Henry, and French Strother. *I Was Sent to Athens*. Garden City, New York: Doubleday, Doran, 1929.

Mugridge, Ian. *The View from Xanadu: William Randolph Hearst and United States Foreign Policy*. Montreal: McGill-Queen's University Press, 1995.

Murray, Ken. *The Golden Days of San Simeon*. Garden City, NY: Doubleday, 1971.

Musk, George. *Canadian Pacific: The Story of the Famous Shipping Line*. Toronto: Holt, Rinehart and Winston, 1981.

Myers, William Starr. *The Foreign Policies of Herbert Hoover, 1929-1933*. New York: Charles Scribner's Sons, 1940.

Nasaw, David. *The Chief: The Life of William Randolph Hearst*. New York: Houghton Mifflin, 2000.

Neatby, H. Blair. *William Lyon Mackenzie King, 1924-1932: The Lonely Heights*. Toronto: University of Toronto Press, 1963.

Newman, L. Hush. "Butterflies to Chartwell." *Finest Hour* 89 (Winter 1995/96): 34-39.

*1929 Financial Report of Armour and Company*. 1930.

Northedge, F.S. *The Troubled Giant: Britain Among the Great Powers, 1916-1939*. New York: Frederick A. Praeger, 1966.

O'Connor, Richard. *Courtroom Warrior: The Combative Career of William Travers Jerome*. Boston: Little, Brown, 1963.

Olson, Lynne. *Troublesome Young Man: The Rebels Who Brought Churchill to Power and Helped Save England*. New York: Farrar, Straus, and Giroux, 2007.

Osterbrock, Donald E., John R. Gustafson, and W.J. Shiloh Unruh. *Eye on the Sky: Lick Observatory's First Century*. Berkeley: University of California Press, 1988.

*Oxford Dictionary of National Biography*. Web. 2012.

*Paintings in the Collection of Joseph Widener at Lynnewood Hall*. Elkins, PA: privately published, 1931.

*Parliament Buildings: Les Edifices du Parlement*. Ottawa: House of Commons, 1980.

PARLINFO—Parliamentarian File. Web. 2012.

Patillo, Roger. *Lake Louise at Its Best: An Affectionate Look at Life at Lake Louise by One Who Knew It Well*. Aldergrove, B.C.: Amberlea Press, 2000.

Pilpel, Robert H. *Churchill in America 1895-1961: An Affectionate Portrait*. New York: Harcourt Brace Jovanovich.1976.

Platt, Frederick. "Horace Trumauer's Mansions in Elkins Park." *Bulletin of the Historical Society of Montgomery County, Pennsylvania* 30, no. 4 (Spring 1997): 252-299.

Procter, Ben. *William Randolph Hearst: Final Edition, 1911-1951*. New York: Oxford University Press, 2007.

Pugh, Garth, ed. *"A Tower of Attraction": An Illustrated History of Government House, Regina, Saskatchewan*. Regina: Government House Historical Society, 1991.

*Rand McNally Guide to Chicago and Environs*. New York: Rand McNally, 1927.

*Rand McNally Guide to Los Angeles and Environs*. New York: Rand McNally, 1925.

*Rand McNally Guide to New York City and Environs*. New York: Rand McNally, 1929.

*Rand McNally Guide to San Francisco, Oakland, Berkeley, and Environs of the Bay Cities*. New York: Rand McNally, 1927.

Reardon, Terry. "Winston Churchill and Mackenzie King." *Finest Hour* 130 (Spring 2006): 24- 27.

_____. *Winston Churchill and Mackenzie King, So Similar, So Different*. Toronto: Dundurn, 2012.

Reksten, Terry. *The Dunsmuir Saga*. Vancouver: Douglas & McIntyre, 1991.

Render, Shirley. *Double Cross: The Inside Story of James A. Richardson and Canadian Airways*. Toronto: Douglas & McIntyre, 1999.

_____. *No Place for a Lady: The Story of Canadian Women Pilots, 1928-1992*. Winnipeg: Portage & Main Press, 1992.

Richardson, A.J.H. "Guide to the Architecturally and Historically Most Significant Buildings in the Old City of Quebec with a Biographical Dictionary of

Architects and Builders and Illustrations." *Bulletin of the Association for Preservation Technology* 2, no. 3/4 (1970): 3–144.

Roberts, Brian. *Randolph: A Study of Churchill's Son*. London: Hamish Hamilton, 1984.

Roberts, H. Armstrong. *Resorts in the Canadian Pacific Rockies*. np: Canadian Pacific Railway, 1924.

Roskill, Stephen. *Naval Policy Between the Wars, Volume I: The Period of Anglo-American Antagonism, 1919–1929*. New York: Walker, 1968.

Routsila, Markku. "Churchill and Wilson." *Finest Hour* 92 (Autumn 1996): 18–23.

Ryder, David Warren. *"Great Citizen": A Biography of William H. Crocker*. San Francisco: Historical Publications, 1962.

*San Francisco Bay Toll-Bridge, the Longest Bridge in the World: Souvenir Program, March 2, 1929*.

Sandys, Celia. *Chasing Churchill: The Travels of Winston Churchill*. New York: Carroll and Graf, 2003.

Scharff, Robert, ed. *Yosemite National Park*. New York: David McKay, 1967.

Schwarz, Jordan A. *The Speculator: Bernard M. Baruch in Washington, 1917–1965*. Chapel Hill: University of North Carolina Press, 1981.

*Seventh Annual Round the World Cruise, Empress of Australia*. np: Canadian Pacific, 1929.

Smythe, John. *The Victoria Cross, 1856–1964*. London: Frederick Muller, 1965.

Soames, Mary. *Clementine Churchill: The Biography of a Marriage*. Boston: Houghton Mifflin, 1979.

_____. *Winston Churchill: His Life as a Painter*. London: Collins, 1990.

Socolofsky, Homer E. *Arthur Capper: Publisher, Politician, and Philanthropist*. Lawrence, KS: University of Kansas Press, 1962.

Stacey, C.P. *Quebec, 1759: The Siege and the Battle*. New York: St. Martin's Press, 1959.

Stanway, Paul. *Alberta in the 20th Century: A Journalistic History of the Province*. Edmonton: CanMedia Inc., 2005.

Sterling, Christopher H. "Churchill Afloat: Liners and the Man." *Finest Hour* 121 (Winter 2003-04): 16–22.

Stump, Al. "Winnie's Big Misadventure." *Los Angeles Magazine* 32 (September 1987): 164–171.

Swanson, Walter S.J. *The Thin Gold Watch: A Personal History of the Newspaper Copleys*. La Jolla, CA: The Copley Press, 1970.

Swettenham, John. *McNaughton, Volume I: 1887–1939*. Toronto: Ryerson Press, 1968.

Thomas, Gordon, and Max Morgan-Witts. *The Day the Bubble Burst: A Social History of the Wall Street Crash of 1929*. Garden City, NY: Doubleday, 1979.

Tilman, Jeffrey T. *Arthur Brown Jr., Progressive Classicist*. New York: W.W. Norton, 2006.

Tolppanen, Bradley P. "The Accidental Churchill." *The Churchillian* 3, no. 4 (Winter 2012): 6–13.

_____. "Churchill and Chaplin." *Finest Hour* 142 (Spring 2009): 16–21.

Townend, Peter. *Burke's Peerage & Baronetage, 104th Edition*. London: Burke's Peerage Limited, 1967.

Turner, Robert D. *The Pacific Empresses: An Illustrated History of Canadian Pacific Railway's Empress Liners on the Pacific Ocean*. Victoria, BC: Sono Nis Press, 1981.

*Unknown Chaplin*. New York: HBO Video, 1983.

*Visit to the Bethlehem Plant of Bethlehem Steel Company*. Bethlehem, PA: Bethlehem Steel Co., 1923.

Von Baeyer, Edwina. *Garden of Dreams: Kingsmere and Mackenzie King*. Toronto: Dundurn, 1990.

Walder, David. *The Chanak Affair*. New York: Macmillan, 1969.

Wallace, David. *Lost Hollywood*. New York: LA Weekly Books, 2001.

Ward, Norman, and David Smith. *Jimmy Gardiner: Relentless Liberal*. Toronto: University of Toronto Press, 1990.

Ward, Stephen R. *James Ramsay MacDonald: Low Born Among the High Brows*. New York, Lang, 1990.

Warren, Kenneth. *Industrial Genius: The Working Life of Charles Michael Schwab*. Pittsburgh: University of Pittsburgh Pres, 2007.

Warrender, Susan. *Alberta Titans: From Rags to Riches During Alberta's Pioneer Days*. Canmore, Alberta: Altitude Publishing, 2003.

Weller, Cecil Edward, Jr. *Joe T. Robinson: Always a Loyal Democrat*. Fayetteville: University of Arkansas Press, 1998.

Wheare, K.C. *The Statute of Westminster and Dominion Status*. London: Oxford University Press, 1942.

Wheeler-Bennett, John W. *Disarmament and Security Since Locarno, 1925–1931*. New York: Howard Fertig, 1973.

*Who's Who 1929*. New York: Macmillan, 1929.

Williams, M.B. *Kootenay National Park and the Banff Windermere Highway*. Ottawa: F.A. Acland, 1929.

Williamson, Philip. "Safety First: Baldwin, the Conservative Party, and the 1929 General Election." *The Historical Journal* 25, no. 2 (June 1982): 385–409.

Wrigley, Chris. *Winston Churchill: A Biographical Companion*. Santa Barbara: ABC-Clio, 2002.

*Year Book of the American Iron and Steel Institute 1929*. New York: American Iron and Steel Institute, 1930.

Young, Kenneth. *Churchill and Beaverbrook: A Study in Friendship and Politics*. New York: Heinemann, 1966.

Zieroth, Dale. *Nipika: A Story of Radium Hot Springs*. Hull, Quebec: Minister of Supply and Services Canada, 1978.

# Index

Numbers in ***bold italics*** indicate pages with photographs.

Abernathy-Lougheed Logging Company  123
*Aftermath*  9, 85, 112, 196
Aitken, Robert G.  148–149
Alberta  56, 76, 90, 92–93, 96–98, 100–103, 106, 112, 172, 203
Alberta Military Institute  99
Allard, A.B.  74, ***75***, 78
*American Impressions*  9
American Iron and Steel Institute  110, 225–228
American Rolling Mills  112
American Smelting and Refining  203
Amery, John  21, 164
Amery, Leo  8, 19–27, 29–30, 61, 114–115
Anderson, James T.M.  86–87, 89
Anderson, W.A.  121
Anglo-American relations  1, 9, 44, 52–53, 79, 85, 160, 169, 171, 174–175, 189–190, 195, 201, 226, 232
Anscomb, Herbert  127, 129–130
*Answers*  23
Archibald, E.J.  27
Armour, Philip D.  188
Armour and Company  188
Ashley, Maurice  115, 144
Asquith, Herbert  32, 74
Associated Screen News  108, 127
Astaire, Adele  194
Australia  9, 36–37, 47, 49, 54, 63, 79, 148, 171

Badgerow, Sir George  19, 62
Bahamas  3, 228
Baker, J.H.  40, 95, 108, 127, 143
Bakersfield  183
*Bakersfield Californian*  1, 183
Baldwin, Stanley  8, 18–22, 32, 48–50, 62, 80, 86, 100, 142, 169, 193, 227, 233
Balfour, Lord  73, 81, 83

Baltac Oil  103, 112, 179, 203, 222, 229
Banff  24, 97, 107–111, 113–114, 117
Banff Springs Hotel  107–108, 110, 114
Bankers' Club  195
Barrymore, Ethel  180, 189
Barrymore, John  115, 155, 168, 180
Barstow  184
Baruch, Bernard  9–13, 30–31, 135, 141, 156, 169, 184–186, ***187***, 188–189, 191–194, 196, 202–204, 210–212, 217–219, 222, 224, 226, 228–229, 232
Battle, Rex  61
Battle Abbey  212
Beacon Hill Park  130
Beatty, Edward W.  42–43
Beauchesne, Arthur  29, 32, 35
Beaulieu  139
Beaverbrook, Lord  3, 9, 11, 15, 22, 35, 53, 87, 105, 169, 194
Beery, Wallace  167–168
Bell Syndicate  9, 202, 203, 206
Bennett, R.B.  35, 53, 105
Benoit, R.A.  29
*Berengaria*  193, 196–197, 203, 230, ***231***, 232–233
Bermuda Conference  3
Bethlehem  219–220
Bethlehem Steel  12, 179, 219–220, 225–226
Biltmore Hotel (Los Angeles)  171, 173–174, 180
Biltmore Hotel (New York)  206
Bingham, William James  119, 122–123, 125
*Birds of Western Canada*  83
Birkenhead, Lord  15, 32, 38, 48–49, 55, 95, 128, 178–179, ***193***, 194–197
Birley, Sir Oswald  113
Blackstone Hotel  189

Blair, R.M.  54
Blenheim Palace  7, 152, 197, 228
Bloody Angle  215–216
Bodkin, Thomas  109
Boer War  7, 13, 25, 36, 74, 85, 99, 101
Bohemian Club  146, 148
Bond Club  195, 203
Boothby, Robert  15
Borden, Robert  28, 53, 56, 76
boxing  177, 189
Bracken, Brendan  15, 194
Bracken, John  78
Brett, Robert  ***93***, 95, 97
Brian, Mary  167
British Columbia provincial exhibition  119–122
*British Columbian*  120–121
British Empire—Dominion relations  28, 44, 48, 54, 63–64, 74, 79–81, 88, 90, 96, 121, 125
British Public Schools' Club  129
Brockington, Leonard  99, 100, 105
Brownlee, John E.  95, 97
Brownsea Scouts  96
Bruce, Robert Randolph  125–127, 129–130, 163
Bryan, John Stewart  212–214
Buchan-Hepburn, Patrick  13
Bull Creek Flat  138–139
Burlingame  141–143, 149–150, 163, 181, 183
Burns, John  107, 110
Burns, Pat  99–100, 107
Bury, Ambrose U.G.  92, ***93***, 94–95
butterflies  116, 139, 155
Byrd, Anne Douglas Beverly  213–214
Byrd, Harry Flood  211–213, ***214***
Byrd, Harry, Jr.  214–215

Calgary  56, 77, 82, 91, 93, 97–101, 103–107, 115, 150

Calgary Board of Trade 99
*Calgary Daily Herald* 99, 102, 105
California 4, 9–12, 31, 104, 109, 133, 135–144, 146–148, 151, 155–156, 160, 162–163, 165–166, 168, 170–172, 174–175, 180–185, 203, 210, 225, 229–230, 232
California Club 171, 174–175
Campbell, Gerald 135–138, 146–147, 150, 154, 169, 174
Campbell, Ronald Ian 208, 217
Campbell, W.W. 141, 148–149
Camrose, Lord 8–9
Canadian Clubs 42–43, 52–53, 60–62, 64, 81, 83–85, 99, 105–106, 127, 129–130
Canadian National Railway 65–66, 94
Canadian Pacific 5, 10, 12, 18–19, 29–30, 37, 40, 42, 61, 71, 74–76, 82, 86, 88, 92, 97–99, 105, 107, 113–114, 116, 118, 125, 127, 130, 132, 143
Capper, Arthur 208
Carlton Hotel 217
Carlyle, William Levi 98, 102–103, 115
Carrel, Frank 35
Carroll, Amazelie 35
Carroll, Henry George 35–36
Casa Del Desierto 184
Casa Del Monte 153, 184
Casa Grande 151–154
Catalina Island 138, 172–174
Cazalet, Victor 17
Central Park Casino 196
Chaffey, Andrew M. 171–172, 174
Chamberlain, Austen 22, 142, 150
Chamberlain, Neville 30, 108, 169
Chanak Crisis 49, 51, 81
Chaplin, Charlie 6, 165, 167–168, 174–178
Charles Scribner's Sons 9, 212, 227
Chartwell 10, 13, 49–51, 67, 108, 110, 115, 155, 169, 178, 186, 197, 228, 232
Chateau Frontenac 30–31, 36, 38, 40
Chateau Lake Louise 114–115, 117
Chateau Laurier 51–52
Cherbourg 6, 18, 21
Chicago 4–5, 9–11, 156, 171, 183–192, 225, 232
Chicago Club 189
*Chicago Daily News* 186–187
*Chicago Daily Tribune* 186, 190
*Chicago Evening Post* 186–187
*Chicago Herald and Examiner* 186–187
Chicago stockyards 184, 187–188
Chidsey, Donald Barr 198
Chidsey, G. Alan 198
Chorley Park 60; *see also* Government House (Ontario)
Christ Church Cathedral 128, 130
*Christina* 4
Church, Tommy 68
Churchill (Manitoba) 88, 104

Churchill, Clarissa 14, 197
Churchill, Clementine 5–7, 14–15, 18, 21, 23–24, 26, 31, 36, 39–41, 45, 51–52, 55–56, 60, 64, 74, 76–77, 84–85, 87–89, 96, 102–104, 107–108, 111–113, 117–119, 122, 136, 142, 144–146, 148–149, 153, 156–157, 162–163, 178–179, 184, 192–193, 196, 202–203, 207, 217–218, 227, 232
Churchill, Diana 5, 6, 14, 179
Churchill, Gwendeline Theresa Mary 14–16, 109, 232
Churchill, John George Spencer "Johnny" 1, 5, 14–17, 19, 22, 24, 26–27, 30, 32–34, 39, 43, 55–56, 77, 88, 90, **93**, 95, 102–105, 110–112, 115–116, 127, 129, 132–133, 138, 143–144, 146, 152–156, 158–159, 161, 164–165, 167–168, 171–172, 174–176, 178–180, 182–184, 186, 188, 190, 192, 194–198, 232
Churchill, John Strange Spencer "Jack" 1, 3, 5, 13–17, 21–22, 24, 34, 36–37, 39, 43, 56, 67–68, 72, 74, **75**, 89–90, **93**, 95, 97, 105, 110–112, 114–116, 129, 132–133, 138, 144, 146, 150, 158, 161, 172–173, 175, 178, 180, 184, 186–187, 195–197, 201, 206–207, 210, 218–219, 222, 227, 229, 230, 232
Churchill, Lady Randolph 7, 13–14, 107, 132, 175, 198, 206
Churchill, Lord Randolph 7, 8, 15, 20, 107, 124, 132
Churchill, Peregrine 14
Churchill, Randolph 1, 5, 15–17, 21–27, 30–31, 33, 36–37, 39, 41–43, 47–48, 50–52, 56–60, 64–69, 74, **75**, 76–80, 88, 90, **93**, 95, 100, 103–106, 108, 110, 112–116, 118, 120–121, 123–125, 127–140, 143–146, 153–161, 163–165, 167–168, 172, 174–175, 177–180, 184–186, 188, 192, 194–197, 207, 232
Churchill, Sarah 5, 6, 184
Citadel, Quebec 3, 34, 38
*Citizen Kane* 151
*City Lights* 176, 178
Clark, William H. 52–53
*Cock-Eyed World* 176, 177
cocktails 143–144
*Collier's* 185, 202, 203
HMS *Colombo* 136–138
Colville, John 13, 15, 179, 211
combine 87, 90, 97
Commercial Club 187, 189, 191
Compton, Juliette 176–177
concentration camps 188
Constasino, Mario 228
Coote, A. Leslie 121
Copley, Ira C. 172–173
*Cosmopolitan* 21, 152, 189, 202
Cotton Club 196
Coultis, Sam G. 101–102
Cowlishaw, Alfred H. 127

Coyne, James B. 76
Craig, Allan 126
Crane, Mrs. Richard 213
Crawford, J.W. 105–106
Crescent City 136
Crocker, Ethel 142–144, 148, 150
Crocker, Ethel Mary 143
Crocker, Helen 143
Crocker, William H. 11–12, 141–146, 148, 150, 163, 232
Cromer, Lady 127, 129
Cromer, Lord 127, 129
Cuba 3, 5, 9
Cunard Steamship 8, 230
Cunningham, Cecil 159
Currie, Sir Arthur 37
Curtis, Charles 217–218
Curtis Brown 163, 185, 189, 202, 229
*Cynthia* 129

*Daily Graphic* 3, 9
*Daily Telegraph* 8–9, 33, 71, 74, 81, 85, 87–88, 90, 96–97, 130, 139, 146, 148, 172, 176, 179, 190, 201, 212, 216, 230
Daniels, Bebe 167
Danville, Kansas 186
D'Arcy McGee, T. 53, 56
Dardanelles 7, 24
Davies, Marion 151–153, 158–159, 161, 164–165, **166**, 167–169, 176–177, 180
Davis, Ellen 202
Davis, John W. 202, 206, 225, 227
Davis, Pierpont V. 195–196
Dawes, Charles M. 133–134
Dawes Committee 170, 199
Day, Rodney 198
Dean, E.W. 122, 125
d'Egville, Sir Howard 29
de Latour, George, 139–140, 143
DeMille, Cecil B. 159, 177
Dempsey, Jack 189
de Pins, Francis 139
de Pins, Galcerand 139
Detroit 10, 34, 191
Dewar, Kenneth G.B. 24, 144
Dobson, Claude C. 137–138
Doherty, Manning 99–100
Doughty, Arthur 50
Doukhobors 118
Dove, Billie 167
Drake Hotel 187–188
Dunsmuir, Laura 127
Duveen, Lord 113
Dyer, James 76

Earhart, Amelia 202
Eayrs, Hugh S. 63
Eden, Anthony 198
Edinburgh University 86, 232
Edmonds, Sir James 144
Edmonton 56, 77, 82, 86, 89–98, 104
*Edmonton Bulletin* 93–94, 96, 98
*Edmonton Journal* 89–92, 94, 96
Edwards, Gus 159

# Index

E.F. Hutton 142, 179–180, 210
Egbert, William *93*, 95, 97
Egypt 9, 22, 25, 27, 44, 59, 63–64, 67, 72, 79–81, 85, 110, 124, 128, 144, 148, 227
Eisenhower, Dwight 3
elections 8–9, 13, 15, 21–22, 35, 42, 46, 53, 64, 68, 78, 85–86, 89, 160, 162, 167, 197, 199, 201–202, 204, 206, 217
Elkins Park 218
Ellis, Diane 167, 176
Emerald Lake 113–114, 117
Empire Club 60, 63–64
Empire Parliamentary Association 29
Empress Hotel 127
*Empress of Australia* 5, 12, 14, 18, *19*, 20–21, 23–24, 26–27, 29, 43, 48, 62, 67, 114
E.P. Ranch 98, 102–104; *see also* Prince of Wales Ranch
Epping division 8, 149
Equitable Building 193, 195, 224
Esquimalt 126, 128
Eton 15, 46, 96, 181
Eureka 137–139
Eureka Inn 136–137

Fairbanks, Douglas, Jr. 159, 176
Ferguson, George H. 62, 64, 67
Feversham, Lord 181–182, 187, 192, 207–208, 210, 217–219, 222, 225, 230
Fischer, Louis 198
Fishing 14, 34, 36, 129, 136, 173
Flavelle, Sir Joseph 62–63
Fletcher, Robert 74, *75*, 78
football 179, 223, 227
Forbes-Robertson, Maxine Frances Mary 47, 52, 53
Forestry Farm, Sutherland 87
Fort Saskatchewan 96–97
Fort William 71–72, 81
Foster, Monte 173
Fourth Hussars 55, 76, 134, 198
France 3, 7, 15–16, 30–31, 42, 44, 50, 55, 64, 84, 124, 129, 139, 164, 169, 192
Fraser, Abraham L. 138–139
Fraser, Alexander 58, 60
Fredericksburg 215–216
*Fredericksburg Free Lance-Star* 1, 216
free trade 7, 20–23, 27, 35, 44, 54, 73
Freeman, Douglas S. 212–213, 216
Freeman-Thomas, Inigo Brassey 47
French language 30–31, 74
Fuller, Sir Cyril T. 47–48, 53

Gallipoli 14, 109
Gamble, Joseph 46
Garbo, Greta 159, 165
Gardiner, John G. 84–87, 89
Garrison Club 34
Gary (Indiana) 189
*Gary Post-Tribune* 189
General Assembly of Virginia 216

*General Baquedano* 125
Georgeson, F.W. 137
Gibson, Charles Dana 199
Gilbert, Martin 22
Gillespie, A.C. 92, 95
*Globe and Mail* 36, 61, 64
Goolrick, C. O'Conor 215
Gordon, Kilbee 163
Government House (Alberta) 47, 57, 92–93, 97–98
Government House (British Columbia) 47, 57, 126–127, 129–130
Government House (Manitoba) 47, 57, 76, 78
Government House (Ontario) 47, 57, 58, 64, 67–68; *see also* Chorley Park
Government House (Ottawa) 52; *see also* Rideau Hall
Government House (Saskatchewan) 47, 57, 83–84, 86
Graebner, Walter 72
grain 71–72, 75–76, 81–82, 87–88, 96, 99, 106, 130
Grand Canyon 9, 10, 31, 183–185
Grant, George 37, 72, 119
Grants Pass 104, 135–136
*Grants Pass Daily Courier* 136
Grauman's Chinese Theatre 176
Gray, A. Wells 120–122
Gray, Lawrence 159
Grayson, Cary T. 211, 212, *213*, 215–216, 232
*Great Contemporaries* 9
Greenly Island 26
Greenwich 227
Griesbach, William 95, 97
Grouse Mountain 122
Guest, Amy 201–202, 227
Guest, Cornelia 94, 96
Guest, Freddie 11–12, 201

Haggard, Godfrey 190
The Hague Conference 42–44, 83, 88, 124
Haig, Douglas 24
Haig-Brown, Roderick 129
Haldane, W.H.M. 127–129
Halifax 28, 119
Hall, Grant 37, 40, 127
Hamilton 60, 66–67
*Hamilton Herald* 66–67
*Happy Days* 172–173
Hargal Oil 103, 112, 179, 203, 222
Harlem 196
Harrow 13, 16, 20–21, 29
Harvey, John 130
Hatley Park 129
Hearst, Blanche 153–156
Hearst, Dorothy 196
Hearst, George 153, 154, 156
Hearst, John Randolph 196
Hearst, Millicent 153, 157, 207, 210–211, 228, 232
Hearst, William Randolph 6, 9, 11, 15, 52–53, 147, 150, *151*, 152–161, 163–170, 176, 184, 191, 196, 210

Hearst, William Randolph, Jr. 156
Henderson, Arthur 25
Herron, William Stewart 100–101, 103
*High River Times* 101
*History of European Morals* 115
*History of the English-Speaking Peoples* 211, 227
Hoak, John 126
Hollywood 6, 9, 11, 107, 115, 129, 152–153, 155, 159, 161, 164, 170, 176–178, 180
Hoover, Herbert 4, 6, 12, 53, 79, 142, 170, 183, 187, 189, 195, 199, 206–209, 217–218
Hotel Commodore 225
Hotel Macdonald 94, 97
Hotel Saskatchewan 84–85
Hotel Vancouver 119, 122–123
Hotel Weylin 199
Hubbard, George D. 133–134
*Humboldt Standard* 137, 139
Humphreys, Arthur Selden 129
Humphreys, Kathleen 129
Hutchinson, Earl 76

*I Was Sent to Athens* 222
Imperial Conference of 1926, 28, 50, 64, 79, 81
India 7, 16, 20, 22, 30, 41, 47, 55, 76, 124, 134, 144, 155, 174, 177, 193, 233
Institute of Politics 13
Ireland 47, 52, 63, 92, 152, 165, 175, 208
Italy 14, 16, 42, 155, 179
Izard, Edward W. 126

Jack, Richard 110
Jackson, John H. 65–66
James, Robert Rhodes 20, 194
James Richardson & Sons 75, 92, 112, 122
Japan 18, 52, 62–63, 128, 155, 175
Jerome, William Travers 206, 225
Jones, Tiny 180

Kahn, Otto H. 11, 156, 191, 201, 206–207
Keary, W.H. 121
Kemp, J. Colin 43
Kenora 76–77
King, James H. 121, 125–127
King, Nellie 121, 125–127
King, William Lyon Mackenzie 3, 6, 35, 47–48, *49*, 50–51, 53–57
Kingsmere 48–51
Knowles, R.E. 30–32

Labrador 26, 148
La Guardia, F.H. 206
Lake Louise 97, 110, 114–117
Lake of the Woods 76–77
Lake Superior 70–71, 81, 87, 89
Lanctot, Charles 35
Langley, W.H. 130
Laniel, Joseph 3
Lapointe, Ernest 50, 53

# Index

Larkin, Joseph 30–31
Latta, Robert 18–19, 21, 26–27
Lauff Hotel 136
Layton, Elizabeth 40
lecture tours 1, 3, 5, 12, 28, 39, 41, 48, 74, 106, 131, 135, 144, 175, 184–186, 197, 228, 233
Lee, Sammy 159
Legislative building (Alberta) 97–98
Legislative building (British Columbia) 126
Legislative building (Manitoba) 76, 98
Legislative building (Saskatchewan) 85, 98
Lett, Larry 85
Lewis, H. Edgar 219
Lick Observatory 12, 145, *147*, 148–149
*Life of Brigham Young* 164, 232
*Life of Lord Randolph Churchill* 124, 163
Lindemann, Frederick 15, 149, 157, 196
Litchefield, Alderman 130
Livesay, D.K. 68–69
Lloyd, Harold 167
Lloyd, Lord 22
Lloyd George, David 8, 15, 22, 32, 46, 48–49, 200, 212, 215, 227
logging 10, 34, 70, 122–123
London Naval Conference 201, 217–218
*London Times* 13, 25
Long, Ray 202–203
*Loretto* 183–184, 207, 210, 219, 221
Los Angeles 5, 10–12, 31, 154, 158–161, 163–165, 167–168, 170–174, 176–183
*Los Angeles Examiner* 160, 163, 175, 177–178
*Los Angeles Times* 1, 161, 171, 173, 177
Lougheed, Nelson S. 123
Love, Bessie 167
Luke, Lord 19, 43
Lynnewood Hall *218*, 219

MacDonald, Foghorn 50
MacDonald, Ishbel 199, **200**
MacDonald, Ramsay 8, 31, 47, 53, 62, 77, 144, 183, 187, 189, 199, **200**, 201
Mackaill, Dorothy 167
Mackenzie, Helen 125–127, 129
Mackenzie, William Lyon 48
MacMillan, Frank R. 86–87
Macmillan, Harold 132
Malkin, William H. 122
*The Man from Blankley's* 180
*Manchester Guardian* 25, 173, 200
*Manitoba Free Press* 74, 80
Mariposa County Courthouse 181, **182**
Mark Twain Society 144
Marlborough, Duke of 7–8, 17, 88, 105, 197–198
*Marlborough: His Life and Times* 8, 23–24, 48, 89, 115, 144, 162, 181, 203, 229, 232
*Marlborough, Portrait of a Conqueror* 198
Marsh, Eddie 23
Massey, Vincent 65, 208
Matheson, Samuel 78, 80
Mattopan 202
Mayer, Louis B. 159, 160–161
McAdoo, Eleanor 161–164
McAdoo, William Gibbs 11, 144, 161–164, 174–175, 185, 232
McCormick, Robert B. 190
McCutcheon, John T. 190
McDowell, C.G. 193
McFarland, John L. 99–100
McGill, John 134
McGowan, Sir Harry 163, 178–179, 196–197, 203
McGregor, James D. 76, 78
McKinley, William 208
McLaglen, Victor 176
McLennan, Donald R. 11, 186, 188
McLeod, John H. 99–103, 112
McNaughton, Andrew 50–51, 53, 56
McNeil, Captain 121
*Meet General Grant* 185
Meighen, Arthur 106
Mellon, Andrew W. 208, 229
*Merced Sun-Star* 183
Metro-Goldwyn-Mayer 159–161, 163–164, 170, 177
Meyer, Ben R. 172–173
Miller, Adolph Caspar 217
Mills, Sir Frederick 227
Mitchell, Charlie 228
Moir, Phyllis 39–40
Money, Noel 129
Montgomery Ward 179, 210, 229
Montmartre Café 164
Montmorency Falls 34
Montreal 13, 24, 26–30, 32, 34–37, 39–45, 56, 63, 70, 78, 88, 143, 226
*Montreal Daily Star* 27, 44
*Montreal Gazette* 43–44
*Montreal Herald* 43–44
Moore, Joseph H. 149
Moorside 50
Morgenthau, Henry 222
Morley, Lord 23
*Morning Post* 25
Mount Amery 20, 29
*Mount Royal* 37, 38–41, 57–60, 65–67, 70–72, 74–76, 82–83, 86–92, 98–99, 104, 107, 117–119, 127, 135
Mount Royal Club 42
Mulock, Sir William 67
Murray, Walter Charles 86
Murray, W.W. 41
*My African Journey* 9

Napoleon 73, 167–168
*Nash's Pall Mall* 23, 185
Nast, Conde 194, 210
Nast, Leslie 194, 210
National Council of Education 13, 60, 74, 78, 123–124, 127–128
naval disarmament 51–53, 63, 66, 79, 81, 83, 85, 96, 124, 128, 183, 187, 190, 195, 200–201, 218, 226
Nest Club 196
New Place 142–143
New Westminster 120–122, 126
New York 3–5, 9–11, 23, 39, 66, 88, 110, 136, 142–144, 153, 156, 159, 163–164, 172, 178, 183, 189, 191–196, 198–200, 202–204, 206–208, 210, 221–223, 227–228, 230, 232
*New York Evening Post* 204
New York Stock Exchange 186, 222, **223**, 224, 228
*New York Sun* 196
*New York Times* 9, 199, 204, 228
*New York World* 194, 228
New Zealand 47, 49, 63, 139
Newfoundland 3, 26, 28, 233
Newlands, Edina 84
Newlands, Henry 84–86, 89
Newton, Kansas 186
Neylan, John 154, 169
Niagara Falls 34, 58, 60, 65–68, 89, 132, 184
*Niagara Falls Evening Review* 66
*Niagara Falls Gazette* 66
Niblo, Fred 159, 161
Nipigon 71

Ocean House 164–165, 168, 171, 177
oil industry 92, 97, 99–104, 106, 115, 125, 130, 172, 184
Old Contemptibles Association of British Columbia 121
Onassis, Aristotle 4
Osborne, Frederick Ernest 98–100, 105–106
Ottawa 3, 14, 28, 31, 45–49, 51–58, 78, 80, 83, 104
*Ottawa Evening Citizen* 45, 48, 54
*Ottawa Journal* 7, 45, 54, 81
Overseas Educational League 13, 78
*Overtones of War* 83
Oxford 15–17, 68, 96, 138, 157, 179, 196–197, 228

Pacific Telephone and Telegraph Company building 145–146
Pacific Union Club 144
Page, James R. 170–172, 174–175
painting 9, 16–17, 50, 74, 109–110, 113–116, 122, 150, 156, 173, 197
*Painting as a Pastime* 109–110, 116
Palestine 124, 136–137, 144, 147, 195
Palliser Hotel 105
Parfitt, Fred 130
Paris Peace Conference 28, 170, 186, 211
Parliament building (Ottawa) 54–55
Parsons, Louella 177
Pattullo, Thomas Dufferin 128–129

# Index

Pebble Beach 150, 232
Philadelphia 135, 198, 218–219
Phillips, Lee A. 173
Phipps, Eric 31
Phipps, Jay 12
Piez, Charles M. 156, 186, 188–189
Pillsbury, Horace Davis 145–146
Pittsburgh 10, 191, 201
Plain of Six Glaciers 116
Plains of Abraham, Battle of the 29, 32–33, 50
Pollard, Harry 108–109
Pooley, Robert H. 126–127, 129
Port Arthur 70–71, 81
Port Haney 123
Price, Percival 55
Prince of Wales 13, 18, 42, 47, 55, 98, 102, 180, 188
Prince of Wales Ranch 99; *see also* E.P. Ranch
Princess Anne Hotel 215
*Princess Marguerite* 125–126
prohibition 6, 9, 119, 132–136, 140, 143–144, 146–147, 165, 177, 196, 204, 214, 217
Pyper, C.D. 72–74, 79–80, 93

Quainton, Cecil 127–128, 130
Quebec bridge 33–34, 36
*Quebec Chronicle-Telegraph* 27, 35
Quebec City 3–4, 6, 10, 18–20, 22–23, 26–30, 32–36, 38, 40–41, 57, 108, 118–119
Quebec conferences 3, 28, 37–38, 57, 119
Queenborough, Lord 31

radio 39, 62, 75, 77, 90, 94, 104–105, 137, 161, 164, 169, 177–178, 185
Radium Hot Springs 110–113
Radium Hot Springs Hotel 111
Rathbone, Basil 159, 177
Redwood Highway 135–136
Redwoods 10, 137–139
Regina 56, 77, 81–87
*Regina Leader-Post* 82–84
Reid, Richard G. 95, 97
reparations 18, 27, 42, 44, 48, 52, 72, 79, 83, 88, 96, 124, 136, 170, 198–199, 218
Replogle, J. Leonard 194, 219, 226
Reynolds, Helen 135–136
Reynolds, Paul 202
Rich, E.G. 163, 202
Richardson, James A. 74, *75*, 76–78, 81, 112, 115, 179, 203, 222
Richmond 10, 211–213, 215
*Richmond News Leader* 212
Rideau Hall 45–48, 51, 56–57; *see also* Government House (Ottawa)
Rimouski 23
Ritz-Carlton hotel 41–42
*River War* 7
Robb, James 43
Robertson, W.L. 76
Robinson, B.D. 126

Robinson, Billie 217
Robinson, Henry M. 11, 170, 174
Robinson, James T. 217–218, 232
Rockefeller, Elsie 227
Rockefeller, Percy 11, 192, 203, 227
Rodney, Lady Marjorie 94–96
Rodney, Lord George 94, 96–97
Rogers, Aurelia 77
Rogers, Robert 76–77
Roosevelt, Franklin D. 3, 28, 57, 119, 204, 208, 222, 233
Roosevelt, Kermit 194
Roosevelt, Theodore 194, 208, 211
Roosevelt Hotel 177
Roslyn, Long Island 201
Ross, Isabel 60
Ross, William Donald 60, *61*, 62, 67
Rothenstein, Sir John 113
Royal Academy 110, 113, 173
Royal Agricultural and Industrial Society 120–121
Royal Canadian Mounted Police 83, 84, 99
Royal Society of St. George 130
Royal York Hotel 60–62
Royalite Oil company 99–102
Rubin, Benny 159, 177
Rutherford (California) 139

San Diego 164, 178
*San Diego Sun* 178
San Francisco 10–12, 31, 81, 104, 134–136, 138–139, 141–146, 148, 150–151, 154, 156, 171, 179, 181–182, 203, 225
San Francisco Bay Toll Bridge 141
*San Francisco Chronicle* 147
*San Francisco Examiner* 145–148, 151, 153, 173
San Simeon 11, 147, 150–158, 160, 165, 168, 177, 184
Santa Barbara 11, 109, 144, 161–164
Santa Monica 153, 164
Sartain, Geraldine 194–195
Saskatoon 84, 86–91
*Saskatoon Star Phoenix* 86, 88
*Saturday Evening Post* 202–203
*Saturday Night* 28, 64, 102
Savoy Plaza 192, 195, 206, 222, 230
*Savrola* 7
Schultz, Fred A. 115
Schwab, Charles M. 12, 30–31, 110, 183, 191, 207, 222, *225*, 226–228, 232
*Scotsman* 200
Scribner, Charles 163, 203, 227
Scripture, A.W. 62–64
Seal Rocks 145
Seattle 31, 119, 125, 130, 132–135
*Seattle Daily Times* 132
Sherwood Starr Gold Mining Company 203
Shoulder Arms 176
Sicamous 116
Simmons 179, 186, 210, 229
Sinclair Hot Springs camp 111

Singapore naval base 27, 62–63, 79, 83, 124, 128
Skinner's Cove dry-docks 126, 128
Smart, Lilian 136
Smart, Morton 136
Smith, Al 204, *205*, 206, 217
Smith, Emily 204, 206
Smith, Jim 195–196
Smith, Vernor W. 94
Snowden, Philip 27, 42, 44, 72, 74, 88, 124
Soames, Mary 9, 111, 119, 144, 184
Southampton 5, 7, 13, 18–21, 23, 88, 197, 230, 232
*Southern Daily Echo* 5
Spencewood 35
Stafford, Harry 41
Stalin, Josef 3
Stamp, Josiah 199
Stanley, Venetia 31
*Star* 81
steel industry 187, 189, 194, 219–221, 225–226
Stevens, Henry Herbert 124–125
Stevens, J. 99
Stimson, Henry L. 208, 217–218
stock market 1, 6, 9, 21–22, 77, 102, 112, 115, 142, 150, 162–163, 179, 185–186, 189, 203, 210, 222–226, 228–229, 232; crash 222–224, 226–229, 232
*Story of the Malakand Field Force* 7
*Strand* 203
Streetfield, R.J. 45–46, 48, 53
Structure Oil & Gas Co. 102, 115
Styles, Alfred G. 83–85
Sudbury 70
Summerskill, Edith 189
*Sunday Times* 144
swimming 16, 18, 21, 24, 77, 88, 108, 111–113, 127, 138, 143, 155, 165, 168, 178
Swope, Herbert 228

Takakkaw waterfalls 114
talkies 154, 161, 176–177
Tammany Hall 204–206
Taschereau, Louis Alexandre 29, 43
Tate Gallery 98, 113
Templeton 201–202
*That Hamilton Woman* 177
Thom, D.J. 83–85
Thomas, James Henry 21
Thompson, Mary 40
Thompson, Walter 41, 119
Thornton Butterworth 9, 115, 163, 229
*Three Centuries of Canadian Story* 83
Tibbetts, Lawrence 159
Tobin, Patsy 144
Tobin, Richard 11–12, 148, 150
Toerge, Norman 203
Tony's 195–196
Toole, William 99–100
Toronto 13, 28, 36, 41, 57–70, 72, 78, 106, 118
Toronto Board of Trade 60, 64

*Toronto Daily Star* 9, 30–32, 59, 64, 68
*Toronto Telegram* 59–60, 62, 64
Tory, John A. 64
*Tragic Era* 185
Trapp, T.D. 121
Travellers' Club 13
Tribune Tower 190
Trotsky 24, 185
Turner Valley 97, 99–103, 105–106
Twentieth Century–Fox 172
*Twenty-One Years* 16

Union Club 206
United Gas 179
United States Capitol building 217
United States Civil War 4, 211–213, 215
United States industry 190–191
University of Saskatchewan 86–87
*U.R. No. 2* 173

Vallee, Rudy 210
Van and Schenck 159
Van Antwerp, Edith 142, 150, 163, 181–183, 232
Van Antwerp, William 12, 142, 146, 150, 163, 179–183, 185–186, 203, 224, 232
Van Hotel 136, 139
Vancouver 10, 12–13, 37, 81, 108, 118–119, 122–125, 144
*Vancouver Province* 124–125
Vancouver Theatre 123
Vickers, Horace Cecil 21, 156, 207
Vickers da Costa 14, 122, 163, 197, 207, 210

Victoria 4–5, 47, 125–130, 163
*Victoria Daily Colonist* 28, 128
*Victoria Daily Times* 129
Virginia 4, 6, 11, 192, 207, 210–214, 216, 225, 232
von Shroders, Edgardo 122, 125

Walker, Jimmy 204, 206
Walker Theatre 78, 80–81
Walsh, Raoul 152, 155, 168, 176–177
*War* 150
*War Birds: Diary of an Unknown Aviator* 150
war debts 8, 42, 52, 152, 218
Warner Brothers 180
Washington (D.C.) 3–4, 9–10, 12, 47, 65, 119, 125, 136, 140, 148, 165, 192, 199–200, 207–208, 210–211, 215–217
Washington Conference of 1921, 52, 152
Watson, Martin 138, 141
*Way of Revelation: A Novel of Five Years* 150, 163
Wellington, Missouri 186
West, Ray 167
Whalen, Grover 222
Wheeler, John 202, 206
Whitaker, Alma 161
Widener, Joseph E. 218–219
Wiggin, Albert 228
Wiley, Louis 199
Willingdon, Viscount 45, **46**, 47, 53, 57
Willingdon, Viscountess Adelaide **46**, 47, 53, 57

Willits 136, 139
Wilson, Woodrow 161–162, 170, 186, 202, 208, 211, 217
Windsor Hotel 43
Winnipeg 5, 13, 28, 60, 64, 70–72, 74–78, 80–83, 93, 101, 112, 115, 179, 203, 222
*Winnipeg Evening Tribune* 1, 72, 74, 81
Winnipeg Grain and Produce Exchange 75–77, 81
Winnipeg Theatre 74
Wodehouse, P.G. 164, 194
*World Crisis* 8, 45, 56–57, 146, 163, 196, 232
World War I 7, 8, 10, 12, 14, 16, 24, 28, 36, 42, 44, 50, 52, 55, 84, 96, 121, 142, 152, 170, 175, 185–186, 188, 193–194, 199, 202, 208, 226
World War II 1, 3, 9, 21, 30, 33, 38–39, 46, 50, 52, 57, 61–63, 109, 113, 136, 149, 155, 164, 169, 186, 208, 230
Worthington-Evans, Sir Laming 178, 196
Wright, William H. 149

Yarrow, Norman A. 126, 129
Yosemite 142, 180–184
Young, Clement C. 160
Young, Owen D. 42, 79, **198**, 199
Young Plan 27, 42, 44, 74, 79, 124, 199
Youssoupoff, Prince Felix 219
Ypres, Lord 185

*Zionist Record* 144

www.ingramcontent.com/pod-product-compliance
Ingram Content Group UK Ltd.
Pitfield, Milton Keynes, MK11 3LW, UK
UKHW051824130625
459655UK00017B/186